Sharing Secrets with Stalin

Sharing Secrets with Stalin

How the Allies Traded Intelligence, 1941–1945

Bradley F. Smith

 University Press of Kansas

Published by the University Press of Kansas (Lawrence, Kansas 66049), which was
organized by the Kansas Board of Regents and is operated and funded by Emporia
State University, Fort Hays State University, Kansas State University, Pittsburg
State University, the University of Kansas, and Wichita State University

Library of Congress Cataloging-in-Publication Data

Smith, Bradley F.
    Sharing secrets with Stalin : How the Allies traded intelligence, 1941–1945 /
Bradley F. Smith.
        p.   cm.
    Includes bibliographical references.
    ISBN 0-7006-0800-1
    1. World War, 1939–1945—Secret Service. 2. Military intelligence—History
—20th century. I. Title.
D810.S7S5544 1996
940.54'85—dc20   96-2395

British Library Cataloguing in Publication Data is available.

Printed in the United States of America

10 9 8 7 6 5 4 3 2 1

To Bradley and Harry Moen

Contents

Preface

World War II was a great engine of mid-twentieth-century carnage and change. It killed at least 40 million people directly or indirectly, while altering the manner of life of the survivors and their institutions in all corners of the globe. Its cost in money dwarfed that of all other international conflicts, and it radically altered the balance of power, pushing aside the traditional great powers and clearing the way for the Soviet and American superpowers to hold away for half a century. Technological changes tumbled forth in forms ranging from jet aircraft to sulfa drugs, all of which quickly altered daily life. Extermination camps, kamikazes, and the atomic bomb raised deep and troubling questions about the nature of human beings and of modern society.

The conflict of 1939–1945 also produced a significant and long-lasting revolution in intelligence that drastically increased the range and volume of nearly every country's collection of secret information. Traditional forms of secret data accumulation, such as agents and double agents, were supplemented by many less glamorous but highly useful intelligence activities, including a detailed daily analysis of the enemy press and the creation of vast censorship organizations, which, along with preventing the leak of sensitive information, collected intelligence about the enemy and about domestic public opinion.

On occasion, belligerent governments were less than pleased by the intelligence they collected from such unorthodox sources as censorship, and they were embarrassed by the public's views that such secret intercepts revealed. For example, British intercepts in May 1941 showed that much of the British public was outraged by the secret shenanigans and special arrangements used by the British government regarding Rudolf Hess, not because they believed that Whitehall was conspiring with the Nazis (as would be alleged later), but because ordinary Britons believed that Hess had been treated much too generously. One intercepted letter from a man in northern Britain fairly exploded, "They're feeding that swine on Chicken and eggs. . . . Here [we] got to do without chicken, fish, eggs and heaps of other things."[1]

Such revelations regarding what common people thought of the new world of covert operations, deception, and worldwide secrecy were, however, largely allowed to fall by the wayside, thereby inadvertently laying the basis for a half century of conspiracy theories and secrecy revelations. The governments were caught in a high-tech struggle for survival, and there was little time or opportunity to ponder such side effects. Speed and technology turned the conflict into a vast panorama of mobility and firepower covering vast distances. Developments ranging from blitzkrieg to intercontinental air travel nearly all depended on radio communications, which produced a revolution in secret communications intelligence as interception ("Y") specialists tracked enemy radio traffic and cryptanalysts tried to break the increasingly sophisticated high-tech cipher systems used by their opponents.

The high-tech developments in cryptanalysis, just like a government's use of censorship for intelligence gathering, were not immediately apparent to most people because every belligerent was careful to keep these "unacknowledged" activities as invisible as possible for as long as possible. Only in the 1980s (despite the continuation of some highly restrictive secrecy policies on the part of nearly all governments) did portions of the most secret aspects of World War II intelligence innovation begin seeping, and occasionally gushing, into the public domain.

We now know that the wartime use of machine ciphering systems by nearly all the major powers exposed their secret communications systems to highly sophisticated, and often highly successful, attacks by the high-tech cryptanalysis of their opponents. The American MAGIC assault on Japanese diplomatic ciphers and the British ULTRA penetration of the German Army, Navy, and Luftwaffe machine ciphers have recently become common knowledge among people interested in World War II. Many people now recognize not only that ULTRA and MAGIC helped the Allies triumph but also that these cipher-breaking systems were important steps in the process that led to the appearance of digital computers, which have revolutionized many aspects of postwar life.

ULTRA and MAGIC also point to another significant and long-lasting change that World War II produced in intelligence. Machine cipher-breaking operations required not only great skill and highly sophisticated technology but also large teams of scientists, technicians, and analysts as well as enormous support staffs to sustain these efforts. Intelligence organizations in every country grew swiftly between 1939 and 1945 as each nation sought to expand both its traditional and its high-tech means of attacking the secret message traffic of its opponents. There was also a vast increase in the numbers of secret agents and photo reconnaissance personnel, as well as humble toilers such as file clerks and analysts of the enemy press, all of whom were indispensable to the functioning of this new secret world.

Faced with burgeoning costs and enormous personnel requirements, government leaders were forced to look more sympathetically on the sharing of intelligence with their allies. In some cases, this cooperation reached levels of intimacy and mutual confidence that had not been reached by allies and partners in earlier wars. That seems to have been the case regarding British intelligence sharing with the Dominion partners Canada, Australia, and New Zealand, as well as the secret intelligence partnership that existed in full form between Britain and the United States from 1943 to 1945.

These Anglo-American and Anglo-Dominion secret cooperative arrangements were so close and apparently so important to the successful war effort of the West that, following V-J Day, tales of their intimacy and effectiveness attained nearly mythic proportions. Since Britain, the United States, and the Dominions continued to function as a secret intelligence–sharing combine throughout the years of the Cold War as well, details of their wartime cooperative endeavors remained largely secret. In consequence, Anglo-American intelligence cooperation in World War II has become to many people a rather amorphous benchmark of what "real," or at least "highly significant," sharing of intelligence should be, even though we have little hard data on which to judge just how cousinly these relationships actually were. Certainly some questions remain regarding British-American trust and comradeship due to newly released documents that show that the British government was decoding and reading American secret diplomatic traffic until at least two weeks prior to Pearl Harbor.

The Anglo-American and Anglo-Dominion special intelligence relationships were nonetheless comprehensive and successful enough to overshadow the wartime intelligence-sharing efforts of other participants on both sides of the Allied-Axis dividing line. In consequence, little systematic study has been given to the subject of intelligence cooperation between other countries during World War II, and such topics as Anglo-French and German-Japanese-Italian intelligence sharing are in their infancy. Scholars such as John Chapman are leading the way, and intelligence history journals such as *Intelligence and National Security* (U.K.) and the *Journal of Intelligence and Counter Intelligence* (U.S.) are beginning to remedy this situation.[2]

The sharing of intelligence between the Soviet Union and the Anglo-

Americans has been almost completely ignored, except for occasional published forays into OSS-NKVD relations and a short account of one person's part in such sharing activities, *The Strange Alliance* (1947) written by the former chief of the American Military Mission in Moscow, Maj. Gen. John R. Deane. Obviously, Cold War animosities have played an important role in maintaining this long silence. As the years of East-West tension rolled on, it became increasingly difficult to imagine that Moscow, London, and Washington had ever managed to cooperate on anything, especially not on a matter as sensitive as secret intelligence. As recently as the 1980s, when many intelligence secrets were already beginning to see the light of day, Supreme Court Justice Powell flatly denied that the Americans had ever provided the Soviets with high-grade intelligence during the war. Sherman Kent of the CIA solemnly entoned that the Russians had made no attempt to assist the British or Americans with intelligence at any point between 1941 and 1945.[3]

But specialists who have probed broadly and deeply into British and American war documents in the National Archives and the Public Record Office have long suspected that there was something wrong with this picture of East-West intelligence abstinence in the years 1941–1945. The War Diary of the British Military Mission in Moscow has been open to research for over fifteen years, and the dispatches that the U.S. Military Mission in Moscow sent to Washington have been available for twenty. Even a cursory examination of these collections is enough to indicate that East-West wartime intelligence cooperation did exist.

By extending the research net to the dozens of record categories available in the National Archives, the Public Record Office, and other American and British archives, it has been possible to assemble a large quantity of documents, supplemented by interviews, that reveal that the sharing of intelligence among Moscow, Washington, and London was extensive and, at critical junctures of the war, may have played a role in the Allied victory. Since a few East-West intelligence transmissions occurred even before Hitler's attack on Soviet Russia (22 June 1941) and then continued to the last week of the war against Japan, they throw light on Allied activities during most phases of the great midcentury conflict.

These documents also suggest that East and West were not always as hostile as has been suggested. Nor does it appear that they were as determined to march off into mutual hostility in the summer of 1945 as many Cold War traditionalists and revisionists have maintained.

When the Cold War ended in the early 1990s, it was hoped that officials in Moscow would open up their archives to help round out the picture of East-

West intelligence cooperation during the 1941–1945 era. It has gradually become clear, however, that the Russian authorities are less than enthusiastic about permitting Western specialists to examine original Russian intelligence documents from the World War II period. Their cooperation with selected Western researchers has been limited to allowing access to NKVD materials and military "studies" on operations. Even these materials have usually been removed from their archival context and presented individually to particular journalists or scholars.

Unfortunately, despite a series of queries and petitions by the author, Russian officials have refused to permit access to any of their relevant army, navy, or air documents. No Russian official contacted by the author, except for the helpful Adm. Igor Amasov, would even acknowledge that Russian records of East-West intelligence cooperation during World War II actually exist in post-Soviet Russia. Faced with such a stone wall of Russian resistance, it has been necessary to try to tell this story from Western sources alone. That limitation is certainly not ideal, but it is not necessarily a mortal distortion, because copies of many wartime Russian intelligence materials provided to the West during the war are still available in Western archives. On balance, therefore, it seemed best to base this account on Western materials in the hope that these revelations of wartime cooperation may prompt a change in attitude in Moscow. When such a change does occur, all parties will be able to agree that international cooperation can pay handsome dividends, even when it is carried on by differing political systems and against great odds.

A number of generous individuals assisted in the preparation of this volume. I am especially grateful to all those who tried to arrange my entrée to military intelligence materials in Russia: Prof. Robert Love, U.S. Naval Academy; David Priestland, Lincoln College, Oxford; John F. Sloan, Springfield, Virginia; Prof. Hans A. Jacobsen, Bonn; Charles Palm and Agnes F. Peterson, Hoover Institution; Kent D. Lee; Jonathan Haslam, Kings College, Cambridge; Charles Burdick, Andrew Elez, and Robert Kane in the United States and Britain; Adm. Igor Amasov, Gen. D. Volkogonov, Yuri G. Kobladze, and Prof. N. G. Sevostianov in Moscow; Brig. Gen. Gregory Govan, U.S. military attaché in Moscow; and Lt. Gen. V. Pronin, Russian military attaché in London. Pat Kennedy Grimstead strove valiantly on my behalf. My thanks also to the late John Costello and Col. David M. Glantz for advising me of their Russian research experiences.

In addition, I received valuable assistance from archivists at the National Archives, especially Dr. Timothy Mulligan, who assisted me at many critical points, and William Cunliffe, David Pfeiffer, Richard Boylon, Timothy Nenninger, and Kathy Nikastro. Scholarly colleagues were also helpful, especially Profs. Warren Kimball in the United States and D. C. Watt in London. Mark Seaman of the Imperial War Museum was, as usual, the source of a great deal of generous assistance, as was the late Robert Cecil, adviser and friend, who generously shared his work and ideas on World War II and postwar intelligence.

To all these colleagues and bringers of aid and comfort, my heartfelt thanks. Thanks also to the Institute of Historical Research, the British Library, and the Public Records Office in London, which provided havens in which to research and write, and to the following institutions, which granted permission to quote from manuscript materials: Yale University and the Library of Congress in the United States, and the Imperial War Museum, Kings College of London University, and the British Library of Political and Economic Science in the United Kingdom.

Finally, to my wife, Jenny Wilkes, who helped type and proofread, as well as clarify my often muddled thinking, a special note of gratitude. And thanks again to my old and sage friend Charles Burdick, and to the Graham Benson family who gave me shelter in which to write.

Abbreviations

ABC	America, Britain, Canada
AFHQ	Allied Force Headquarters
ASDIC	Antisubmarine detection
BL of PS	British Library of Political Science
BNLO	British Naval Liaison Officer
CA	California
CAM	Cambridge
CCS	Combined Chiefs of Staff
CIGS	Chief of the Imperial General Staff (British)
CNO	Chief of Naval Operations (U.S.)
COI	Coordinator of Information (U.S.)
COS	Chief of Staff (British)
CSDIC	Combined Services Detention Intelligence Centre (British)
DB	Diplomatic Branch, National Archives (U.S.)
DD	Deputy Director
DMI	Director of Military Intelligence
DNI	Director of Naval Intelligence (British)
EW	European War

FO	Foreign Office
G-2	U.S. Army Intelligence
JCS	Joint Chiefs of Staff (U.S.)
JIC	Joint Intelligence Committee (British and U.S.)
JP	Joint Planners (British and U.S.)
JPS	Joint Planning Staff (British and U.S.)
LSE	London School of Economics
MEW	Ministry of Economic Warfare (British)
MI	Military Intelligence (British)
MI 3	Military Intelligence Subsection, Order of Battle (British)
MI 6	Military Intelligence Subsection, Secret Service (British)
MID	Military Intelligence Division (U.S. Army)
MIS	Military Intelligence Service (U.S. Army)
MOI	Ministry of Information (British)
MR	Military Reference Branch, National Archives (U.S.)
NA	National Archives (U.S.)
NID	Naval Intelligence Division (U.S.)
NKVD	Soviet secret police
OB	Order of Battle
ONI	Office of Naval Intelligence (U.S.)
OPD	Operation Division (U.S. Army)
OSS	Office of Strategic Services (U.S.)
PHP	Post Hostilities Planning
PRO	Public Record Office (British)
PS	President's secretary (U.S.)
PSF	President's secretary's files (U.S.)

R&A	Research and Analysis Branch, OSS (U.S.)
RAF	Royal Air Force (British)
RDF	Radio Direction Finding
RG	Record Group, National Archives (U.S.)
SC	Special Communications
SHAEF	Supreme Headquarters, Allied Expeditionary Force
SI	Secret Intelligence Branch, OSS (U.S.)
SIS	Secret Intelligence Service (British)
SOE	Special Operations Executive (British)
SOE-NKVD	Special Operations Executive, Soviet secret police
SS	Schutzstaffel (German)
USAAC	U.S. Army Air Corps
VCNS	Vice Chief, Naval Staff
VCIS	Vice Chief, Imperial Staff
WM	War Ministry
WO	War Office (British)
WP	War Planners (British)

Public Record Office Collections

ADM 1	Admiralty and Secretariat
ADM 116	Administration and Secretariat, Cases
ADM 199	War History, Cases and Papers
ADM 205	First Sea Lord
ADM 223	Naval Intelligence Papers
ADM 237	Operations, Convoys
AIR 2	Registered Files

AIR 8	Chief of Air Staff
AIR 19	Private Office
AIR 20	Unregistered Papers
AIR 40	Directorate of Intelligence
AIR 46	AIR Missions
AVIA 39	German Electronics and Signals Organization
CAB 2	Imperial Defence to 1939
CAB 62	Non-Intervention in Spain
CAB 65	War Cabinet Minutes
CAB 66	War Cabinet Memoranda
CAB 79	COS Minutes
CAB 80	COS Memoranda
CAB 81	COS Committees
CAB 84	JP Staff Committees
CAB 104	Supplementary Registered Files
CAB 105	War Cabinet Telegrams
CAB 119	Joint Planning Staff
CAB 120	Ministry of Defense
CAB 122	Joint Staff Mission
CO 273	Colonies, Straits Settlements
CO 323	Colonies, General
DEFE 1	Postal and Telegraph Censorship
FO 115	United States
FO 181	Russia
FO 298	Germany
FO 371	General Correspondence

FO 418	Russia, Confidential Print
FO 800	Private Collections
FO 954	Avon Papers
HO 45	Home Office
HS 4	SOE
HW 1	GC and CS to Prime Minister
INF 1	MOI Correspondence
PREM 3	Operations
WO 32	Registered, General
WO 106	Operations and Intelligence
WO 160	1914–1918, Miscellaneous
WO 165	War Office Directorate, War Diaries
WO 176	War Dairies, Smaller Units
WO 178	War Diaries, Military Missions
WO 193	Directorate of Military Operations
WO 204	AFHQ (World War II)
WO 208	Military Intelligence
WO 216	Chief of the General Staff
WO 219	SHAEF (World War II)
WO 259	Secretary of State, Private Office Papers
WO 287	"B" papers

1
Overture

The fact that Britain and the United States became partners with the Soviet Union in the summer of 1941 was one of the most improbable events in the history of twentieth-century international relations. During the previous quarter century, Moscow had rarely missed an opportunity to condemn the British and Americans governments, denouncing them as the purest embodiments of capitalistic exploitation and malevolence toward people's democracies. Throughout the 1920s and 1930s, London and Washington frequently replied in kind, denouncing Soviet Russia as an evil and murderous empire bent on the destruction of all things good and dear, as well as devoted to limitless ideological and perhaps military conquest. In the three years following the outbreak of Lenin's revolution in 1917, the British took the lead in an international military campaign against the Soviet Union, trying—in Churchill's later inelegant phrase—to strangle Bolshevism in its cradle while carrying out extensive anti-Soviet intelligence operations on the edges of the newly formed USSR.[1]

Authorities in the American government, being more cautious and less flowery and lacking London's infatuation with intelligence, busied themselves chasing Reds at home and played only a modest role in the effort to contain the Soviet system between 1917 and 1919. When this effort failed, Washington adopted a policy of oppositional fantasy, officially denying the existence of the Soviet government until President Franklin Roosevelt finally extended recognition in 1935.

Both of the Anglo-Saxon countries were swept by varying forms of Red scares following the armistice of 1918, and during a brief period after the affair of the Zinoviev letter in 1927 (when Soviet officials seem to have tried to whip up the British radical Left), London broke off diplomatic relations with Moscow. The year 1927 also saw developments that helped freeze East-West relations. Stalin's program of rigid and centralized economic planning, the Five-Year Plan era, began then, as did the Moscow Comintern campaign against every Left-leaning movement throughout the world that refused to submit itself to all the twists and turns of the propaganda line charted by the Communist Party of the Soviet Union.

The London and Washington governments responded to the apparent rise of this ever more serious "Communist threat" by trying to isolate the USSR and by doing everything possible to prevent the export of Communist subversion. Since the Soviet Union stretched across the Eurasian land mass and lay in close proximity to many areas Britain considered to be vital—the Black Sea, the oil resources of the Middle East, northern China, and the Afghan gateway to India—London was especially anxious that every hint of Soviet expansionism be contained. Moscow's call for international revolutionary action by people without power or prospects was especially menacing to the British government, for it was not difficult to imagine India, Africa, and China, as well as the English Midlands, one day being swept by a Communist whirlwind. British military and economic strength was stretched thin at home and abroad during the 1920s and even more so in the depressed 1930s. Whitehall was consequently very nervous about the possibility of Soviet Russia making a two-pronged assault on Britain's vulnerable colonial position by combining traditional great-power military and economic pressure with various forms of revolutionary ideological warfare.

As a consequence, the Special Branch of the Metropolitan Police was reorganized and given a new charter in April 1919, a charter that had a select distribution within Whitehall but included Secretary of War Winston S. Churchill among its recipients. The charter declared that "under the charge of Mr. Basil Thomson as Director of Intelligence," the new department would collect intelligence relating "to threatened disturbances (whether arising out of labour troubles or otherwise), seditious meetings and conspiracies, and revolutionary movements at home and abroad." Thomsom was specifically charged with the duty of preparing "periodical digests of home and foreign intelligence as to seditious propaganda and revolutionary movements."[2]

Faced with the perceived threat of leftist disturbances at home and colonial uprisings abroad, the British government throughout the 1920s and 1930s pursued radicals in the courts by repeatedly strengthening its antisubversive measures. When the governor of the Straits Settlements inquired of the Colonial Office in April 1927 whether "propaganda inciting to world revolution" was seditious,[3] London quickly provided him with information to answer such questions and suppress those who threatened to start revolutionary trouble. Similarly, in 1938 and 1939, when doubts were raised about the power of colonial governments to inspect telegrams to counter subversion, Whitehall immediately took steps to guarantee that the administrations of all British colonies had such power under the Official Secrets Act.[4]

Although not as frightened by the possibility of Soviet international adventures as was the British government, Washington was nervous about Comintern activities in Latin America, especially the Caribbean, and in the Philippines. Like those in Whitehall, American officials were also suspicious of Soviet intentions in China, where every trace of propaganda urging class war evoked deep apprehension in Americans ranging from missionaries to bankers and Pacific Rim expansionists (who, in a subsequent generation, would be labeled the "China lobby").

With respect to Soviet-inspired subversion within the Western countries themselves, the American government may have been a trifle less apprehensive than the British about the vulnerability of the working class to the blandishments of Soviet propaganda, but America experienced a raging Red scare in the early 1920s, and the fear of the Red peril remained both widespread and intense throughout what Moscow scornfully called American ruling circles. U.S. leaders publicly and privately deplored the evils of Bolshevism and used their influence and money to counter the activities of groups toned from pink to red. In consequence, the political coloration of most American, as well as British, local governments was distinctly non-Red. Throughout the 1920s and 1930s, the police forces of both countries energetically combated all groups and individuals that showed an inclination to raise the Red flag, and in nearly every local American community, the forces of law and order, especially religious and business groups, vigorously struggled to curtail public expressions of support for Communism or the USSR.[5]

Military officials of the United States and Britain tended to be strongly anti-Communist and highly suspicious of Soviet Russia. Much staff planning carried out by Britain during the interwar period focused on the possibility of Red incursions into Central Europe or the Middle East, as well as on the possibility that Moscow might attempt to flex its revolutionary and military muscles at the expense of the small states stretching from Finland to Austria. These nations had been established with the help of the Western powers in 1919 in part to act as a *cordon sanitaire* barrier against an advance of the Red pestilence toward the heart of Central Europe. In the United States, military planners were much more concerned about the possible advance of the Red tide of "have-not" Communists across the Rio Grande into the American Southwest, but in both London and Washington, the perceived reality of a Soviet military and revolutionary threat gave security planning an anti-Red coloration throughout much of the 1930s.

But this sad development was not merely a product of blindness, military inadequacies, and anti-Communist bias among the generals of the 1920s and 1930s.[6] Many senior political figures in Britain and America, such as Winston Churchill and Henry Stimson (who would emerge in the 1940s as British prime minister and U.S. secretary of war, respectively), also had faultless credentials as determined anti-Communists. The Foreign Office and the State Department were always at least as busy as the military during the interwar era trying to cope with the reality, or the possibility, of a Soviet threat. The personal and professional views of such young Soviet specialists in the State Department as Charles Bohlen and George Kennan had been shaped by the shock of the Russian revolutionary experiences. Their close association with anti-Communist emigrés and their extended service in Finland and the Baltic states, the front line of Western political defense against Soviet incursions in the 1920s and 1930s, were the crucible of their worldview.[7]

The interwar police and security services of Britain and the United States were even more busy during this period monitoring Communist activities, tracking suspected Soviet agents and fellow travelers, and sharing information with other governments on Communist Party members and subversives. The Foreign Office and the Security Services of Great Britain had arrangements for the exchange of information regarding Communist Party members and subversive suspects with a number of Western and Central European governments, as well as with the United States. Information on individual Communists regularly passed back and forth between diplomatic posts in London and Washington, as well as among Washington, London, and other Western capitals (especially those of the imperial mother countries, Belgium, Holland, and France) from the end of World War I until 1940–1941.

Although many segments of the British and American governments were colored by anti-Soviet activity in the 1920s and 1930s, one should be cautious about glibly condemning this hostility to Soviet activities or dismissing all Western bureaucrats and politicians as blind and mindless anti-Communists who were unable to distinguish between phantoms and actual threats to Western security. Communist revolutionary activity, especially that orchestrated by Moscow, did pose unprecedented challenges to Western governments, particularly during the instability of the immediate post–World War I era and the traumatic depression of the 1930s. Furthermore, during Stalin's Five-Year Plan era of the 1930s, the economic and military power of the USSR did rise, and this increase in strength was paralleled by the use of savage repression and mass murders, the ferocity of which surpassed even the wildest imaginings of the traditional Red haters.

In the face of these Soviet challenges and horrors, some individual conservative politicians managed to remain reasonably calm and level-headed. From at least as early as 1924, for example, that most stern and taciturn of conservative American presidents, Calvin Coolidge, regularly read the *Daily Worker,* and both Coolidge and his secretary of state, Charles Evan Hughes, noted from time to time that they found the official organ of the Communist Party of the United States to be interesting reading. This calm, self-enlightening response to a bewildering challenge illustrates the fact that despite all their worry and scheming, at no time after 1921 (with the possible exception of the British reaction to the 1927 Zinoviev affair) did the central government of either of the great Atlantic powers fall into a ragingly aggressive anti-Communist panic.[8]

It is appropriate to note, however, that by 1941, a large portion of the senior- and middle-level civil and military officials of Britain and the United States had long been deeply enmeshed in shadow conflicts with the USSR or planning for a possible military showdown with Stalin's Russia. Such people were little inclined to trust Soviet policies and generally dismissed Stalin as a crude and ignorant butcher. When the panzers turned east in June 1941, they believed that the Red Army had little or no chance of stopping Hitler. Over the next four years, some of these people changed their minds and gave Stalin, the Soviet government, and especially the Red Army high marks for courage and military competence. Yet throughout the war years, those in Western governments who knew the most about the USSR and shouldered most of the responsibility for direct dealings with the Russians had some of the strongest suspicions about Soviet aims, methods, and reliability.

In the pre–June 1941 period and on through the wartime "alliance," Soviet hostility and suspicion toward the West were even more rife. The Soviet system was based on a belief in inevitable and permanent conflict with the capitalist states, which were seen as viscerally hostile to Communism and endlessly preparing to carry out attacks on the Soviet motherland. Western intervention in the civil wars of 1917–1921, the *cordon sanitaire* erected in 1917–1919, the security operations carried out in the West against Communist parties, and the numerous expressions of Western opposition to the USSR were seen by the majority of Soviet officials (and perhaps by a majority of the Soviet population) as manifestations of Western capitalism's determination to destroy the Marxist-Leninist motherland by fair means or foul.[9]

The fundamental conviction that the West was up to no good with respect to the first workers' revolutionary state, which had deep roots in Marx's thought as well as Lenin's views and life experience, was seriously intensified once Stalin took the helm in 1927. The program of building socialism in one country drew a sharp line not only between the USSR and the Western capitalist states but also between the USSR and every non-Russian political organization or leftist theory. Additionally, Stalin's increasing use of real or imagined foreign devil threats led the Soviet government to emphasize the existence of a host of Trotskyists, Whites, Mensheviks, and imperialists, all of whom were accused of being linked to the West, being in the pay of the capitalists, and striving to abort the advance toward the socialist paradise being engineered by Comrade Stalin. The "Great Leader" pulled out all the stops in the decade and a half before Hitler's attack on the USSR, trying to convince the Russian people that every setback and shortcoming at home, as well as abroad, was caused by the machinations of the capitalists and their bewildering array of treacherous fellow travelers within and without the USSR. Nor was Stalin content to depend solely on propaganda to drive this message deep into the hearts and minds of those at every level of the government and the Party bureaucracy, as well as into the hearts and minds of the Russian people. The gulag, the security organs, the torture chambers, and the occasional battered defendant in the show trials all proclaimed the message that harboring doubts about whether non-Communist, especially Western, political leaders were evil was a very hazardous activity.

As the persecutions and economic developments continued in the 1930s, those who were opposed or who had secret doubts about the course of events in the USSR either became silent or disappeared. Step by step, a society, a party, and a government bureaucracy were created in which negative thoughts ceased to be expressed; younger cadres entered a professional world in which doubt about the system, and its black and bleak vision of the outside world, became quite literally inconceivable. Thus, when Hitler struck in June—after a bit of shuffling to explain how the Great Leader had been so wrong about the Fuehrer—it was easy for the Communist Party and the state propagandists to trumpet the message that the outside world had shown itself to be even more diabolical and hostile to the Soviet motherland than the Party and state leaders had always claimed.

Despite the enormous force of anti-Westernism in Stalin's Soviet Union and the fear of the Red menace that dominated much of Anglo-American government and society, feelings of bitter hostility were not universally harbored in either the East or the West. Most Western countries had maintained diplomatic relations with the USSR throughout the interwar era, as did Britain from 1927 and the United States from 1935. Although many of the diplomatic representatives appointed by the two sides may have played the game tongue in cheek, they did play the wartime game. There were also genuine enthusiasts who sincerely tried to bridge the gap between Stalin's world and that of the West. Along with the assorted visitors to the Soviet Union in the 1930s who, like the Fabian socialist writers Sidney and Beatrice Webb and George Bernard Shaw, thought that they detected the seeds of an earthly paradise, there was one American ambassador, William Bulitt, and one American military attaché, Col. Philip Faymonville, who were very impressed by the Soviet system. Although certainly not in the league of these fellow travelers, Maxim Litvinov, the Soviet foreign minister in the middle and late 1930s (and later Soviet ambassador to the United States), was an advocate of East-West cooperation; he obviously liked Western democrats and tried to build bridges between the Soviet system and the democracies.

Furthermore, the British and French had managed to cooperate fairly effectively with the Soviets on some aspects of political and military activity in the mid-1930s, although these efforts were largely obliterated from Western government memories by the mid-1940s. For example, the Popular Front phenomenon pivoted on British, French, and Soviet cooperation at the League of Nations, which seemed to be the wave of the future until the Western states and the USSR went their separate ways over the Spanish Civil War in 1936–1937. But in that mid-1930s period, which might be termed the first East-West, anti-Nazi, anti-Fascist confederation, the Soviets even opened up aspects of their military organization to Western observers. High-ranking French and British officers (including Col. G. de Q. Martel, who would return to Russia as an abrasive leader of the British military mission in Moscow during 1942–1943) managed to gain so much information on the Red Army and Air Force as observers of the 1936 Russian maneuvers that their bulging files continued to be the basis for Whitehall's intelligence picture of the Soviet military even in June 1941.[10]

These tender shoots of East-West goodwill sprouting in the 1930s were nipped in the bud by the purges of 1937, which led Western intelligence leaders to believe that the Red Army had been seriously weakened by Stalin's fury. Even then, some East-West military contact persisted until 1939, when Stalin made a desperate effort to divert Nazi expansionism away from Russia's borders and to pick up some territorial plums in the process. Throughout the spring and summer of 1939, the British and French dickered warily with the USSR in an effort to create an East-West alliance that might contain Hitler. But the Western powers were unable to make a truly bold approach to Moscow because of their fear and loathing of Stalin, their doubts about Russian power, and Stalin's sensible but ominous demand that the Western powers approve the stationing of Red Army forces in the Baltic states and eastern Poland. Racked by apprehension that such a deal would merely trade a Russian threat for a German one, the Western negotiating team did not leave for Moscow until 5 August 1939 (and then by ship), which meant that serious talks did not begin in Moscow until mid-August 1939.

Hitler had not been content to wait and see whether the Soviets and the West would finally put together an alliance that would thwart his designs on Poland. Throughout the early summer, cautious and low-level German probes, beginning with economic questions and moving on to international security and zone of influence matters, had taken place in Germany and Russia. Then in the fourth week of August, Joachim von Ribbentrop, Hitler's foreign minister, suddenly flew to Moscow, and in a whirlwind of negotiation, the two countries agreed on the terms of an economic partnership, a nonaggression pact, and secret clauses that guaranteed Stalin zones of influence and control in Poland and the Baltic states. The signing of this Nazi-Soviet pact (23 August 1939), which eliminated the last obstacle to Hitler's invasion of Poland, forced Britain and France to go it alone in a futile effort to stop Nazi expansion while the Soviet Union reaped a harvest of territorial acquisitions, including eastern Poland and the Baltic states.

The Soviets were compelled to pay a substantial price for this acquisitive adventure, however. No other turn or twist of the Party line ever seemed so murderously cynical as this one. Membership in Communist Parties around the world plummeted as many of those who had believed the Party to be the firmest bulwark against Nazism left in droves. Conservative political leaders in the West, who had always taken a jaundiced view of the moral reliability of Stalinism, now seemed to believe that their worst fears and dire predictions had been fully confirmed. During the Anglo-French "Phony War" against Hitler in late 1939 and early 1940 when the two sides sat idly along the Maginot Line, the British government continued to try to block Soviet expansion. The War Office provided assistance to Afghanistan to strengthen its position against Russia, just as it had been doing since the mid-nineteenth century in the fair days of the tsar and the raj.[11] The Special Branch also went about its customary business of pursuing the king's ideological enemies, much as it had been doing during the previous twenty years. Initially, and not surprisingly, it showed more enthusiasm and skill in tracking Communists than it did in controlling Nazis and their sympathizers. On the day Britain declared war, 3 September 1939, the Special Branch had a secret informant at the meeting of Communist Party officials held at Marx House in London, who reported the details of the Party's plan to liquidate the above-ground Communist Party before British officials moved against it. The Special Branch agent also reported that although the formal Communist Party would disappear, a secret Party nucleus would be retained to support the British war effort (regardless of the Nazi-Soviet pact) and "prove to the British working class that not merely can Communists attack fascism verbally but they do not shrink from fighting on land, sea and air." The Special Branch quickly fell in with the new Party line. In a report of 29 September 1939, it stressed that although the Party was still united "in opposition to the [British government]," it also "advocates the prosecution of the war with utmost vigor."[12]

The British government especially resented the fact that while Britain faced one whole year of mortal peril (using Churchill's phrase) and the Communist Party applauded British efforts, the USSR continued to provide diplomatic and economic assistance to Hitler. London also continued to view with apprehension Soviet Russia's perpetration of "anti-British activities" in Asia, which persisted throughout the "Phony War" period of 1939–1940.[13]

Over the summer and autumn of 1940, as the British braced themselves to withstand the blitz and possible invasion, the Soviet Union continued to sell large quantities of strategic materials to Germany, thereby nullifying much of the effect of Britain's blockade of Hitler's Reich. The United States was just beginning to rouse itself from two decades of isolationist illusions and had started to supply Britain first through cash-and-carry and then in the spring of 1941 through lend-lease, so Soviet Russia did not win praise from the American government for its continued massive and profitable assistance to Nazi Germany.

Resentment against Soviet Russia's role as a safe, tame, and manipulative benefactor of Hitler, when combined with Allied military failures against Germany, dampened any enthusiasm Whitehall might have felt for the USSR because it had not tried to use the Communist Party to undermine the British government. Between October 1939 and April 1940, during Russia's embarrassingly inept effort to invade Finland, a number of far-fetched proposals were worked out by various cabinet committees in London to attack Soviet oil production and western Russian supply routes. British military intelligence services took advantage of the war in the far north to gather substantial secret information about the Soviet armed forces and their armament.[14]

Even after British popular enthusiasm for challenging Stalin for the sake of "gallant Finland" had evaporated due to Field Marshal Mannerheim's acceptance of Russian armistice terms in March 1940, the Royal Air Force (RAF) continued to make detailed plans for raids on the Soviet oil center at Baku. This planning also occurred well past the point when it had become abundantly clear that the RAF of 1940 was incapable of finding and hitting industrial targets successfully in Central Europe, much less Eastern Europe. Yet even after the Air

Ministry bowed to the force of unpleasant reality following the fall of France and gave up its dreams of long-range bombing operations against Russia, Britain's covert warfare activists in the Special Operations Executive (SOE) continued to float up proposals for hopelessly impractical and politically dangerous sabotage operations against the USSR.[15]

Despite all this hazardous British military busyness, for a brief moment in October 1940, Anglo-Soviet military relations showed signs of improvement, and Moscow even raised the possibility of an exchange of air force visits. By the end of 1940, however, both the British and Soviet attachés were again caught in a grim tit-for-tat battle between the two governments. Neither Moscow nor London conceded attaché access to secret information or military installations unless such concessions were made reciprocal. The British military attaché finally managed to visit a Red Army tank unit in December 1940, but only because the Russian attaché had been granted a comparable visit in Britain.[16]

London was especially cautious about revealing secret information to Russian and other foreign attachés during this period, because Britain not only was at war but also feared an imminent German invasion. Ironically, this fear would not disappear until Hitler chose to use his offensive power to invade Russia rather than Britain in June 1941. But until that actually happened, the Russians were also highly cautious in dealing with British officials, because they wanted to do nothing that might raise the ire of their powerful and dangerous Nazi ally, who was obviously casting about in search of the most suitable place to use his massed panzers.

All this caution, worry, and tension made a posting to Moscow more tense and unpleasant than usual for British military and diplomatic representatives during the last months before Hitler launched Operation BARBAROSSA. On occasion, the pressure caused British representatives stationed in Moscow to snap and lash out at the home departments for asking them to do things that were simply impossible in the frozen political climate of 1940–1941. In August 1940, a British Ministry of Information representative in the Russian capital sent a sarcastic reply to his ministry, explaining why he could not meet his superior's request that British war films be shown in Russian cinemas:

> To tell you the full reasons for the complete impossibility of show-
> ing British propaganda films in the U.S.S.R. would entail a long
> disquisition on the origin, constitution and political characteristics
> of this country. Very briefly, however, the Soviet Union is con-
> trolled by a dictator (M. Stalin), propaganda is entirely in the hands

of his party (the Communist Party), which also controls all cinemas. The Communist Party disapproves of all capitalist states and particularly of the Empire. It therefore does not permit the showing of any foreign propaganda films. There is no law to prevent the showing of such films: no such law is needed, any more than a law is needed to prevent Soviet citizens from singing "God Save the King" in Red Square.[17]

Ministry of Information officials in London were, like Queen Victoria a century earlier, not amused by this exasperated outburst. But the poor information officer had given a clear picture of the plight of British officials marooned in the Russian capital during the last months before BARBAROSSA, as they simultaneously dealt with cold suspicion and hostility from the Soviets and insufficient moral support or understanding from harried British officials at home.[18]

But beginning in June 1940, a powerful and quite surprising British voice was raised in favor of trying to reach some form of cooperative arrangement with the USSR. On 25 June 1940, shortly after becoming prime minister, Winston Churchill shoved aside his impressive anti-Communist credentials and made a direct appeal to Stalin (via the new British ambassador in Moscow, Sir Stafford Cripps) for an Anglo-Soviet arrangement to contain Nazi expansionism in Europe. Cripps managed to see Stalin, but in the view of some Foreign Office officials, he so watered down the prime minister's proposal that the Soviet dictator was able to sidestep it with ease and a minimum of embarrassment. There the matter of an Anglo-Soviet rapprochement rested until April 1941, when the ULTRA penetration of German ciphers began to provide Churchill with solid evidence that Hitler had made up his mind to attack the USSR. Following the Nazi devastation of Yugoslavia and Greece, Hitler had chosen not to decrease his military forces in the east but to build up an armored strike force on the Soviet border. When ULTRA began to show clear indications of this German redeployment toward the USSR, Churchill started once again to weigh the possibilities and military implications of joint belligerency with Stalin. In early April 1941, he sounded out his chief of air staff, Marshal Sir Charles Portal, on the strength and quality of the Red Air Force. Even when Portal responded that it was not very good, although it had some bomber capacity, Churchill was not put off, musing that "a lot of German war industry should be vulnerable [to the Red Air Force], especially if we are busy from the other side."[19]

In this mood of hopeful musing, Churchill sent Cripps a message for Stalin that contained ULTRA information (attributed to a trusted agent) that the German army command was moving the Third Panzer Division and other offensive formations to the Soviet border. The British ambassador in Moscow, who probably did not grasp the existence or significance of the ULTRA heart of this message, decided that it was not deliverable to Stalin in its original form. After much muddle and toning down, punctuated by Churchill's irate protests from London, Cripps finally passed the message on rather casually to a Soviet deputy foreign secretary, so there is no clear proof that it ever reached Stalin or that, if it did, he gave this message any special credence.

Over the next six months, Churchill continued to rave that Cripps's decision not to insist on seeing Stalin to deliver the prime minister's message had been a colossal blunder, an act of insubordination, and a contributing factor to the complete surprise of Hitler's BARBAROSSA attack on 22 June 1941. But Anthony Eden maintained at the time that Stalin was too well insulated in 1941 to hear what he did not want to hear or believe what he did not wish to believe. The Soviet leader refused to give credence to a multitude of other warnings received in the spring of 1941, and it is highly unlikely that the April message from Churchill—an old Soviet hater whose self-interest clearly lay in embroiling Soviet Russia in a war with Nazi Germany—would have had much chance of pulling the blinders from Stalin's eyes and dreams.[20]

The important part of this incident was the fact that by the early spring of 1941, the prime minister had already decided to mute his anti-Communism—at least for the time being—and was ready to welcome cobelligerency with the Soviet Union, even though on 23 May, the Joint Intelligence Committee (JIC) had second thoughts about whether Hitler would actually attack the USSR.[21] In May and June, Churchill had little patience for those who doubted that Hitler was about to throw Stalin into the arms of Britain. On a memo by the Polish general W. Sikorski that deprecated the possibility that Germany would move east, he noted, "I do not feel convinced by it. At any rate either war or showdown is near."[22] Like a number of others long hostile to the USSR, Churchill was convinced that this time the Soviet Union was the innocent and injured party and Hitler the undeniable aggressor. Even the extremely anti-Soviet American military attaché in Moscow felt compelled to observe in April 1941 that the "disposition of troops, attitude and military doctrine [of the] U.S.S.R. [is] fundamentally defensive."[23]

By early June 1941, although the SOE was still putting up plans for covert operations against the USSR and the JIC had no confidence in Russia's capacity to resist—"the Red Army is unlikely to offer successful resistance in open warfare to an army so highly mechanized or ably led as the German Army"[24]—higher Whitehall authorities had little doubt that Britain would have to establish some form of partnership with Soviet Russia once Hitler attacked. By 11 June, enough German secret messages had been broken to convince British intelligence authorities that the German secret service was throwing every available agent against the Russians.[25] On the following day, the cabinet directed the chiefs of staff to give "preliminary consideration" to the organization of a military mission for Moscow to be dispatched when the Germans struck.[26] On 13 June, Foreign Secretary Eden met with the Soviet ambassador in London, Ivan Maisky, and informed him that Germany was definitely concentrating against the USSR and that, "in the event of such hostilities, we should be ready to send a mission representing all three services to Russia, not because we pretended to any superiority in the art of war over Russian commanders, but because it would be composed of officers who had the most recent experience in actual conflict with the German forces"[27] (an inflated claim, for none of the senior British officers sent to Moscow after 22 June had any recent combat experience against the Wehrmacht).

On 14 June, the JIC once again looked at the likely course that a Russo-German war might take and concluded that it would require no more than six to eight weeks for Hitler's legions to polish off the USSR.[28] On the same day, the chiefs of staff nonetheless ordered their planners to consider dispatching such a mission to Russia, which they designated 30 Mission to distinguish it from other numbered military missions sent to the four corners of the world. The only stipulation was that no one who had been in the ill-fated mission that had tried to conclude a mutual defense agreement with the USSR during the Polish crisis of August 1939 should be included this time. The Joint Planning Staff (JPS) turned its attention to the question of the purpose of the mission to Moscow on 14 June as well, initiating its deliberations with the rather sour comment that Eden should not have jumped the gun by promising Ambassador Maisky that a mission would be sent. The JPS believed that such a mission should be seen as a "favor to Russia" and that its major purpose was to "keep the pot boiling" in the east by encouraging Russian resistance. The JPS anticipated that the Soviets would have little chance against the Wehrmacht regardless of what the British did, but if the Red Army did better than expected, the presence of a mission would show that Britain had tried to help, and the Russians would gain "the benefit of our experience in fighting the Germans."[29]

By 16 June, the British government was certain that a German attack on the USSR was imminent. It was also sufficiently sure of how it should react to that event that the prime minister cabled President Roosevelt and informed him that the Wehrmacht was definitely moving east and that Britain would "give all encouragement and any help we can spare to [the] USSR."[30] The American military authorities thereupon set about making their own pessimistic estimates regarding the Red Army's chances. U.S. Army G-2 had already concluded that Russia's "inherent inefficiency" denied it any chance of success, and Secretary of War Henry Stimson predicted in his diary on 17 June that Russia would "surrender" to German pressure even before the Wehrmacht attacked. But just as Churchill went against his naysayers, Roosevelt rejected the views of his gloomy advisers and informed Churchill that he would support "any announcement" welcoming Russia "as an ally."[31]

The civilian ministers of the British government who would have to cope with any political controversies regarding cobelligerency were apprehensive about the prospect of marching together with Stalin's Russia. A Foreign Office meeting held on 17 June to consider the propaganda implications of linking arms with the USSR was replete with wrangling and agonized pessimism concerning the central problem of how to cope with Soviet entry into the war in such a way as "to prevent a wave of disappointment when the Soviet resistance breaks."[32] The staff of the Ministry of Information, which met on the same day to consider possible propaganda problems, was chiefly worried about the political explosiveness of joining with the Soviets. "In view of the emotions associated with the general concept of Soviet Russia," the ministry concluded, "it will not be possible to treat Russian belligerency with the same evasiveness which we for so long applied to Abyssinia." Furthermore, the ministry was tormented about where to draw the line of partnership when Britain became an ally of Russia: "Should [Soviet Ambassador] Maisky be admitted to the St. James Palace Group [of Allied ambassadors]? Should the *Red Flag* [the Soviet anthem] be played on Sunday evenings? Should the Communist Party be recognised and admitted to the T[rade] U[nion] Congress?"[33]

These were weighty matters indeed, but ones that could happily be avoided by military men. On 19 and 20 June (still two to three days before the German attack on Russia), the Joint Planning Staff and the Chiefs of Staff Committee worked out the general principles for the posting of a military mission to Russia and ordered that it be dispatched to Moscow immediately after Hitler attacked. The chiefs believed that the value of this mission "would not be great," for the USSR faced rapid collapse; the JIC estimated only three to six weeks of resistance. The mission was to be sent primarily "on the grounds of need for intelligence," specifically, information on the Soviet Union and its military forces rather than those of the Nazi enemy. If Russian defenses turned out to be better than expected, the mission might help in overall strategy coordination between East and West, but the chiefs of staff were too pessimistic about the Red Army to harbor much hope of Soviet resistance. To only one aspect of the Soviet government were they prepared to grant serious respect: the chiefs specifically excluded from the mission any subversive activity specialists, because "the Russians will be suspicious from the outset and if subversive activities were traced to any one member, the mission as a whole would be compromised [because] the OGPU [in this period, actually the NKVD] are known to be efficient."[34]

Since the Soviet secret police organization was the sole promising feature of Stalin's Russia identified by the chiefs on the eve of BARBAROSSA, the Joint Planning Committee thought that the best course for the British military mission would be to run for it when Russian resistance collapsed. If this were done, portions of the mission might "continue to operate in such parts of Russia which remained free from German occupation[,] where they would not only stimulate resistance, but would provide us with intelligence when all other sources of information had dried up."[35]

On the Sunday morning that BARBAROSSA began (22 June 1941), the prime minister publicly proclaimed that Britain welcomed the Soviet Union to the anti-Hitler coalition and promised aid to the USSR, a gesture that stirred considerable popular enthusiasm in Britain and compelled the prime minister to secure retroactive cabinet approval for his action on Monday, because his colleagues had not agreed to it beforehand. The U.S. government and much of the American public also welcomed Russia's entry into the war on the side of the Allies, and the Communist Party abruptly halted its antiwar propaganda. But on both sides of the Atlantic, the generals and admirals lagged far behind public enthusiasm and the more measured satisfaction of the politicians. Secretary of War Stimson confided to his dairy on 22 June, "I cannot help feeling that it [BARBAROSSA] offers us and Great Britain a great chance provided we use it promptly." On the following day, the secretary tried to get the U.S. Army G-2 and War Plans Division to make an estimate of what awaited the Germans in Russia. Although Stimson "cross examined them fully and didn't let them get tangled up by the irrelevant speculations that they are so prone to indulge in," the best prediction the U.S. Army staff could produce was that "Germany will be thoroughly occupied in beating Russia for a minimum of one month and a possible maximum of three months."[36] The next day, the U.S. Army Air Corps produced its own waffling report on Soviet air strength, declaring that the Red Air Force had 8,000 aircraft and 16,000 regular officer pilots, but adding that no one seemed to know "how good these pilots are."[37]

During this critical period, the planning staff of the British military mission in Washington at least equaled the Americans in gloom and doom. This group of British planners merely adopted the pre-BARBAROSSA estimate made in

Whitehall that the Soviets might last three to six weeks. It added a number of dismal prophetic comments regarding the resistance potential of the Red Army: "Russian arms of all types are not likely to oppose effective resistance to the German assault"; "it is not expected that the German war machine will be seriously weakened in the long run"; and "the likelihood of the Russians being able to cause much embarrassment to the German High Command is very doubtful."[38]

Nonetheless, in Moscow, even as Stalin and the Russian Army high command fell into just the kind of funk that the Western military doomsayers had predicted, the Red Navy cleared the decks for action and sought to cooperate with the U.S. and Royal Navies. The Red Navy high command contacted Ambassador Cripps in Moscow and asked him to request that the Royal Navy designate a line of demarcation in the far north so that the new East-West partners might avoid inadvertent clashes. On that same day (23 June), the Admiralty replied positively to this approach, stating that for the time being, the Royal Navy would stay out of the far north and leave that operational zone to the Russians.

On the day after the start of BARBAROSSA, the only British high official in London who actually held out a helping hand to the Soviets was, however, the foreign secretary. Anthony Eden contacted Soviet Ambassador Ivan Maisky and told him that the British government believed that the two countries were now partners (Eden did not say "Allies"), that London would do what it could to assist the USSR, and that a three-services British military mission would be sent to Moscow if the Soviets agreed to receive it. Maisky may well have been gratified by Eden's friendly and supportive approach, because the Soviets certainly needed all the help they could get, and also because the Kremlin initially seems to have believed that the Nazi attack was part of a broad conspiracy that would be supported by all the capitalist opponents of the USSR. Five months later, former Soviet Foreign Secretary Maxim Litvinov confided to a British official in India that when he had heard the first news of Germany's offensive against Russia, he had been convinced that Hess had made an arrangement with Britain. Litvinov was both surprised and relieved when Churchill made his speech of support for the USSR.[39] Understandably, then, Maisky warmly assented to all that Eden suggested and added that his government wanted to reciprocate. "Not that there would be strict reciprocity in every detail," Maisky emphasized, but officials of the Soviet government "did not feel that they could receive help without also giving help." Eden was obviously delighted with this Soviet attitude, and the British military authorities were quickly given a green light to prepare their mission to Russia. But the principle of reciprocity had been laid down by the Soviet authorities and agreed to by Eden, and it would be used by Moscow to lever the British into making concessions on a broad range of military activities and assistance during the remainder of the war.[40]

Such long-range worrisome considerations were far from the thoughts of those in Whitehall, however, during the fourth week of June 1941. On 22 June, Hitler had crossed his Rubicon, and many people in Britain felt a burst of hope. A colonel in British Army intelligence noted in his diary on the following day, "I have a conviction that this is Hitler's mistake." Many believed instinctively that Nazi Germany might well have taken on one enemy too many.[41] The War Office promptly authorized its attaché in Moscow, Col. E. R. Greer, to collaborate with the Soviets on enemy order of battle information and instructed him that if the Russians so requested, information on the airborne methods that the Germans had used against the British in Crete could be handed over. But Greer was also told not to disclose any information on "our unavoidable weaknesses" in the Crete campaign or any current details of British "order of battle or plans in the Middle East or elsewhere."[42]

British military intelligence information was going to be passed to the Russians, but it was going to be done carefully and selectively. The British code- and cipher-breaking authorities similarly approached the Soviets with no more than deliberate speed. According to the British official history of intelligence in World War II, on 22 June 1941, the Government Code and Cypher School ceased all work on Russian codes and ciphers. This assertion may well be correct, but it is also clear that British interception and recording of Soviet encoded traffic did not cease in June 1941. In any event, the British authorities tried to be helpful with regard to the security of Russian codes and ciphers. On the day Germany attacked the USSR (22 June), the Foreign Office directed its embassy in Moscow to warn the Russians to improve the security of their codes and ciphers:

> We know that during the Soviet-Finnish War [1940] the Finns were reading all the Russian service cyphers. It appears that they can still do so. For example, we learn that a message from the Soviet Third Army Headquarters at Grodno reporting very serious damage to many airdromes of the W.[estern] M.[ilitary] D.[istrict] and asking urgently for assistance had been intercepted and read by the Finns by 11:00 a.m. today.[43]

Similar instances in which the British warned another government, no matter how friendly it was, that its codes and ciphers were not secure are rare.

Indeed, during World War II, it seems to have occurred only when Britain was providing another government with secret information that might have been put at risk unless its partner's codes and ciphers were made safe.[44] That the Foreign Office would issue such a warning to the Russians prior to any secret information being dispatched to Moscow indicates that, with the beginning of BAR-BAROSSA, at least the Foreign Office was taking Russia seriously. That this message also tacitly informed Moscow that the British had confidential sources of information about Finland (probably cryptanalytic) was a further vote of confidence in the USSR and indicates that London believed that Russia knew how to play the great ingelligence game and how to keep a secret.

Other inhabitants of Britain's secret world were, however, equally quick to search out possibilities for secret shenanigans in Russia. The day before the start of BARBAROSSA, the minister of economic warfare (the parent ministry for Britain's covert operational organization—the Special Operations Executive, or SOE) notified the British embassy in Washington that "in the event of a Russo-German war," and if the Soviets agreed, Britain planned to send oil demolition experts from the Middle East into southern Russia.[45] The SOE quickly established the nuclei of a dual organization, one portion of which was to be centered in the Middle East, where the demolition teams were preparing for action. The other portion was in Moscow, where a pair of British SOE officers were to coordinate with the Russians. On 23 June (the day after the German attack), the Joint Planning Staff in London prepared a paper advising that the SOE should be ordered "as a matter of urgency" to make preparations for infiltrating sabotage agents into the Caucasus.[46] Three days later (26 June), the British commander in the Middle East urged that Armenians be mobilized to assist the Soviets in destroying the oil-producing facilities in the Caucasus, if necessary, to keep them out of German hands. On that day, arrangements were also made for the dispatch of two SOE oil demolition specialists to Moscow, assigned to the embassy under the cover of "commercial secretaries."[47] The Foreign Office then worked up a plan to replace the Russian oil losses that would result from the demolition by shipping oil via Vladivostok, although, as a Foreign Office official noted, "it is not our present intention to make a *free gift* of the oil."[48]

The prospects for these oil obliteration operations were far from promising. It is difficult to imagine how Stalin could have been expected to go along with a scheme whereby British demolition specialists—foreign, capitalist, and imperialist—would blow up Russia's oil supplies and Whitehall would then sell the Russians substitute oil. Early in July, the head of the newly formed British military mission in Moscow was "very disturbed" about the plan, if for no other reason than that it "would be a great psychological mistake" to indicate to the

Russians that Whitehall believed that "a speedy Russian collapse is in-evitable."[49] The feeble cover that was supposed to disguise British demolition personnel quickly dissolved on 6 July, when one of the "commercial secre-taries" who was to organize the operation arrived in Moscow in military uni-form, which surely must have alerted the NKVD. The Soviet authorities nonetheless sought to make the best of the situation and actually put one of the British oil demolition specialists to work in Moscow helping the Russian Naval Air Staff to identify suitable oil targets for Red Air Force raids on Rumania. But when Ambassador Cripps suggested to Stalin on 22 July that British experts should work with the Russians on demolition preparations for the Cau-casus, the Soviet leader not surprisingly replied that demolition was a matter for the Soviet government to decide, and if the need arose, the Soviets them-selves would blow up the Baku oil fields.[50]

What neither the Russians nor the British demolition experts in Moscow had been told, however, was that the British Middle East Command and SOE were also developing a completely separate oil demolition scheme for the Caucasus, code-named the "G(R) 16" Mission, which planned to fly bands of Kurds, Armenians, and perhaps Georgians from Iraq into the Caucasus to blow up the oil fields when the Germans began to enter the region. In late summer, the Foreign Office and some British Army staff officers in Whitehall became worried about the risks of not informing the Russians of these Middle East demolition activities. During August, keeping the G(R) 16 Mission hid-den became even more difficult, because Britain and Russia were moving closer to joint action to neutralize possible Axis subversive pressure from Iran and to occupy that country in order to use it as a supply route into south-ern Russia. Inevitably, this planning forced Moscow and London to take a closer look at Axis subversive activities in the Middle East. Between 2 and 16 August, for example, the Soviets supplied the British with information on real or possible German-inspired threats from Iran, Afghanistan, and the Turko-Syrian border. But even with Soviet agents obviously sniffing close to the activities of the G(R) 16 Mission, Churchill personally ordered that no one was to tell the Russians of the plans to destroy the Caucasus oil fields, and this ban remained in force even when the two countries launched their joint occupation of Iran on 25 August.[51]

In the third week of September, the chiefs of staff were still fussing about prospects for Caucasus oil production and even contemplating sabotage opera-tions against Donets Basin coal production. But the Red Army managed to hold on grimly throughout the icy month of November, and on the penultimate day of that month, it drove the Germans out of Rostov, inflicting the first major defeat on the German army in the war. In the process, it saved Caucasus oil and prompted British authorities to dismantle the G(R) 16 Mission.[52]

The risks that had been run, and the ultimate uselessness of the SOE oil demolition arrangements made in Moscow and the Middle East, nonetheless failed to deter the SOE from trying to arrange other subversive operations in Russia during the late summer of 1941. In early August, Ambassador Cripps had suggested that the SOE send someone to Moscow to discuss subversive propaganda with the Soviets, an idea that apparently left the director of the SOE's propaganda activities "frightened out of his wits." But the minister in charge of the SOE, Hugh Dalton, advanced this idea and also made arrangements to attach someone to the embassy staff in Moscow to liaise with the NKVD, which was, in addition to being the Soviet secret police, the agency used by the authorities to aid and encourage resistance activity. As early as 23–24 June, Dalton recorded in his diary that he wanted to attach someone to the embassy staff in Moscow who could cooperate with the NKVD. The original idea was to use "some Slav, perhaps Czech" tough to work with the Soviet secret police, but after a bit of confused consultation, a regular army sapper, Col. Robert Guiness, who had been attached to the SOE was flown in during late June to act as temporary SOE representative in Moscow.[53]

Matters rested there until the first week of August, when Dalton and his aides seriously began to weigh the appointment of a permanent SOE representative in Moscow. In the course of this deliberation, various advantages seem to have been considered. Among them was one that appeared during a private dinner that Dalton had with Sir Stewart Menzies, "C," the head of the British Secret Intelligence Service (MI 6), on 6 August 1941. The two British shadow warfare chiefs agreed that although the British Communists would be useless for either espionage or covert warfare activities, Communists from other countries might be highly valuable agents, especially in France and Germany. This may well have been the genesis of a program adopted during the later stages of the war, through which the NKVD provided agents that the SOE trained and equipped at bases in the United Kingdom and the RAF subsequently airlifted to drop points on the Continent.[54]

Whether or not the hope of tapping Soviet Russia's reservoir of secret Communist agents was the primary motivation for sending a permanent SOE representative, Dalton decided in the summer of 1941 to appoint another veteran of earlier battles against the Communists, and a man with some clandestine operational experience, to direct SOE operations in Russia. Brig. George Hill was as near as one could come to being a professional and notorious practitioner of dirty tricks, especially those aimed against the Bolsheviks. He had even written a book about his anti-Communist derring-do. But the Soviets' need for assistance made them willing to overlook virtually all past sins if they thought that those whom the British sent were professionals with skills that might assist them in their hour of greatest need. The Kremlin therefore lodged no complaint against the posting of Hill to Moscow as chief of the SOE's "Sam" Mission there.[55]

Hill was sent to Russia by sea and arrived in Moscow sometime in September. Once there, he seems to have spent most of his time engaged in endless rounds of waiting and liaising, with little of practical value to show for his efforts. But long before Hill actually arrived in Moscow, another much more important gesture of British willingness to collaborate had materialized in Moscow in the form of a combined-services British military mission. The mission had to be organized and its staff selected very quickly, while the differing interests of the Royal Navy, Air Force, and Army were hammered into some form of workable consensus. This task had also been performed in an atmosphere of impending doom, because virtually all British military and civilian leaders clung rigidly to their pessimistic forecasts that Soviet Russia had no chance against the German Wehrmacht. On 23 June, British Army intelligence (MI 14) had concluded that German armor might reach Moscow "in three weeks or less, though allowing for a reasonable resistance by the Russian Army, they would probably take as much as five weeks."[56] The permanent undersecretary of the Foreign Office (Sir Alexander Cadogan) noted with relief on 25 June, when BARBAROSSA was only three days old, that the Germans had not conquered Russia yet. Meanwhile, across the Atlantic, the War and Navy Departments of the United States gave the Soviets only four weeks to three months before the Germans would overwhelm them. Such gloomy predictions, along with strong British governmental suspicion of unsavory ideological activities, led Eden and Minister of Information Duff Cooper to limit "publicity about Russia" to "cultural material of the pre-1917 era." The BBC began its pro-Soviet war broadcasts with performances of the *Cherry Orchard* and readings from *War and Peace*.[57]

The military authorities were rather more realistic in their preparations for the dispatch of 30 Mission to Moscow, but even they were not able to get everything right. Originally, the joint planners wanted to send Gen. D. G. Johnson as overall head of the mission, with Rear Adm. J. G. A. Miles, Brig. R. C. Firebrace, and Air Vice Marshal A. C. Collier (who had been air attaché in Moscow during the 1930s) to lead the navy, army, and air sections, respectively. The support staff was to consist of an equal number of staff and intelligence officers, a submarine and minesweeping specialist, plus radio operators, cipher personnel, clerks, and batmen.[58]

This plan originally called for a mission of fifty-odd army personnel, with smaller RAF and navy delegations, but in the end, an advanced high-level cadre of nine officers was flown from Scotland to north Russia, accompanied by the British ambassador to Moscow, Sir Stafford Cripps, who was returning to his post after a short sojourn in Britain. This advance guard landed in Archangel and quickly journeyed to Moscow by air, where they were introduced to Molotov rather than Stalin. They immediately held their first staff conference with Gen. G. K. Zhukov and Lt. Gen. I. Golikov in Moscow on 28 June, just six days after the Germans attacked the USSR.

The advance party was led by Gen. Noel Mason Macfarlane, who, at the urging of Gen. Sir John Dill, had been appointed mission chief instead of General Johnson, for reasons that are not altogether clear. Brigadier Firebrace had also been excluded from the mission, being appointed instead to direct British Army liaison activities with Soviet military officials in London. Collier and Miles assumed control of the air and navy branches of the mission, and the army section was later turned over to Col. E. R. Greer, then serving as British military attaché in Moscow.

The decision to break the mission in half—sending the advance party via the northern route by air and allowing the remainder to go by sea (some enlisted personnel and junior officers going around the Cape and not arriving until late 1941 or early 1942)—was in part due to the difficulty of flying large numbers of British personnel into Russia at a time when long-distance air travel was in its infancy. The original idea had been to fly the whole mission in from the Middle East by securing Iranian permission for flights over that country. But the British embassy in Teheran insisted that the Iranian government would never permit flights that were intended to assist its dangerous Communist neighbor. Ambassador R. Bullard initially suggested to the Foreign Office that it would be better not to even raise the issue, because if the aircraft flew high enough, Iranian air security was so poor that the flights were "unlikely to be detected by the Iranians."[59]

This was too adventurous a course for Whitehall, however, which chose the safer, if inconvenient, approach of splitting 30 Mission into airborne and seaborne contingents. British officialdom was perhaps inclined to take this cautious course because the dispatch of a military mission to Moscow was such a delicate matter, and untoward incidents had to be avoided. Whitehall also may have needed extra time to screen personnel especially carefully. Once word had gotten out that Britain was sending a mission to Moscow, applications arrived from some "unbalanced members" of the general public who wanted, for a variety of unfathomable reasons, to take part in their own mission to Moscow.

Military officialdom therefore took its time, making certain that the candidates for membership in the mission were reliable and had appropriate technical and staff expertise, along with as much Russian language skill as possible.[60]

Paradoxically, this close screening process meant that in the pursuit of competence and experience, the mission, throughout the four years of its existence, would contain a large number of individuals with prior experience in Russia. This meant that the majority of them had fought in Russia against the Communists in the last stage of World War I and the civil wars, came from emigré families, or had served as members of official delegations to Communist Russia in the 1920s and 1930s, when Anglo-Soviet relations had been frosty in the extreme.

The anti-Soviet complexion of 30 Mission personnel did not appear to augur well for its long-term prospects. That liability was compounded by the sizable contingent of professional intelligence men in the mission, which inevitably increased Soviet suspicions. The original War Office plan had even included a paragraph stating that the mission "will be bringing one special portable wireless transmission set disguised as an ordinary suitcase."[61] Fortunately, saner minds prevailed, and after a discussion between Ambassador Cripps and War Office planners about Soviet security practices, the secret suitcase was left at home.

The curriculum vitae of the chief of the mission, Gen. Noel Mason Macfarlane, as well as those of other members of the mission, was, as the general himself later put it in an unpublished memoir, too closely associated with the "I" side of army life to make Macfarlane's appointment as head of the mission reassuring to the extremely suspicious men who made up Stalin's court. Macfarlane had held two attaché posts, including Berlin in the 1930s, and had then directed the intelligence section of the British Expeditionary Force in France and Belgium during the ill-fated campaign of 1940. He was an energetic, rather eccentric, and unstable individual who loved amateur dramatics, did not suffer fools gladly, and carried a heavy touch of playacting over into everyday life. Later, during the long, acrimonious exchanges over Soviet demands for a Second Front, in which Moscow hurled insults at the inactivity of the British, Macfarlane's foppishness was a serious liability. But it must be said in his favor that he took his liaison duties seriously, and while he was in Moscow he struggled valiantly, but in vain, to learn the Russian language.[62]

Macfarlane realized that his appointment might be unwise and urged the chief of the Imperial General Staff, Gen. Sir John Dill (with whom Macfarlane was on first-name terms), that it would be better to send someone less tainted by extended intelligence service. Dill not only brushed aside Macfarlane's reservations and confirmed his appointment but also sent a message to Moscow telling Marshal S. K. Timoshenko that during the French campaign, Macfarlane had been "some time head of the intelligence" section of the British Army on the Western Front.[63] The purpose of this message was presumably to convince the Russians that Macfarlane had extensive knowledge of combat against the German Army, but its effect was probably to increase the urgency of the Kremlin alarm bells announcing that a group of hostile capitalist intelligence agents was on the way.

Any government faced with the crisis that confronted the Soviet Union in June 1941 would have been given food for thought by messages such as that from General Dill. But no government in modern times was more paranoid than the early wartime regime of Stalin's Russia. The fact that the first military mission sent to Moscow was openly led by a longtime professional intelligence man probably seemed to Stalin and his staff to be as much a provocation as an offer of assistance.

If the Soviet authorities had been given an opportunity to examine the instructions that were issued to the mission (as their secret agents in London or the Soviet citizens employed in the British embassy may well have allowed them to do), many of their deepest fears and suspicions would have been fully confirmed. Macfarlane and his team were provided with four sets of instructions, one for Macfarlane himself, and one for each of the three service subsections (navy, army, and RAF).[64] Each set of instructions had its own special elements and variations of language, but there were important common features. As their first-priority assignment, all segments of the mission were ordered to toil against the odds and prolong Russian resistance for as long as possible, even though none of them believed that it would last long. When that effort failed, they were directed to encourage last-ditch resistance in any areas of Russia where military operations against the Germans might still be possible. Both Macfarlane and the head of the naval mission, Admiral Miles, were instructed that their highest priority was to ensure that the Red Fleet was scuttled. After that, when all else was lost, it would be every man for himself. Before his departure from England, Macfarlane was told by General Dill that his best chance of escape would probably be to work his way south on foot for a thousand or so miles and then hike over the mountains to India.[65]

These instructions were certainly not cheery reading for the members of 30 Mission, nor would they have heartened any Russians who learned of them. The Soviet authorities also would not have been overjoyed with the second-priority assignment given to each section of the mission (except, oddly, the RAF), which was to supply London, specifically the chiefs of staff, "with information and intelligence [that sensitive word again] both on Russian and German operations and on the course of the campaign."[66] Whitehall wanted as much advance warning as possible regarding when and where the Red Army was likely to breathe its last. In the meantime, it sought as much information as possible on both the Wehrmacht and the Red Army so that Britain could adjust and improve its own military methods and defensive deployment against Hitler.

Most of the other provisions of the instructions would not have offended even the most paranoid Stalinist. However, their hope stated that British and Russian strategy could be coordinated by the mission, or that British officers might be attached to Russian armies, never came close to realization. The directive to the RAF mission chief that he should coordinate shuttle bombing of Rumanian oil fields, employing RAF and Red Air Force long-range bombers, had no success either, although a modified form of this idea was ultimately implemented by the U.S. Army Air Force in 1943–1944.

Nonetheless, by 28 June 1941, the British government had taken a great leap and committed itself to attempting to join the USSR in a common struggle against Nazi Germany and Hitler's fellow travelers Italy, Rumania, Hungary, and Britain's earlier favorite, Finland. But no joint command was established with the Russians such as would be formed with the Americans when they entered the war. In 1942, the British Chiefs of Staff Committee and the newly created American Joint Chiefs of Staff would be combined into an Anglo-American supreme command (the Combined Chiefs of Staff), but the Soviets were not included. In addition, no warm bond was miraculously created between Churchill and Stalin such as already existed between the prime minister and President Roosevelt (although Churchill had recurring fantasies that he would join Stalin in a warm embrace as late as mid-1942). There was also no Anglo-Soviet agreement on common principles to guide wartime political activities or to act as an idealistic foundation for planning the peace, such as the Atlantic Charter would provide for the United States and Britain when it was signed off Newfoundland in August 1941. Whitehall had not relinquished its deep suspicion of Stalin and the Comintern, nor its unease that the working-class people of Britain might be a bit too pleased by the establishment of a common front with socialist Russia. For its part, across the East-West divide, the Soviet leadership made little effort to conceal the dislike and distrust, spiced with disdain, with which it viewed the British Empire and all its works.

In late June, Britain had not even begun to sort out its military, economic, or cultural policies toward the USSR. But under Churchill's energetic and surprisingly enthusiastic leadership, the British government had begun a course of hesitant support for the Russian defense effort. Whitehall genuinely condemned Hitler's attack on Russia. It also resolved not to say nasty things about Stalin and Stalinism in the immediate future, and it promised to check the military supply cupboard for anything that might assist the Russian defense. But it remained profoundly pessimistic about the Soviet Union's power to defend itself against Hitler's blitzkrieg, and from the opening days of the campaign, Whitehall was braced for the probability of a sudden Soviet collapse, as had already occurred in Poland, the Balkans, Norway, France, and the Low Countries.

The British 30 Mission, whose top-level staff arrived in Moscow in the fourth week of June, was therefore in the forefront of the great experiment that would determine whether democratic and imperial Britain could successfully cooperate with Communist Russia and, against the obvious odds, actually defeat Nazi Germany. But in truth, the military mission had very little largesse to give. Cooperation regarding military supplies would require considerable negotiation and would be plagued by formidable shipping difficulties, as well as a maze of procedural and technical differences between the two countries. Britain had very few weapons or military personnel to spare, and what it did possess was devoted to the defense of the home islands, the lifeline, and the Empire, which would most certainly become Hitler's main target if and when Russia collapsed.

In addition, the much vaunted British experience in fighting the Germans turned out to be largely irrelevant, except for the British expertise in air warfare and their undoubted advantage in naval skill and experience. In the most crucial matter, however—that of mass armored warfare involving millions of men, dreadful weather, primitive communications systems, and vast distances—the knowledge and experience of the British Army members of the mission, and of their masters in the War Office, were largely beside the point. The efforts of General Macfarlane and his colleagues to teach the Russian military how to fight the Germans in defense of their homeland were spectacularly irrelevant, to the point of offensiveness.

Beyond the unquestionably important fact that 30 Mission created a symbolic partnership with Russia and would act as a brokerage house for an increasing flow of largely American-produced supplies, Macfarlane's team served primarily as a double conveyor belt system for secret information. It tried to perform the assignment it had been given to discover everything possible about the Russo-German war and send it on to Whitehall. More importantly, in midsummer 1941, it would take on the especially delicate task, not foreseen in its original instructions, of passing to the Soviet high command a broad and deep flow of secret intelligence regarding Germany and its Axis partners Italy, Rumania, Finland, and ultimately Japan. From midsummer onward, Macfarlane's team would also transmit to Whitehall the secret intelligence the Russians gave it in exchange. Therefore, for the next four years, the mission (joined in mid-1943 by a comparable U.S. military mission team) served as the main clearinghouse for secret East-West intelligence cooperation during World War II.

2
Searching for an Intelligence Partnership, 22 June–9 July 1941

On 22 June 1941, the Wehrmacht threw against the Russians the largest and most powerful offensive force the world had ever seen. Three massive army groups, consisting of 152 divisions (19 of them panzer divisions) and totaling 3 million men, struck the stunned and ill-prepared Soviet defenses. In the north, Field Marshal Ritter von Leeb rolled toward Leningrad, aided by a Finnish Army determined to recover the territory it had lost to the Russians in the Winter War of 1940. At the southern end of the advancing line, Field Marshal Gerd von Rundstedt's Army Group South, aided by a half dozen Rumanian divisions, massed on the Russian border to pin down Soviet units; drove toward the Ukraine, encircling vast numbers of Soviet troops; and roared on in the direction of the Black Sea, the Crimea, and ultimately the Caucasus. The German Army Group Center, under the command of Field Marshal Feodor von Bock, simultaneously smashed through Belorussia and drove northeast in the direction of Smolensk and Moscow.[1]

Behind the Stukas and panzers of each army group came the SS *Einsatzgruppen* death squads, charged with exterminating the Soviet system and preparing the Russians for submission and helot status in a Thousand Year Reich. For Communists, Jews, Gypsies, and other "undesirables," the *Einsatzgruppen* brought mobile killing teams that slaughtered "racial enemies" in the hundreds of thousands. In 1942, when such methods proved unable to keep up with the killing quotas, they were supplemented first by mobile gas vans and then by extermination camps such as Sobibor, Treblinka, and Auschwitz. BARBAROSSA was truly an ideological and racist war without limit, reservation, or mercy.

Unprepared, badly led, untrained to combat blitzkrieg warfare, and initially paralyzed by the suddenness and ferocity of the German attack, Russian frontier forces were overwhelmed by shock and German power. Even Stalin's iron will seems to have faltered in the face of blitzkrieg, as the Soviet leader slumped into a deep, dark, and debilitating depression. But even in the worst moments of the first German onslaught, many Red Army soldiers stood their ground, fought, and died. The German advance was thereby slowed, and the basis was laid for a great swell of national pride, determination, and bravery that would soon flow over Soviet Russia and become the most important single factor in the defeat of Nazi Germany in World War II.

By the end of June 1941, Stalin had pulled himself together, and on 10 July, just as the bitter battle for Smolensk began, he swept aside the existing structure of the armed forces high command. Stalin himself became commander in chief, with Marshal B. Shaposhnikov as his military aide and mouthpiece. Two and a half weeks later, Gen. K. Zhukov was made roving troubleshooter for the Stalinist command system, with Gen. A. M. Vasilevski providing the military brains needed to outplan and outmaneuver Hitler and his brilliant staff. However, these changes in the Soviet command structure could not immediately stop the German advance or lessen the frightful wave of death and destruction that was engulfing Russia and its army. By the first week of July, von Bock's Army Group Center had completed the Smolensk encirclement, and another 100,000 Soviet military prisoners were driven off for slave labor or death. Three weeks later, in the far north, the Germans closed the noose around Leningrad, cutting the city off from the rest of Russia. Leningrad's martyrdom had begun, and its civilian population would die in the hundreds of thousands over the next two years.

In spite of Hitler's apparent triumphs and the astronomical number of Soviet military and civilian casualties, however, BARBAROSSA did not go according to plan, even during its first two months. The Red Army did not collapse, and the Soviet system was not broken. Russian generals quickly found their way, and many Red Army units fought ferociously, even in hopeless situations that would have broken the will of lesser armies. The Russian soldiers were far better and more dedicated fighters than the Germans had expected, and there were far more of them than had been allowed for. The Germans had assumed that they would face roughly 200 Red Army divisions, but by mid-August, 360 divisions had already been identified. The Germans also learned that the Russians had some first-class equipment, including the T-34 tank, and a well-armed tactical air force.

Faced with this peculiar balance sheet of triumphs and unforeseen difficulties, Hitler hesitated in the fourth week of August. Having won the Smolensk battle, albeit at a high cost in men and machines, his generals wanted to push on immediately against Moscow, where Russian defenses seemed to be thickening and becoming more formidable by the hour. But the Fuehrer overruled his staff and opted for a sweeping southerly diversion to chew up the Soviet military reserve, seize the Ukraine, destroy the foundations of Russia's heavy industry, and open the door to the Caucasus oil fields, which at this moment were also being eyed by the various demolition enthusiasts of Britain's SOE.

The senior German generals bitterly and vainly condemned the decisions to go south, and most historians have subsequently endorsed their view. By failing to strike immediately against Moscow, Hitler lost his best chance to achieve a total strategic triumph over the Soviet Union in 1941. In October, when he turned back against the Soviet capital, the Red Army was wiser in the ways of modern war, was better dug in defensively, and had the force of the Russian winter on its side. Yet it must be acknowledged that at the time of Hitler's decision, and during the Nazi southern advance in late August and early September, it was difficult to believe that the Germans were on a losing course. Once again, the German generals seemed to outsmart their Russian rivals at every turn, while the panzers and the Stukas struck with bold efficiency and huge encirclement operations added hundreds of thousands of Red Army soldiers to the German bag of prisoners of war.

A strong current of military opinion in London during the summer of 1941 was inclined to believe that the rapid German advance and the huge numbers of prisoners indicated an imminent and smashing Nazi triumph, both before and after Hitler made his fatal decision to move south in late August. Throughout July, the military estimates prepared by the War Office mainly pondered what would happen following the inevitable collapse of Soviet resistance west of the Urals. On 3 July, one estimate concluded that it was "possible" that "organized and coordinated Russian resistance would end" within a few weeks, and the Russian government would then be compelled to take to the woods and try "to continue the struggle in much the same way as the Chinese Government is carrying on the war against Japan."[2]

Shortly after the preparation of this estimate, the British Joint Planning Staff met with the U.S. military mission in London, and although the British were rather coy about providing a definite prognosis on the duration of the Russo-German war, the Americans concluded "that the British view is that a German success is in the offing; the doubt is as to when." The generals and admirals in Whitehall confided to the American mission that the only aid that they were prepared to give Russia consisted of "extending encouragement" coupled with RAF attacks on Germany's Baltic ports. On 10 July, a colonel in MO 1 (the main operational subsection of the War Office) dismissed Russian resistance and any possibility of serious Western aid to the USSR by declaring, "if they are going to fight they will fight, but for their own lives and not to help us defeat Germany." This colonel went on to say with astonishing optimism that "we are doing quite nicely against Germany, particularly in view of ever increasing American aid and the practical certainty that the U.S.A. will sooner or later come into the war."[3]

British civilian officials generally appear to have been quicker than those in the military to read the signs correctly and conclude that the Soviets were actually doing better than had been anticipated. Alexander Cadogan noted in his diary on 3 July that the Russians were obviously putting up a fight, because embassy telegrams from Moscow had become less depressing. V. F. W. Cavendish Bentinck (secretary of the Joint Intelligence Committee) concluded on 10 July that even on the basis of the dismal estimates arriving from the War Office, there was no possibility that the Germans could reach the Caucasus in less than six weeks.[4]

Shortly thereafter, the parliamentary secretary confided to the director general of the Ministry of Information that he was disturbed by the thought that there was no British propaganda section dealing with Russia, nor, as far as he knew, had "any steps been taken to create one." It was not until August that the Ministry of Information was prepared to face the fact that the Soviets were doing rather well and that the British public knew this and "believe[d] in social action and admire[d] Russia." Only then, in order to "counter subtly a drift to communism" due to the Soviet Union's military achievements, did the Ministry of Information conclude that it would be best to employ subtly ambiguous pro-Russian propaganda, because such "oblique" materials would fill "the vacant mind and prevent therefore, devils from entering in."[5]

Gradually, the British military leaders also began to acknowledge that the Red Army was putting up a better fight against the Nazis than they had thought possible. The first step in registering this gradual recognition of Soviet military achievements was the acquisition of an appropriate map. Although the War Office had been anticipating BARBAROSSA for weeks before the German attack, no one had secured detailed maps of the USSR. On 3 July, a War Office official bewailed the fact that they did not have a single Russian military map: "We are completely in the dark as to what is the state of their triangulation . . . and we have no conception as to what map work has been undertaken for the last twenty or more years."[6]

Despite this long delay in acquiring the means to trace the course of the eastern campaign, British military planners had gradually come to admit that the Russians were doing surprisingly well. By 26 July, MI 3(c), the Army staff intelligence section concerned with the Eastern Front, acknowledged that Germany's initial goals had not been reached but also moaned about Soviet appeals for assistance. If London did not send material in large enough quantities, "the Soviet authorities and their sympathizers in this country" would accuse the War Office of being "Fascists, White Guardist, and class conscious." But the Soviet system had not collapsed, Russian morale was high, and the British intelligence analysts accurately predicted that the Germans would soon have to make the hazardous choice of either conquering land or destroying Russian military forces. A month later, on 27 August, MI 3 and MI 14 (the general Order of Battle Branch) produced a major joint assessment that summed up the situation on the Eastern Front by declaring "that no forecast as to the future can usefully be made, but it must be borne in mind that winter is approaching." This admission that the Russians had changed the odds to roughly even, with the weather perhaps tipping things in their favor, constituted a striking shift in the settled opinion of the British military establishment.[7]

Unquestionably the speed with which this change occurred was largely due to the intelligence related to the Eastern Front, which the British authorities acquired from ULTRA decrypts. Bletchley Park had secured considerable vital intelligence regarding German operational movements and intentions through its ability to read the general Luftwaffe liaison cipher, code-named "Red" by the British, as well as the Luftwaffe's ground-air key (code-named "Kestrel" by Bletchley) used in the east from June 1941 to September 1942. In addition, the first German army operational cipher cracked by Bletchley was the army cipher (code-named "Vulture" by the British) used for BARBAROSSA, which was broken on 27 June 1941 and was read intermittently thereafter until June 1944. Supplementary details also came from the reading of diplomatic codes. In addition to access to Japanese codes provided by the American gift of a MAGIC machine in early 1941, the British were reading coded diplomatic traffic from Germany, Italy, and a wide range of other countries, including Portugal, Saudi Arabia, and Turkey. Such information was pure gold, and a month or two of considering it should have been enough to convince the War Office that all was not going well for the Germans on the Eastern Front.[8] In addition, the British were acquiring secret information from both intercepts and the conscious sharing of information by the military representatives in Moscow of their small allies, especially the Poles, Czechs, and Greeks. The Czech military attaché in Russia, Colonel Pika, was an especially prolific source regarding Russian operations and intentions, and many of his reports had been provided to Whitehall by the Czech government in exile even before the launching of BARBAROSSA. As General Macfarlane reported from Moscow on 18 August 1941, the ability of the Polish and Czech military representatives "to get good information both official and unofficial is much better than mine," and the British military and air attachés in Finland also seem to have been able to secure truly useful information during the early stage of the eastern war.[9]

In addition to these indirect and cryptanalytic sources of information on the Russian campaign, the Anglo-American authorities were given confidential data on developments in the Russo-German war by three official military liaison posts established, at least in part, to provide just such information to London and Washington. These three units were a Russian military mission in London (which arrived in Britain on 12 July), the office of the American military attaché in Moscow, and the British 30 Mission, which was also in Moscow.

Of these three organizations, the American military attaché's office easily won the prize for the Western agency that produced the smallest amount of useful intelligence in the first phase of the Russo-German war. The American military attaché, Maj. Ivan Yeaton, knew rudimentary Russian but was a passionate hater of the Soviet system; he was unprepared to concede anything to Stalin or his aides, even after they went to war against Hitler. In consequence, he was given an especially difficult time by the Soviet authorities. Yeaton's assistant attaché, Maj. J. A. Michela, was only slightly less hostile to the Soviets than his chief and did little to soften Yeaton's hostile and controversial stance. The American ambassador was also of marginal help. Lawrence Steinhardt was a punctilious, old-fashioned diplomat, totally lost in the peripheral formalities of his office and disinclined to push members of his mission to try to work with Soviet officials. On the one occasion during the summer of 1941 when the U.S. government seriously attempted to work out a program of assistance to the USSR (Harry Hopkins's supply mission of late July), Hopkins carefully kept all the civilian and military naysayers at the U.S. embassy in Moscow at arm's length.[10]

As the summer campaign in Russia progressed, the U.S. Army authorities in Washington, pushed by Secretary of War Stimson and the president, repeatedly told Major (and then Colonel) Yeaton to try to cooperate with the Red Army high command and to exchange all information with the British military mission in Moscow except cryptanalytic (i.e., MAGIC) intelligence. But Yeaton claimed that he could do nothing, even if he wanted to; in the second week of July, he had burned all his files in the belief that the feeble Soviets would immediately collapse and the Nazis would soon be in Moscow. The War Department again told him to cooperate with the British mission in exchanging information with the Russians. At first, Yeaton replied that this would cause problems, because Ambassadors Steinhardt and Cripps were mutually hostile. A bit later, he refused to try because he believed that General Macfarlane and his team were too optimistic about Russia's prospects. Yeaton even insisted that before he could do anything with the Soviets, Washington would have to put restrictions on Russian officials in the United States in order to compel Moscow to grant the U.S. attaché a visit to the front. When G-2 and the State Department agreed even to this demand, Yeaton reversed himself and predicted that the Soviets would not let him see anything of value in any case. After the Soviet authorities overlooked all his obstructiveness and allowed him to visit Red aircraft factories, where he saw with his own eyes modern aircraft being produced even in damaged installations, Yeaton maintained that the Stalinist system was weak, the great majority of the people completely disillusioned, and the Nazis therefore sure to win because anti-Soviet fifth columns were in full operation in the Baltic states as well as in the Ukraine and Georgia.[11]

The War Department in Washington was doubtful about Yeaton's fifth-column tales, since the British mission in Washington had heard nothing of the kind from its own people in Moscow. So when the U.S. military attaché in Moscow tried to explain away his failure to obtain intelligence from the Russians by claiming that the Soviets could trade such information only for intelligence on Japanese forces in Manchuria, G-2 immediately sent him its summaries of these forces, identifying, among other units, six Japanese infantry divisions, two armored and two cavalry brigades, plus 350 military aircraft at five named Manchurian locations.

This move seems to have spiked Yeaton's pipe, but there is no indication in the files that he ever tried to swap this secret information on the Japanese for secret German order of battle information held by the Russians. That failure appears to have settled the attaché's fate, for shortly after listening to his prophecy that no large volume of supplies could ever be shipped into Russia through such a cold and dreary place as Archangel, G-2 ordered Yeaton to give up his post in Moscow and return to Washington on 21 October.[12]

Fortunately for Allied prospects, not all American officials who appeared in Moscow in the summer of 1941 were so closed-mindedly opposed to the USSR. In particular, President Roosevelt's special emissary Harry Hopkins, who traveled to Moscow in July despite a near-fatal illness, did his best to be positive about the Soviet Union and its chances against the Nazis. Hopkins certainly took too rosy a view of Stalin and was partly hoodwinked by the Soviet leader's cheerful predictions of future Soviet successes. But Hopkins was proved right when he concluded that the Yeatons and Steinhardts were suffering from tunnel vision and that the USSR would withstand the German assault. He also benefited the Allied cause by selling the reality of Soviet strength to both Churchill and Roosevelt, an achievement that exposed Hopkins to considerable good-natured ribbing because of his alleged conversion to Stalinism. His British hosts on the August 1941 journey to the Atlantic Charter meeting off Newfoundland went so far as to make a straight-faced apology to Hopkins for showing the movie *Mr. X,* which portrayed his Kremlin "pals" in a bad light.[13]

Although Harry Hopkins was instrumental in moving Russia up to the front ranks of American aid projects in the summer of 1941, the Soviets themselves had not been shy about promoting their cause in Britain and the United States and securing as much military hardware and vital raw material as possible even before the Hopkins visit. When a Russian military mission suddenly arrived in Britain on 8 July (the Kremlin having given the British authorities only two days' warning that it was on its way), they came—in the words of the British liaison officer assigned to them—clutching the idea that "Great Britain was a vast storehouse of munitions." Within a short period they were disabused of this idea, and the Soviet mission soon underwent a number of changes to meet the real situation that prevailed in the United Kingdom. Ten days after the mission's arrival, its commander, Gen. F. I. Golikov, moved on to Washington, where he headed the Russian supply mission in the most bountiful environment of the United States. Golikov was replaced as head of the Soviets' London mission by a taciturn rear admiral, N. M. Kharlamov, who held that post until the end of the war. Under Kharlamov's direction, the mission gradually tipped the emphasis of its activities from acquiring supplies to securing useful information, especially technical data and operational intelligence.[14]

Prime Minister Churchill initially welcomed the appearance of the Soviet mission in Britain. The Foreign Office also looked on it favorably, as did the chief of the air staff, who remarked, "it is to our advantage that the Russians should have as many successes as possible, and for this purpose we must take some risks from the security of intelligence point of view." But the Joint Planning Staff, speaking for those in the military hierarchy whose doubts and suspicions were still firm and clear, declared that although it was British policy to keep the Soviets fighting "for as long as possible," Britain was "not allied with Russia nor do we entirely trust [the] country"; in consequence, "we cannot be completely frank to the Russian Mission."[15]

The wariness of British military officials regarding the Soviet mission was not lessened by the fact that when it arrived at Kings Cross station on 8 July it had been greeted by a group of British leftists "with clenched fists and singing Communist songs." But it would be inaccurate to overemphasize the British government's fears of subversion. Two weeks later, when it seemed possible that a portion of the Soviet Baltic fleet might be relocated to a British port, a member of the Royal Naval staff sanely remarked that it was "not considered likely that a few hundred Russian sailors will corrupt or contaminate the country." The director of military intelligence (DMI), General Davidson, clearly tried to be positive, stressing on 11 July that the British authorities must focus on two main purposes for the Russian mission in Britain: keeping the Soviet Union in the war ("if we can prolong Russian resistance even for a few days, by good handling of their mission, it may be worth anything") and, equally important, trying "to gain certain intelligence."[16]

In that spirit, the Russian mission was installed in a stately building on Kensington Palace Gardens, and the foreign secretary met with General Golikov and his deputy, Admiral Kharlamov. In the course of the first meeting, the Soviets provided the British with a broad yet quite comprehensive summary of the German Army's order of battle in the east. Golikov and Kharlamov then went on to meet with a high-level, three-services British group to discuss Soviet plans for the capture of Petsamo and the island of Spitsbergen in the Arctic. Spitsbergen was subsequently captured but could not be held due to lack of air cover, and by 1942, both small German and Norwegian units were stationed on the island, the latter supported by the Royal Navy. During the July 1941 discussion, Golikov gave British officers the Soviet estimate of German ground, air, and naval forces in the Norwegian far north, as well as information on the German mainline ground communications there. Three days later (12 July), Kharlamov and Golikov met with the vice chief of the Imperial General Staff and, in exchange for the current British estimate of the overall German order of battle, the Russians supplied a detailed breakdown of German units and their commanders across the Eastern Front.[17]

The mood of agreeable sharing and exchange in London lasted through early August 1941. Discussions occurred on the bombing policies of the two countries, and at least until the end of July, intelligence was exchanged regarding bombing targets. On 29 July, the British handed the Soviets a copy of London's picture of the current Luftwaffe order of battle and granted them a general meeting with MI 14 on 2 August, as well as supplying the current British order-of-battle estimate of the Japanese Army two days later. The Admiralty answered Russian questions about Italian navy vessels in the eastern Mediterranean at the end of July, and in early August a Soviet test pilot arrived in Britain to fly nine British and American aircraft as part of a deal brokered in Moscow by the British military mission in exchange for test pilot trials of combat aircraft from the U.S. Army Air Corps, the RAF, and the Red Air Force.[18]

Following this spurt of mutual generosity, intelligence exchange with the Soviet mission in London slowed for reasons that were both complex and easily predictable. The Kremlin had not given the Soviet mission much freedom of action. Approval from Moscow had to be secured before Kharlamov and his colleagues could offer the British any information that was the least bit out of the ordinary. In the view of one British officer, few Russians would risk exceeding instructions; they had been brought up in such an atmosphere of secrecy, with the threat of shooting hanging over their heads, that they would answer nothing on their own responsibility. Another impediment to easy exchange was that the official British organization established to deal with the Soviet mission, the Russian Liaison Group, was staffed from top to bottom by a group of British officers who had specialized in Russian affairs. Most of them had the customary pedigree for this line of work—service against the Bolsheviks during the civil war or family ties to anti-Bolshevik emigrés. Like the head of the Liaison Group, Col. W. O. Firebrace, they had difficulty keeping in check their anti-Bolshevik feelings and defeatist opinions regarding Soviet chances against Germany. But to be fair, Firebrace usually tried to go the extra mile, and on 21 July he remarked, "I must say that this continued optimism is having an effect on me."[19]

But the rigidity, timidity, and doubt were not the only factors that worked against successful exchanges in London. General Macfarlane unintentionally gave the effort a near-fatal blow on 16 July when he told Lt. Gen. A. P. Panfilov in Moscow that the DMI in London would give the Golikov-Kharlamov mission "the gist of all the information" that was being sent by London to Macfarlane.[20] Henceforth the Soviets were under little pressure to pay for what they received from the British in either Moscow or London, because they knew that the same information was being dished up to them in both locations.

An even more basic reason that little successful exchange could be carried out in London had to do with British interservice rivalry. Soviet authorities in both Moscow and London had made it perfectly clear that they had great respect for the Royal Navy and some respect for the RAF but harbored little more than contempt for the British Army. The Russians wanted to work primarily with the Admiralty, but Whitehall insisted that the War Office should be the "predominant partner" in dealing with the Russians and should control the three-services Liaison Group that dealt with the Soviet mission in London. The British generals worked energetically to entice the Soviets into asking for visits to British Army installations in the hope that Moscow would then give Macfarlane comparable visits to Red Army bases. But as a brigadier in the War Office observed on 8 August, "the fact is they are not interested in the doings of our army, and they are quite clever enough to see that our attempts to force them to visit units are probably intended to extract a quid pro quo." Shortly thereafter, a Foreign Office official lamented, "I fear that our Army does not impress or much interest the Soviet authorities . . . there is nothing to be done I fear." Two weeks later, one of the Russians told Firebrace privately that the Soviet mission believed that the British Army and the tactical sections of the RAF were "on leave." Firebrace was so alarmed by this remark that he urged the DMI to come clean with the Soviet mission, using "Most Secret [i.e., ULTRA] sources," if necessary, to prove to the Soviets that Britain was simply too weak to take immediate action on the Continent against the German army. But Whitehall was unable to bring itself to walk down that risky and humiliating road, and the dreary, centralized, and largely useless liaison efforts between Firebrace and the Soviet mission continued.[21]

But the senior British service believed that it could do good business with the Soviets in London and walked beyond Firebrace's liaison machinery to deal directly with its Russian counterparts. By May 1942, the Admiralty had begun its own weekly intelligence meetings with the Red Navy in London, outside the combined-services liaison channels. Here important intelligence was exchanged up to the end of the European war, especially information regarding the safe passage of the northern convoys and intelligence on German naval disposition in the Baltic, which affected both countries. But because the Admiralty felt compelled to operate beyond the combined-services exchanges in London in order to work effectively with the Red Navy, the other British services were unable to ride the coattails of the senior service and secure useful benefits for themselves.[22]

The poor showing of the intelligence-exchange efforts in London, added to the dismal performance of the U.S. attaché office in Moscow, meant that in 1941, the only hope for significant East-West intelligence exchange lay with the newly arrived British military mission in Moscow. That mission initially hoped to carry out a number of liaison activities with the Soviets, including joint strategic planning, exchange of technical information, and provision of British knowledge about Axis war making acquired during the first twenty months of the conflict. But it took less than a week of meetings with the Soviet staff to prove to the British in Moscow that the Soviets were "not much interested in British war experience." The Red Army chiefs also revealed striking inconsistency in their figures on the forces committed against them, altering their estimates of the number of German divisions in the east by 160 in one twenty-four-hour period (General Zhukov estimating 110 German divisions on 29 June, and General Golikov pegging it at 270 on the following day). Since British specialists believed that the actual total of German divisions in the east lay between 140 and 160, the wild swings in Soviet figures were not at all encouraging.[23]

The British mission in Moscow was further put off by Molotov's demand on 29 June that the British open a Second Front to relieve the pressure on the USSR. This was the first of many increasingly strident calls for a Second Front, whose cumulative effect over the next three years was to sour East-West relations. In June 1941, however, the principal effect of Molotov's restrained and confidential first appeal seems to have been to further undercut Macfarlane's hope of broad cooperation with the Soviet military, based on the assumption that Britain would be the senior partner in the anti-Nazi cause.

Always high-strung, Macfarlane was unnerved by these developments as he tried to keep up with the different personalities and shifting moods of the men who made up the Soviet military and naval staffs. He struggled through three difficult days trying to find common ground with Marshal Timoshenko and General Zhukov (27–29 June), then he was tossed to the more affable General Golikov, only to discover that this man, whom Macfarlane believed was the "star turn" of the Russian military staff, was being posted to liaison duties in London and Washington. In consequence, the mood of the British military mission staff went down and up like a yo-yo. The sailors were initially offended that the Red Navy appeared to be uninterested in the information the Royal Navy provided on the German fleet. After complaining about Soviet inefficiency, arrogance, and secretiveness, Macfarlane grumbled to the DMI in London, "you know these people, so [there is] no need to explain." Yet when Golikov provided a moment of cordiality, Macfarlane was completely transformed, welcoming the fact that the "atmosphere was distinctly improved" and rejoicing that Golikov was "friendly" throughout their meeting and had shown "quiet confidence." He even concluded one message home with the observation that although the Russians were "desperately reserved and suspicious . . . our relations are frankly extraordinarily good if you take past history into consideration." In such moments of elation, Macfarlane lectured the home authorities (for his telegrams were routinely sent not only to the DMI and other branches of the War Office but also to the chiefs of staff, the Joint Intelligence Committee, the Foreign Office, and frequently the prime minister) on the need to avoid excessive pessimism regarding the USSR's ability to resist because "it won't help them. It won't help the war. It won't help us and the little we can do."[24]

But whatever the admonitions from the British military mission in Moscow, nothing could prevent Whitehall from promoting peculiar projects with serious potential for raising Soviet hostility and jeopardizing the position of the military mission, along with any hope of useful exchange in Moscow. Even before the start of BARBAROSSA, the Royal Navy became obsessed with the idea that it needed to station one of its officers in Vladivostok. On 26 June, the JIC, prompted by the Royal Navy and the Foreign Office, approved a proposal that the Russians should be asked to permit the stationing of a second British military mission in Vladivostok. Since 30 Mission had not yet even arrived in Moscow and the USSR had long been reluctant to allow foreign military representatives in Siberia (although a U.S. consul's office was there)—not only because it was a strategically sensitive area but also because the NKVD was still busy with its grisly work in the gulag—this suggestion showed poor judgment. Coming at a time when Moscow was also anxious to avoid anything that might encourage the Japanese to take offense and invade Siberia, it was close to provocative.

When British officials in Tokyo were sounded out on the idea, Ambassador Sir R. Craigie replied that any effort to put a British military mission into Siberia would be "absolutely certain" to create "all kinds of difficulties" for the British in Japan. Macfarlane and Ambassador Cripps were equally opposed to the scheme. Cripps pleaded with London "not [to] regard the present circumstances as an opportunity to obtain intelligence" in Siberia, because it would create nightmarish opposition to 30 Mission and the British embassy.[25]

During early July, the Soviets hinted that they might be willing to swap some information with the British regarding the Japanese—which might have obviated any significant need for a mission in Siberia. At the same time, Cripps and Craigie repeated their admonitions against Siberian adventures. But the Foreign Office blundered on. Even as the British military attaché in Toyko was acquiring useful indications of Soviet Far Eastern planning from his "Russian colleague,"[26] Eden told the Soviet ambassador on 15 July that Britain wanted consular offices in Baku and Vladivostok. On 26 July, the Foreign Office came up with another scheme, proposing that India, of all places, should be represented in the British military mission in Moscow. This proposal sent imperial officials into a frenzy of activity as they envisioned the perils that might follow if thousands of Soviet commissars were officially encamped by the Ganges or the Nile. Finally, in mid-August, the Admiralty rejoined the Foreign Office on the comic stage, suggesting that in return for intelligence opportunities in Siberia, the Russians should be offered information regarding British forces in Malaya—an area that was even further from Russian centers of interest than India or Egypt.

The Moscow military mission ultimately managed to placate the Soviets by sidetracking all these proposals, but the Siberian mission affair was an important indicator of the kind of unrealistic pressure that was exerted on Macfarlane's staff by Whitehall. Even in late September, the Admiralty attached a naval intelligence officer to the Beaverbrook-Harriman economic mission to

Moscow (which Churchill and Roosevelt saw as the best hope for creating a close partnership with the USSR), the officer's sole function was to try to convince the Russians to "insert" him into Siberia."[27]

It is small wonder that Macfarlane often acted as if he were on a tightrope, with the difficult Soviets at one end and the home authorities—demanding and uncomprehending—at the other. In a desperate effort to explain the nature of the difficult spot they found themselves in, Macfarlane and his staff concluded that a mysterious force called "the Kremlin" was the principal cause of their troubles. On 29 June, Zhukov had promised the mission daily intelligence exchanges, and Macfarlane had therefore asked the DMI to send on to the mission all possible "material of hot value." When, on 30 June, the Red Army failed to provide the information that Macfarlane had requested regarding the German order of battle and the depth of the German advance, the mission chief concluded that the "Kremlin has clearly put on the brake." Four days later, in a private summary letter to the DMI, Macfarlane opined that the Russian generals wanted to play ball, but they "couldn't do a thing without the Kremlin's knowledge and sanction." The 30 Mission chief thought that the Kremlin leaders were no longer in "a position to double cross us, but you can't trust the Kremlin one inch . . . they are all oriental and self-centered and satisfied and look upon us as a junior member of the firm who is not pulling his weight but is hoping for a partnership."[28]

Believing that henceforth he would be locked into a serious struggle with the Kremlin, the British military mission chief desperately sought British assets that could be used as bargaining chips to make the Red Army and the Kremlin sit up, take notice, and accept Great Britain as a full and, most important, equal partner in the struggle against Germany. Since British forces were then engaged in combat against the Germans only in very limited zones—on the high seas, in Bomber Command's operations, and against the small German Afrika Korps in Egypt and Libya—it was difficult to make a case for the United Kingdom as a real comrade in arms with the Red Army, which was suffering millions of casualties. When, on 3 July, Macfarlane tried to counter Russian claims of British military idleness, the only item of importance that he could come up with was RAF activity over Germany. Macfarlane's problem was compounded by the fact that in the summer of 1941, little headway had actually been made in delivering war supplies to the USSR. Preparations for aid to Russia were in their infancy, as was the convoy system, and once the Hopkins and Harriman-Beaverbrook supply mission appeared in Moscow in late summer and autumn 1941, it was obvious to all—including the Kremlin—that the major source of supply assistance to Russia would not be Britain but the United States.

These unpleasant truths rankled both in London and within the British Moscow mission, but the fact remained that Macfarlane and his team had very few cards with which to play. Out of a combination of necessity and desperation, the mission therefore always came back to intelligence exchange as the best available method of aiding the Russians and demonstrating Britain's military prowess and importance. As both Whitehall and the mission knew, it was a risky enterprise from the beginning. Every important piece of intelligence rested on some form of secret source, ranging from secret agents to radar detection, but at the heart of Britain's intelligence treasure trove lay the ULTRA secret.[29]

The small circle of British officials with knowledge of the ULTRA secret was determined that it would not be compromised, whatever the cost. An American mission had been shown peripheral aspects of the ULTRA decryption and evaluation process in early 1941, but the British kept the United States from naval ULTRA decryption procedures until autumn 1942 and from the process used to break German air and army codes until mid-1943. Under these circumstances, with Britain still struggling to hold its own in the battle of the Atlantic and bracing for a possible German invasion, sharing the secret of ULTRA openly with the Soviets, of all people, was simply out of the question.[30]

When the military mission was dispatched to Moscow in June 1941, great care had been taken to ensure that Macfarlane and his staff would receive a rich and broad flow of British intelligence material regarding the eastern campaign. On 26 June, the JIC ordered the Admiralty and the War and Air Ministries to prepare their own daily intelligence summaries for dispatch to the respective sections of 30 Mission. This information was enciphered and sent to the military and naval attachés by means of commercial telegraph. The chiefs of staff emphasized that with regard to this information, as well as any British technical information that might be considered for transfer to the Soviets, the guiding principle would be to "provide such detailed information as would already be in the hands of the Germans." Nothing that the Germans were still ignorant of would be shared with the Soviets, in part, as the DMI noted on 27 June, because of the "insecurity of Russian ciphers."[31]

Therefore, on this account too, the British were initially adamant that no chances be taken with ULTRA. On 28 June, Prime Minister Churchill had declared that he was "satisfied" with the arrangements made for transmitting ULTRA to the British military attaché in Moscow, because every item would be submitted to him before it was dispatched. On 30 June, the chief of staff ordered the Joint Intelligence Committee and the director of MI 6 (Sir Stuart Menzies—"C") "to work out a scheme" for transmitting "highly secret information" to Macfarlane, "who is anxious to have full information on German operational moves." Macfarlane had been given special instructions about the importance and delicacy of ULTRA information and would "pass on nothing to the Russians likely to compromise our sources of information." MI 6 established a special direct wireless communication link with the mission in Moscow, and all messages were initially enciphered in one time pad in the War Office, placed in a double envelope headed "Colonel H. C. Hatton-Hall, M.C., Broadway buildings," and sent to MI 6 at 54 Broadway, SW 1, London.

This link was restricted to "MOST SECRET operational messages." All the information was carefully "wrapped up" (i.e., there was a cover source indicated), and the only indirect indication of its ULTRA origin was the inclusion of the phrase "from most reliable sources." On 1 July, the chiefs of staff ordered that in addition to the "most secret" messages sent to Macfarlane by the individual service ministries via this route, the Joint Intelligence Committee should also send a daily combined intelligence telegram. The circuit was soon overloaded, and Ambassador Cripps in Moscow requested the installation of an encoding-decoding machine (Typex) to ease the load. During the first week of July, a ciphers officer, Capt. J. V. Fox, arrived in Moscow, and by 22 July 1941, the Typex machine was working; the mission was henceforth connected to London by an almost instantaneous most secret link. But even the bulk of information from most secret sources was still sent in one time pad, and after 19 August, all such information for Macfarlane's personal use was marked "A."[32]

The British military mission was therefore well armed with intelligence information, but it was also severely restricted in what it could pass on to the Russians because of the overriding demand of ULTRA security. This tension between tight security and a desire to establish good working relations with the Red armed forces by providing valuable assistance placed the mission in a real dilemma. From the earliest meetings, the Russians made it clear that they were desirous of receiving secret Western intelligence, and it also seems clear that the Soviets had a genuine, if inflated, respect for the intelligence prowess of the infamous British Secret Service. During the first meetings Macfarlane held with Soviet staff officers, he gave the Russians some material on German deployment and order of battle in the east. Zhukov, in particular, responded positively to these gifts, agreed to daily meetings to exchange intelligence, and provided Macfarlane with scraps of spot items in return, most of which concerned possible Axis moves in the Mediterranean and the Middle East. The Soviet deputy chief of army staff also emphasized that the Russians were anxious to receive British secret information on German deployment at the Eastern Front and any available data regarding possible increased Japanese concentrations in Manchuria.

Macfarlane understood that Zhukov "was out for all he can get" and called on the London intelligence chiefs to send everything possible to the mission. "Without something with which to barter," Macfarlane stressed, "we shall achieve nothing," and "intelligence seems to be almost the only medium we possess for barter." But before Whitehall had a chance to respond to 30 Mission's proposal for tough intelligence horse trading with the Soviets, the mission had its first meeting with General Golikov, who managed to charm away much of Macfarlane's belligerence and his desire for stiff bargaining by suggesting that they just send intelligence to each other without formal meetings. Macfarlane passed over "a lot of useful information" that he thought was "clearly appreciated" by the Soviets, who gave the British "a ration" of intelligence in return, which the 30 Mission chief characterized as "somewhat meagre" but "nonetheless . . . quite useful stuff." Follow-up discussions then occurred between the representatives of the separate services of the two countries.[33]

During the air force meeting, the RAF representative, Air Vice Marshal Collier, turned over all the papers on German aircraft, bombs, and ammunition the mission had brought from Britain, plus the complete British version of the Luftwaffe order of battle as of 22 June. The Red Air Force representative at the meeting supplied no intelligence information at all to the British, but he did request additional data on the Luftwaffe order of battle as well as the latest information the British had on current German aircraft production figures.

In the naval meeting, the British furnished the Russians with intelligence on German mining techniques, antisubmarine tactics, and German mining operations off Murmansk. The Red Navy supplied nothing in return and showed no immediate signs of special gratitude. But shortly after the session ended, the Red Navy "gratuitously" sent the Royal Navy section of the mission a number of documents on German U-boat building and the antiaircraft defenses of Kiel.[34]

In the army session, the Soviets requested more data on Japanese troop movements, along with information on developments in Anatolia and the eastern Mediterranean, the German armored order of battle in the east, the eastward movement of German units stationed in France, and full details of German airborne tactics, especially those employed recently in Crete.

Although the Red Army and Air Force failed to supply the British with any intelligence documents during this series of meetings, in the course of the discussion they did (perhaps inadvertently) make the important admission that some of their information on German air and ground tactics had been acquired from intercepted messages. This was the first direct indication that the Soviets possessed an intercept service, a discovery that increased the possible benefits that might accrue to Britain if a broad intelligence exchange could be established with the Soviet authorities.[35]

In light of the Soviets' mention of radio intercepts and the more cordial tone that prevailed at the Moscow meetings, no more was heard of Macfarlane's proposal to get tough with the Russians. After a discussion with Golikov on 1 July, the British military mission chief reported that the Russian general "seemed politely and regretfully disappointed that we had nothing of real interest to give him today." During the meeting, Golikov specifically thanked the British for the intelligence information they had supplied, describing it as "most useful" and expressing his relief that British intelligence had detected no indication that the Japanese were concentrating forces in Manchuria in preparation for an attack on Siberia.[36]

The Soviet general also asked for British assistance in determining the results of recent Soviet air attacks on the Ploesti oil fields. Golikov indicated that he was very anxious about the likelihood and timing of German advances toward the Caucasus and Persian oil fields. He expressed a desire for British assistance in determining the scale of German oil and lubricant reserves and in estimating how long the Germans could sustain their attack on the present scale. The matter of German oil reserves was something that British intelligence organizations had lavished a great deal of attention on, and as SOE plans for adventures in the Caucasus had indicated, London was highly sensitive about anything that hinted at a German plan to advance toward the great oil installations of the Near East and southern Russia. Therefore, on these points, 30 Mission was in a good position to provide Moscow with valuable information, and it apparently did so.

There were additional indications of the Soviets' willingness to cooperate with 30 Mission in the first week of July. On the fifth, the British naval mission gave the Soviets a sample ASDIC underwater sound detection device, and the Red Navy officers who received it were obviously "delighted" with this gift.[37] On the following day, Red and Royal Navy officers held an extended working session as the British sought to introduce the Soviets to the complexities and technical dimensions of the naval war raging in the North Sea.

On 8 July, Capt. F. B. Birse arrived from the Middle East to handle order of battle exchanges with the Soviets, and on the same day, the mission received more evidence that the Russians did have a "Y" (intercept) service. Macfarlane immediately telegraphed the chiefs of staff, requesting permission to offer "collaboration over low grade material" plus exchange of Russian and British "Y" officers. If this move proceeded satisfactorily, Macfarlane wanted to offer some details of British "Y" successes in the hope that they would pave the way for the dispatch of a British "Y" group to the USSR.[38]

Unfortunately, none of these good omens developed quickly enough for 30 Mission to use them to produce a closer relationship with the Russian staff. Birse spoke good Russian, but he had not been formally trained in order of battle work and had to learn about the subject on the job. His skeptical and suspicious Russian counterparts were far better informed than he was about the German Army and intelligence methodology. The Whitehall administrative wheels also turned so slowly that it was impossible to seize the opportunity for "Y" cooperation. This delay may have been nearly fatal, because the decisive moment for intimate Anglo-Soviet intelligence cooperation seems to have come in the first week of July.[39]

During a regular meeting between Golikov and Macfarlane, the Soviet general asked for "any information on German losses since the start of the campaign," plus the current British estimate of total German airborne and parachute units.[40] These requests were easy for 30 Mission to accommodate, but Golikov also made a point of claiming that in the battle of the Pripet Marshes, the Germans had not yet crossed the Berezina River. Macfarlane was skeptical of this claim and asked the War Office for "WI" (wireless intelligence) indicating "for my own information" whether this claim was correct.[41]

This seemingly routine query apparently set off a chain of events that would have serious, perhaps mortal, consequences for close Anglo-Soviet intelligence cooperation throughout the early stages of the war. Since the beginning of the eastern campaign, Whitehall had become increasingly nervous about the embassy's security and doubly nervous about providing the Soviets with Ultra information, because of the proven insecurity of some Russian ciphers as well as lingering fears that the Soviets might still double-cross the West in the manner of August 1939. As indicated above, Churchill initially seems to have overridden military staff worries and insisted that some Ultra be sent to Macfarlane to provide his staff with a comprehensive overview of events, since the Soviets were not coming clean about what was happening on the battlefield. The prime minister had also approved occasional transmission to the Soviets of well-wrapped-up Ultra spot items, usually attributed (in a phrase invented by "C") to a well-placed source in Berlin, when they seemed especially important. But when Golikov indicated that the Russians wanted the intelligence exchange door opened more widely in early July, the chief of the Imperial General Staff (CIGS) and Churchill were overcome by their suspicion of the Soviets and their nervousness about Ultra security. On 4 July, the mission was informed that the CIGS had ruled that Ultra information "of immediate operational value" could not be given to the Russians. Three days later, the DMI informed Macfarlane that Churchill himself had decided that it was "impossible to accede to your request to pass on to the Russians ULTRA of immediate operational value."[42]

The British government thereby sharply limited the extent of intelligence cooperation with the Soviets, although it would later experience short-term changes of heart. Less than twenty-four hours passed in early July before the existence of this limit was made obvious to the Russians. On 8 July, Macfarlane had a meeting with Gen. Aleksei Pavlovich Panfilov, a tank man, who had just taken over liaison duties with the British mission due to General Golikov's departure to liaison posts first in London and then in Washington. Panfilov arrived at the meeting with a strong hand to play and a willingness to bargain. A few days earlier, Macfarlane had indicated to Golikov that the British had evidence of Wehrmacht divisions being held in reserve in eastern Germany and were interested in swapping it for any information the Soviets had on these units. Panfilov told Macfarlane that he had "precise information of [the] number and location of 15 of these divisions," but the British team was unable to rise to the occasion because of Whitehall's ban on giving ULTRA intelligence to the Russians. As Macfarlane reported to London, "I do not think they will give this much detail to me unless we provide them with locations in return and I realize this is impossible."[43]

So the moment passed, and Panfilov and Macfarlane went on to more routine matters, such as the number of German invasion barges in the Black Sea, the best methods for destroying oil installations in areas being evacuated, and the likelihood of German operations against the Caucasus. Macfarlane continued to defend his corner, and when Panfilov asked for information on Iran, Turkey, and Bulgaria, as well as for the details about recent German air raids on Britain, the British general asked for a quid pro quo. But this was in part play-acting by a man whose chief hobby was amateur dramatics. The British held only a small handful of bargaining chips in their relations with the USSR—few supplies to give and even fewer prospects for a successful landing on the Continent. Intelligence, especially ULTRA intelligence, was the one valuable commodity they possessed, but the Whitehall ban had tied Macfarlane's hands. The mission could not play in an intelligence free-for-all with the USSR, and without that possibility, there was little chance that Macfarlane's team would ever reach a position at the Soviet high table. So in the late summer of 1941, 30 Mission had little choice but to trudge on, suffer the coldness and arrogance of the Soviet liaison staff, and see what could be squeezed out of the limited intelligence trading assets it still possessed.

3
Moaning and Dealing, July to Mid-September 1941

On 11 July, just as 30 Mission began the second and more sharply defined and limited round of attempting to create effective liaison with the USSR, Macfarlane's organization received a new charter intended to help guide it through its many difficulties. This directive, prepared by the DMI and the vice chief of the Imperial General Staff (Lt. Gen. H. R. Pownell), was sent to Moscow over the signature of the chief of staff, Gen. Sir John Dill. Macfarlane and his team were ordered to concentrate their energies on two main tasks: keeping "Russia in the war as long as possible" and, "as a by-product," learning "certain intelligence" about the German war machine. To carry out the first task, Macfarlane was given a bit more latitude by "C", who authorized him on very special occasions to give the Soviets the gist of some ULTRA items wrapped up "in the genuine camouflage given to our allies" (i.e., a high-placed source in the German government). All other concerns, ranging from technical exchange to preparing for demolitions in the Caucasus, were to take second place, because London believed that keeping the USSR in the war was transcendentally important and would be an extremely difficult task. The CIGS thought—wrongly, as it turned out—that the Germans had already "broken through Russian defences in the Smolensk area" and that, although the Soviets had now been driven into "their old defence areas," they probably had no strategic reserves to prevent the Germans from cutting them to pieces in open field operations.[1]

With this dismal estimate ringing in his ears, Macfarlane attended a liaison and order-of-battle meeting with General Panfilov on 12 July. For the first time, the Russian general identified the main Russian army groups along the Soviet western front, as well as their commanders: Timoshenko in the center, K. E. Vorosilov in the north, and S. M. Budenny in the south. Macfarlane responded by providing the Soviets with an estimate—just received from Whitehall—of German army groupings in Finland, as well as reports of Turkish troop movements, German activities in Iran, and, in response to an earlier Soviet request, Britain's embarrassing failure to defeat the German airborne attack on Crete. Panfilov tactfully made no remarks about the Crete disaster and indicated general agreement with the British estimate of German forces in Finland.[2] This was not a glorious beginning to a new era of intelligence exchange, but Panfilov was a bit more considerate than he had been in the recent past.

Also on 12 July, the cooperative momentum received an important push when Macfarlane and Air Marshal Collier finally had their welcoming audience with Stalin. According to his unpublished memoir, Macfarlane began this meeting by voicing his pleasure at having an opportunity to cooperate with the great Red Army against the common foe. Stalin allegedly replied to this overture by remarking how splendid it would be if he could believe Macfarlane, but he added that in any case, the two countries were now comrades and must have no secrets from each other. Then he bade the Britians a hearty welcome.

Although momentarily rocked back on their heels by his bluntness, Collier and Macfarlane were impressed by Stalin. After running through a series of hollow and self-deprecating remarks, including a characterization of the USSR as a backward country, the Soviet leader rattled off performance statistics of Soviet front-line aircraft and details of antitank warfare. He also proposed that test pilot flights be exchanged, with British pilots flying a series of front-line Red Air Force planes, and a Soviet pilot being authorized to test-fly British and American aircraft in Britain. Collier was immediately sold on the idea, and after the Kremlin meeting, he urgently recommended to London that the offer be accepted. The deal was soon done; a Soviet test pilot was sent to Britain, and on 11 August, the Russians authorized British test flights of four Soviet aircraft, including the advanced MIG 3 fighter.[3] The British test pilot was also allowed to visit a Soviet aircraft factory and to examine a broad range of Russian air equipment. By August, RAF central intelligence already had reports on the test flights of Russian aircraft and related equipment in its files.[4]

The meeting with Stalin was even more significant for the impact it had on Macfarlane. The British general was deeply impressed, if not smitten, by his conversation with the Soviet leader. Writing to the CIGS (General Dill) shortly after the meeting, Macfarlane fairly gushed his enthusiasm:

> Stalin is intensely interesting to meet. He has I should say a first class brain, a great deal of knowledge of all sorts, with a really good memory, and—most striking of all—he is the only one of the Kremlin lot who looks you straight in the eye and does not think twice every time before opening his mouth.

Although Macfarlane still thought that "the Voroshilovs, Timoshenkos and above all the Budennys are utterly outclassed by the Lists and Rundstedts and Reichenaus," he concluded that the combination of Stalin and Shaposhnikov would "between them represent quite a good generalissimo," and the Red Army therefore had a better chance of containing the Germans than the naysayers in Whitehall imagined. Macfarlane was now convinced that there would be no "big double cross [of the Allies] by the Kremlin or the Army, who stand to lose all if they allow defeat to make them lose their grip on the country. I don't think they will admit defeat even if they have to move a long way East."[5]

This belief that both the Soviets and the Nazis were determined to fight to the finish, and Macfarlane's newly acquired respect for Stalin, seem to have lifted and lightened the general's spirits in the second half of July. Like a bird embarking on the nesting season, he resolved to make the best of his exile in Moscow. On 13 July, with unconscious symbolism he reported to the DMI that the mission was lacking bedding. Finding it impossible to secure what he needed in Moscow, Macfarlane asked that bed linen for the whole mission be sent from London as soon as possible.[6]

Macfarlane not only got his bedding, but he also received an intelligence bonus. London had just identified a group of Soviet naval ciphers that the Germans were reading with ease and sent the relevant information on to the mission. Macfarlane sensed that this was a valuable card to play and immediately handed the information to the Red Navy staff, which was "very disturbed" but also "most grateful." Inevitably, this bit of generosity made London appear efficient, helpful, and perhaps all knowing; in Russian eyes, it probably enhanced the attractiveness of the British as intelligence partners. Fortunately for Whitehall and the mission, the Soviet Navy did not know how much better the British were at acquiring such information than protecting it effectively. Although the tightest security had been imposed in London, including a demand stamped on the document that all copies of the dispatch to Macfarlane be destroyed, at least *twelve* copies of the document remain in Air Ministry files.[7]

Building on the goodwill they had acquired by sharing their knowledge of Red Navy cipher vulnerability, Macfarlane and Colonel Greer—armed with ULTRA information about German armored units on the Eastern Front—had a pair of useful meetings with General Panfilov on 15–16 July, during which the British officers also supplied information on German monthly tank production. In return, Panfilov cited indications that the Germans faced fuel and ammunition shortages and also acknowledged that previous Soviet estimates of German divisions in the east had been too high. They now pegged it at 180, including 21 armored.

This was a sensible, matter-of-fact exchange of information, but perhaps the very normality of it caused Macfarlane to fall again into one of many dark moods, which would increasingly become his trademark. Writing to the DMI on 18 July, he complained that in the 1930s he had been "90% more useful and able to help in Berlin, our obvious potential enemy, than in the capital of this latest ally of ours." Grumbling about the Soviet staff, he characterized his earlier chum, Golikov (currently in London), as "Kremlin and crooked"; Panfilov, whom he would soon be cursing as stupid and obstructive, was currently portrayed as "a much straighter and better fellow." Yet even the best of the Red Army officers failed to measure up in Macfarlane's eyes because, as he observed to the DMI, all Soviets seemed "terribly oriental and parochial."[8]

Such outbursts were probably little more than safety valves for Macfarlane's intense emotions and strong temper, but they made it difficult for him to act as a sensible leader of his liaison team or as an accurate reporter to his London superiors. No one in 30 Mission needed such inflammatory explosions from on high as they struggled to liaise with Russian officials, who were usually difficult and always wary. Overdramatizing the problems he faced obscured Macfarlane's capacity to see opportunities to cooperate with the Russians. The steady stream of negative comments that he dispatched to London may well have increased Whitehall's tendency to underestimate Soviet chances in the war and led British authorities to undervalue the Russians' willingness to cooperate.

Obviously, Stalin's officials were difficult and paranoid. The system continued to repress and torture many of its own people, persecute minorities, and bar self-determination for all elements of the population, including the Mongolians, the Volga Germans, and the Baltic populations. Suspicion of the West and resentment at Britain's failure to undertake land operations on the Continent to draw German forces away from the Eastern Front remained palpable. Moscow repeated ad nauseam that the lack of a Second Front indicated that the capitalist "allies" were only feigning cooperation and remained committed to the hope that the Nazis and the Communists would ultimately destroy each other.

Soviet resentment and suspicion, however, were often tempered by realism, as well as by a recognition that some modus operandi had to be arranged with the West to defeat Hitler and limit Soviet losses. On the same day that Macfarlane delivered his first great midsummer moan (19 July), Soviet liaison officers partially satisfied some of the mission's most urgent informational requests. Two skilled Red Air Force colonels (Istignev and Pugachev) were added to the Soviet air liaison team run by the taciturn Colonel Petrov. They immediately gave the British specifications of the bomb types being used by the Germans on the Eastern Front, a summary of the strength of the Luftwaffe units facing the Russians, and photos of the bomb damage that the Red Air Force had inflicted on Ploesti (to prove to the skeptical British that the Russian air raid there had been successful).[9]

This was an important initiating move toward more effective East-West air force order-of-battle cooperation. On the same day on which it was made, General Panfilov, in a discussion with Macfarlane, confirmed a British intelligence estimate of the location of German headquarters in Finland (Rovaniemi), as well as the position of the German 17th Army on the southern front. Panfilov also revealed that two more German divisions, the 25th and 125th, had just been transferred from France to Russia. More significantly, the Red Army liaison man offered to provide full details of identifications and groupings of German divisions in the east if the British would provide the German Army order of battle in other areas (Western and Central Europe and the Mediterranean), along with the location of German corps and army headquarters and reserve units in central Germany.

All such Russian proposals were difficult for the British to accept, however, because of the ULTRA secret. On 16 July 1941, Churchill wanted to send the Soviets ULTRA information that their forces at Smolensk were to be encircled by the 4th Panzer Army ("Surely we ought to give them warning of this," he stated), but "C" was "of the opinion that the source would definitely be imperiled if this was done," and the warning was not sent. "C" also refused to send a message to 30 Mission on 17 July until a statement that the 4th Panzer Army was encircling Smolensk was removed. Nonetheless, the Air Ministry and the War Office believed that Panfilov's proposal might be the long-awaited chance to create an intimate intelligence partnership with the Soviet authorities, and the DMI agreed to be more generous in sending intelligence to the British Moscow mission. General F. H. N. Davidson was even willing to include some "most reliable secret" spot items and intelligence originating from "our occasional agent" (i.e., ULTRA), doing what he could to find loopholes in the prime minister's ban on ULTRA transmissions to the Soviets. Then, after two or three days in which the mission exchanged only routine information and assorted complaints and grumbles, the Soviets cleared the way for even more serious intelligence cooperation.[10]

During the regular meeting with Macfarlane on 22 July, General Panfilov began by tracing the broad course of the battle in the east. Claiming that the Red Army had identified 206 German divisions, he remarked that "a fair proportion of German armoured divisions only had one tank regiment" and expressed optimism about the Red Air Force's battle with the Luftwaffe. He then went on to advance important new proposals on the sharing of secret information. First he suggested that the Russians should concentrate their air order-of-battle work on the area east of Berlin, while the British did the same to the west of the German capital. The two sides would then exchange their results and conclusions. The British mission seemingly agreed to this arrangement in principle, subject to the approval of the Air Ministry. Panfilov then made another intelligence gift to the British in the form of a report containing "detailed information of [the] German divisions identified on the Eastern front," which concluded that there were 139 operational divisions plus five to seven divisions in reserve. This instance of Russian honesty and generosity initially prompted sarcastic remarks in the mission, because Panfilov had recently claimed that the Germans had "206 divisions on [the] Eastern front." This apparent discrepancy would ultimately be clarified—the larger Soviet figure counted all units that had appeared in the east, including those that had subsequently been rotated to other areas.[11]

Macfarlane and his staff were generally pleased and encouraged by Panfilov's initiatives, especially the information regarding the German Army order of battle. Since Whitehall's general estimate of German order of battle within the Reich and all fronts other than the east had just reached the mission, Macfarlane exclaimed, "it will now be possible to make a detailed analysis and to produce for the Russians information regarding [the whole] German Order of Battle." Two days later (25 July), he again exclaimed to the DMI that the Russians were fighting "flat out" and that his newfound favorite, Joseph Stalin, was "taking charge himself." The latter was an especially pleasing development, because as Macfarlane observed on 31 July, only Stalin "can say what he thinks and give a direct answer."[12]

Indeed, the British Army staff of the mission responded to the Soviets by handing over "a great deal of OB [order of battle] information" on 25 and 26 July, and the Red Army quickly reciprocated. In a general meeting between Panfilov and Macfarlane, as well as in an OB meeting between Birse and the Russians in late July, the Soviets furnished general information on the battle raging near Murmansk and on German chemical warfare units, and they estimated that the "whole Japanese Army is being brought onto a war footing," with new divisions being formed in Japan and the Kwantung Army in Manchuria preparing for maneuvers.[13]

The British air mission was finally allowed to visit a Soviet military airfield, and Air Commodore Collier acquired details on German heavy bomber development from a Soviet Air Force general who had visited German production sites shortly before 22 June 1941. More significantly, since it suggested that

Moscow was increasingly serious about OB cooperation, Birse obtained a breakdown of all the divisions committed by the Germans in the areas of Army Group Center and North (except the Finnish front), with clear distinctions drawn between divisions that had definitely been thrown into battle and those that were only probable. The Red Army staff further promised that comparable information regarding German Army Group South, as well as the Finnish and Rumanian fronts, would be provided shortly. Macfarlane thought that these achievements warranted a bit of crowing, and he reported to the chiefs of staff that the mission was "now in a position to exchange important information" and therefore had great hope that the OB contacts would produce "valuable results."[14]

For the first time, the army portion of 30 Mission saw signs of hope that it might reach the level of intimacy and cooperation with the Soviets that the Royal Navy had been enjoying since the arrival of its mission team in the USSR. On 11 July, the Royal Navy staff in Moscow had been given some "details" on the construction of the German battleship *Bismarck* by the Red Navy staff, and three weeks later it had received a photostat of "what appeared to be some form of damage control handbook" from the same German super battleship. Although the Royal Navy had already sunk the *Bismarck,* it was always eager for information that would help explain the secrets of the German capital ships, especially *Tirpitz,* the perennial threat to British operations in northern waters.[15]

By mid-July, the Soviet naval authorities provided the British naval mission with detailed summaries of where the Germans were and were not laying mines in the northern sea lanes. Later in the month, the Red Navy passed on intelligence summaries indicating where the strongest German forces were located in the far north—Varanger, Kirkennes, and Petsamo—information intended to assist a British carrier-based air attack that was launched shortly thereafter.

In this Royal Navy action, Soviet-sourced intelligence was of secondary importance, compared with the information acquired from what the Admiralty would later call "the very early cryptographic success" the British had achieved in far northern waters. It also needs to be emphasized that the Soviets had an enormous vested interest in British naval activity there, for only the Royal Navy had the wherewithal necessary for the running of the northern convoys (convoy number PQ 1 being dispatched on 1 September). So important was the convoy issue to the Russians that besides Royal Navy officers being allowed to survey in detail northern Russian naval and port facilities, on 20 July, RAF Group Capt. F. L. Pearce was permitted to examine the defenses, especially the air defenses, of both Archangel and Murmansk.[16]

Yet the cordial reception extended to the Royal Navy by the Soviets went well beyond northern supply matters. On 19 July, officers in the naval section of 30 Mission were invited to visit Russian ships without having to wait for reciprocal visiting facilities to be granted to Red Navy officers. During the last week of July, arrangements were made for the dispatch of a British naval liaison officer to the Black Sea, which was one of the great British liaison triumphs of the war. A series of British naval liaison officers would remain in the Black Sea area for three years, acquiring rare and valuable intelligence on southern Russia. Such reports are sprinkled throughout British and American intelligence and operational files from 1941 until at least late 1944.[17]

In consequence, the Royal Navy was the point man of the British intelligence liaison effort in the Soviet Union. Ambassador Cripps noted on 29 July that "naval co-operation is excellent." The office of the director of naval intelligence (DNI) observed on the following day that "the head of the Naval Section of the British Mission to Russia is being informed that the information which has been forwarded is of good value."[18]

Even the combination of naval liaison triumphs and the rising level of success achieved by the army and air sections of the mission was still insufficient in late July to convince leading British officials in Moscow and London that the Soviets were doing an effective job against the Germans or that they were being reasonable partners in the exchange of intelligence. The DMI was a perennial prophet of doom regarding Russian ability and willingness to cooperate, diligently picking apart Russian claims of defensive successes in his reports to Macfarlane, most of which bore instructions to "burn after reading" but were often routinely kept in the files. Not until the end of July did General Davidson concede that the Soviets had done better than he had expected, were using their tactical air force well, and were not panicked by armor penetrations.[19]

Others in Whitehall, while remaining blissfully ignorant of the problems faced by 30 Mission, nonetheless wanted Macfarlane to help the British military authorities solve special problems. On 26 July, for example, the inspector of chemical warfare requested permission to attach an officer to Macfarlane's staff simply because "we are lamentably short of information on German chemical warfare techniques and equipment"; he hoped to get enlightenment in Moscow, as "gas warfare may break out on the eastern front." Indeed, although no chemical warfare officer was attached to 30 Mission, the Soviets did answer British questions on German poison gas methods, and even the British official history of intelligence in World War II acknowledges that up to the end of 1941, the most reliable information that Britain had on German gas warfare methods came from the Russian front.[20]

The Air Ministry, however, set the record for asking 30 Missions for the most sensitive information about the USSR. Two weeks after a proposal to exchange "Y" with the Russians had gone up to the chiefs of staff for consideration, the Air Ministry blithely tried to start over by asking Collier, "Can you find out tactfully whether the Russians have a 'Y' service?" It followed up this remarkably out-of-date query with the bizarre admonition that the RAF believed that the mission should proceed tactfully in this matter because the Russians would probably be difficult. Air Commodore Charles Medhurst even declared on 27 July that the Air Ministry harbored the wildly unrealistic hope that someday it would be allowed by the Soviets to station its own "Y" operators in Russia. Four days later, even though the chiefs of staff had still not assented to a "Y" exchange, Macfarlane went ahead and proposed to the Soviets that such cooperation be undertaken.[21]

As if to make certain that the Foreign Office was not left out of the vaudevillesque British attempt to achieve multifacted intelligence cooperation with the Soviets, Ambassador Stafford Cripps chose the fourth week of July—the point at which 30 Mission began to enjoy better OB exchanges with the Soviets—to lament in a report to Whitehall that the Russians were stonewalling the mission and not providing any intelligence. Claiming that only economic and naval liaison were "functioning properly," Cripps asserted that Macfarlane was being held at arm's length and that "air liaison virtually does not exist." Four days later, in a letter to Eden, Cripps proclaimed that although "naval cooperation is excellent" and the mission may well have gotten over "the difficulties with air," on the military side, things were unsatisfactory; "[the Soviets] have never opened up at all," Macfarlane was "largely disregarded," and Cripps himself was completely frozen out.[22]

Such comments were an unintended parody of recent developments. During the previous week, Moscow had provided the army and air sections of the mission with considerable information of value, including the detailed OB of German Army Groups North and Center, as well as arranging the exchange of test pilots. Cripps's dire assessment was not even accurate as to his own situation. On the following day, he blithely requested that Vyshinsky search through Russian postal censorship records for the period before 22 June in the hope of finding items that might be of interest to British intelligence and security agencies. Indeed, on 31 July, Cripps received two such letters from Vyshinsky referring to German anti-British activities in Afghanistan.[23]

It is not possible to determine from available records whether the letters that Vyshinsky gave to Cripps on 31 July were of any particular value to British officials. Panfilov told Macfarlane on 10 August that German postal censorship was too tight to permit much useful information to be gained from captured letters to and from German soldiers. Nor is it possible to establish whether the Soviets subsequently provided Cripps with additional material from their censorship files. But what is obvious is that the Soviets did more for Cripps and the British military mission than his anguished and complaining messages to Eden and the Foreign Office indicated. Like Macfarlane and Collier, Cripps was hostile to Soviet Russia, deeply offended by what he perceived as Russian rudeness and arrogance, and angered by his inability to break through their cold reserve. He seems to have felt, in words later used by Admiral Miles, that much of the problem arose from the "lack of breeding" among Soviet officials and officers, which had "resulted from the elimination of the educated classes." The embassy and the mission were therefore left to face "men of peasant stock disguised as officers" who were "gauche, ill mannered . . . and uncultured."[24]

By late July, all British officials in Moscow, both military and civil, had joined voices in pouring out to London their unhappiness, their grumblings, and their resentment about the Soviet cold shoulder damaging their pride. This chorus of lamentation—Macfarlane on 31 July referring to the mission's situation as "our concentration camp"—meant that Whitehall failed to receive what its Moscow representatives were supposed to provide—a calm, clear picture of what was actually taking place in their relations with the Russians and on the Eastern Front.[25]

The main reason that such information was not forthcoming was, quite obviously, the Soviets' obsessive secrecy and their distrust of the British. That they would not give any indication of their own strength and military dispositions especially frustrated and angered the Britons in Moscow, and when the Soviets suggested that this reluctance was due to poor British security—citing press leaks and indiscretions by the BBC—it only raised the temperature of British anger and frustration. We now know that the Soviet authorities had good cause to question British security, if for no other reason than the existence and espionage activities of Philby, Burgess, and Maclean.

Overall, it seems clear that the British military mission and the embassy staff compounded the injuries they suffered and the obstacles they faced by nursing their complaints and wounded pride. They thereby failed to indicate clearly to London at the end of July that substantial progress had been made. The army and air sections, as well as the navy section, were firmly linked to the appropriate Soviet liaison offices, and all of them were providing sensitive information to the Soviets and receiving such material in return.

On the receiving end of the mission's dispatches, the anti-Soviet attitudes in Whitehall compounded the trouble. When on 7 August the mission reported that Muscovites took German air raids calmly, the DMI noted that this was "not surprising when one realizes what the Russian people have already been through, a series of purges, bullyings, 'visits to Siberia,' etc. etc."[26]

Yet late summer 1941 actually turned out to be one of the high points in the British effort to establish effective cooperation with the USSR during World War II. In addition to the intelligence about the enemy that was exchanged during this period, the Russians somewhat relaxed the customary secrecy regarding their own operations. In early August, the Soviet high command indicated to the British mission that the Smolensk sector was the scene of the crucial battle. Shortly thereafter, the Soviets also correctly informed Macfarlane that the German attack in the south was of increasing importance. By August 17, the Soviet high command concluded that the Germans would make their main thrust against Kiev and then move against the Caucasus—a full two weeks before Hitler would echo that judgment by delaying the attack on Moscow in order to throw his full offensive power against southern Russia.[27]

As summer moved toward autumn, the Soviets suffered one serious reversal after another, with Leningrad encircled (except for Lake Ladoga) on 8 September, Kiev falling on 19 September, and the Germans entrapping 660,000 Soviet troops in the great southern encirclement on 24 September. Beginning in September, Nazi police messages from Russia, which Bletchley had just broken, indicated all too clearly the human price of Nazi victories. They routinely included passages such as "Jews shot, 1246" on 1 September and "3,000 Jews shot" on 6 September.[28]

While these disasters were taking place on and off the battlefield, Anglo-Soviet intelligence exchanges continued, with the Royal and Red Navies once more leading the way in effective collaboration. The closeness of the two navies was increased by the beginning of northern convoys in September, with no convoy ship losses occurring in 1941. In the north, the Royal Navy allowed Soviet officers full access to British vessels, and at Scapa Flow, Admiral Kharlamov was permitted to survey a number of British heavy ships. A steady flow of information reached the British from various Red Navy offices throughout the month, including a copy of the Soviet recognition manual, a register of German ships sunk by the Russians through 9 August, a report based on radio intercepts (probably "Y") indicating German ships in the Bay of Salonika, lists of German airfields in Norway, documents on German defenses in the Baltic, and an estimate of the likelihood of German military operations against Murmansk. On 3 September, a Royal Navy team visited a Russian destroyer. In the technical realm, the British provided information to the Soviets on current Western minesweeping technology; in exchange, the head of the British naval mission, Admiral Miles, discovered that the Soviets were developing an anti-magnetic minesweep at Archangel "which might possibly develop into something as good [as], if not better" than, the minesweep equipment currently being used by the Royal Navy. As a result of this discovery, Miles suggested to Whitehall that "we ought now to put all our minesweeping cards on the table." Some high-level British mine-detection equipment was consequently given to the Red Navy during September.[29]

Again, however, the labyrinthine bureaucracy of Whitehall stopped a simple swap of minesweeping technology from being consummated. The British, and later the Americans, continued to dawdle over such an arrangement throughout late 1941 and well into 1942. But the British naval mission in Russia had established such close and effective relations with the Red fleet that despite the muddle and delay, naval intelligence benefits continued to flow to both sides. During August and September, the Admiralty and the prime minister became gravely concerned about the fate of the Red fleet in the Baltic if Leningrad should fall. At the same time, the naval situation in the Black Sea turned more serious as the Wehrmacht drove on toward Odessa. In the far north, the possibility loomed of a German threat to Murmansk. Admiral Miles succeeded in securing assurances from the Soviet chief of naval staff that the Russians would never allow the Baltic fleet to fall into German hands, and even though Red Army morale in Odessa was shaky, the Red Navy in the Black Sea declared its determination to fight on, whatever the cost. In the north, the Royal Navy continued to have excellent relations with the Soviet fleet. A senior British naval officer there declared on 20 September, "I am lucky in having a [Russian] C-in-C, [A.] Golovko, who is about 40 years of age, just promoted to Vice Admiral, fully alive to the situation, astute rather than clever, A[ssistant] N[aval] A[ttaché] Madrid for a time and realizes there is room for improvement" in the Russian fleet. On the following day, the Soviets in the north showed that they were skilled at more than bonhomie by counterattacking and blunting the German offensive aimed at Murmansk.[30]

Capt. G. B. H. Fawkes, the British naval liaison officer (BNLO) in the Black Sea area, provided even more detailed assurances that the Soviets were fully prepared to scuttle their ships if they were in danger of falling into German hands. The British naval mission in Moscow did its best to stiffen Russian resolve to hold on in the Black Sea by passing along a series of assurances that Turkey would definitely not join in the German attack. It was Captain Fawkes, however, who was in the best position to judge the realities of the naval situation. He had good personal relations with the Red Navy staff, including a personal meeting with the local Soviet director of naval intelligence in early

September, and he had been allowed an eight-day survey cruise aboard a Soviet destroyer. Also, starting at the end of August, Fawkes received voluminous spot information on the German and Red Navies in the area and was routinely issued a copy of the Soviet Black Sea fleet's "Daily Intelligence Summary." Fawkes suspected that he received such good treatment because of the intelligence on Rumanian and Bulgarian Black Sea defenses he had presented to the Russians as soon as he arrived. The Soviets were so grateful that Fawkes was soon able to send home detailed reports on German and Russian naval equipment, including a twenty-five-page analysis of Russian submarines, with a three-page detailed list of Red Navy ships in the Black Sea area, including tonnage listings for most of them, and a general order-of-battle report on the Russian Black Sea fleet. Summing up his mission's position in October 1941, Fawkes declared, "I am certain we had [during the summer] far more knowledge of the current situation than most of the senior officers of the Soviet Black Sea Fleet."[31]

Fawkes's dispatches were thus unusually important, as the Admiralty soon realized. In early September, it ordered that they be sent from Odessa directly to London rather than being routed through the military mission in Moscow. BNLO Black Sea reports were then distributed to a broad range of Whitehall offices and departments, including the Air Ministry and the War and Foreign Offices, with spot items appearing in the prime minister's files and some reports going on to the Americans beginning in 1942.

Consequently, Fawkes was not put off by occasional Russian lapses in liaison protocol. As he reported to the Admiralty, not only had he received much valuable intelligence, he had also been allowed an amazing degree of freedom and access by the Soviets—even giving lectures to the Soviet submarine forces. He was quite certain that a Russian Navy submarine officer would not have fared as well if he had arrived at "Portsmouth during the height of an invasion scare." He also understood that some of the Russians' suspicions and wariness of close liaison relationships could be explained by "their being completely unused to contact with any foreigners, their intense secrecy [and] their fear that some weakness or inefficiency on their part may be revealed and their preoccupation with, and apprehension of, the undoubtedly grave situation in which their country found itself."[32]

The British definitely benefited from the Royal Navy's high standing with the Soviet authorities. V. Cavendish Bentinck, the secretary of the Joint Intelligence Committee, remarked on 12 September that the Russians "respect our navy and think they can learn a lot from our sailors" but "think they have nothing to learn from our soldiers except evacuation." The comparatively strong position of the naval mission in Moscow was nonetheless undermined by Whitehall's eternal desire to get a naval team into Vladivostok. The DNI, Admiral Godfrey, continued to be the obsessive driving force behind this effort, and over Macfarlane's objections, Godfrey bombarded the mission with advice and documentary materials that he thought might act as a quid pro quo to get the Soviets to open the door to Siberia.[33]

Godfrey's August Vladivostok onslaught came at a time when the mission was experiencing internal difficulties. In a moment of sympathetic weakness brought on by Macfarlane's laments, the CIGS had told the 30 Mission chief that he would soon be allowed to come home to get a bit of rest and that there might be a reexamination of British military policy toward the USSR as well as 30 Mission's relations to the Soviet staff. But the prime minister sharply rejected the idea. "I thought he was a very tough man and sent [him] there for that reason," Churchill minuted on 8 August; he added, "if he comes home now he will not go back." Dill then beat a hasty retreat, acknowledged that Macfarlane was "rather a tense sort of person," and agreed that he should stay in Moscow.[34]

Although Macfarlane took this decision well, the personnel and housekeeping situation he confronted in Moscow during late August was far from reassuring. Admiral Godfrey had just thrown another curve at 30 Mission by indicating that he intended to attach one of his old favorites, Ian Fleming, to Macfarlane's team. This suggestion threw the mission into an uproar. Admiral Miles believed that Fleming was being sent to act as Godfrey's secret agent and to spy on the staff. Macfarlane feared that Fleming would launch madcap espionage activities in the USSR that would destroy any prospect of working effectively with the Soviets.[35]

In the end, Fleming was not sent to Moscow, but Godfrey's follies and the difficulties within the mission had come at an especially difficult time. In mid-August, the mission was trying to strike a deal with the Soviets on the highly sensitive matter of "Y" material. On 12 August, a three-man team from 30 Mission (Macfarlane, Greer, and Colonel Exham) met with Col. D. P. Estigneney to request permission to establish a British Army–RAF "Y" observation group in Russia and to exchange British and Soviet "Y" officers. To sweeten the deal, the Britons handed the Soviets a copy of the British library of German "three-letter" codes. Two days later, General Panfilov responded by expressing how "very glad" the Soviet military was to receive the three-letter code library, but he rebuffed the idea of a "Y" exchange. The British authorities nonetheless dispatched army and RAF "Y" officers to Moscow to try for a deal. Squadron Leader G. R. Scott Farnie, the RAF officer, arrived from the Middle East during the second week of September, but the army specialist, Edward Crankshaw (later a renowned journalist and historian of modern Russia), did not even leave for the USSR until 19 September. Even so, the RAF "Y" team pushed on without waiting for Crankshaw. Macfarlane and Farnie met with Panfilov and an unidentified Soviet "Y" officer on 11 September. The British team had been ordered by the Air Ministry and the War Office not to touch the question of "E" (i.e., ENIGMA-ULTRA) traffic,"[36] so this first East-West meeting on code and cipher breaking was limited to sketching out the organization and form of the British "Y" effort, together with an offer to provide the Russians with details of British intercept and low-level code-breaking activities. From the bits of information the Soviets disclosed about their own "Y" operations, Farnie and Air Vice Marshal Charles Medhurst (in London) concluded that "Russian 'Y' was not developed to the extent of our own." But the British authorities were careful not to close the door on future cooperation, and a week later, the mission passed on to the Soviets more "Y" and "E"-related information just in from London, this time indicating to the Soviets that the "Germans are intercepting Russian operation[al] orders."[37]

On 18 September, the Soviets were given more detailed evidence of the Germans' ability to read Russian operational orders. This time, the Soviets were "very pleased" by their British partner's generosity and "guaranteed" that the British source of the information would "be completely safeguarded." During the next few days, although some members of the mission continued to complain that the Soviets were unwilling to undertake serious "Y" cooperation, members of the Soviet liaison group were alarmed by what they called "anti-Soviet" statements allegedly made by three members of the British mission (including a cipher officer). The Soviet "Y" team nonetheless handed over information that the British described as "very satisfactory," and arrangements were begun to allow Farnie to visit a Russian "Y" station. Although the Soviets had not "committed themselves to continuous exchange of 'Y' information," the air mission was pleased with the overall results and quite optimistic about the future. Macfarlane observed that "the Russians appreciated our desire to cooperate and realized its value." The mission chief went on to predict that when Crankshaw arrived, "I think he will find things easier than Scott Farnie did, as the Russians appear more interested in the army interception business than in its air counterpart and they also have more knowledge of the former."[38]

Nonetheless, the Soviet authorities remained unwilling to commit themselves to long-term "Y" exchange. As summer faded into autumn, and vital battles took shape in southern Russia and on the high road to Moscow, a number of other areas of disagreement or irritation between East and West came into the open. When Panfilov's deputy, Colonel Istignev of the Red Air Force, met with Macfarlane on 14 August, he stated the traditional Soviet grievance simply: "We are fighting one of the biggest fights in history," the Soviet colonel declared, and though the Soviets realized that Macfarlane wanted closer cooperation, he could "expect no improvement as long as the British Army is doing nothing on land to help us in our struggle."[39]

The response of 30 Mission was to beg Whitehall to be more forthcoming with the Soviets, who had "put up a far better show than we thought possible," even though "by democratic standards they are a bloody double crossing autocracy less vile than the Nazis only in that they were less prepared to back propaganda war with military aggression." The head of the military mission had nonetheless come to believe that it would be wise to be more open with the Soviets both in providing intelligence and in being frank about British weaknesses. On 31 August, Macfarlane even went so far as to suggest the establishment of a joint planning staff with the Russians, a kind of Combined Chiefs of Staff or Combined Planning Staff, such as the British would not establish even with the Americans until early 1942.[40]

On 24 August, Colonel Firebrace, from his post as liaison officer with the Soviet mission in London, echoed Macfarlane's call for the British government to be more open with the Russians, indicating the weakness of Britain's economic and military position. Whitehall received such ideas coolly, however. In late August and early September, the DMI minuted that Macfarlane's criticism were "not altogether fair," because London wished only to withhold information from the Soviets that would disclose Britain's "most secret sources." General Davidson did grant, however, that there might be some merit in indicating Britain's weakness and why it was impossible to undertake offensive action against Germany in the west. But the bulk of the Whitehall establishment thought otherwise, and on 14 September, Macfarlane was informed by the Foreign Office that joint planning with the Soviets was not "expedient" and that Moscow would not be given an in-depth explanation of why Britain could not carry out a cross-Channel offensive. In this same period, Churchill himself told both Cripps and Stalin that Britain was unable to launch an offensive in the west, even though he sympathized with Cripps's desire to do something more positive as the ambassador confronted "the agony of Russia." When Cripps found, during a Kremlin meeting on 7 September, that Stalin himself was depressed and tired, this merely brought forth a dismissive diary remark by the permanent undersecretary of the Foreign Office (Alexander Cadogan) that even the Communist dictator had been bluffing and was now spent.[41]

In retrospect, it seems probable that the British decision to play its weak hand close to its chest was an error. The Russians had seen enough to know that they were not being cut into Britain's most sensitive intelligence material. Their fantasies about the powers of Western capitalists and their belief in the West's ingrained wiliness surely merged in Stalin's mind into a firm belief that Britain was holding back in the hope that the Eastern totalitarian giants would destroy each other. Obviously, as events of the postwar era would show all too clearly, even if a firmer East-West partnership had been formed in the dark days of September 1941, there were no guarantee that it would have worked effectively when the endless defeats were followed by the great wave of Allied victories. If Britain had found the will to walk the extra mile in the late summer of 1941, the military side of the wartime partnership might have worked more effectively, and the intelligence activities of the British mission might have gotten a new lease on life.

Once Whitehall shut the door on coming clean with the Soviets, however, it took away the mission's means to work with maximum effectiveness and gave a green light to the anti-Soviet feelings that always bubbled just below the surface in many offices in London and in the British mission in Moscow. In mid-September, Cripps was back to his old refrain that the mission had received "very little" from the Russians, and although some in the Air Ministry thought that complaining when the Russians were doing the dying "was not the way to treat a friend," Vice Air Marshal Collier called for the Air Ministry "to put the screws" to the Russians by withholding all intelligence and technical information until they were more forthcoming with information the British wanted.[42] Simultaneously, the War Office abruptly slapped down Macfarlane's suggestion, made on 20 September, that the mission be allowed on occasion to reveal to Moscow the source of special cryptanalytic intelligence. All British authorities, including Macfarlane, then churned out reams of outraged and denunciatory refutations when Panfilov had the temerity to pour oil on the flames by bitterly accusing the British of failing to provide useful intelligence. As Panfilov saw it, most of what the British had given to the Russians was "too general and of no concrete value" in the life-and-death struggle in which the Soviets were engaged.[43]

But throughout August and the first three weeks of September, as would happen repeatedly during the years 1941–1945, even as East and West traded accusations and recriminations—Macfarlane referring contemptuously to the Kremlin gang and characterizing Molotov as one of the most unpleasant creatures he had ever met—they blithely went on doing intelligence business as if their relations with each other were all sweetness and light. During the first two weeks of August, the Russians provided the mission with more German OB than they received, punctuated by complaints about the failure of the British to reply in kind. Macfarlane conceded to Whitehall that "the Russians are coming across well" and that the two sides now had a "good joint order of battle show" in operation. When on 4 August the long sought German OB data on Western Europe finally arrived, the 30 Mission chief exclaimed, "this is what the Russians have been pressing us to provide and its arrival will be a great help in our relations."[44]

After taking a full two weeks to work up the new OB material, during which perfunctory meetings with the Soviets continued, Macfarlane finally handed it over on 18 August. The result was a good meeting "in which the Russians made some provisional comments on German OB both in eastern and western Europe" and indicated that the British information was "much appreciated."[45] A week later, Panfilov provided data on the location of two German regiments on the Eastern Front (the 25th and 74th Infantry Regiments) long sought by the British, and he even admitted that a Soviet press reference to the location of the 21st Panzer Division had been in error. On 23 September, the Soviets further conceded that the British OB summary of German units in Western Europe was more accurate than their own.

Such effective and polite OB exchanges continued through late August and well into September. Macfarlane reported on 31 August that "our order of battle contact is now working well with great advantage to both sides." The mission and the War Office rated this achievement so highly that on 1 September, another officer took over the mission's OB work to allow Birse to be sent back to Britain. There he would receive a short course in OB intelligence methods to better prepare him to rejoin the mission and carry out OB business with maximum effectiveness.[46]

The late summer establishment of good OB cooperation in regard to Germany led the Soviets to take the bold step of suggesting similar cooperation in regard to Japan. Obviously, both the British and the Soviets, as well as the Americans, were worried about Japan's intentions in summer 1941. The Soviets feared a Japanese attack from Manchuria (Manchuko), and the Western powers were apprehensive about Japanese expansion in Southeast Asia and the Pacific following the occupation of Indochina during July. On 26 August, General Panfilov supplied a summary of Japanese divisional totals in Manchuria to 30 Mission; in return, he requested a copy of the British OB estimate of the Japanese Army. Three days later, 30 Mission received from London the OB information the Soviets had requested and soon presented it to Panfilov. On 8 September, the British and Russian OB teams met to hammer out their differing views on Japanese OB and managed to narrow the gap to four divisions (the

Soviets pegging the total Japanese divisions at 65 and the British at 61), with the Soviets contending that the Japanese had three more tank regiments in Manchuria than the British thought possible. A week later, London provided an even more detailed summary of Japanese OB; this too was shared with the Soviets.[47]

The mission had trouble, however, keeping its Japanese OB exchanges with the Soviets on track due to the adventurist notions and follies of Whitehall. On 31 August, Macfarlane felt compelled to send a rather stern message to the CIGS, pleading with him to stop trying to link such exchanges with requests for "information from the Russians about their own disposition in the Far East." He explained that "the Russians will never reveal their own dispositions and intentions," nor would they allow a British mission there.[48]

Problems also arose with respect to exchanges of military technology. Considerable technological information was given to the Soviets by British officials during the summer of 1941, and similar arrangements were made by the mission in Moscow during the same period. The information covered antiaircraft equipment, aspects of army radar, and the specifications of RAF bombs. The mission sent home drawings of the Soviet system for obscuring blast furnaces from aerial observation in early August, and the specifications of Russian gasolines and oils in midmonth. From time to time, the Soviets also indicated to the British when the Germans put new equipment into action, such as the appearance of the K-2 tank in early August.

But technical mismatches frequently occurred. In early September, when the Soviets asked for advice in constructing antitank obstacles, the War Office sent via the mission instructions for the construction of elaborate tubular steel scaffolding barriers. Macfarlane ruefully replied that he had passed on the high-tech information, but the desperate Russians "did not react," perhaps because "they were thinking more in terms of logs than of steel."[49]

When the desire to obtain technical secrets moved into the realm of high technology, problems again appeared. One method of trying to resolve technical exchange questions was to invoke the "reciprocal" principle that Ambassador Maisky had advanced in his conversation with Eden at the time of the German attack in June.[50] From time to time, it was cited by both sides. It was invoked when implementing the exchange of test pilot flights of front-line aircraft that had been suggested by Stalin in mid-July, and in the series of exchange visits to aircraft manufacturing plants that took place in August, thereby making possible the preparation of a twenty-page Air Ministry secret paper called "Equipment of the Russian Air Force."[51]

But as the British chiefs of staff had grasped from the earliest days of cobelligerency with the Soviets, the principle of quid pro quo could work only in areas where technical levels, secrecy policies, and the importance each country attached to a particular device or procedure were roughly equal. On 30 June 1941, therefore, the chiefs had approved a formula whereby they would provide the Russians detailed technical information only on devices that were "already in the hands of the Germans."[52] Although this was a prudent policy position, in practice, it meant that one's comrade in this peculiar partnership would receive vital technical information only after the enemy did.

This principle obviously caused offense when the Russians sought to acquire Western innovations, but it also gave them a handy means of thwarting unwelcome requests for Soviet technical developments. Moscow possessed some valuable technical secrets; by 20 September 1941, even the Americans had learned that the Soviets were using radio-controlled land mines, and Washington was curious about their operation. But well before this, the British had been forced to recognize that the Soviets knew how to play their hand well when the West evidenced interest in their secret technical achievements. On 11 August 1941, Collier and Macfarlane were given a demonstration of the Russian "rocket bomb" being fired by "tank-busting" planes of the Red Air Force. The two British officers were pleasantly surprised by what they witnessed, Macfarlane calling it "a weapon which is already most impressive, and may well develop into a decisive factor" in air warfare.[53] But after initial sounding out, Collier and Macfarlane concluded that the Soviets would not part with the specifications of the rocket bomb unless they received a very valuable quid pro quo. Moscow had long known that the British had highly developed radar equipment, and they immediately indicated that they would be willing to reveal the secrets of the rocket bomb only in exchange for those of the RAF's most secret night-fighter radar system. Faced with this offer, both the Air Ministry and the chiefs of staff balked. The secret of the night-fighter detection apparatus was unknown to the Germans, and the RAF was employing it only in combat over the British Isles, for fear that the Germans would discover the secret if the apparatus were recovered from a crashed British plane. Therefore, to give it to the Russians for use in the fluid conditions of the Eastern Front would invite German capture. Whitehall was compelled to say no and to explain its refusal by citing the principle that technical developments should be exchanged, except for those secrets that the enemy was ignorant of. When Macfarlane screwed up his courage in the third week of August and finally explained the British viewpoint to the Soviets, the Russian military authorities, with vast experience in secrecy and its implications, were not the least offended. They merely asked that this highly important principle be put in writing, a suggestion that made Macfarlane, and apparently the War Office, even more nervous. For the moment, the British allowed the whole question of high-technology exchanges to be quietly dropped from consideration.[54]

Britain also failed to follow up a later Russian initiative that straddled the line between intelligence and psychological warfare.[55] In mid-August, General Panfilov claimed that the Soviets had "considerable evidence of unrest in Berlin and Hamburg," as well as reports of troubles among Hitler, Goering, and the generals. As was established after the war, all such reports were false, but even without conclusive evidence in hand to refute these Russian reports, the military mission refused to pursue this chimera. It seems not to have informed the SOE mission in Moscow of this initiative. At the time, the SOE mission leadership was being changed, as Brigadier Hill finally arrived and Colonel Guiness was recalled.[56]

But the British military mission was not always willing to stand aloof from sources of secret information that were outside routine channels. Macfarlane believed that the Czech and Polish missions in Moscow had better contacts and sources of information than he did, and he cultivated close relations with General Anders and Colonel Pika. Since both the Polish and Czech governments in exile were also relaying many of their Moscow missions' reports to the British authorities in London, little of the information that Macfarlane acquired was likely to have been especially important, or even accurate. On 10 August, however, the 30 Mission chief learned from "a source in close contact with personnel returned from the front" that the German infantry was not full of fight and did not "like the bayonet." The same report alleged that there were complaints in Russian ranks about the inadequacies of the Soviet high command and the failure to provide the Red Army with enough flak to help counter German air superiority.[57]

Such tattle about the Soviet Army merely whetted Macfarlane's longing for a chance to see the great eastern war in person. From the moment he had arrived in Moscow, he pleaded for a chance to go to the front and judge for himself what was going on there. By 5 August, the oft-repeated refrain of Macfarlane's requests, and the Soviets' refusals, had become so routine that Cripps minuted to the Foreign Office, "I can't help feeling that General Macfarlane somewhat exaggerates the need that he should visit the front. Is it really as important as he seems to make out?"[58] But the military mission kept right on probing, trying to lever Panfilov into granting the long sought visit to the front. On 4 August, the War Office added Macfarlane's determination by declaring that there was no sense letting him come home until he had somehow arranged to visit the front.[59]

On 17 August 1941, Collier and Macfarlane received an appetizer. They were authorized to spend the night with a Soviet mobile antiaircraft battery fifteen kilometers northwest of Moscow during a Luftwaffe attack on the Russian capital. Then, as even the British press was immediately informed, at 5:00 A.M. on 20 August, the British military mission chief, accompanied by Colonel Greer, was allowed to visit a front-line Red Army combat unit that had just successfully counterattacked north of the Dnieper. This division had faced a difficult task and performed well, and in chats with troops and junior officers, Macfarlane was impressed by their high morale and toughness. In a series of "absolute priority" telegrams home, he reported on this happy occasion; praised the Red Army's adequate, if simple, logistical support system; and noted that the Russian troops were warily respectful of the Germans' use of massed mortars.[60]

Having thus broken the barrier regarding visits outside Moscow, Macfarlane was soon authorized to travel to Tiflis in Georgia, where he surveyed the situation and consulted with a British liaison officer stationed there. These survey visits in late August, and on into September and October, seem to have enhanced Macfarlane's optimism and good cheer. He observed to London on 22 September, in the last of his summer messages, that he was now certain that the Russians would fight on to the end and that Leningrad "will never surrender," to which the DMI penned the note, "I agree."[61] But not even this conclusion—which was a complete reversal of the pessimistic predictions with which all British officials had greeted the Nazi attack on the USSR less than three months before—was enough to turn Macfarlane into an optimist about East-West relations. He stuck to the view that such relations would remain poor because the Soviets were so difficult and because Britain seemed unable to "prove to Moscow that no Second Front was possible."[62]

But if this account of Britain's efforts to create an effective intelligence partnership with the USSR during the summer of 1941 must end on a note of disappointment, with an undertone of bumbling and closed-mindedness, a last look at the American stance regarding East-West intelligence exchange may serve to keep the British activity in perspective. On 15 September 1941, the U.S. assistant secretary of war, John J. McCloy, met in Washington with a Soviet liaison team to discuss supplying American bombers to the USSR. McCloy sidestepped Russian requests for heavy bombers (B-17s and B-24s), instead offering the Russians medium bombers (B-25s and B-26s), with an invitation to choose which planes they wanted after witnessing an improvised air show.

The Soviets agreed to this arrangement and then, near the conclusion of the discussion with McCloy, raised a far more important issue. Out of the blue they announced that the USSR desired "to initiate *preliminary* staff discussions regarding military action against Japan." McCloy, presumably somewhat surprised by this statement, sidestepped it only by managing to reply that "he would like to have defensive aerial measures against Japan discussed,"[63] which apparently meant that he was interested in planning joint air operations or air reconnaissance. This appears to have been the ideal opening for the West to make a deal with the Soviets that would enhance its information about Japanese intentions as well as increase its power to intimidate Tokyo, just when relations with Japan had become strained and the prospects ominous. But McCloy and the U.S. government simply let this Russian initiative pass by—the available documents state only that "the subject was not further developed."[64] Coming as it did just eighty days before the Japanese attack on Pearl Harbor, this American failure to jump at a chance to cooperate regarding information on Japan shows all too clearly the barriers that stood in the way of effective East-West wartime intelligence and operational cooperation. It also suggests that the failure to overcome such obstacles may well have increased the pain and cost of the conflict for all the Allied powers.

4
The Turning Points of
Late 1941, Mid-September to
the End of 1941

World War II was so multifaceted, and so extended in time and space, that it gave rise to dozens of critical junctures or crises, each of which was vitally important to a particular group of belligerents. But if one considers the broad sweep of the war's history, it is difficult to avoid the conclusion that the late autumn of 1941 and the early winter of 1941–1942 was when the course of the war was most significantly wrenched in new directions, with consequences that would fundamentally shape the next four years of combat and the postwar era as well.

The most dramatic and surprising of these events was Japan's attack on Pearl Harbor (7 December) and the subsequent Japanese advance across the Pacific and through Southeast Asia. This development instantly transformed the conflict from a regional European struggle into a truly world war, raising the stakes and complexities for people everywhere. It vaulted a shocked and angry America into the conflict in a way that guaranteed that the people and the government of the United States would be united in support of the war effort. That, in turn, meant that 10 to 12 million men would ultimately be added to the armed forces of the Allies. Even more importantly, the world's largest agricultural and manufacturing system would henceforth be harnessed to the task of smashing Nazi Germany, Fascist Italy, and Imperial Japan.

In addition to this most basic change, decisive events occurred in the autumn of 1941 on the Russian front that would shape the future course of the war and the nearly half-century-long postwar era that followed. On 2 October 1941, Hitler threw the full force of German blitzkrieg power (Operation TYPHOON) at the center of the Russian line in an all-out effort to break the Red Army, conquer Moscow, and deliver a massive blow to the Soviet system before the arrival of the dreaded Russian winter.[1] This was the big gamble of the European war, and Hitler lost it. The Red Army was initially battered by TYPHOON, bloodied and forced to fall back on the Soviet capital. But even as retreat occurred in the center, the Russians made gains on the flanks, advancing here and there around Leningrad and actually retaking the vital southern city of Rostov on 29 November. But the decisive Russian achievement was the grinding down of von Bock's Army Group Center through stubborn Russian resistance, aided by autumn mud and then paralyzing cold. On 5 December, Zhukov's great counteroffensive fell on the Germans, smashing von Bock's battered and frozen units in what was clearly the first Allied offensive triumph of World War II.

This success, like the entry of the United States into the conflict, would have important effects both during and after the war. On 5 December, Hitler lost the strategic initiative in the European war, and though he tried to recover it in the summer campaign of 1941, which culminated in his second big eastern defeat at Stalingrad, at no time after 5 December 1941 would the second great twentieth-century conflict be "Hitler's war," to do with as he would. The Russian victory before Moscow virtually guaranteed that Stalin's Russia would emerge from the war as a truly great, if not yet super, power.

Thus, in the brilliant light of hindsight, the autumn of 1941 seems to have been a turning point of modern history. But to the individuals on the ground, including those struggling to produce effective East-West intelligence cooperation, it was often just one more phase in a difficult and frequently frustrating struggle. Many of the characteristics that had marked the East-West cooperative efforts in the summer continued to apply in the autumn. The Americans remained unwilling or unable to play a leading role in the intelligence-sharing process, and Moscow rather than London continued to be the main scene of Anglo-Soviet exchanges. The British mission was still frustrated by Soviet reluctance to permit its members to wander freely through Moscow and the rest of Russia, although some opportunities to observe Red arms and installations did arise when mission personnel were sent on assignments beyond Moscow, Archangel, or Murmansk.[2]

With regard to technical exchanges, although both sides were quite generous in sharing weather data, information on chemical warfare, and the specifics of German military technology (ranging from aerial torpedoes to tanks and self-propelled guns), exchange of advanced technological secrets continued to pose serious difficulties. Despite repeated British appeals, including direct intervention by Ambassador Cripps, the Russians refused to provide technical information on the rocket bomb. The British, although giving the Soviets ASDIC, declined to disclose the workings of their most advanced torpedoes or other secret aspects of RAF equipment. By early December, the Admiralty finally formulated a statement to guide its personnel in coping with Soviet equipment requests. "Nothing under development" was to be disclosed to the Russians, nor were they to receive any item that was "not in service" or had "not got into enemy hands."[3]

During this period, there was also little change in the attitude and activities of the chief American military representative in Moscow. Colonel Yeaton continued to loathe the Soviets and refused to credit them with any ability or success. Yeaton spent September and October regularly recommending that Washington not send supplies to the USSR because the Germans would soon overrun the whole country. Beyond these dismal tidings, he had little to report except to complain periodically that the Red Army was giving him no information at all. From some unidentified source, he did manage to acquire the German Army staff handbook on European Turkey, however, and he may have picked up other isolated tidbits as well.

After Yeaton was withdrawn during the winter, Colonel Michela continued on as attaché, introducing only minor variations on the theme that the Soviets were uncooperative, incompetent, and doomed. As the battle for Moscow reached its climax, Michela repeatedly cautioned Washington against sending any form of military assistance to the Russians on the grounds that the Soviet authorities would be unable to use it properly. In early October, U.S. Army Air Corps Maj. Gen. J. E. Chaney visited Soviet aircraft factory number one near Moscow and reported that it was producing ten or more modern aircraft per day. Michela replied to Washington that "his report astounds me" and hinted darkly that the wily Soviets might have hoodwinked Chaney.[4] All levels of G-2 in Washington were overwhelmed by negative and defeatist thoughts about the USSR in the autumn of 1941. When Averell Harriman and Lord Beaverbrook visited Moscow in late September and early October, a broad-minded general in the army's Office of the Chief of Air Staff (Gen. Martin F. Scanlon) found it necessary to send Harriman private and confidential reports to indicate that not all American military officials thought that the Russian situation was as hopeless as Yeaton and Michela indicated.

In late winter, although no new deal occurred, American supplies to Russia increased and new personnel were added to both the American military attaché's office and the U.S. supply mission. As a result, indirect sources of intelligence about Russia and the war against Germany improved. In December 1941, the U.S. naval attaché, Comdr. Ronald Allen, sent home the first detailed American reports on the north Russian ports and navigation on the Volga. The newly arrived assistant military attaché, Col. James Boswell, was dispatched on a courier mission to Vladivostok, where he established that the Soviets in that region were so dependent on trade with Japan for their survival that it was highly unlikely that they would offend or challenge the Japanese in any way. The Soviet military attaché's office in London indicated to American authorities there that Moscow's hostility to East-West intelligence exchanges was softening and that "as soon as United States munitions were being received in large amounts it would disappear altogether."[5]

Yet even after Pearl Harbor, the Soviets remained wary of doing anything that might annoy the Japanese, although other legations in Moscow were not so reticent. In late December, the Swedish mission provided Clinton Olson of the American economic mission with a detailed summary of the damage that the Japanese authorities believed they had inflicted on the U.S. Navy by their attack on Pearl Harbor. This report was sent to Washington posthaste and immediately found its way into the files of the office of naval intelligence (ONI).

But as things improved for some Americans in Moscow, Michela continued to report home that the Soviets had defeated *him,* declaring on 1 December that "unless some means can be found to break [the] present Soviet attitude this office is helpless." G-2 nonetheless kept him in his post, even though Macfarlane's staff found Michela so negative that they refused to distribute crucial intelligence material to him. Michela therefore sought out bits of information wherever he could find them, including the Polish General Anders. During November, Michela's favorite source of information about the Soviets, especially concerning their alleged weakness in Siberia, was the Japanese military attaché. The near total uselessness of the American military intelligent establishment in Moscow during the autumn of 1941 was thereby revealed most clearly. Michela continued to cite the Japanese attaché in Moscow as an authoritative and open-minded source on the USSR right up until three weeks before the attack on Pearl Harbor, even though the Soviet Union was at war with Japan's German ally and Japanese-American relations were so dire as to be headed for catastrophe.[6]

Another aspect of the inter-Allied intelligence exchange effort blundered along in the byways during the autumn, much as it had during the summer. The British authorities discovered that the earlier Soviet attempts to tighten their code and cipher security had not been sufficient to thwart the code-breaking efforts of the German B. Dienst. On 13 November, 30 Mission again informed the Soviets that Germany was cracking Russian codes, and once more the Soviets expressed their gratitude for the information. But the creation of a code- and cipher-breaking cooperative agreement continued to elude the British and Russian governments. In early November, Macfarlane believed that "a proper contact" regarding "Y" exchange might be possible in Moscow, but the opportunity was allowed to pass, partly because when the British Army "Y" expert,

Major Crankshaw, finally arrived in Russia, his services were required by the British forces in the north. Perhaps because of the resulting delays, hope for a comprehensive "Y" deal evaporated.[7]

A general and comprehensive "Y" deal between Britain and Soviet Russia was probably inherently impossible in any case, because of the great political differences and suspicions that divided the two countries. Britain was so far ahead of Russia (and most other countries) in code and cipher breaking that the two reluctant and differently placed allies found it impossible to conclude even a wide-ranging "Y" deal. But the obstacles were increased in the autumn of 1941. The Red Army staff was stretched to the limit during the decisive battles with the German Army and was consequently even more prickly and suspicious than usual.

All these troubles and frustrations were seriously compounded by the Soviet decision on 14 October, two weeks after the beginning of TYPHOON, to carry out a partial evacuation of Moscow. Many nonessential Soviet government offices were relocated further east, and the same fate befell the auxiliary staffs of foreign embassies, including the British military mission. On 16 October, it was transferred to the provincial town of Kubyshev, near Omsk, a thousand miles east of Moscow. Although the move to Kubyshev gave members of the mission an opportunity to observe much of Russia and some Soviet military equipment, the transfer was so sudden that adequate preparations could not be made for a smooth transition or a continuous liaison with the Soviet high command. Serious mistakes were also made by the British authorities in Moscow. The general archives of the embassy were destroyed "in error," along with many order-of-battle files plus the whole RAF section war diary for June to mid-October, because mission members believed that Moscow was about to fall to the Germans.[8] Once in Kubyshev, Macfarlane was appalled by the chaos and inefficiency of the local administration and was horrified to discover that because the Soviet high command was not in Kubyshev, he was now cut off from effective liaison. On 21 October, he still did not know where the main Soviet government was actually located and began to protest to London that something must be done to get him back in touch with the Russian high command. Eden thought that his loud complaints were "a little heavy-handed," and when the prime minister learned what was going on, he minuted to the CIGS on 26 October:

> General Macfarlane is making altogether too much fuss. Considering the thin ice we are on in Russia while we are doing so little for them, he should be told to go easy.[9]

Three days later, the DMI ordered Macfarlane to simmer down, and after another two weeks, he instructed him to show more reasonable patience.

Whitehall was surely correct in holding that Macfarlane's needs and the activities of the mission were of marginal importance when the USSR was fighting the battle that would decide its own fate and, in large measure, that of the whole Allied cause. But the chief of 30 Mission had been placed in a difficult situation by the evacuation to Kubyshev. During the six weeks he was there, he acquired virtually no intelligence sufficiently valuable to warrant sending it on to London. Whereas the mission's navy branch could deal with the Soviet chief of naval staff, who had also been transferred to Kubyshev, and Collier of the air staff enjoyed effective liaison arrangements because the Soviets needed him to facilitate the shipment and maintenance of RAF equipment, Macfarlane was left alone with, as he muttered, only "one nitwit" to deal with. Finally, in December, he and the section heads simply left the rest of the mission in Kubyshev (until mid-January) and hitched a ride on the plane of the head of the Polish government in exile, Gen. W. Sikorski, who happened to be passing through Kubyshev. Thus they managed to get back to Moscow and reestablish direct contact with the Soviet high command.[10]

While Macfarlane and the British Army team had been virtually incommunicado in Kubyshev, the Royal Navy mission and its subsections in the Black Sea and the north had flourished. Although unable to secure everything the Admiralty wanted, the main mission obtained, among other items, reports on German submarine and auxiliary vessels in the far north and a detailed description of an operation that the Germans had recently conducted against Oesel Island. The Royal Navy responded by providing information on German anti-aircraft methods, data on German flak in the Baltic from both Polish and British sources, a report on German fleet dispositions, and details of northern German minefields. From the British Navy missions in the far north, the Admiralty received considerable useful information, including detailed dispatches on conditions and defenses of the Russian ports, plus the names and ranks of top Russian Navy officers, German order of battle, and the movements of German ground and air forces in the northern area. The British northern navy team was given a tour of the Soviet destroyer *Sokrushitelni* in late September and, in December, received cruise reports from Russian patrol boats, contact statements from Russian submarines, and a three-page cruise report by the Soviet submarine *Seawolf*. The Royal Navy secured so much information on Russian ships and bases in the north that by 25 October it began to pass some of these items on to the Americans. Soon, that old enthusiast for all things nautical, Franklin Roosevelt, opened a special file to hold the photos and statistics regarding the Red Navy that he received from the British authorities and later from the American merchant and escort vessel crews and the U.S. Navy missions, which went into north Russian ports.[11]

In southern Russia, the British Navy liaison office in the Black Sea area continued its winning ways, even though Commander Fawkes was temporarily replaced. The combined intelligence reports issued daily by the Soviet naval commander in the Black Sea were routinely given to the British, along with a substantial volume of OB intelligence on the Black Sea navies of Germany's allies—Rumania and Bulgaria—plus masses of OB information on the armies of all the Axis states fighting against the Soviets in southern Russia. Even this intelligence bonanza was not sufficient to prevent the Admiralty and its liaison officers from treating the staff of the Russian Navy with condescension. Following a late December dinner held for the Soviet navy mission in London, an Admiralty official prepared a three-page report entitled "The Russian at Dinner." This document declared that "since we shall have to live with the Russians in a rapidly contracting world, we must break down their isolation if we are to avoid fighting them," but it went on to state that the Russian officer was "altogether . . . very pleasant, somewhat childish, and rather pathetic."[12]

This patronizing attitude also lay at the root of the absurd British persistence in wanting to station one of their missions in Siberia, even though the Soviets were fighting for their lives and had repeatedly refused to sanction such a move. In mid-October (just prior to 30 Mission's deportation to Kubyshev) and again in mid-November, the chiefs of staff hounded Macfarlane to seek Soviet approval for the stationing of a British mission in Vladivostok. Again Macfarlane sought to head off the folly of the chiefs. This time, he suggested that it might be better to ask the Soviets to accept a temporary British intelligence team in Vladivostok to carry out on-the-spot exchanges of intelligence relating to Japan, "because they already appreciate our order of battle and other intelligence here."[13] This suggestion was doubly silly: the Soviets would surely have seen that it was merely a ruse to fulfill the British Siberian passion, and by early November, exchanges of intelligence on Japan had already begun in Moscow.[14]

On 4 November, Britain supplied the Soviets with a copy of its OB summary of the Japanese Army. This initiative was taken to help the Soviets and to enhance intelligence cooperation with them, at a time when Britain was increasingly worried about Japanese expansion, just a month prior to Pearl Harbor. The War Office also hoped that if the Soviets were pleased with this intelligence material they might reciprocate and fill Britain's nearly empty larder of secret information on the Japanese armed forces. As MI 2c (the army intelligence section concerned with the Japanese Army) noted in early December, the most recent Japanese Army list that British military intelligence possessed was dated 1935. On this matter, the Soviets responded quite generously, and by 5 December, a more recent edition of the Japanese Army list was in the hands of the British military mission in Moscow.

Immediately following the attack on Pearl Harbor and the start of the Japanese sweep through Southeast Asia, the Soviets were unusually generous to the Western powers regarding Japanese intelligence. It was not in the USSR's interest to see its Western comrades weakened when the Germans were at the gates of Moscow, and Stalin was presumably worried that Japan might strike north as well as south. On 22 December, Col. G. Pugachev and a colleague from the Russian mission in London visited the War Office and the Air Ministry to discuss Japanese order of battle with British officers. On 11 December, the Soviets had paid back the British for their kindness in warning of the vulnerability of Russian codes by informing London that on 15 November, Theodor Kordt in Shanghai had given the Japanese the key to a British code that had been broken by the German B. Dienst. At the same time, the Soviets provided a summary of overall Japanese army deployment in Southeast Asia and named the commanders of the four Japanese Army contingents in that area. On the last day of the year, the British naval mission in Moscow was given a survey of the whole Japanese naval radio network as of October 1941, with a warning that "all Japanese warship call signs had been changed."[15]

In post–Pearl Harbor Washington, East-West exchanges of intelligence materials on Japan also occurred. On 16 December, U.S. Army intelligence secured from the British delegation in Washington the identities of the Japanese commanders in Malaya, which the British had acquired from the Russians. On 22 December, American intelligence returned the favor by providing the Soviets with the general characteristics of the Japanese midget submarine that the U.S. Navy had captured in Hawaii. The head of the new American intelligence agency, Col. William "Wild Bill" Donovan, of the Office of the Coordinator of Information (COI), also had a private discussion with the Russian naval attaché, Capt. I. A. Yegorichev, during this period. But Donovan was uncharacteristically cautious on this occasion and made no effort to secure intelligence from the Soviets, although nine days later (11 December), he proposed sending two COI "representatives" to scout out the USSR, only to have this plan rejected by the president.[16]

In the last months of 1941, the British government showed a comparable coyness as it tried to work out propaganda policies that would show that London was supporting the government of the USSR but at the same time giving no encouragement to the British or any other Communist Party. After much to-ing and fro-ing on this problem, the prime minister's intelligence aide, Maj. Desmond Morton, advocated attaching an intelligence "expert" to the Ministry of Information to advise it on "the theory and practice of the Komintern" and to help it develop propaganda policies that would expose "the British people to the difference between the Russian Government and the 'Komintern.'" The prime minister supported Morton's proposals, but it must be acknowledged that this effort to square the circle actually accomplished very little. British public opinion swung enthusiastically in support of the USSR in 1941–1942, and there was a steady drift toward the Left in British politics during the last three years of the war.[17]

British cooperation with the Soviets in another form of political-military operation, which it had traditionally shunned as morally and legally dubious, also failed to achieve its problematic objective during late 1941. The operation's aim was to kill the German Army high command and Adolf Hitler, not by means of a coup or a direct attempt at assassination, but through heavy bombing of locations where they were thought to be. On 11 November, with Churchill's approval, 30 Mission was directed to tell the Russians that the Nazi leadership would be meeting in "a special train" at Orscha in Belorussia during inspections of the Eastern Front. One day later, on 12 November, "Colonel Greer handed over [to the Soviets] important information regarding a meeting between the German High Command and all commanders on the Russian Front to be held at Orscha."[18] Three weeks later, coincidentally on Pearl Harbor day, the British military mission reported to London that the Russians had "bombed Orscha . . . heavily on the night of 13 November," but the Russian staff had concluded "from information of Hitler's movements, subsequently obtained," that it was "unlikely that he was at Orscha on the day in question."[19] The British continued to provide the Soviets with information on the location of German headquarters in the east in late 1941 and 1942. This was, of course, useful for OB identification but also may have been helpful in pinpointing future Soviet efforts to eliminate the Nazi leadership through air raids.

Such semi-covert activities represented atypical aspects of the Anglo-Soviet intelligence partnership in 1941, although the British continued to work on the possibility of carrying out joint psychological warfare campaigns with the Russians. The SOE, together with MI 6 and the NKVD, also moved ahead with bizarre attempts to use British logistical support, training facilities, and airlifts for Soviet agents going into Europe. But all such adventuresome and unorthodox operations, as well as most of the more conventional intelligence-sharing activities involving Britain and the USSR, paled in comparison with the scale and success of the exchange of order-of-battle information.[20] In the latter part of

1941, the sharing of OB intelligence continued to be the lifeblood of the Anglo-Soviet secret partnership, just as it had been during the summer and early autumn. Yet just as the leaves had begun to fall in the autumn of 1941, a crisis arose regarding OB.

On 19 September, the Soviets asked for and received a ration of information on German OB on the Russian front. All seemed satisfactory and harmonious, even though the War Office continued to complain about inordinate delays by the Soviet staff in dealing with British intelligence requests. Then, in a discussion between Ambassador Cripps and Stalin that occurred on the following day, matters took a sharp turn for the worse. This meeting was a festival of complaints, with Stalin grumbling about the failure of the Americans to send him enough war supplies, and Cripps bemoaning the Soviet refusal to share the secret of the rocket bomb with the British.

When Cripps also accused the Soviets of failing to cooperate adequately with the British military mission, Stalin replied, quite reasonably, that the Soviet staff was more concerned with the enormous battles raging across Russia than it was with the British military mission. But then he went on to lodge two countercomplaints about 30 Mission. First he declared that "not all members of the British Mission [had] conducted themselves as they should," and that some of them had been guilty in Soviet eyes of anti-Soviet propaganda in conversations with Soviet naval officers.[21]

This classically Stalinesque accusation led to considerable anguished and agitated exchange between London and 30 Mission during the ensuing weeks. The Foreign Office was especially reluctant to have any of the accused Royal Navy officers removed from Russia because, as Cavendish Bentincka observed on 10 October, "we have been receiving more information from the naval officers at Murmansk and the Black Sea than from any other quarter." But Churchill was not prepared to quibble with Stalin, although he deluded himself with the notion that the Russians "are far more dependent upon us than we are upon them." On 2 October, he ordered the recall of those British personnel whom the Soviets considered persona non grata.

Stalin gave Whitehall a second sharp tweak by asserting that "the information supplied by the British Military Mission had not always proved reliable" and suggested that this might be explained by the presence of pro-Nazi agents within the British military intelligence service. Specifically, Stalin charged that "some time ago," Macfarlane had supplied information to the effect that the principal German thrust in the northern battlefront would be somewhere between Leningrad and Moscow, "whereas in fact," the Soviet leader asserted, "the blow had been directed against Moscow itself." Stalin also claimed that "the British Mission had supplied information that the main thrust in the south would be against the Crimea, and that a landing from the sea would certainly be attempted"; actually, the German "main blow had been directed against Kiev."[22]

These accusations stung the British military intelligence establishment to the quick, led Macfarlane to protest formally to General Panfilov (who professed complete ignorance of Stalin's assertions), and earned the chief of 30 Mission a reprimand from the DMI and CIGS for not lodging even more detailed and precise refutations of Stalin's accusations with the Soviet staff. Beyond that, Eden and Cripps exchanged wordy messages exploring whether the Soviet high command sufficiently appreciated the intelligence information they were receiving from Britain.

The British intelligence authorities' effort to vindicate themselves led to a detailed review of the intelligence on German operational intentions that had been sent to 30 Mission and handed on to the Russians between 26 June and 19 September. As part of this review, on 29 September, the staff of the CIGS listed the details of ten telegrams sent to 30 Mission in the summer and autumn of 1941 pointing in the direction of German offensive plans or likely intentions. Significantly, only three of these (dated 9 and 14 July and 9 September) bore the heading "Most Reliable Report" or from "Most Reliable Occasional Source," indicating to Macfarlane that these items came from ULTRA sources. One other item was headed "Appreciation of Situation" (26 June 1941), suggesting that it may have been merely a War Department estimate and was unlikely to have been based directly on highly secret sources. One other telegram (9 August) claimed only to be based "on considerable evidence."

The ten telegrams throw light on a number of matters that were important in estimating the significance and accuracy of the British intelligence contribution to the Soviet cause during the first four months of the Russo-German war. Clearly, the information provided by the British regarding German intentions vis-à-vis Moscow and Leningrad at the end of July was at least partly off the mark. A non-ULTRA British document had declared that the German "main air effort [had been] transferred to the Leningrad front" and the German land effort would "presumably soon follow." Stalin was wrong in claiming that this document had indicated that the main German blow would fall "between" Moscow and Leningrad—the document declared that it would be Leningrad.[23] But the British intelligence information was also wrong, because the Germans certainly did not rank Leningrad as a higher lead target than Moscow. Similarly, in regard to Stalin's accusation concerning the Crimea, in two non-ULTRA items sent in mid-August and on 9 September, the British asserted that the Germans were aiming at the Crimea and were preparing a seaborne expedition, but the 9

September ULTRA item also declared that the Germans would strike south against Kiev as part of a "decisive operation to win the war."[24]

So Stalin was surely justified in charging that Britain's intelligence was not always 100 percent accurate or precise, and the British authorities were equally warranted in claiming that among the items they sent east, Germany's intentions were accurately indicated—at least at some point. But it is evident as well that the British did not send the Russians much information on German intentions (ten items in two months) and that the material they did send was not always crystal clear. In the light of subsequent claims that large quantities of ULTRA were sent to the mission and, in the pro-British version, passed on to the Soviets or, in the anti-British version, withheld from the Soviets, it is important to note that a total of only three ULTRA items on German intentions were sent from London to Moscow in two months. This strongly suggests that ULTRA's role in the early phase of the eastern war may have been grossly exaggerated. But when all the investigations were concluded in October 1941, the mission decided that its "forecasts of German future action were a hundred percent right in every case." Macfarlane came out of this affair believing that all the trouble had once again been caused by the Kremlin gang rather than by the Soviet high command, the British, or even Stalin himself. Therefore, one must acknowledge that the affair inevitably caused a good deal more confusion, resentment, and suspicion to be stored up for the future.[25]

But with the resilience and willingness to struggle on that seemed to characterize relations between 30 Mission and the Soviets in 1941–1942, the two sides were soon back to useful OB exchanges as if nothing untoward had happened. On 24 September, the mission concluded that "the difference between our and the Russian conception of German order of battle has now been reduced to a comparatively small number of divisions and the free and full exchange of information had produced excellent results." The materials shared and the estimates evaluated ranged from German panzers near Leningrad to possible German reinforcements for Finland. But of course, the Soviets were not told that London's OB picture of 283 *Russian* divisions (presumably based on "Y" and ULTRA sources) had also been sent to the mission by the War Office on 26 September 1941.[26]

Between 25 September and 2 October, the primary focus for Panfilov and Macfarlane was the Germans' preparation for the TYPHOON offensive against Moscow, which the Soviets and 30 Missions tracked in detail. On 24, 25, and 27 September, the British mission gave the Soviets information on "the German concentration now thought to be taking place in the central sector," including flak and Luftwaffe information as well as details of Panzergruppe 3, all of which Panfilov promised would go "straight to M. Stalin and Marshal Shaposh-nikov." In this period, Macfarlane was careful not to hand over intelligence materials unless they had a high level of accuracy. The Soviet staff members—seeming to understand this, and realizing that with TYPHOON looming they needed all the help they could get—were not only pleasant to the British staff but also confirmed many British reports and sought to obtain from the British every bit of intelligence available, including information on German casualties, OB on German units in the Reich and the occupied territories, and the organization of Rumanian, Bulgarian, and Italian formations in western Russia.

In the first six days of the German offensive (TYPHOON), the military mission passed over to the Soviets additional intelligence details, but what could be delivered was somewhat limited by a chiefs of staff decision in early October that the Russians "should *not* be given" the most recent JIC appreciation of future German plans.[27] In consequence, although the Soviets asked for even marginal information on German activities and tipped off the British to the like-lihood of an imminent German attack in Libya (a tip that turned out to be false), Macfarlane had no additional high-level intelligence to give the Soviets. He pleaded with London for any hot "Y" intelligence that might help the Russians, while admitting to the DMI that he could not "pretend to be able to give you a useful appreciation, in fact you are in a much better position to make one than I" (a remark that prompted the DMI to add a self-satisfied one-word comment, "yes," to the telegram and to crow rightly to the Foreign Office that prior to the start of TYPHOON, British intelligence had sent to the Soviets via Macfarlane telegrams that foretold the exact concentration of German armored groups for the attack on Moscow).[28]

In the beginning of the second week of TYPHOON, and again a few days later, Macfarlane received more "very important information . . . from the War Office which gave the outline German [attack] plan and [the] grouping of their armored divisions for their attack on Moscow." The mission immediately handed this material to Panfilov and subsequently relayed a second batch of such material to the Soviet high command. The Russians (not surprisingly) were "very pleased" to receive it and certainly made good use of it in the fol-lowing weeks, but neither Moscow nor London has seen fit subsequently to admit that British military intelligence made a major contribution to the Soviet intelligence pool in the battle that saved Moscow. The British say virtually nothing about it, even in their official histories, and Marshal Zhukov subse-quently claimed that his intelligence data for the battle came from Red Army "front intelligence."[29]

Unfortunately for Macfarlane, he had little opportunity to brag about this

TYPHOON intelligence triumph. In mid-October, just after the Air Ministry provided a final summary of German aircraft production and the British general had a final chat with General Golikov (recently returned to the USSR from Washington and currently commander of the 10th Red Army) regarding the movement of German divisions (including *Totenkopf*) from France to the Russian front, Macfarlane was shipped out of Moscow and dumped in Kubyshev. During the seven weeks that the main mission was out of Moscow and TYPHOON continued, the air section managed to supply the Soviets with extracts from an Air Ministry summary paper, "An Appreciation of German Air Strength," and various other bits of documentation on the Luftwaffe. In November, Macfarlane also discussed with the Russians various secondary matters, such as Finland's partial demobilization and the OB of the lesser Axis states (Bulgaria and Rumania). By 11 November, the air mission had acquired a Soviet paper on German air tactics, and on 19 November, Major Birse and Colonel Gusev managed to resume general OB cooperation on the German Army. The Battle of Moscow era was not a time when 30 Mission provided significant intelligence materials to the USSR, however. [30]

October–November 1941 was a tense period for Allied leaders both East and West. Stalin obviously carried the greatest burden of responsibility and strain as TYPHOON moved on, for the Soviet leader was more aware than anyone else of the scale and ferocity of the German attack. British and American leaders, although not facing the same back-to-the-wall situation as Stalin, were seriously worried by TYPHOON and doubtful of the Soviet capacity to absorb the German attack. On 16 October, U.S. Secretary of the Navy Frank Knox sent an enigmatically reassuring message to the First Lord, A. V. Alexander: "As I write, the news from Russia is exceedingly depressing. However, in view of the fact that most of us expected Russia to put up very slight resistance when the war started, it is useful at this moment to remember that the partial defeat of the Russian Army which seems now to be achieved, has been bought by Germany at a frightful price." A week later, the prime minister and the DMI exchanged estimates of the likelihood that Moscow would fall before winter. The prime minister was inclined to "put it even"; the DMI, noting that the "uncertain factor of weather will play a big part," nonetheless "reckon[ed] the chances at slightly greater than even—say 5 to 4 on its capture."[31]

Not until 1 December did the JIC conclude in report number (41) 452 that the Russian front would stabilize, that is, that the Red Army would hold before Moscow, by mid-December. After that date, the JIC declared, large-scale operations would be confined to southern Russia, where the Germans might be successful enough to seize Rostov.

As early as 8 November, however, Churchill was circling phrases like "roads have again deteriorated" and "heavy fighting" in the reports from German intercepts secured from the Eastern Front and sent by "C," and JIC 452 turned out to be a multiple disaster.[32] Three days after it was completed (5 December), Zhukov made an unconscious mockery of it by launching the greater counteroffensive that tore huge holes in the center of the German lines and threw the Wehrmacht well back from the gates of Moscow. At the same time, in the south, the Red Army had also been on the march, and it was the Red Army, not the Germans, who seized Rostov and held it throughout the winter. By 18 December, the prime minister was drawing more circles around the incorrect predictions in the report and minuting the military authorities that "this requires revision in the light of what has happened since!"[33] But by that time, the Soviets had also had their crack at JIC (41) 452, and they discredited it even more thoroughly than did the prime minister. Shortly after he returned to Moscow from Kubyshev in early December, Macfarlane met Panfilov and showed him a copy of the report. When they met again on 7 December (perhaps the JIC's Pearl Harbor day), the Russian general flatly rejected the British contentions that the Germans would be able to go on the defensive in front of Moscow and that they would be able to recover from the loss of Rostov and launch a summer offensive in the south.[34]

Such reproofs may well have been resented by a British military establishment, which had initially been rather slow to provide the Soviets with secret information to assist Zhukov's advance, preferring instead, as Cavendish Bentinck remarked on 15 December, to indulge the British "mania for offering the Russians advice and technical experts, neither of which they want, and which only arouse their suspicions."[35] In the second week of December, MI 14C (the army OB section in London concerned with the eastern war) held ULTRA evidence that the Germans were trying to extricate the armor of the main panzer group from Klin and pull it back to Tula, but Macfarlane, for no readily explicable reason, had specifically been barred from informing the Soviet high command. However, the air mission did give the Soviets full summaries on the condition of the Luftwaffe in the east, and by 20 December, the DMI, 30 Mission, and the Soviet high command had all come to the conclusion that the Germans would make their stand in the Smolensk area. The DMI observed that unless the Germans succeeded in taking Sevastopol in their current assault, they would be forced to go into winter defensive quarters in the south as well. In the fourth week of December, MI 14 gave the Soviets a valuable study on the probable German winter defensive line for Army Group Center, another on German intelligence methods, and a third on Wehrmacht systems for mobilizing new forces, as well as a forecast of German intentions for a spring offensive in the east. By the last day of the year, the OB specialists in the Soviet mission in London had finally been assigned to specific British MI 14 specialists covering OB for Germany (Captain Chapman), Italy (Capt. F. J. Rendall), and Japan (Capt. J. E. Ridsdale).[36]

From their perspective and within the narrow limits of their assigned duties, the British military intelligence authorities had valid reasons for being satisfied with their accomplishments in the autumn and winter of 1941. They had acquired a great deal of information on the German side of the eastern war and had cautiously passed on some highly valuable portions of it to the Soviet high command via 30 Mission and the Soviet liaison mission in London. They had thereby assisted the Soviet Union in taking the measure of the German offensive and in facilitating the initial advance of Zhukov's counterstroke. Having played a useful part in these successes, 30 Mission itself was enjoying a comparatively sunny midwinter period in its intelligence partnership with the Soviet high command.

But during the last three months of 1941, the Western missions in Moscow had not always received a clean bill of health from the authorities in Washington and London or from the various British and American civilian authorities who visited Moscow. During the Beaverbrook-Harriman mission, sent to arrange economic assistance for the USSR (28 September–4 October 1941), Beaverbrook would have no close contact with Ambassador Cripps, Macfarlane, or any other high British officials in Moscow, presumably because of Soviet complaints about these personifications of British officialdom. Nonetheless, the War Office used the occasion—and the cover—of the Beaverbrook mission to send oil demolition specialists to and from Moscow, and as part of the economic discussion, an RAF officer attached to Beaverbrook joined the American general Chaney to inspect Soviet military aircraft production.[37]

Beaverbrook and his team concluded from their stay in the USSR that the overall Soviet military situation was far from hopeless, and Moscow was therefore deserving of renewed economic support. Harriman shared this view but was more forthright in pointing out the deficiencies of his own country's diplomatic mission, as well as what he saw as the shortcomings of the British civil and military missions in the Soviet capital. In his personal notes, Harriman observed that if he had had the power, he would have recalled the American ambassador Steinhardt as well as Cripps and Macfarlane. In Harriman's view, the British ambassador was a dithering snob, and Macfarlane, although appearing to be good humored, was exceedingly dense and seemed determined to act as if he were a peacetime attaché. Later, when departing from north Russia,

Harriman penned additional withering portraits of British naval officers in Archangel, declaring that one of them should have been expelled, not because of his anti-Soviet activities, as Moscow had charged, but because he was patently incompetent.[38]

Harriman's confidential strictures failed to produce any changes in the personnel of the British missions, but they did lead to alterations in the American arrangements in Moscow. When Harriman returned to the United States, Col. Philip R. Faymonville was left behind in Moscow to act as the American lend-lease administrator, and this "Red colonel," as conservative members of the American military establishment dubbed him, outraged G-2 and other Washington traditionalists by what they considered to be his excessive sympathy for the USSR.

During the Harriman-Beaverbrook meetings with Stalin, one or two other significant points arose that would have an impact on the prospects and credibility of the Western liaison teams in Russia. On 28 September, Harriman asked Stalin to provide information on Soviet weather reporting and air bases in Siberia for use by the U.S. Army Air Corps in the event of war with Japan. He also raised the possibility that the Alaska-Siberia link might be used as a plane ferrying route for sending aircraft to the USSR. Stalin sniffed derisively at the possibility that the Alaska-Siberia connection would be an efficient route for ferrying planes to Russia, but in the end, he agreed in principle to provide the air base and weather information as part of contingency planning for joint operations against Japan.[39]

Thus was born a complicated and contentious issue that would occupy Washington and Moscow until the end of the Pacific war. Despite Stalin's doubts, considerable war material was ferried to the USSR by this route. American liaison teams worked with Russian authorities in Siberia, building air bases for joint operations against Japan in 1945, and the U.S. Army Air Corps even had weather stations operating in the region until shortly after V-J Day. But to achieve this modest level of joint military and logistical activity required interminable bargaining, extending from late 1941 throughout the subsequent three and a half years of World War II.

The other issue arising during the Harriman-Beaverbrook-Stalin talks that had an even greater impact on the British and American missions in Moscow was the possibility of direct British military intervention in the eastern war. On 28 September, Beaverbrook offered Stalin joint Anglo-Soviet strategic discussions and even invited the Russians to send a mission to London "to consider the British problem" (i.e., Britain's limited resources, far-flung commitments, and inability to mount a cross-Channel invasion). Beaverbrook also proposed that such a Soviet mission to London could "give advice on what might be done" about this "British problem," a suggestion that surely would have made that old nationalist and anti-Communist Tory Winston Churchill apoplectic. Beaverbrook then proceeded to explain to Stalin that the British were building up their military forces in Iran. In addition to preventing consolidation of pro-Axis forces in this country, which was vital to the Allies, and perhaps opening a southern supply route into Russia, these units might join up "in the Caucasus with the Russians." What Beaverbrook did not say was that British interventionist activities regarding the Caucasus were wrapped up with schemes to demolish the Soviet oil industry if the Germans came too close and also, perhaps, with wilder schemes, rejected even by Macfarlane, for the buildup of British influence in Transcaucasia following a Soviet collapse.[40]

But Stalin disposed of the British dreams of a Caucasus intervention deftly and effectively by observing that "there is no war in the Caucasus but there is in the Ukraine."[41] Beaverbrook tried to dance around Stalin's invitation for Britain to share directly in the ferocity and horror of the Eastern war by asking whether the Soviet leader thought that Britain could invade Europe through France. Stalin replied that he didn't know enough about the situation to say, "but why not send a [British] force to Archangel or the Ukraine?" This invitation was especially surprising, coming from one of history's most secretive and murderous dictators, and also because it specifically requested that British forces be used in two of the areas where Western units had strived to crush the USSR in 1918–1919. The proposal was nonetheless met by a deafening silence, first from Beaverbrook and then from London.[42]

Five weeks later (23 October), Stalin and Molotov returned to the charge. In a meeting with Cripps and the Labour Party's Walter Citrine, the Soviet leaders noted that they had received no response to their request for "the assistance of 25 to 30 [British] divisions on the Russian front." In reply, Cripps waffled regarding the lack of an answer, noting merely that Britain did not have that many divisions to send anywhere. He then hastily urged London to make some reply to Stalin; "surely it is possible," he wrote, "to send either to Murmansk or through Iran at least one or two fully armed divisions to fight on the Russian front."[43]

But the British authorities still did nothing in response to the Soviet request for British troops, even though in the last week of November, British demolition experts were invited into the Caucasus by Vyshinsky, only to find that their skills were not required due to the successful defensive work of the Red Army. Finally, on 3 December, Churchill and his advisers examined the possibility of sending British units to Russia and decided that no troops could be spared. This conclusion was reinforced four days later by the need to rush reinforcements to Southeast Asia in the wake of the Japanese attack on Pearl Harbor and the consequent Japanese advance in Malaya. But still the Soviet authorities were not clearly told of London's decision, or the reasons that the British could not take up Stalin's unique invitation.[44]

Eden visited the Russian capital in an effort to conclude an Anglo-Soviet alliance, and in "an atmosphere of alcoholic cordiality," Stalin again raised the issue of British troops fighting on the Russian front (8 December). He declared that if the proposed military agreement between the two countries was to be "a live document . . . some British troops should be sent to the Soviet front." The Soviet leader reminded Eden that he had repeatedly requested "that some British troops be sent into the Soviet Union in order to take up positions at a specified part of the front." But since London had reservations, he now asked that arrangements be made for a joint Anglo-Soviet special operation "against Petsamo and the north of Norway." Shortly thereafter, in the same session, he went on to stress that he would still like British troops to be brought into Russia via the northern ports to take up positions with the Soviets on the Leningrad front, perhaps opposite Finland. "But," Stalin added, "I think you would prefer not to do that" (a masterful understatement); so the troops could be "placed somewhere [else] on the Leningrad front," he said, perhaps "some place like the Estonian front."[45]

Again the British authorities sidestepped Stalin's invitation to join the eastern Armageddon. During a 19 December trip to view the city of Klin, which the Red Army had just "liberated" from the Germans, a shaken Eden, accompanied by Macfarlane, Collier, and Miles, was forced to recognize what the war in the east was really like when he found the city completely obliterated. Apart from the depressing reality of this experience, Eden was caught in an especially difficult position, because the Soviets had just presented him with a draft alliance under which Britain would have to guarantee the Soviet borders of 1941, including continued Soviet repression of the Baltic states and eastern Poland, which the Russians had occupied under the terms of the Nazi-Soviet pact.[46]

Churchill was in Washington, meeting for the first time with the Americans as post–Pearl Harbor warring allies. His host, Franklin Roosevelt, was adamantly opposed to any secret wartime territorial deals and guarantees that conflicted with the principles set forth in the Atlantic Charter. The cabinet in London was consequently unable to function—Eden could not be authorized to agree to anything of significance—and political paralysis was added to a host of other military, manpower, and supply reasons for Britain's refusal to send troops to Russia.

But even though all these considerations made eastward dispatch of British forces difficult, and London had many good, moral, and humanitarian reasons to stand clear of the war in the USSR, in retrospect, the failure to take up Stalin's invitation seems to have been one of the lost opportunities of the wartime era. If British units had been sent to the east, that development would certainly have compelled the Soviets to extend more cooperation to the Western military authorities in 1941–1943, just as increased cooperation resulted from American use of Russian air bases for shuttle bombing of the Reich in 1944. Joint Anglo-Soviet ground operations in the east during 1941 would inevitably have forced the Soviet high command to share with London more information on Soviet forces, weaponry, and order of battle, as well as more intelligence on Nazi Germany. Such a move might also have obviated Alan Brooke's postwar complaint that he "never received a Russian order of battle showing their dispositions" during the whole war.[47] Beyond all such potential military gains, the possible political effects of joint Anglo-Soviet defensive operations in Russia, followed by a joint advance across the western half of the Soviet Union and perhaps into the eastern portion of Nazi-occupied Europe—the region later subjugated behind the "Iron Curtain"—could have been truly earthshaking. Such an action might have altered the Soviets' ability to pretend to their people that the Red Army alone had won the war and that no choice existed for the peoples of the USSR and Eastern Europe except that between Stalin and Hitler.

Compared with such broad possible consequences of the decision not to send British troops to the Eastern Front, the actual impact of that decision on 30 Mission and the process of East-West intelligence cooperation was more limited, though still significant. Between June and December 1941, the Soviets repeatedly acted as if their war was totally sealed off from the one that Britain was waging against Nazi Germany. Yet at least in theory, Russia and Britain were partners with interacting mutual interests that might expand in the future. From December 1941 onward, however, the eastern and western zones of Allied conflict against the Nazis were ever more fundamentally divided, even though Western material aid to the USSR increased sharply in 1943 as American military production took off. With no intermixing of military forces, the principle of local control and mandatory use of quid pro quos would reign with overwhelming force, as Stalin repeatedly bludgeoned the Western powers with the claim that the Soviets were carrying the weight of the German war and demanded that they open a "Second Front" against Hitler's fortress Europe.[48]

In this situation, the Western missions in Moscow inevitably fell on harder times. This was especially true of the British Army team, which had always been on the thinnest ice and now carried the stain of refusing to come east and fight side by side with the Red Army in the "real" war. Stalin knew that the West dared not let him fail and that it must provide him with technical and intelligence assistance, because all hope for Allied victory on the Eastern Front lay in his hands. He was not only master of his own house; the West had guaranteed him complete control of his own battlefield. Therefore, beginning in early 1942, Macfarlane and his American colleagues were about to learn just how stubborn, single-minded, and crudely forceful Stalin could be when he held the aces and the West had thrown away one of the high cards that might have made the Soviet leader play his hand more cautiously.

5
Difficult Times,
January–June 1942

Disaster was the watchword for the Allied cause in the first six months of 1942. From the Atlantic to the Pacific, from Southeast Asia to southern Russia, the armed forces of Germany and Japan scored a string of devastating triumphs. The Japanese roared through the central Pacific; they cleared the British from Hong Kong and Southeast Asia, the Dutch from the East Indies, and the Americans from the Philippines and their central Pacific bases of Wake, Guam, and Midway. For the British, the ultimate humiliation was the destruction of the *Repulse* and the *Prince of Wales* by air power alone, with no Japanese ship coming within range of the mighty guns of the British men-of-war, and the shocking collapse of Britain's greatest overseas bastion, Singapore, which the Japanese Army seized quickly and with a minimum of casualties.

The great American catastrophe of the period was, of course, Pearl Habor itself. Although the destruction of much of the Pacific fleet caused grief to the people of the United States, more importantly, it provided an explosive demonstration of the country's vulnerability. Pearl Harbor proved beyond a doubt that the United States could no longer stand aloof from the most dangerous and destructive aspects of world affairs. After six months in which their only consolation was that their forces held out longer on Bataan than did the British in Malaya or the Dutch in Batavia, the Americans achieved a stunning victory at Midway by sinking three carriers and blunting the offensive power of the Japanese Navy. Even then, the Americans were unable to quickly take the offensive in the Pacific. The American people also had to witness their economy and society fumble and stumble toward full mobilization in early 1942. Meanwhile, German U-boats made a mockery of American claims of invulnerability by sinking hundreds of thousands of tons of shipping within sight of the harbor lights of East Coast ports from New York to Charleston.

This "happy time" for the U-boats along the East Coast of the United States was a bad time for Britain as well as for America. In early 1942, the United Kingdom desperately needed American supplies to sustain the bomber offensive, build up strength for an eventual "Second Front" landing in northern France, and maintain British forces in Southeast Asia, the Middle East, and North Africa. With the loss of Malaya, Britain was compelled to defend a line in Burma as far to the west as possible in order to prevent Japanese penetration into India. Japanese conquest of the oil fields of the Netherlands East Indies meant that Britain also had to hold the Middle East and the oil fields there at all costs. But the British had only minimal forces sprinkled across the Middle East. German armies in southern Russia threatened to drive into the Caucasus from the north, seize the oil there, and then go on to Iran. To complicte matters further, in North Africa, Erwin Rommel and the *Afrikakorps* administered one humiliation after another to the British Eighth Army, continually threatening to take Suez, cut the lifeline to India, and drive into Palestine and Jordan.

In sharp contrast, during the winter of 1941–1942 on the Eastern Front, the Red Army had sought to break the German siege of Leningrad; destroy Army Group Center, which was stalled before Moscow; and retake the Don line as well as the Crimea in the south. Initially, all three German Army groups were in jeopardy, and the horrors of the Russian winter inflicted dreadful casualties on Hitler's legions. The Red Army offensives shuddered to several halts in March, however. Then, in the spring of 1942, overruling the judgment of his intelligence staff, which had concluded that the Germans would strike in the south, Stalin gambled that Hitler's main move would be the resumption of Army Group Center's attack on Moscow. To counter this presumed threat, the Soviet leader ordered a series of spoiling offensives that were so clumsily organized that 30 Mission was able to warn the Soviet high command that the Germans were fully aware that Timoshenko was soon coming. Massive German counterattacks against Timoshenko's drive toward Orel and Kharkov occurred right on schedule, costing the Soviets a quarter of a million losses.[1]

On 18 May, Macfarlane told Panfilov that the main spring-summer German offensive would be aimed at the southern Don and Caucasia,[2] but in the run up to this attack, Manstein inflicted additional losses of a quarter of a million Red Army men in the Kerch-Crimea disaster. By 1 June, the British JIC had concluded that the Germans would soon strike for Stalingrad, and although this JIC study earned the praise of the prime minister, it was not given to the Soviets. In late June, after a protracted and heroic defense, Sevastopol finally fell, and the German Central and Southern Army Groups tore a huge hole in the Russian line at Voronezh. Wide-open blitzkrieg warfare was possible once more, and with Manstein's armor in the van, the German armies simultaneously drove south and east toward the Caucasus oil fields and Stalingrad, on the way to a gigantic encirclement operation against Moscow.[3]

By the time the Soviets faced up to the great Stalingrad crisis, the Americans had finally found their Pacific sea legs at the Battle of Midway. But the Soviet disasters in southern Russia during May, June, and July significantly outweighed this American achievement. Once again, Hitler had badly beaten Stalin on the Eastern Front, and this time he was seriously threatening to win the European war in one bold stroke.

Given the course and scale of events in the German-Soviet conflict during the first half of 1942, British and American efforts to achieve some form of systematic intelligence cooperation with Moscow had little chance of achieving dramatic success. Not only did Stalin and his aides have much more pressing matters on their minds, but London and Washington lacked significant leverage, because Western supplies were still little more than a trickle into Russia even in mid-1942. London had already cast away a highly useful card by refusing to send troops to the Eastern Front, and throughout the first half of 1942, the British and Americans put on a dazzling display of military incompetence that covered every corner of the world from Libya to Pearl Harbor.

Diplomacy also did little to smooth the way for effective intelligence cooperation in the first half of 1942. The American diplomatic and attaché missions in Moscow continued to present a picture of warring factions that were only mildly differentiated by the intensity of their loathing for their Soviet hosts. The appointment in March of a new, charming, gregarious, and clever British ambassador in the person of Sir Archibald Clark Kerr (replacing the austere Stafford Cripps) may have helped the British cause a bit—Stalin seems to have genuinely enjoyed his company and his pipe tobacco—but the Western powers made a diplomatic hash of Molotov's visits to London in April and to Washington in May. The United States assured Molotov that there would be a Second Front in 1942, whereas the British said first that there might be and then that there might not be, neither of which helped convince Moscow that the West was helpful or even competent. The British managed to conclude a twenty-year peace and friendship treaty with the Soviets in May, but as both sides knew, this merely postponed the divisive issue of the Soviet Union's future western borders and the vital question of what form the postwar world order would actually take.

Those in the forefront of the Western intelligence-sharing effort, especially Mason Macfarlane, were in for a long winter and spring. The head of 30 Mission attempted to alert Whitehall that it needed to make a rapid political move toward Moscow to convince the Soviets of Britain's good intentions, telling the

CIGS on 8 February that "the whole trouble has been the long time it took those in London to realize that these people could and would fight." But by then it was probably too late, if the chance ever existed, to convince Moscow that Britain was ready to play serious ball.[4]

The Soviets occasionally asked 30 Mission for German OB information in January, and Macfarlane dutifully relayed these requests to London in the hope of acquiring useful trade bait. In return, the DMI sent large quantities of the materials he requested, and MI 14(b) in London also granted the Russian mission at least one meeting on German OB in January.[5] When the situation in Russia became more serious, the Soviet mission in London also had a torrent of OB meetings—at least four in April and May, and another three in June. In Moscow, the Soviets were provided with information on the German First Panzer Army on 27 January, but Birse did not get his first 1942 meeting with a Soviet OB expert until 5–6 February. Twelve days later, the Red Army anxiously requested British estimates of German force totals (Army, Luftwaffe, Navy) for spring 1942, and on 24 February, Macfarlane managed to work in a bit of cordial OB chitchat with Marshal Shaposhnikov during a Kremlin party.[6]

On 9 March, Birse had one OB meeting, then after a two-month gap, the British managed to get another that was marginally effective. The best the British could do during the interval was to give the Russians spot data on the eastward movement of German flak, while receiving occasional hints about German OB from Panfilov. Then, when the situation in south Russia again became grave in the late spring, the British provided the Soviets with more OB meetings in London (one in April, four in May, and three more in June). Birse had another ineffective meeting on 4 May and then, finally, secured useful OB meetings on 25 May and 13 June. These meetings were followed by a Soviet appeal for a return to intimate OB collaboration. The British were cautious, however. Even though the situation was better in June than in January, the 1942 output had been rather feeble, despite the fact that crucial battles were raging all over central and southern Russia.[7]

Macfarlane had some general discussions with Panfilov that touched on the overall battle situation during January and February. Predictably, in that period of Soviet triumphs, the Red Army general was all optimism, seeking every bit of British information about German defensive positions. During these discussions and meetings with the chief of the Red Army's artillery section during February, Macfarlane succeeded in acquiring some data on German artillery. The DMI and 30 Mission also managed to arrange for exchanges of technical data on German land mines, in addition to holding very successful talks on Soviet and British chemical warfare measures and exchange of technical data on Soviet and British tanks. In April, the Soviets gave the mission a fine collection of German artillery ammunition, and in May, members of the mission were allowed to tour the Soviet tank center at Gorky. This combination of East-West contacts must have worked to Britain's benefit.[8]

As for the broad strategic questions, both the British and the Russians seem to have wallowed in uncertainty and a lack of information during the winter of 1942, although the British had some peculiar sources of intelligence (in addition to ULTRA). In March 1942, the Government Code and Cypher School was picking up tidbits on Japanese intentions relating to Russia from the dispatches of the Turkish ambassador in Tokyo. In late February, in an effort to fill the large informational gap regarding German intentions, MI 3 imagined that it was the German general staff having to decide where to strike in the spring. MI 3's conclusion was that southern Russia "was likely to be chosen," and on 3 March, General Macfarlane learned from Panfilov that the "Soviet Staff appears to think that unless all our oil calculations are wrong the most likely and logical objective for the German offensive in the spring is the oil fields of Caucasus or Iraq." Two days later, however, the Soviet military authorities asked 30 Mission for any information it had on German spring intentions, because Moscow claimed to have none. On the following day, Panfilov "admitted" to Macfarlane that the Red Army had no "concrete information" on the Germans' spring intentions.[9]

As we now know, this muddled probing and theorizing was beside the point, because Stalin had incorrectly concluded that the Germans would strike in the center and had opted for a preemptive strike in the south. That miscalculation would cost the USSR hundreds of thousands of dead and vast territories. Among the British, there were so many illusions and fantasies about the Red Army and the realities of war in the east that Whitehall was little better off than Stalin in trying to figure out what would occur in the eastern battles or what the chances were of arranging East-West intelligence sharing. The DMI repeatedly carped at 30 Mission because so much information had been sent to Moscow and so little had been acquired in return. During late March, General Davidson even sent Macfarlane another JIC paper on Axis intentions, urging that it be used as trade bait to loosen Russian tongues, although the previous attempt to barter with a JIC paper during the Battle of Moscow had been a fiasco.[10]

While welcoming this and all other materials that were sent to him, Macfarlane sought once more to explain to London that the Soviets simply would not play by fixed rules. He also advanced various explanations for Soviet obstructive behavior, including the failure of the British to launch a Second Front, the Western refusal to formally concede Soviet territorial demands, and the British intimacy with the Americans, whose insecurity, Macfarlane had persuaded himself, was anathema to Moscow. What the 30 mission chief did not grasp until it was too late was that British inefficiency also played a part, along with Stalinist rigidity and paranoia. Not until 1 June, for example, did the mission learn that while it had been trying for months to use British battle information from Libya as trade bait to entice the Soviets into giving out more of their own OB data, Whitehall had blithely been handing this material over to the Soviet mission in London without asking for any quid pro quo.[11]

The British head of the mission in Moscow was further blinded by transcendental fantasies of his own, including the contention, advanced in February 1942, that Germany still considered Britain rather than the USSR to be its most dangerous and principal enemy. In March 1942, he made the even more outlandish observation to the War Office (after the *Einsatgruppen* killing teams had been active for nine months, and London had been reading much of their radio traffic recounting the murders) that "apart from isolated instances, I do not, repeat not, personally think that we are yet justified on the evidence available in accusing [the] Germans of being more brutal than is to be expected in a war in partisan infested country under very difficult supply conditions."[12]

In this realm of boundless ignorance and fantasy regarding the ground war in the east and the murderous ferocity of Hitler's Germany, it is not surprising that some of the most useful information that Macfarlane sent to London in the winter of 1942 came from the eyewitness evidence he acquired during his second visit to the front. This visit occurred between 29 January and 2 February on the front of the 5th Army near Gyhatck. The 30 Mission chief acquired extensive information regarding German tactical methods, ranging from the mass use of mortars to the fortification of villages in winter. He also obtained considerable detail on Soviet combat techniques, including special methods for utilizing barbed wire, as well as technical information on Soviet equipment and materials, especially winter lubricants. Impressed by the high morale of Russian troops, Macfarlane concluded that the Red Army now really had "its tail up" and was fighting very well. But his report may have lacked credibility, because as he confided to the vice CIGS on 1 February, "on my last night with the Russian 5th Army I passed out completely. I have no knowledge of the facts but am told I was laid to rest by the Deputy Army Commander and the Army Commissar" after consuming "400 grams of vodka, among other things."[13]

Five months later, in June 1942, Col. K. G. Exham, the military attaché and head of the army section of 30 Mission, visited the Soviet 5th Army near Borodino. Although he was accompanied by the perennially pessimistic American military attaché Colonel Michela and another American officer, on this occasion, too, positive reports regarding the Red Army, its abilities, and its morale were sent to London.[14]

Yet in surveying the sweep of 30 Mission reports during the first six months of 1942, it is obvious that Macfarlane and his colleagues sent little information home and missed much that was important. The 30 Mission army team actually seems to have secured nearly as much information from the Russians about the Japanese Army as it did about the German one, although Moscow was not at war with Japan and was striving mightily to keep Tokyo from striking into Siberia. In late January, General Panfilov asked the mission for technical information on the Japanese prussic acid hand grenade, and London pressed 30 Mission to get all the information it could from the Russians about Japan. On 28 January, and again on 17 February, the War Office included Japanese Army OB information in its briefing of the Russian military mission in London. On 7 February, 30 Mission had its first meeting with an unnamed Soviet specialist on Japanese Army OB and found him "informed, friendly, and prepared to cooperate on [a] bargain basis." Four days later, the War Office sent the mission a complete summary of its picture of Japanese Army OB. This was duly given to the Russians, who, on 10 March, gave the mission another Japanese Army OB meeting and, on the following day, provided the mission with a detailed critique of the British OB summary, confirming most of the British conclusions but correcting a number of divisional identifications and locations, especially in Manchuria and China. In May, the British Army authorities supplied the Soviet mission in London with two additional OB reports on the Japanese Army.[15]

This was a highly useful and mutually profitable (and heretofore unknown) form of East-West intelligence partnership. It indicated that the Soviets were perfectly capable of carrying on effective army intelligence exchanges when they chose to do so. It also parenthetically indicated the torturous ambiguities that Whitehall brought to nearly every aspect of close cooperation with the USSR. When Macfarlane sought to initiate these OB exchanges regarding Japan, the Joint Planning Staff had been quite reluctant to do so, observing that "in view of the usual Russian attitude towards military conversations, we cannot exclude the possibility that General Panfilov's request [for information on the Japanese Army] has been inspired by the Russian Government"; it then added, "it is therefore important that General Mason Macfarlane should be warned of this possibility."[16] When such mad Whitehall attitudes—of course virtually every move Panfilov made was inspired by the Russian government—were combined with the heavy-handedness of Macfarlane and the secretive paranoia of Stalin, it is quite remarkable that East and West managed to exchange any order-of-battle information at all during the first half of 1942.

Fortunately, the Royal Navy continued to enjoy effective cooperative relations with its Soviet counterpart, and this connection yielded useful information. The British naval liaison officer in the Black Sea had especially rich pickings, acquiring detailed descriptions and even photographs of German acoustic and photomagnetic mines. This officer—currently a Captain Ambrose—was also allowed a detailed survey visit of a Russian Air Force fighter base and regularly sent London OB and movement reports on German and Rumanian ground, air, and sea units in southern Russia, especially those related to the battles for Kerch.[17] The British senior naval officer in north Russia did equally well; although initially unknown to both the Red Navy and the head of the British naval mission in Moscow (Admiral Miles), a Royal Navy "Y" interception station (feebly camouflaged under the cover name "Wye Cottage") had just been set up at the Royal Navy Polyarnoe headquarters at Archangel. This station was soon collecting large amounts of secret German naval radio traffic from northern Norway and the Arctic, which was outside the range of the radio interception network in Britain and was consequently especially valuable to British "Y" analysts and code breakers. Admiral Miles broke "the news" of the existence of the Polyarnoe "Y" station to the Red Navy commander on 10 February 1942, "rather than [have the Russian high command] receive [the news of] it later in the form of a complaint" from below. Fortunately for the British, the Russians raised no objections, presumably because intelligence from German naval "Y" was essential for the Arctic convoys. "Wye Cottage" was therefore allowed to carry on its secret labors.[18]

Although not as valuable as the intelligence yield of the Polyarnoe "Y" station or that provided by the naval liaison office in the Black Sea, the British naval mission in Moscow secured a broad range of useful details from the Red Navy, including reports on the damage the Russians inflicted on German merchant vessels and navy ships during the first six months of the war, general data on the German naval building program, and some information on the German cruiser *Seidlitz* being completed in Bremen. On 16 June, the Soviets gave the British naval mission intelligence books on naval antennae and on magnetic and acoustic mines. Regarding the war in the Pacific, during January and February, the Red Navy turned over some data on Japanese naval construction and the Japanese naval supply system in Manchuria; in April, it passed on an eyewitness account of the Doolitle raid. Precise details concerning German operations in both northern and southern Russia, which a Red admiral claimed came from "wireless intelligence," were also passed on, and these inclined the Admiralty to believe that "the Russians have broken German high grade ciphers." When, on 15 June, the Red Navy gave the British the text of a German Navy message sent from Wilhelmshaven to the U-boat station at Kirkenes, the 30 Mission war diarist merely noted, "this is another indication of the efficiency of Soviet 'Y.'"[19]

The Royal Navy supplied the Soviets with such large quantities of information on enemy navies that, beginning in March 1942, the Admiralty maintained special lists of Soviet naval intelligence requests, along with indications of the action that had been taken on each. To facilitate the exchange of these and other naval materials, beginning in April, the Admiralty held a special meeting each Tuesday with Admiral Kharlamov in London. Considerable British data were provided on Japanese weapons, including midget submarines, torpedo boats, and incendiary bombs, as well as information regarding the Japanese battle fleet, the size of Japan's merchant navy, and the organization and operation of the Japanese landings in Malaya and the Philippines. Intelligence on German naval weapons that was passed on to the Russians in the first half of 1942 included material on clockwork timing fuses and delayed-action bombs. In February, the Admiralty also supplied the Red Navy with its regular Germany-Poland intelligence report on the eastern Baltic, along with details of mined areas off the coast of Norway and German naval defenses and antiaircraft units in Leningrad and Estonia. The Admiralty even took the politically sensitive step of supplying the names of all Latvian and Estonian ships that had been seized by the British. In January and again in June, it gave the Soviets information on Finnish shore batteries and ports, although Britain was, of course, not at war with Finland, and the Finns held an especially warm place in the hearts of the British and American citizenry.

In January 1942, the Admiralty supplied the Soviets with information on secret Red Navy documents that the Germans had captured in the Black Sea area—information that the British had likely traced through radio intelligence.[20] This incident produced fulsome expressions of Russian gratitude, and the two navies again clasped hands in southern Russia during February when the Red Navy's Black Sea squadron was forced to flee into the Mediterranean. This time it was the British who lavished praise; the Royal Navy commander in chief in the Mediterranean signaled home that "the excellent handling of Russian ship and seamanlike conduct of their crews" had impressed all the British officers.[21]

By June, the Royal Navy had decided to share all aspects of its technical equipment with the Russians, as long as the items had been used against the enemy and the Germans and Japanese already knew how they operated. Even when the Red Navy refused to extend the sharing partnership to "Y" intelligence traffic in the Far East, the Royal Navy took it with good grace. The

Moscow naval mission declared on 9 June that "excellent relations . . . [continued to] exist as far as Germany and to some extent Japanese intelligence is concerned."[22]

The principal combat operation that brought the Royal and Red Navies together in close cooperation and affected the sharing of intelligence continued to be the running of the northern convoys. This was still virtually the only artery of supply through which Western assistance could reach the USSR, and since the first sixteen convoys, comprising a large number of Soviet as well as Western merchant ships, had arrived without serious incident, the Royal Navy clearly deserved to stand in high favor with the Red Navy and the Soviet government. But as the DNI, Capt. E. G. N. Rushbrooke, observed in February 1942, this was a thin thread on which to erect naval intelligence cooperation, because safe operation of the convoys was far from a sure thing, and the Soviets were obviously willing to play politics with intelligence. Moscow was withholding intelligence from Macfarlane, Rushbrooke contended, in part to put pressure on the British to open a Second Front, and the Russians might do something similar to the Royal Navy if an analogous situation arose. In March, another senior British naval officer predicted that the honeymoon period of Anglo-Soviet naval intelligence cooperation would end quickly if the Admiralty called a halt to the convoys in the face of increasing German air and U-boat attacks.[23]

In fact, relations in Archangel were far from harmonious, with political difficulties and brawling sailors upsetting the normal tomblike calm that prevailed in Soviet cities. In early April, when ULTRA indicated that the Germans were about to go all out against the convoys, using Kirkenes in far northern Norway as their main base, Churchill sensed that the resulting heavy losses could produce more trouble with the Soviets. The prime minister sought to offset this by explaining to Stalin the great risks the British were running in sending the convoys, and after the loss of HMS *Trinidad* due to lack of air cover for PQ 15, the Soviets partially made good on their promise to provide air support, flying 2,028 sorties for PQ 16. But most of these Red air operations were reconnaissance flights, which still left the Archangel convoys without incoming fighter cover.[24]

The Admiralty and other British government departments were therefore braced for trouble in July. Only Macfarlane, wrong once again, thought that "Joe Stalin was a big enough man" to understand if the Admiralty should decide that the convoys must stop. Following the disastrous losses of PQ 17, when Churchill ordered the halt of the convoys, Stalin's rage knew no bounds. The Royal Navy and Army sections of the Moscow mission encountered more trouble than before in operating an intelligence partnership with their Soviet counterparts.[25]

All this might suggest that the ebb and flow of Soviet willingness to exchange intelligence were caused chiefly by political considerations, ideological hostility, the lack of a Second Front, and the value of the convoys, spiced by wild-card factors such as antipathy toward individuals such as General Macfarlane. But when one examines what happened to air force intelligence and "Y" cooperation during the first six months of 1942, such conventional explanations and attractive symmetries immediately vanish. In this period, headway toward effective partnership continued to be made, and the RAF portion of the mission in Moscow actually did better in its intelligence relations with the Soviets than it had in the past. Due to long-standing RAF suspicion and offended outrage at Soviet coldness and abrasiveness, this increase in cooperation is hard to detect under the cloud of complaints and lamentations enveloping the surviving files. Indeed, the air mission, which was still divided between Kubyshev and Moscow during the first three months of 1942, was less than dazzlingly successful in solving a series of by this time traditional problems. Living conditions continued to be spartan, and supplies were so short that on 19 April, the Air Ministry received a pathetic plea from its Moscow mission to "please send a bag of latrine paper," because such niceties "were unobtainable in any form."[26]

Air mission visits to Russian installations and direct observation of Soviet, or even German, aircraft and equipment continued to be difficult, and the RAF was more than once inclined to protest. Air Commodore W. E. Cheshire was allowed to visit a fighter station at Tushimo, twelve miles northwest of Moscow, in March, and he also sent home identification reports on German aircraft displayed in a Moscow park. But some members of the press believed that even the Tushimo visit had been merely a staged performance, with Red Air Force planes brought in for the occasion and then immediately removed after Cheshire's departure. There was no doubt, however, that the teams of British air technicians and engineers sent to assist the Soviets in the assembly and maintenance of British equipment given to the Red Air Force—such as the "Swallow" party, which visited a number of Russian air bases during the early spring—provided the air mission and the Air Ministry with valuable data on the Red Air Force. This was especially so in May–June 1942, when, along with the technicians, Cheshire rejoined the ranks of visitors observing a series of bases belonging to the Red Air Force and the Red fleet air arm. Still, those pursuing air intelligence always had a difficult time. Wing Comdr. H. H. Hilliar was not allowed to get within ten yards of any Soviet aircraft during a base visit in late

May, and those trying to secure tidbits of technical data through social contacts with Russian fliers also faced perils. More than one RAF officer ended his tour with a serious drinking problem after duty in Russia.[27]

Overall, the air mission had marginal success in acquiring information regarding Soviet aircraft production, air combat methods, and secret equipment. An instructive chat between Collier and a Red Air Force general occurred in March, during which the Soviet officer observed that the Russians were having good success against German planes on the ground when they used cannon and splinter bombs. The Luftwaffe was not doing as well in bombing Red airfields, because its large bombs were better at making craters than damaging aircraft. The mission also received a few vague generalizations from Soviet officials regarding Russian output of military aircraft. But although Cheshire, Collier, and their staffs tried to answer Soviet questions about Axis and Japanese aircraft output, the Red Air Force was generally satisfied to sit contentedly atop its secrets, including synthetic rubber production, and let the British mission keep begging to gain access to Russian weapons and technical assets.[28]

This posture was made ludicrously easy for the Red Air Force, because ever since Macfarlane first witnessed a demonstration of the rocket bomb, 30 Mission had made it obvious that the British would pay a high price to acquire its secret. So although the RAF occasionally provided the Soviets with information on German secret devices—some of which had considerable value, such as the *Verlobungsring,* which served German aircraft as rudimentary radar in flights over water—the Red Air Force dribbled out its rocket bomb treasure in dribs and drabs to keep the RAF team partially satisfied yet still hungry. On 6 January, Cheshire received a detailed Russian report on the rocket bomb, but no technical drawings or sample parts were provided. In May, British personnel witnessed rocket bombs being installed on Hurricanes that had been given to the Russians, but again, no detailed technical information was provided. Only on 23–24 June 1942—nearly a year after Macfarlane originally viewed the rocket bomb in action—did the mission finally receive a sample bomb as well as full blueprints of the bomb and its launching mechanism. On this occasion, the Soviets also threw in a description of their 37-mm aircraft cannon, along with a sample of their 12.7-mm machine gun and complete operational instructions.[29]

Although the air mission seemed quite gratified by this final triumph in the great chase after the rocket bomb, its acquisition actually seems to have had little impact on the development of Western air armament. The Air Ministry probably made a far greater contribution to the Allied victory by taking the lead in arranging exchanges on more mundane matters, such as weather information. In early January, three soviet meteorologists went to Cairo to discuss sharing weather information and to observe Western meteorological methods. Two weeks later, the British chiefs of staff authorized the establishment of a Russian weather station in Spitsbergen that would benefit both the Red and the Royal Navies as well as aid the successful operation of the northern convoys. In mid-April, an arrangement was made to exchange Indian weather information for that from Tashkent, and by 23 April, a more comprehensive exchange agreement was concluded covering eighteen to twenty weather stations in southern Russia, Iran, and throughout the Middle East. This meant that by early May, largely through the efforts of the air mission, Russia and Britain were trading weather information covering all of Russia, Western Europe, and the Middle East—a full two years before a general Russian-American weather deal was concluded. London and Moscow both employed standard reciphering weather code pads provided by the British government to exchange weather data.[30]

This information exchange was a genuine success, and in early February, the air mission tried to repeat its weather coup by concluding a quick map exchange agreement. But the Soviets were slow to react, and Collier's group also had trouble preventing its outstations from destroying all prospects for an agreement by trying to acquire Soviet maps by surreptitious means. Such disappointments were, however, more the exception than the rule in the air mission's information-gathering efforts during the first half of 1942. On 1 January, Collier began to meet regularly with a member of the Red Air Staff, Major General Beliaev. Before, during, and after these meetings, Collier continued to sing the traditional RAF song that the United Kingdom gave more than it received—noting a year later that although some exchange of Luftwaffe intelligence took place in early 1942, it was "desultory," a one-sided affair, "with the Russians much in credit."[31] The British Air Ministry would also waste considerable time trying to refute Beliaev's hypothesis that the Luftwaffe had been slowed down on the Eastern Front by synthetic fuel problems in cold weather. Nonetheless, Collier and Beliaev carried out extended intelligence exchanges over a two-month period and laid the basis for more fruitful air intelligence swaps in the spring and summer of 1942.

During their initial meetings, Beliaev occasionally seemed to be simply one more overly optimistic Russian, which characterized most Soviet officials in January, following the German defeat before Moscow. But from the beginning, the Soviet general was prepared to discuss the current battle situation with Collier and immediately admitted that Zhukov's offensive had not been a decisive strategic triumph. Collier was heartened by this frankness and concluded his report on the meeting with the line, "suggest the time has come for barter." In early March, Beliaev again showed his levelheadedness by observing that the Germans were still very strong on the central front, while also conceding that in the near future there was little chance that the Soviets would advance sufficiently in the north to relieve Leningrad. Prospects for an immediate advance in the south did not look bright to Beliaev either; he observed in passing that Red Air Force losses in the first four months of the war had been "immense."[32] In late March, he made the startling admission that the Germans had the "advantages of flexibility and power to concentrate quickly." He said, "in this respect they . . . proved themselves superior to the Russians last summer," and "they would thereby be able to regain the initiative once again."

These were highly unusual admissions for an officer in Stalin's court, and Collier, who was one of the most staunchly anti-Soviet members of 30 Mission, gradually came to recognize that Beliaev was "generally honest in his views of the military situation." Collier held that Beliaev was primarily "a Russian patriot" who "desires above all to see the destruction of the enemy," and "his military judgement is partially swayed by the desire to thrash the enemy." In his rosier moods, Collier even conceded that this was a virtue, because "it is this mad desire and determination to destroy [the] enemy which has given the Red Army the confidence and strength [it] exhibited in the last eight months of operations."

It is therefore possible that an element of mutual respect, and perhaps a small trace of simple human affection, played a part in turning Collier and Beliaev into fairly effective partners. But whatever the cause, on 25 June, Beliaev told Collier that the Red Air Force wanted to exchange papers with the RAF on their war experiences during the previous six months.[33] He also declared that the Red Air Force had recently carried out raids on four locations where British intelligence had reported large numbers of German aircraft. Two of the raids had been successful (Smolensk and Schatalovk—southeast of Kursk), and the Soviets were sufficiently pleased with the results for Beliaev to invite the British to participate in a general exchange of OB material on the Luftwaffe.

The Air Ministry, goaded by Cavendish Bentinck of the Foreign Office (and secretary of the JIC), soon expressed its willingness to participate, and before long, high-grade intelligence was on its way to 30 Mission. On the day before the Beliaev-Collier meeting, at least one ULTRA decrypt indicating a movement of German aircraft from the Crimea to Kharkov had been sent to the mission by none other than Group Captain Winterbotham, the man who would later reveal the ULTRA secret. This document was headed "Most Secret" and bore the bold-lettered instructions "DESTROY BY FIRE AFTER READING." Yet it remained in the files, as did a similar item dated 14 February on the Saki airfield in the Crimea.[34] With this level of intelligence available, it was an easy matter for the mission to provide useful information to the Soviets (even if the British seemed to have trouble carrying out security instructions), and on 29 January, the Red Air Force was presented with papers on German air organization in Finland and on Rumanian antiaircraft units. The Soviets also began to put probing and detailed questions about recent British air operations over Germany to 30 Mission, perhaps because they were trying to test the accuracy of their own, presumably agent-based, intelligence sources.

When on 1 February 1942 a Soviet officer told Collier that the Red Air Force had given the British useful intelligence and wanted the air mission to respond, mission personnel were genuinely shocked. Four days later, Collier dismissively declared that the only reason any cooperation existed was "because we are giving everything and getting nothing in exchange." But a week later, the Russian air mission in London, with unconsciously perfect timing, rebutted this remark by giving the Air Ministry a summary of the Soviet OB estimate of the Luftwaffe deployment on the Eastern Front. On that same day in Moscow, a pair of Russian Air Force colonels provided the British with useful Luftwaffe information, and this exchange opened the door to a brighter period of Anglo-Soviet cooperation on Luftwaffe order of battle.[35]

On 11 February, the first formal Anglo-Soviet meeting on German air OB occurred in Moscow, with Collier representing the British. Most of the meeting was taken up with general questions about German reserve strength and OB queries about the location of Luftwaffe bomber units, as well as various aspects of German fighter tactics. Yet overall, the British and Soviet officers found enough common ground for Collier to cautiously speculate that, by April, the Red Air Force might be superior to the Luftwaffe on the Eastern Front. The British walked away with their share of treasures, since the Soviets gave them two Luftwaffe documents that had been captured in recent ground operations.

While Collier began to revise the British OB picture of the Luftwaffe on the basis of the data provided by the Soviets, the Air Ministry grasped that these meetings could lead to an intelligence breakthrough. Arrangements were consequently made to send a specialist air OB officer to Moscow to handle exchanges on the Italian, Japanese, and German Air Forces. During the second Anglo-Soviet air OB meeting on 18 February, much time was spent determining which of the previous British warnings to the Soviets forecasting specific German air attacks had been correct and which had not, with the total apparently falling somewhere around 50–50. The third meeting, which occurred on 24 February, was largely taken up in discussions of Luftwaffe OB on the Eastern Front, especially unit numbers and call signs, and at its conclusion, both

British and Soviet officers expressed a desire to extend the meetings to cover the Japanese Air Force. The Soviets also raised the delicate question of including the Finnish Air Force.

But British reserve remained and was in part justified on 25 February, when at a Kremlin reception it became obvious to the Britons that one of the Russian OB officers they had been working with did not even know the commander in chief of the Red Air Force, Gen. Col. P. F. Zhigarev, by sight. This development prompted Collier to exclaim, "no wonder we never get any useful information from [the Red Air Force] Liaison Department!"[36] But such negative developments and caustic observations did not stop the cooperative momentum, because the most skeptical and anti-Soviet member of the air mission staff, Collier himself, was sent back to London in early March.

That month, the air mission was given documents on the movement of German flak units, and Red Air Force officers passed over a captured German document listing some RAF call signs. The Soviets also requested details of a recent RAF raid on the main Renault factory in France, again apparently trying to check the reliability of one of their secret agents. During the fourth meeting, on 24 March, the Soviets answered some British questions about German fighter aircraft used on the Eastern Front and provided estimates of German losses. But they again failed to supply information on the Japanese Air Force.

At this point, Air Commodore W. E. Cheshire took over as head of the air section of 30 Mission, and he decided to push the Russians. In late March and early April, the British posed specific questions on Japanese air OB and German air raids in Russia. The Soviet response was to hand over on 14 April a detailed report on a recent German raid on Murmansk and to hold an extended meeting on Japanese OB with the British on 18 April. During this meeting, the Soviets presented their estimate of total Japanese aircraft in Manchuria, Korea, and the Pacific and a list of the location of known Japanese air bases in Manchuria and Korea. They pegged the Japanese aircraft losses in the first four months of the Asia-Pacific conflict at between 800 and 900 aircraft of all types (which was probably too high).

Although it was very general, this information on the Japanese Air Force was all that the British could reasonably have hoped for. Russian air intelligence cooperation with the British was still in its infancy, and the USSR was not at war with Japan. London therefore directed the Moscow mission not to push further on this question, which would be handled by Macfarlane in the event he was granted another opportunity for a face-to-face meeting with Stalin.[37]

The decision to drop Japanese OB matters came near the end of the spring

1942 era of reasonably close air intelligence cooperation, except for two unorthodox transmissions of British information to the Soviets. On 17 June, the Soviets were given "Most Secret Information," probably of ULTRA origin, indicating that the number-two man in the Reich and head of the Luftwaffe, Hermann Goering, would soon be headquartered at Poltava. The Soviet air officers who liaised with 30 Mission were very interested in this information, which was not surprising, since the Russians had earlier prized similar data regarding Hitler's movements. On 29 March, in a discussion with the new British ambassador (Sir Archibald Clark Kerr), Stalin had frankly stated that he wanted to kill the Nazi leaders ("He was extremely anxious to see Hitler dead") and sought British help in locating them. The Red Air Force therefore bombed Poltava on the basis of the British information, vainly trying to kill Goering, although his death at this stage of the war, and this stage of his psychological and narcotic disintegration—whatever the morality of the operation—would hardly have been a great boon to the Allies.

In May 1942, the air branch of 30 Mission also informed the Soviets that the British had learned from a "secret and reliable source" (probably ULTRA) that Fliegerkorps VIII was being transferred to the Crimea, which indicated that a German offensive was about to begin. This was definitely a matter of high policy and, in this case, of high-level Stalinist folly. Manstein was getting set to roll on the course that would take the Germans to the gates of Stalingrad in two months, but in facing that threat, Stalin refused to listen to anything as remote as British intelligence, even if it was highly accurate.[38]

So the air intelligence honeymoon of spring 1942 ended on a rather sour note of differing perceptions, differing values, and elements of mutual suspicion. In summing up the exchanges that had occurred over the previous four and a half months, Cheshire bemoaned the relatively small amount of secret information that the Red Air Force had provided to the British, compared with that which the British had given to the Russians. But not all those in the Air Ministry shared Cheshire's dismal view of what the Russians had done and its significance. Commenting on Cheshire's message, the vice chief of air staff, Gen. W. G. Freeman, noted on 15 May:

> We do not for a moment contest his view that from the point of view of intelligence—per se—the Russians are getting better than we are. But there is also the other side—they are fighting and we are not and surely this merits some quid pro quo.
>
> I was quite prepared to accept this small minded outlook from

Collier who left this country at a time when the immediate collapse of Russia was almost a foregone conclusion. But Cheshire, I think, left this country [when] the U.S.S.R. were doing their bit and a great deal more and apparently recognized by all except Cheshire.[39]

General Freeman's point was a fair one, although it was easier to embrace the big picture while seated in the relative calm and safety of Whitehall than it was for those who had to suffer the slings and arrows of Soviet abuse and coldness in Moscow. In addition, it is quite clear, even from the currently available open records, that although the British provided the Red Air Force with far more intelligence than they received during the first half of 1942, they acquired some useful information from the Russians, especially relating to German air OB on the Eastern Front. The Soviets seem to have been going through a transitional period; they saw the advantages of more openness in intelligence sharing, but when confronted with situations in which they would actually have to exchange "state secrets" with the British mission, they most frequently recoiled.

This tendency of the Soviets to take one step forward, followed by hesitation and occasionally one or two steps backward, revealed itself most clearly between January and June 1942 with regard to that most arcane and complicated of intelligence matters, "Y" intelligence. In December 1941, following the earlier work performed by Scott Farnie, Edward Crankshaw had begun negotiating with the Red Army and Air Force on "Y," first in Moscow and then in Kubyshev. During the Kubyshev discussions, the Soviet "Y" expert, a Major Tulbovitch, had given Crankshaw a recently captured German Army call-sign book (Edition E), which the British authorities had found highly valuable.

Crankshaw returned to Moscow on 11 January but was felled by illness, and meetings with Major Tulbovitch did not resume until 31 January. In the interval, difficulties emerged on the British side regarding the highly secret Typex cipher and MI 6 radio communications system, because of the moves from Moscow to Kubyshev and then back to Moscow. Also at this time, the whole system of military, naval, and air relations with MI 6 was undergoing reform in London. To top off the complexities and complications, some at Bletchley seemed to believe that the Soviets were actually highly adept at code breaking and were even able to read stale ENIGMA. On 20 January, the Admiralty therefore asked Crankshaw to see what he could do to secure from the Soviets information on Japanese codes. Apparently alarmed by this question, and in order to clarify his position, Crankshaw asked London about the "advisability of raising high level 'Y' problems" with the Soviets and received the reply "that no such action should be taken."[40]

In consequence, Crankshaw's range of activities was sharply narrowed, but the problems and frustrations did not disappear. One of the main sources of trouble was the Admiralty's continuing belief that Britain could benefit from the widespread "Y" organization that it thought the Soviets maintained in the Far East, even though Moscow seemed to be increasingly wary about antagonizing the Japanese. In addition, neither the mission chiefs nor Crankshaw had been properly briefed on precisely what information Farnie had given to the Russians regarding the relationship between Luftwaffe call signs and the fuselage markings found on crashed German aircraft. Knowledge of this relationship would greatly assist Russian "Y" staff in determining which Luftwaffe squadrons were actually operating in Russia at any given time and would also help them match up the various radio call signs with particular squadrons. Crankshaw met with the Russian "Y" representative, and the Soviet authorities were sufficiently appreciative of British efforts to arrange a special exhibit of captured German radio equipment for their benefit. But Crankshaw thought that the Red Air Force continued to be seriously confused about the relationship between German squadron markings and call signs, and this added to an already murky situation.[41]

In early March, Crankshaw toyed with the idea that the best way to produce a breakthrough with the Russians might be by trading Japanese Navy "Y," and he proposed setting up such a liaison arrangement through Comdr. A. T. Courtney in the British naval mission. But by mid-March, Crankshaw had changed his mind, concluding that an even better area in which to establish a working partnership would be secret German police radio traffic. On 15 March, he asked London for authorization to cut a deal by offering the Russians the keys to the main German police codes. Approval was apparently granted, for after a meeting with Major Tulbovitch on 23 March, Crankshaw fairly crowed that the Russians had agreed to the deal on police codes. In his view, this would provide an invaluable precedent for other forms of "Y" cooperation, as well as offering an insight so far denied into the efficiency or otherwise of Russian "Y."

By mid-April, Anglo-Soviet "Y" cooperation regarding German police traffic was functioning smoothly. The Russians were "pleased with what they are getting out of this traffic," showed less impatience than Crankshaw had anticipated, and convinced many British officials by "the speed and thoroughness" with which they tackled the German police traffic that the USSR must have "extensive resources in sets and operators." The atmosphere was therefore "decidedly improved," and as Crankshaw enthused, "for the first time the Russians have unbent sufficiently to ask me for advice on certain matters as from man to man." In appreciation, and also perhaps as a reward for the conclusion of the recently signed Anglo-Soviet alliance, the Russian "Y" authorities presented the British with two thank-you gifts—captured copies of the German "Y" handbook, and the German Army instructions for the drafting of signal plans—gifts that 30 Mission characterized as "invaluable." In June, Crankshaw was also given the ultimate vote of confidence when he was allowed to visit a Soviet "Y" station.

These successes marked the high point of 30 Mission's efforts at intelligence cooperation during the first half of 1942. In early May, Crankshaw noted that Tulbovitch was still "showing goodwill," and Crankshaw himself was "satisfied with [the] progress" that had been made. Soon afterward, with a dubious sense of timing, London decided that Crankshaw should return home to receive new instructions and additional information to enable him to answer some of Tulbovitch's questions. The Soviets agreed to this arrangement and promised that upon Crankshaw's return he would be allowed to see Soviet "Y" stations at work. But travel procedures and bureaucratic systems were too slow in 1942 to make lightning journeys of a thousand miles possible, and when Crankshaw returned to Russia, the Soviet attitude toward "Y" cooperation would be sharply changed.[42]

Nonetheless, the harmony and mutual profitability in the realm of "Y" that had been achieved in the spring of 1942 underscored what 30 Mission and the British military and naval departments in London had accomplished regarding East-West intelligence cooperation since the beginning of 1942. A large volume of diverse intelligence materials, ranging from items on German naval technology to "Y" information, had been received from the Soviets, and even more varied intelligence documentation had been supplied to Moscow. Organizations loosely connected to the military mission and the British embassy, such as the assorted oil demolition teams, Hill's SOE unit, and the various military sub-missions in other parts of the USSR from Murmansk to Tiflis, had also picked up bits and pieces of information on both the Russians and the Germans. Other British organizations in Moscow had also scored occasional successes. The Ministry of Economic Warfare had even managed to persuade the Soviets to hand over fifteen bags of Japanese mail (from the trans-Siberian railroad) in April so that they could be screened for economic and military secrets. Colonel Pika and the Polish emissaries continued to engulf the Foreign Office and other British departments with reports on conditions in Russia and the prospects for future cooperation with the USSR.[43]

In addition to what the mission could acquire and the information that could be levered out of Kharlamov and his colleagues in London, the British government also had other—usually extensive and often highly reliable—sources of information about the war in the east. From the earliest days of 1941, the British authorities had placed great importance on POW interrogation as a source of intelligence and had bugged holding cells and prisoner meeting rooms to acquire information. By 1942, these activities, as well as simple open interrogation methods, were yielding substantial intelligence about immediate combat operations in which Axis personnel had been captured, as well as about conditions in Germany and on other fronts where the POWs had been posted.[44]

"Y" intelligence about Russia, much of which came from the Middle East, in addition to that from the Polyarnoe station and other Royal Navy sources, also yielded highly useful information about both German and Russian operations. Most important of all these special intelligence sources relating to the Eastern Front was, of course, ULTRA, which continued to yield a massive flow of information about the enemy taken directly from high-grade German code and cipher messages, as well as considerable data about Soviet operations and the strengths and weaknesses of the Soviet armed forces.

Whitehall had therefore come to view 30 Mission as a useful, but not necessarily indispensable, source of intelligence. As the war in the east rolled on, with the Red Army usually doing better than the British had anticipated, the reality of Soviet power and the need to consider relations with the Russians for both today and tomorrow became increasingly important. In early 1942, British leaders began to have second thoughts about whether bullying the Soviets into providing secret information was really worthwhile. At this point in the war, the Ministry of Information (MOI) was complimenting itself on what it believed was a successful campaign to sterilize the British war effort of any possible Left-Right ideological conflicts and prevent the British Communist Party from cashing in on the battlefield successes of Stalin's Russia. One top MOI official remarked on 20 January that he thought that Communism was in the doldrums with the British public. A month later, the MOI had further reason for self-congratulation regarding Britain's partnership with the USSR, because Moscow turned over copies of the propaganda it was dropping over German-occupied Europe.[45]

Although the Foreign Office continued to worry about the possibility of a Stalinist superpower emerging in Eastern Europe, it hoped that the Soviets would extend a hand to the West, recognize Britain as an equal partner, and agree not to assert its might either in Allied councils or on the map of Europe and Asia. Eden had returned from Moscow in January somewhat chastened by his difficulties with Stalin over Eastern European borders, as well as by his inability to conclude a comprehensive treaty of alliance. He was nonetheless quite optimistic about the course of change in the USSR, noting what he believed to be an "absence of constraint between Stalin and his advisers," compared with what he had witnessed during his visit to Moscow in 1935. The foreign secretary seems to have found the most seriously troubling aspect of his visit to be that Soviet bands had played "God Save the King" on many occasions while he was in Moscow, but there was an "embarrassment that we could not return the compliment by playing the 'International.'"[46]

At a time when attitudes and dreams such as these prevailed in London, Macfarlane's style was definitely out of step. After his initial effort to charm the Soviets into cooperation had failed, his modus operandi became hectoring the Soviets into giving him visits and intelligence documents. By February, the British embassy in Moscow observed that the Soviets were suspicious of the military mission to an "unbelievable degree." This situation had been made worse by wild schemes and adventures, such as the oil demolition activities in the Caucasus, and by the fact that Macfarlane and his team were saddled with responsibility for arranging the evacuation from Russia of Polish military units, an operation perfectly tuned to arouse Soviet suspicion and paranoia.[47]

In early 1942, Macfarlane sank into a state of depression over the prospects of his mission. In March, when the DMI made a last effort to save him by proposing that the mission try to arrange a swap of information on the complete military and economic situations of the USSR and Britain, the 30 Mission chief dismissed the idea as completely impossible. On this occasion, Macfarlane's view was actually quite sensible. He argued that only through the creation of a joint planning mechanism—an East-West Combined Chiefs of Staff—would there be any chance of the Soviets revealing information about the vital elements of their war machine. But since London had always vetoed any such idea, Macfarlane thought that nothing could be done except to work "the information business here as much as possible on a bargain basis" and hold back information for haggling purposes when such action did not "handicap the Russians operationally."[48]

This response quite likely decided Macfarlane's fate. Important people, including the prime minister, had already suggested that he be replaced, and Gen. Sir Alan Brooke had been forced to fall back on the dubious word "temperamental" to characterize Macfarlane while trying to defend him in the face of Churchill's criticisms. But when the 30 Mission chief admitted in his dispatch that he believed that intelligence intended for the Soviets should be "held back," his cause was probably lost. A large Foreign Office exclamation mark was inked in the margin next to this pair of words. The wolves immediately began to gather (including the DNI, who still harbored resentment that his plan to station an attaché in Vladivostok had failed to materialize), all of them calling for Macfarlane's blood. On 23 March, Eden asked the War office to replace him, and on 1 April, the foreign secretary carried the issue to the prime minister, who agreed in principle that a change should be made. By this time, everyone from Soviet Ambassador Ivan Maisky in London to Clark Kerr in Moscow knew that Macfarlane was on his way out, and a large assortment of names was soon circulating—candidates for new head of 30 Mission. Maisky instantly vetoed Colonel Firebrace, whose coolness to the USSR was much too obvious. Eden and the chiefs of staff thought that Admiral Miles, or any other admiral, would do because of Soviet respect for the Royal Navy. Then, in late April, the whole question of the replacement was vaulted into the realm of the preposterous when Churchill and others became fascinated with the idea of sending Maj. Gen. C. Gubbins to head 30 Mission. Gubbins was another old anti-Bolshevik warrior who currently acted as the supremo of Britain's subversive warfare organization (SOE) and was ideally suited to awaken every possible form of suspicion and hostility among the Soviet authorities.[49]

After six weeks of confused wrangling, nothing had been definitely settled except that Macfarlane would be withdrawn and Admiral Archer would serve as acting head of the mission until Whitehall could pull itself together and name a successor. Most of the problems that weakened 30 Mission had been aired during March and April, including the fact, cited by Clark Kerr, that the mission had both supply and intelligence functions. This made the supply men look like secret agents to the Soviets, and the intelligence men appeared to be using supplies to lever secret information out of the USSR. The Foreign Office also managed to get on the record its doubt that any intelligence of sufficient value and importance could be secured in Moscow to warrant risks being taken to secure it. In early May, Clark Kerr even proposed solving both the mission's and the embassy's problems by recognizing that the Soviet Union would be the "predominant power" after the war and signing the treaties that the Soviets had proposed in December 1941. Kerr, although feeling "sorry for the Baltic peoples," also recognized that "being sorry will not help them," and Britain should therefore pursue its own interests.[50]

Such radical and icy suggestions never had a chance of being adopted, and both London and 30 Mission were soon back on the course of muddling their way through East-West intelligence exchanges. They still grasped the larger hope that Germany would somehow be beaten without destroying Britain or unleashing an all-powerful USSR on the rest of Europe. After a final meeting with Panfilov in which the two men swapped misassessments of what was likely to happen on the Eastern Front during the summer, Macfarlane left Moscow on 19 May and reached London shortly thereafter. Until taking up his new and comparatively harmless task as governor of Gibraltar (where he played an enabling role in the 1943 invasion of Italy), he spent a month telling the joint planners, the chiefs of staff, the prime minister, and anyone else who would listen that the Soviets had been fooled by Manstein's offensive and might well be knocked out over the summer. This blend of uncontestable fact about the past and inaccurate forecasting of the future served as a fitting monument to the first year's work of 30 Mission. It also clearly indicated that the British had failed to use the mission's presence in Moscow to secure a monopoly on Western intelligence cooperation with the USSR.[51]

During 1941, American isolationism, closed-mindedness, inexperience, and incompetence had left the field virtually free for the British to do what they would. But between January and June 1942, the U.S. embassy in Moscow, as well as various governmental departments in Washington, began to form some tentative but potentially effective intelligence connections with the Soviets. In so doing, they began to lay the foundation for a serious challenge to British intelligence relations with the Soviet Union.

The first six months of U.S. belligerency had certainly not been a happy time for American arms. Nor had it put an end to bureaucratic confusion and rivalry among the leaders or abolished the maze of competing departments and bureaus in Washington. The War Department seldom spoke to the Navy Department, everyone tried to muscle in on the State Department's direction of foreign policy, the president said all things to all men, and White House favorites such as Harry Hopkins and Henry Morgenthau pursued the great sport of empire building with little regard for custom, the chain of command, or even the cabinet system of government.

In regard to relations with the USSR, this meant that the president and Hopkins were inclined to put Russia near the top of the list in terms of economic and military supplies because, as FDR told an informal meeting of the U.S. chiefs of staff on 10 April, "the Russians are killing more Germans and destroying more German material than all the other United Nations put together."[52] Traditional U.S. partners, especially the British and the Chinese, were not enamored of this view, nor were those responsible for rearming the United States, such as Marshall, Knox, and Stimson (although the Soviets came to believe that Marshall, in particular, was fair to them and tried to meet their most pressing needs for supplies and military equipment). Furthermore, even such presidential predilections as this one could not override all of Washington's bureaucratic chaos and cannibalism, nor could it root out those individuals deeply embedded in many subdepartmental organizations, such as Colonels Yeaton and J. P. Ratay in G-2, who not only loathed the USSR but still believed that it was incapable of standing up to the German war machine. Finally, just as had been the case with the British a year earlier, as soon as the United States entered the war, many American departments and bureaus concerned with Russian questions were overwhelmed with mad schemes to cooperate with the USSR (William Donovon's COI, the predecessor of the OSS, was already in touch with the American Communist Party in April 1942). They were also inundated with numerous petitions from tsarist emigrés anxious to volunteer for liaison missions to the old homeland.[53]

In Moscow, the U.S. embassy had more than its share of meandering "business as usual" inefficiency, even after Pearl Harbor. Lawrence Steinhardt's ambassadorial term was allowed to run out early in 1942, but the new ambassador, Adm. William Standley (who had accompanied Harriman to Moscow in late 1941), did not take up his post until April. Even after he picked up the ambassadorial reins, Standley faced a virtual American civil war over lend-lease aid and the role to be played by the military attaché's office. Colonels Faymonville and Michela remained at each other's throats, and the embassy staff was frozen in a mood of depression and discouragement by frequent expressions of Soviet hostility. Dismal conversations with members of Macfarlane's team led them to believe that nothing good would come of any Western effort to cooperate with the USSR. To top off the doom and gloom, much of the American embassy staff, including those in the military attaché's office, continued to be stranded in Kubyshev. This situation was so grim that Michela tried to throw in the towel and resign, but G-2 ordered him to stay at his post.[54]

Despite all the resentment, hostility, and failure that dogged the American team in Russia during 1942 (on one Kafkaesque occasion, they accidentally received a MAGIC intercept from Washington with no explanation, simply signed with the name of the Japanese admiral "Togo"), the members of Standley's organization made some significant advances in intelligence collection and exchange. Relations with the British mission were quite good, and although the two "cousins" did not combine their exchange efforts with the Soviets, the British embassy did supply the U.S. naval attaché with information on what Geoffrey Palmer of Clark Kerr's staff called "our little yellow brothers," the Japanese. As Macfarlane reported to the War Office, however, the Soviets supplied the "Americans practically nothing," and Michela himself "showed no enthusiasm when [Colonel] Exham suggested he might like to be put into [the] German Order of Battle picture."

Unlike the British (who were envious), the Americans had a consulate general's office in Vladivostok, and in early 1942, Consul A. I. Ward succeeded in gaining some information on Soviet-Japanese border clashes, as well as on the scale of Soviet military preparations in Russia's eastern provinces. U.S. diplomatic couriers also traveled back and forth between Moscow, Vladivostok, and other points in the USSR, and they picked up useful impressions of conditions prevailing in the far eastern portion of the Soviet Union.[55]

Standley was anxious to arrange intelligence exchanges with the Soviets, and despite his lamentations, Michela actually seems to have secured some useful information from the Red Army. But since there is a large gap in the surviving records—the principal collection of attaché reports sent to Washington between 1 January and 9 March 1942 is missing from the National Archives—a full appraisal of the importance of this material is not possible. Michela definitely received a six-page report on German OB on the Eastern Front from the Soviets on 9 March 1942, and a month later the Red Army apologized for the rough treatment he had previously received and gave him a Soviet rifle, a German machine gun, and six German aircraft shot down on the Eastern Front, including a Heinkel 111 and an ME 109, as a reconciliation present. The Soviets also assured the American military attaché that the planes and other equipment would be shipped to the United States, and this was actually done in June.

By late April, the U.S. Army attaché's office regularly received Soviet weather reports and was also given a Soviet antitank rifle. In early May, Michela was permitted to carry out a detailed inspection of Soviet tanks, and on 17 May, he was provided with the Soviet OB estimate of the Japanese Air Force in the Kuriles and northern China. Two weeks later, Moscow's desire to show favor to Michela reached its climax, when he was given information on the organization of Japanese reserve divisions, data on Luftwaffe OB in Norway, and samples of German gas masks and Soviet and German Army uniforms. Between 20 and 26 June, he also visited the headquarters of the Russian 5th Army and received copies of the Soviet picture of German OB on this sector of the front. This experience left the U.S. Army military attaché with the impression that although Red Army morale was not soaringly high, discipline was "superb," and he reported to Washington that his view of the Red Army was now "somewhat higher" than it had been previously.[56]

By this time, a new U.S. naval attaché, Capt. Jack Duncan, had also arrived in Moscow. He immediately exchanged navigational charts with the Red Navy, received a briefing on the Japanese Navy in the North Pacific, and was asked by the Soviets if the United States wished to assign one of its naval officers to Vladivostok. Although Duncan was unaccountably slow in responding to the latter offer, the Soviets were clearly signaling that they were prepared to be more accommodating to the Americans than to the British. This also may have been the reason for the success of Charles Thayer of the embassy staff in cultivating a number of ostensibly private and personal sources of information within the Soviet press corps and the military branch of the Soviet information service.

Weakly paralleling this surge of Soviet-American intelligence cooperation in Moscow and Kubyshev during the spring of 1942 was a noticeable increase of exchanges in Washington. In 1941, U.S. Army and Navy officers had received from the British copies of reports by Macfarlane and the British naval liaison officer in the Black Sea (this practice continued in 1942), but the Soviet military and naval attachés in Washington gave next to nothing to American authorities through mid-March 1942.[57] But on 25 March and 30 April 1942, the Soviet naval attaché, Captain Yegorichev, was given three ONI reports on Japanese army and air strength. Additional intelligence on the Japanese was provided to Yegorichev, including some on the Imperial Navy. The U.S. Navy Department also gave the Soviets information about German naval construction. On 4 May, Yegorichev finally began to return the favor by providing the U.S. Navy with the Soviet version of the OB of the Japanese Air Force (as of 30 April). Soon after, in the words of G-2, "an amazing change of attitude" came over the Soviet army attaché, who proceeded to furnish the Americans with "considerable valuable information on Sakhalin, the Kuriles, Manchuria, and Korea." On 5 May, the Soviet military attaché "voluntarily" and surprisingly supplied the War Department with Moscow's estimate of Japanese ground strength, as well as the Soviet version of Japanese Army OB. In reply, the U.S. Army gave the Soviets its current OB summary on Japan.[58]

The first six months of cooperative East-West intelligence efforts in 1942 thereby ended with the peculiar result that the Americans were on the upswing and the British were racked with dissension, their military mission was without a leader, and British policy toward the USSR was in near turmoil. During the final six months of 1942 and on into 1943, amid both disappointments and Allied triumphs, the three great Allied powers would begin to jostle more openly for position both within the Allied camp and in regard to their power and influence throughout the world. In this era, the two Western powers would more consciously play politics as they sought Soviet assistance in increasing their military might and attempted to produce an intimacy with Moscow that might stretch beyond the near horizon.

6
Converging and Dividing Paths, July 1942–March 1943

The period from summer 1942 to spring 1943 produced important turns and twists in many aspects of the war. On the battlefield, the Americans began the long road back across the Pacific. The landing on Guadalcanal in August 1942 unleashed six months of ferocious fighting before the Japanese were cleared from the island and the way north and west was open to the Allies. Reversals in North Africa in mid-1942 were serious enough for the Soviets to offer Britain three Polish divisions to provide them with the punch necessary to win. The permanent undersecretary of the Foreign Office, Sir Alexander Cadogan, became so despondent that he confided to his diary that he was willing to try anything, even making the bête noire of the Whitehall establishment, Charles de Gaulle, the chief of the British Imperial General Staff.[1]

In October, the British finally scored a decisive triumph over Rommel at El Alamein, and Operation TORCH put British and American forces into Algeria and Morocco in November. By March 1943, the Anglo-Americans were poised to crush the Afrika Korps in Tunisia, thereby ending the Axis threat in North Africa. At sea, the Anglo-Americans were slowly but surely winning the battle of the Atlantic against the U-boat in 1942–1943. In the skies above German-occupied Western Europe, the U.S. Army Air Corps had joined forces with the RAF, putting to the test the proposition that the massive destruction produced by strategic bombing could play a significant role in winning the war.

Late summer 1942 saw the Germans press on toward Stalingrad, but they encountered such stubborn resistance across the length and breadth of the Eastern Front that all other German efforts to advance in the east had been halted (even though the Germans had penetrated into the Caucasus). Every ounce of German offensive power was hurled at the gateway city to the east and south that bore Stalin's name. The German efforts were in vain, however. On 19 November 1942, the decisive Soviet counteroffensive began, and on 22

November, the jaws of the Soviet encirclement snapped shut, trapping the whole of the German 6th Army. The men of Paulus's command endured two and a half months of great suffering. Finally on 31 January 1943, this man who had helped plan the original German BARBAROSSA attack on Russia in June 1941 laid down his arms. The last 90,000 hungry and frozen men of the 6th Army stumbled into Soviet captivity, and at war's end, only 5,000 of them were still alive. Yet even after Stalingrad, Hitler was far from through. In March, the Germans attacked again, retaking Kharkov and Belograd and leaving Kursk exposed like a great salient in the middle of the Russian line.[2]

Beginning in late 1942 and early 1943, as the Allies began to bring their enormous manpower and economic resources to bear, the scale of operations increased, and the toll of death and destruction multiplied. Although the prospect of Allied victory brightened, concern increased about holding together the "Big Three" and preparing the way for a stable, better postwar world. Political attitudes across the West were shifting as gratitude to the Soviet Union for taking on the Germans lapped over into greater respect for Stalin and the Soviet system. In this period, the Communist Parties of Britain and the United States often acted as if they thought that their hour would soon come, embracing every Soviet sailor who appeared in a Western port in the hope that the Party would be covered with this purest form of reflected glory.[3]

During August, Churchill visited Moscow to try to charm Stalin into East-West cooperation, especially to convince him that TORCH was rather like a Second Front. Roosevelt refused to join the British on this journey, but Averell Harriman again acted as the American minder during this British foray in Russia. In addition, Washington sent a parade of official and quasi-official visitors to Moscow, including Patrick Hurley (who had both extensive diplomatic and anti-Communist experience), Eddie Rickenbacker, and Wendell Willkie. No significant political agreements were made during the Stalin-Churchill talks in Moscow, but the two men took new measure of each other after decades of mutual hostility and suspicion. Much drinking was done, and Churchill rejected formal attire to march about in his coveralls. Among the other surprising occurrences was Stalin's praise for the Allied intelligence services, and Clark Kerr's genuine astonishment at the arrogance and bad manners of the British generals and their staffs. In the end, after clouds of Stalinist anger had been released, the Russians came to accept TORCH as at least somewhat useful in drawing off German divisions from the Eastern Front, even as Moscow continued to call for a real Second Front in northern France.[4]

During January 1943, as the final battle with the Germans in North Africa drew near, Churchill and Roosevelt met at Casablanca, with neither Stalin nor any other high Soviet spokesman present. The primary purpose of this meeting was to display Western collaboration and to resolve the controversies over where Britain and the United States should land next. During the meeting, however, President Roosevelt publicly proclaimed Allied dedication to the principle of unconditional surrender. Whatever the merits or demerits of this announcement (and controversy has raged ever since about whether the unconditional surrender policy was either wise or necessary), the announcement at least confirmed that the Western Allies planned to fight until their enemies were smashed, which may have helped ease long-held Soviet fears that the West might make a separate peace with Hitler.

But the total-victory scenario implicit in the demand for unconditional surrender also meant that the prevailing balance of power would certainly be destroyed by war's end if the Western powers had their way, and future world power relationships would have to be determined by the victorious Allies, including, quite obviously, the USSR. The unconditional surrender policy was therefore an important move toward a general recognition that World War II constituted a real revolution in international power relationships, and that East-West cooperation would be essential for the building of the hoped-for better world. British and American relations with the USSR thus became even more important, because although Churchill was somewhat unwilling to recognize it, Soviet and American power and influence were rapidly rising, while that of Britain was in steep decline.

The effect of these many-sided political developments pulled various aspects of East-West relations in different directions. On one level, the British and Americans, and in some measure the Soviets, acted as if it was now appropriate and sensible for them to try to compromise, since their wartime fates were tied together and someday soon they might have to sit down on the same side of the peace table. This hard fact compelled them to cooperate on a number of political matters, including peace overtures from enemy countries. Indeed, in 1943, they informed each other of a host of such probes made by Hungarians and Italians as well as Germans and originating in locations from Sweden to Buenos Aires.

Whitehall was also aware of the need to assure Moscow that Britain was committed to a fight to the finish against Nazism. When in October 1942 A. A. Milne wandered a bit too far from Poo Corner, declaring in *Time and Tide* that the Soviets should simply be told that a cross-Channel invasion would be too costly (and German radio began trumpeting the story to the world), Mr. C. Warner of the Foreign Office minuted other departments that in this case they should not worry too much about Moscow's reaction, because "the Soviet authorities would remember that A. A. Milne was an appeaser and a poor fish."[5] In a similar vein, three months later, Churchill himself intervened to try to stop British officials from making public statements that sounded anti-Soviet, referring specifically to "a very foolish lecture given by Brigadier Firebrace the other day in which he ran down the Russian Army."[6]

Consequently, it is not surprising that although the total volume of intelligence exchanges seems to have increased during this period, notable difficulties were also present. These were exacerbated by the Soviet campaign to convince the Western leadership that the eastern war had so denuded Western Europe of German troops that a Second Front would be little more than a walkover. Overall, the Soviets were more receptive in principle to intelligence exchanges with both the British and the Americans than they had been in the past, but they continued to be much more cautious than either London or Washington. This was particularly true with respect to information on Soviet armed forces and operations. Although 30 Mission had initiated an exchange with the Soviets regarding the two countries' military formations, providing the Russians with details of British infantry and armored divisions in November 1941, London had to wait ten months before the Soviets supplied comparable information about their own units.

Despite their eagerness to dazzle the Americans with their intelligence prowess, British officials were usually forced to admit to Washington that they had "no authentic Russian picture." Many 30 Mission summaries on the Red Army were as hesitant as one dated 4 September 1942, successive paragraphs of which began "We believe," "I have no information," "Very probably," and "As far as we know."[7] By fitting together bits and pieces from many sources—some of them highly dubious—the British Army intelligence staff prepared a 400-page OB of the Red Army and passed it on to Washington in March 1943. But much of this report was based on out-of-date information due largely to bureaucratic muddle. In January 1943, the War Office intelligence section concerned with Red Army OB was given a large block of Red Army data from "CXX" (i.e., intelligence coming mainly from intercepts of German messages) on Red Army OB. An officer in the War Office Red Army OB section immediately informed his superiors that he was very glad to get the information because he had "not received any of this information before." Then, after admitting that he did not know who in the War Office was actually handling this material, he expressed the strong wish that henceforth "the information derived from the German 'Y' service [be] immediately made available to M.I. 3 (C) at the War Office." So although it is true that in the latter part of the war the British and Americans used ULTRA to secure large amounts of detailed information on the Red Army, that did not begin in earnest until all the crucial battles on the Eastern Front except Kursk had already been won by the Red Army.[8]

On some occasions, though, the Soviet high command deemed it appropriate to respond in detail to high-level British requests for information, such as the series of questions on Russian operations and prospects sent by the DMI to Moscow in January 1943. When such queries arrived, a Red Army spokesman would call in a member of 30 Mission and march through the British questionnaire, describing specific military operations, providing assessments of the enemy military situation, and often citing specific German divisional ID numbers, especially those of units recently transferred from Western Europe. On truly sensitive questions, such as Russian methods of prisoner interrogation, there was seldom parity. Although members of the Soviet mission in London were allowed to be present during a British interrogation of German prisoners in September 1942, 30 Mission never secured a comparable opportunity to observe a full-scale Soviet interrogation in Moscow.[9]

Generally speaking, the Soviets tended to be more solicitous of American than of British goodwill during late 1942 and early 1943. Lend-lease and rising American power certainly contributed to this tendency, even though the British had far richer sources of intelligence information than did the Americans. The British mission in Moscow was therefore in a weaker position than previously. The staff of the British embassy, and presumably the Soviet liaison officials as well, found Admiral Archer easier to deal with than Macfarlane had been, but since the admiral was only an acting mission chief, and since Soviet officialdom was highly sensitive to matters of status and protocol, the Russians showed their displeasure by being even more remote from the British mission. In contrast, the American position was enhanced because Admiral Standley was much more forceful than Ambassador Steinhardt had been. He also had more support from Washington, being an associate of Harriman as well as of the president. And as an old seadog, he enjoyed a special line of approach to the higher echelons of the Red Navy. Furthermore, as the Pacific war progressed, American combat experience, technology, and intelligence sophistication increased as well. When these factors were combined with the massive flow of American supplies entering Russia through the northern ports and Iran in 1943, the United States probably seemed a much more desirable partner to the Russians.

Any tendency of either of the Western powers to go it alone in regard to intelligence sharing with the Soviets was held in check by a number of factors. The combined chiefs of staff system, although it excluded the USSR—an exclusion that Clark Kerr thought was a serious mistake—made extensive

Anglo-American cooperation inevitable. The special relationship between Churchill and Roosevelt also knitted the two countries together, as did Britain's need for American supplies and troops. The American search for British military advice, experience, and intelligence formed another binding link across the Atlantic, and the huge liaison staffs in the British Joint Staff Mission in Washington, paralleled by the large U.S. teams in London's Grosvenor Square, prevented either of the Western countries from wandering very far, or very long, on their own.

This meant that they were both stuck with Soviet reserve and obstructionism unless they could tap unorthodox sources of information about what was going on in Russia and on the Eastern Front. The most abundant such source was still Colonel Pika, who not only had his reports forwarded to Whitehall and Washington by the Czech government in exile in London but also occasionally delivered them directly to the British embassy in Moscow. Kerr's staff, however, was not as enraptured by Pika as it had been in the past. A British embassy official observed in March 1943 that Pika was "neither so intelligent nor so well informed" as his ambassador, Zdenek Fierlinger, who was in fact very pro-Russian. Pika's reports kept piling up in the Foreign Office general correspondence files, but doubts were rising about them in London too. For example, in July 1942, the Ministry of Economic Warfare observed that the Czech embassy had given sharply different versions of one of Pika's reports to the War and Foreign Offices.[10]

Frustrated that neither the Russians nor the Czechs would provide them with truly hot information on what was going on at the Eastern Front, the British military mission from time to time evidenced a desire to take greater risks in securing intelligence. Even after the British embassy and the military mission had assured London that they would not attempt to acquire information on Soviet railroads except through regular liaison channels, the mission went right ahead and did so. Like the Americans, they collected Soviet railroad data from members of their various supply missions; embassy and military staff carefully examined all sections of the Russian railroad network on which they traveled and filed secret reports on what they observed. Of course, if the Soviets had lessened some of their absurdly rigid security controls, or if more anonymous benefactors (such as the person who secretly mailed a copy of the Red Army's current general combat intelligence estimate to the U.S. mission in February 1943) had plied their trade more extensively, the Western military missions would not have had to grumble so much or take so many risks to supplement what fell from the Soviet table.

The British and American missions in Moscow therefore functioned just like cousins should. They had separate organizations, and these organizations were of different types, with the British team centralized and the American still rigidly divided between the naval and military attaché branches. British and American officials encountered one another socially but apparently did not talk much shop and seemingly never exchanged intelligence materials in Moscow during this period. Inevitably, however, both the British and the American missions focused on many of the same materials—order of battle, technical intelligence, and strategic estimates of German and Soviet intentions. Some of the materials they acquired and sent to their superiors were stirred together in London and Washington as the officials at home and the combined chiefs of staff sought to paint comprehensive pictures of what the Soviets were doing and why.

In only one area of pure intelligence activity did the British retain an absolute monopoly, and that was "Y." The Americans had no "Y" representative in Moscow, were not actively pursuing cryptanalytic attacks on German codes and ciphers, had no intercept stations in Europe, and therefore had little of value to offer the Russians. Consequently, the British mission had a free run on "Y," and even before Crankshaw returned from his long visit to Britain, the Red Navy signaled that, like the Red Army, it desired meetings with the British "Y" representative. In the interim, the Royal Navy carried on its extensive "Y" work in northern Russia, a full report on this work being sent to the DNI in midsummer. Following his return on 1 September, Crankshaw met with a senior member of the staff of the northern fleet and had a "long and useful discussion on ways and means of arranging Anglo-Soviet 'Y' cooperation in North Russia." He also made a detailed inspection of the Royal Navy "Y" station at Polyarnoe.[11]

Arriving in Moscow on 4 September, Crankshaw indicated to his Soviet liaison officer that the British government wanted to send a team of cryptanalysts to visit the USSR, but "the most pressing need" was for Crankshaw himself to "be given access to a responsible senior Soviet 'Y' officer with whom he could deal on policy matters outside the competence of Major Tulbovitch."[12] A week later, Crankshaw was told that the regular Soviet liaison officer (a general named Dubinen) would deal with all high-level "Y" matters and that the Soviets were making arrangements for Crankshaw to send "Y" intercepts from the Polyarnoe station to London by air. On that foundation, Crankshaw resumed his regular lower-level meetings with Major Tulbovitch, reporting the results directly to the "Y" authorities in Britain while he awaited the Soviet response to his proposals for British cryptanalysts to visit the USSR.

By October, the "Y" material that Crankshaw acquired was being regularly flown to Britain via Teheran, but his weekly meetings with Tulbovitch had given way to fortnightly meetings. On 11 October, Crankshaw was engaged in "delicate 'Y' negotiations" with the Soviets regarding German Army traffic. Throughout October and November he continued to receive German "Y" information from a Soviet liaison officer. Then, out of the blue, on 1 December the Soviets completely cut off army "Y" cooperation. No sooner did this disaster befall the British team, however, than the Red Navy rushed forward and assured Crankshaw that it wanted to continue sharing "Y" with Britain. The "Y" partnership with the Red Navy continued to operate smoothly over the next two months (mid-December 1942 to mid-February 1943) as Crankshaw did his best to reopen the door to army cooperation by having Admiral Miles give the Soviets some "particularly secret" (but now unidentifiable) "Y" information at the end of December. Soon thereafter, Crankshaw came down with glandular fever. But even though he was out of commission and British Navy "Y" interception was limited to Polyarnoe (no Royal Navy intercept station existed in Murmansk), the volume of "Y" traffic sent to Britain from Russia had doubled by January 1943. In consequence, British officials moved resolutely in late 1942 and early 1943 to buttress their "Y" liaison. On 5 January 1943, Lt. Comdr. Viscount Kelburn was sent to Moscow on a "Y" liaison mission, and after two weeks, Lt. C. D. C. Chalkley was assigned to Polyarnoe to oversee "Y" matters. With the decks thereby cleared, the ailing Crankshaw was allowed to return to Britain on 21 February, and neither he nor any other British Army or RAF "Y" official would return to Russia during the war.[13]

Another threat to naval "Y" cooperation arose in late February 1943. A number of observers asserted that the Soviets demanded the closure of the Polyarnoe intercept station, but in fact, the Soviets continued to raise no objection to British "Y" interception in the north. Moscow's objection was that the Royal Navy had allegedly set up too many powerful and unauthorized radio transmitters at Polyarnoe. Much bureaucratic wrangling ensued, because if two of the transmitters were shut down, as the Soviets demanded, "Y" traffic would have to go out via the much slower and less reliable land line to Moscow for radio transmission to Britain. This was unacceptable to the DNI, and the British fought hard to maintain their transmitters. In late February, the Soviet Foreign Office intervened in support of the Royal Navy's cause, and by early March, Molotov had taken the matter under his wing, immediately approving the operation of the British transmitters and "Y" station. At the end of March, the British naval mission reported that northern "Y" was proceeding so satisfactorily that the Red Navy now requested authorization to send two of its officers to Britain to confer with Crankshaw on both German and Japanese naval "Y" matters. This time, however, it was the British who closed the door of secrecy.

Although the Soviets continued to allow the Polyarnoe "Y" station to do its work, and some sporadic "Y" exchange contacts continued to be made in Russia, the British "Y" board put all Soviet radio intercept requests on hold during the winter of 1942–1943, including any possible Russian "Y" visit to Britain.[14]

By following tight security procedures, the British and Russian authorities seem to have succeeded in keeping all aspects of their "Y" exchanges secret from the Americans as well as the Germans. The Soviet authorities also refused all American requests for Japanese radio equipment (G-2 Washington had told Moscow that American forces had not yet captured such material), but they did give the U.S. mission in Moscow eleven boxes of German radio apparatus. Furthermore, the U.S. Moscow mission seems to have remained unaware that 30 Mission received information from a "Most Secret Reliable Occasional Source" (i.e., ULTRA intelligence) from London for its own use and that Churchill occasionally sent highly wrapped up ULTRA directly to Stalin. Apparently, the Americans were also kept in the dark regarding Maisky's tentative discussions with British authorities on bacteriological warfare in late October, as well as the fact that the British broke off these discussions because they had just made a great leap forward in this field.[15]

Other highly secret Anglo-Soviet exchanges leaked to the Americans very quickly, however. The U.S. mission immediately learned from Soviet sources about the 1942–1943 Anglo-Soviet discussions on measures to be taken if Germany resorted to gas warfare, and Washington demanded to be included if any such talks were resumed. Similarly, although the United States was not anxious to be included in Britain's partnership with the NKVD, the American embassy in Moscow informed OSS in Washington in August 1942 (when some of the first NKVD agents were being sent to Britain) that an SOE-NKVD connection definitely existed.[16]

The U.S. government was especially concerned about being left out of any East-West exchanges regarding technology. In 1942–1943, the British military services continued to fill Soviet requests for unconventional weaponry known to the enemy, including ASDIC and some forms of radar. Churchill also agreed to a more general technological exchange while meeting with Stalin in August 1942. Although Harriman was present during the Stalin-Churchill meeting in which technology exchange was discussed, he did not indicate whether the U.S. government wished to be a party to such an arrangement. The Americans as well as the British were eager to conclude meteorological exchange agreements with the Soviets, and a number of such agreements were reached between July and October. In September–October, the British also acquired samples of Soviet antifreezing oils and lubricants, and the Americans obtained a sample

Red Army soldier's winter kit, along with the Red Navy's complete medicine and surgical procedures pamphlet for ships at sea. Hydrographic information continued to be exchanged with both Western navies, and in September, the Soviet high command agreed to exchange technical films with the U.S. Army. In October–November, the British Moscow mission finally fulfilled one of its heart's desires and made a large map exchange arrangement with the Russians.[17]

Initially, the British, who permitted the Russians at least 200 plant and factory visits in 1942, intended to go much further. Expansive plans were made to send the British technical wizard, Professor Henry Tizard, to Moscow, comparable to the visit he had made to Washington in 1940. But the British services lodged reservations and demanded that proximity fuses, "window" (aluminum strips dropped to jam radar), and a host of other British secrets, including advanced radio direction finding (RDF, which was being withheld from the Russians but was clearly visible on British ships in north Russia and had even been installed on some Russian ships being refitted in British ports), should all continue to be withheld from the Soviets. Then the Americans joined in to attack the proposal. Secretary of War Henry Stimson's scientists were especially worried about it, and on 11 February, the U.S. embassy in London told the Admiralty that no classified American equipment could be included in any Anglo-Soviet exchanges.

Perhaps fortunately, Professor Tizard fell seriously ill, and the British pulled back from technical exchanges with the Russians. Kerr stressed that the British should avoid appearing too anxious, and the prime minister minuted that the ambassador was "absolutely right in this," especially because, as he noted on another occasion, "nothing we tell the Russians can possibly be produced and come into service use for a year or more." No sooner did the British draw back, however, than the Russian authorities, who had previously been cool and obstructionist, suddenly promised to welcome a British technical mission with open arms. Large-scale East-West technical exchange was, however, an idea whose time had not yet come in 1943. Although the British and Americans looked at each other with a generous measure of suspicion, they found it advisable to direct their cooperative proposals with the Soviets into less controversial areas, such as occasional visits to each other's installations rather than high-tech information.[18]

Regarding opportunities to visit installations and outer regions of the USSR, the British and the Americans were far more successful in late 1942 and early 1943 than they had previously been. Besides Moscow and Kubyshev, both British and American personnel were stationed in Murmansk and Archangel. In

August 1942, a U.S. naval attaché, Comdr. C. H. Taecker, was assigned to Vladivostok, making an unintended mockery of the long and vain British effort to get one of their own naval officers into that port.[19]

The British naval liaison officer in the Black Sea, Captain Ambrose, remained at his post, and although he was having increasing trouble with Soviet officials, the First Lord (A. V. Alexander) noted in November that Ambrose "is at present the only source of intelligence about the Russian Black Sea Fleet," providing "valuable information about general operations in the Black Sea." In March 1942, Soviet officials requested all sorts of information, ranging from new German aircraft data to chemical warfare information, from Ambrose. Apparently they assumed that they stood a better chance of getting British intelligence secrets from a Royal Navy officer who had himself been receiving intelligence benefits from the Russians.[20]

Although some of Faymonville's supply personnel still refused to collect intelligence, most other Anglo-American missions and posts in the USSR sent in large numbers of on-the-spot reports on local military and civil conditions, as well as travel reports detailing Soviet air bases, railway lines, and so forth. These reports were forwarded to London and Washington and remain there in open files, silently denying the accuracy of assertions that the West could secure information about travel in the USSR only from highly secret sources such as MAGIC intercepts.[21]

Soviet representatives stationed in the United States and Britain certainly had far more access to bases and manufacturing plants than did Western personnel stationed in the USSR. But in 1942–1943, many of the rigid Soviet restrictions on the movement and observation opportunities of Westerners were relaxed. This era also produced a number of organized Western visits to Soviet military and naval bases, including an inspection by Admiral Miles of the main Soviet naval mine and torpedo factory (as well as the torpedo firing range), a July British air mission survey of the Moscow Air Defense Center, and an examination of a Russian ammunition factory by Colonel Michela.

But aside from the special opportunities for observation provided by Churchill's August mission to Moscow, senior British visitors had little chance of seeing important or sensitive installations. Perhaps the resulting frustration, as well as the Americans' success in getting their men into the Soviet far east, prompted the commander in chief in India to revive the idea of sending a British mission to Siberia. In February 1943, Colonel Exham of the Moscow military mission raised the matter again, incorrectly claiming that prior to Pearl Harbor the Soviets had agreed to let such a British mission go in. The naval intelligence division (NID) once more supported this now obsessive demand, but by this time, Admiral Godfrey was on his way out after too many battles lost within the JIC, and Whitehall was leaning toward caution on all things Soviet.[22]

American visitors crisscrossed the USSR in this period. The Soviet authorities were so eager to open doors to them that in February–March 1943, both Ambassador Kerr and the British JIC noted for the record that the Americans were being allowed many more Soviet facility visits than was the British mission in Moscow. During July, Stalin personally intervened to assure Colonel Michela and Admiral Standley that U.S. fliers would be allowed to accompany Soviet crews charting the Alaska-Siberia aircraft ferrying route. The assistant U.S. military attaché, Col. Richard Park, was also allowed to visit the Stalingrad front with General Hurley; they stayed with the 51st Guards Division in the northern pincer and returned with twenty pages of detailed information on German and Soviet military methods and weaponry.

Another U.S. general, Follett Bradley of the U.S. Army Air Corps, was sent in early 1943 to liaise with the Russians on preparations for Operation VELVET, an abortive scheme to employ Anglo-American air forces in support of the Red Army in southern Russia, as well as on possible Soviet-American air force cooperation in Siberia. Bradley's intelligence triumphs were not as dramatic as those of Hurley and Park at Stalingrad, but he outperformed any previous British or American military representatives in securing detailed information on Soviet military installations, procedures, and equipment.[23]

Hurley, Park, and Bradley were the first American observers to see that Soviet combat units were now using a broad range of lend-lease equipment from the United States, which may in part explain the more forthcoming attitude of many Soviet officials. Gratitude for American supplies, coupled with a desire to smooth the way for additional shipments, were probably significant factors in the Soviet decision to reveal more to American observers in 1943.

But this increased Soviet openness with the Americans also extended to the sharing of information on Axis and Japanese equipment and weaponry, which had nothing to do with lend-lease. In July 1942, the Red Navy furnished details on German heavy ship silhouettes, armor specifications, and general identification characteristics, as well as data on German raiders. During August, the Red Army presented particulars of the German 150-mm heavy gun, which G-2 had requested. In September, the Soviets also supplied highly secret information on German naval mines.

The Red Navy presented the U.S. Navy with summaries of the composition of the Soviet northern and far eastern fleets, summaries that the Soviets specifically requested should *not* be given to the British. But the transcendent act of special technical generosity to the U.S. Navy during the autumn of 1942 was the presentation of a detailed report (probably acquired by an agent) of "the armour of the cruiser *Seidlitz,* of the Battleships *Bismarck* and *Scharnhorst,* and the Aircraft Carrier *Graf Zepplin.*" During the winter of 1942–1943 and into the spring, the Soviets handed over additional German publications on naval construction, as well as data on U-boat refueling practices in the Western Hemisphere. In exchange, the U.S. Navy supplied silhouette information on Japanese and Axis ships, along with bits and pieces of technical data on the German fleet.[24]

During this same era (1942–1943), Britain's 30 Mission enjoyed some of the increased Soviet generosity regarding enemy military and naval technology. A report on panzer division tactics was received from the Soviets, together with a sample of the German 12.7-mm gun. While the Spitfire photo reconnaissance squadron was operating in northern Russia during September–October 1942, the Soviets furnished the British with aerial photographs of this area. As occurred on earlier occasions, the Royal Navy continued to have livelier exchange relationships with the Soviets than did either the British Army or the RAF. The Red Navy provided the Royal Navy with data on German mines and information on the Japanese fleet up to January 1943. But its main contribution on enemy technology, as had been true of its dealings with the Americans, related to German heavy ships. Information on the *Tirpitz* acquired by a Soviet agent went to the Admiralty on 3 August, and in late 1942, the Soviets furnished detailed technical data on the design of all the German heavy ships, including their boilers and auxiliary machinery. The Royal Navy showed its gratitude for these gifts by giving the Russians information on U-boat radio equipment and providing details on German ship construction and the operation of German raiders.[25]

Authentic intelligence treasures appeared from time to time in the general exchanges that occurred between the Red Navy and the British and U.S. Navies in late 1942 and early 1943. But during much of this period, exchange of air and ground order-of-battle information regarding Axis and Japanese forces was shaky and spasmodic. In July and August, after a special Russian request, the Soviet mission in London was granted considerable OB material, including the current disposition of German, Italian, Japanese, and even Finnish forces. In Moscow, the Soviets requested details on Luftwaffe training schools, in preparation for another "special" Red Air Force bombing attack. Birse had his first OB meeting in four months with the Soviet specialist on the Japanese Army, a Major Gerzenstein, on 12 July. Soon thereafter, Colonel Michela was given a one-page Soviet breakdown of the Japanese Army, listing the total number of Japanese units in various categories, from infantry divisions to railroad regiments. Colonel Exham gave the local Red Army commanders in Archangel the latest British information regarding German OB on that section of the front, but aside from vague speculation about enemy movements, he received nothing in return. The Soviets had gone quiet about German OB. Cheshire imagined that their reticence was the result of unhappiness about deficiencies in the convoy system and the lack of a Second Front. But it is more likely that the great battles in southern Russia were too important, and too fluid, for the Red Army command to have much time or desire to carry on fencing matches with the British in Moscow.[26] The Soviets remained mum even when Churchill got into the intelligence-sharing act, telling Stalin in August that from "the same source [i.e., ULTRA]" he had used to warn of the German attack in June 1941, he had learned that the Japanese were resisting German efforts to get them to attack the USSR. Again in September, from the "same source," he told Stalin of German intentions to advance in the direction of the Caspian Sea. Stalin made no reply to Churchill's gifts, but his real opinion of British intelligence men and their secrets emerged during his meeting with Churchill at the Kremlin in August 1942. He reminded the 30 Mission team of how dangerous their work was and "what horrible penalties it might entail," a sally that produced a few nervous giggles and caused Admiral Miles to "go purple in the face."[27]

Nonetheless, 30 Mission continued to do business regarding Japanese OB. Colonel Exham met with Major Gerzenstein on 21 August and 16 September, and the War Office discussed both German and Japanese OB with members of the Soviet mission on 1 September. So promising were these openings that on 25 August 1942, the War Office called on its missions in India, China, New Zealand, and Washington to fetch all the Japanese OB documents they could, because the Russians "cannot understand our lack of documentation" on the Japanese Army, and any such materials "would be of great help" to both the British and the Russians.[28]

The happy OB situation of 30 Mission continued throughout September, with OB meetings regarding the German Army being held on 23 and 29 September, at which the Soviets answered a number of detailed British queries that had been hanging fire for months. No sooner did the British appear to be making headway with the Russians on OB, however, than problems arose with the American cousins. In July, Admiral Miles had erroneously reported to London that the Soviets gave the Americans "practically nothing" in the way of intelligence and that the U.S. mission in Moscow showed "no interest in intelligence cooperation with the Soviets."[29]

Actually, Michela believed that he had finally received War Department authority to keep Faymonville under control, and he therefore began to move energetically into the OB exchange arena. On 1 September, the Soviets handed Michela a short list of German divisions, and a week later, G-2 Washington informed its Moscow mission that the British were gathering OB from the Russians and ordered Michela "urgently" to secure some as well.[30] Ten days later, after a meeting with Red Army officials, Michela sent two pages of German divisional identifications on the Eastern Front to Washington and, in response, received authority to hold fortnightly OB meetings with the Russians as long as *none* of the information acquired was given to the British, a restriction that remained in force until March 1943. Almost instantly Michela launched into OB discussions with the Soviets, who gave him details on a whole series of German regiments fighting on the Eastern Front as of 21 September.[31]

During the subsequent six months, the British and American missions went their separate ways on OB sharing with the Soviets, and neither seems to have gained any marked advantage by going it alone. During most of this period, Soviet attention—as well as that of most of the rest of the world—was riveted on Stalingrad and then on the German counteroffensive at Kharkov. At a time when Moscow wanted information from every possible source, it was not much concerned about Anglo-American troubles or whether the Western powers had formed a common front in dealing with the USSR. By the time of Stalingrad, the USSR held the strong hand on the Eastern Front and was little inclined to pay much of a price for intelligence cooperation with either London or Washington.

Despite G-2's impassioned initial sally, Washington was not keenly interested in pursuing intelligence cooperation with anyone at this time. U.S. Army OB work was still in its infancy, and no systematic Anglo-American cooperation on this subject was going on in Washington, London, or anywhere else. When a 17 October 1942 report from a new U.S. naval representative in Moscow, Comdr. K. Tolley, claimed that the British enjoyed good air OB cooperation with the Soviets—a rather exaggerated claim—no one in the U.S. Army Air Corps or other branches of the compartmentalized American intelligence community seems to have been the least interested.[32]

The one area that G-2 was urgently trying to improve was its Japanese Army order of battle (under the direction of Col. M. W. Pettigrew), even though the U.S. Army had not yet made any serious break-in to Japanese Army codes and ciphers. Pettigrew nonetheless supplied the Soviet embassy in Washington with a two-page summary of the U.S. Army's version of Japanese OB on 30 October 1942, and when General Bradley visited the USSR two months later, the Soviets returned the favor. A senior Russian officer assured the

U.S. Army Air Corps general that the Japanese had "no large air force in Manchuria."[33]

This minuscule exchange of Japanese OB marked the end of the American effort to trade any intelligence with the Soviets for nearly four months. But the British were not inclined to such avoidance or delay. Admiral Miles noted on 1 October that "things were getting better as regards the provision of information concerning the German and Japanese orders of battle." The admiral had learned by hard experience that when the Soviets opened doors it was best not to tarry but to stride briskly through them. There was actually only one full Anglo-Soviet meeting on German order of battle in October (14 October), but on 7 October, General Dubinen confirmed British claims that certain Luftwaffe units had been removed from the Eastern Front. During November, the Soviets were again extremely cautious, and only one more abbreviated session of regular OB meetings occurred. On 17 November, however, Dubinen nonchalantly handed Colonel Exham and his colleagues "a most valuable document" that gave the "latest Soviet details of identifications, together with sources [of] information for nearly all of the 70 German divisions about which the War Office had asked for information." Dubinen's gift led one of the British staff members to exclaim, "this is one of the best pieces of co-operation that we have yet received from the Soviet General Staff." Then on the last day of November, Dubinen's staff also agreed to clarify some of the information on a microfilm of the 1938 Japanese Army list that the Soviets had given to the British earlier, copies of which London had passed on to the Americans.[34]

OB matters then bounced a bit backward in December 1942 and January 1943, just as the British mission was ready to go all-out on German OB cooperation, having received the British version of the German operational plan in the east for 1942–1943 from the War Office on 21 December. Dubinen, always ready to discuss Red Army operations, provided summaries of the situation on the Stalingrad front on 2 December. Two days later, he made a point of answering in detail a request from the Belgian government in exile for information on pro-Nazi Belgian units on the Eastern Front, indicating the locations of the two units the Belgians had inquired about and also revealing the whereabouts of a third unit. One full German OB meeting was held in Moscow in December, and another "good meeting" took place on 6 January.[35] On Christmas Day, perhaps as the ultimate present from an ostensibly atheistic service, the Red Navy declared that it wished to make "cooperation" on German naval OB "closer and more thorough than in the past," whatever happened regarding East-West army intelligence exchange.[36]

Nonetheless, on 10 December, Admiral Miles formally protested to General

Dubinen. The German OB meetings scheduled for each Wednesday were becoming a one-way street, he charged, with Captain Chapman providing substantial information on German OB while the Soviet liaison officer did not even bring "his books of reference or location lists" to some of the meetings.[37] Instead of dealing with these British requests for improvement, the Soviets snubbed Miles's complaints, and Moscow Radio announced in its Stalingrad communiqué of 1 January the whereabouts of two German divisions (6th Panzer and 306 Infantry) whose location Chapman had been seeking in vain since November. Despite a "good" German OB meeting on 6 January 1943, the Soviets added more fuel to the fire by refusing to continue OB meetings on Japan and by once again declaring that German OB cooperation was not working properly because of Britain's failure to launch a Second Front.[38]

In response, 30 Mission finally requested the War Office to retaliate by cutting off Japanese OB cooperation with the Soviets in London as well as in Moscow. Noting that the Soviets were stalling on both German and Japanese OB cooperation, Churchill minuted the foreign secretary on 11 January, "I think we should curl up a bit ourselves,"[39] and implemented a policy of slowdown on OB exchanges with the Soviets in a cabinet meeting on the following day. A month later, on 2 February, the JIC became so fed up with what it saw as Soviet obstructionism that it recommended that "the element of bargaining should be introduced when information is passed to the Russians" and that nothing should be done without a quid pro quo. After three weeks of fuss and consultation, the JIC even drafted a proposed character for 30 Mission, emphasizing intelligence bargaining. In retrospect, the British official history of intelligence continued to make Whitehall's case, thundering against Soviet failings and even asserting that no documentary reports on German OB had been received from the Soviets prior to January 1943. This was certainly off the main point, because most of the OB exchange work in the earlier period had been done in regular give-and-take meetings, without documents being presented by either side.[40]

Despite all this anger and noise in London, little actually changed in the Moscow intelligence exchange process. On 23 January 1943, in obedience to London's direct orders, Admiral Miles tried to pin down Dubinen on whether the Red Army thought that the Germans would hold in the Caucasus, whether the Russians could take Rostow, and how the Red Army managed to cope with the supply problems produced by its 200-mile advance. Dubinen replied that the Soviet staff was uncertain about the chances of taking Rostow (they took it) and thought that although the German situation in the Caucasus "was difficult, it was not critical" (they lost it).[41] Dubinen became heated only in regard to the supply question. Assuming that this was a condescending query about the primitive nature of the Red Army, he replied emphatically that the Soviet advance was supplied like any other army and not by "living off the land."[42]

But the OB exchange machinery continued to clank along. During the regular Anglo-Soviet OB meeting on 3 February, "some" German OB was obtained by the British, and another OB meeting occurred on 13 February. In between these two meetings, the British mission sent Dubinen the summary of an ULTRA report from London setting out the German plan for the evacuation of the Caucasus, which the "most reliable" secret agent had recently "seen."[43]

This rigid routine was suddenly interrupted by a Soviet, rather than a British, initiative. Worried that the Germans might be able to rebuild their battered units quickly, Moscow asked 30 Mission for an immediate special meeting to gauge Germany's manpower and material situation. This request was right up London's alley, and its pleasure at being able to play some of its strongest cards seems to have overcome Whitehall's angry mood and desire for rigid quid pro quos. After some dickering over the time and place for the meeting, the British finally agreed to Moscow in mid-March. Capt. M. M. Chapman, 30 Mission's German OB specialist, then met with a newly appointed Soviet OB expert, Major Lapkin, on 14 March, and in a five-hour session these two men agreed on a general picture of German Army OB and on the strength and placement of German units on the Russian front. This meeting seemingly reestablished the harmonious Anglo-Soviet OB partnership that had existed during the autumn. Exham enthused to the DMI that OB cooperation was "greatly improved" because of the appearance of the man whom one mission member characterized as Chapman's "new friend Lapkin."[44]

Even though the air section of 30 Mission was not as optimistic as the army section about Soviet military power or the level of Red Air Force cooperation, it is fair to say that in March 1943, the 30 Mission leaders felt that they were on something approximating a roll in their intelligence relations with the USSR. The mission therefore assumed rather a superior tone regarding its American colleagues, who appeared to be still lost in darkness and unable to form an effective working relationship with the Russians. In mid-February, Michela, just promoted to brigadier general, had moaned to Admiral Miles that he had been unable to secure secret information from the Soviets. In mid-March, Exham met with Michela, and the two officers tentatively agreed that the Western powers should join forces to press the Soviets into sharing more intelligence with them, but the Foreign Office and the chiefs of staff in London immediately vetoed this idea, presumably feeling that the British were in the stronger position and desiring to keep it that way.[45]

In fact, although the U.S. mission in Moscow was still grumbling that the Russians were being more difficult than ever, and Washington erroneously concluded that the British received German air OB for the whole Eastern Front while the Americans got nothing, Michela and company were really making their first great leap into full-scale German Army intelligence cooperation with the USSR and were well on the way to catching up with the British. On 3 March, Col. James Boswell of Michela's staff held his first German OB meeting with Major Lapkin, the same Soviet intelligence specialist the British were working with. Two days later, Michela and Dubinen joined Lapkin and Boswell for a more wide-ranging discussion intended to explore the question of Germany's ability to rebuild its battered military units—the same question that the British Captain Chapman would explore with the Soviets nine days later. In March, Boswell and Lapkin met a total of nine times to consider German Army OB matters, and though little give-and-take occurred—each side simply read off the answers to the questions that had been posed in the previous meeting—the Americans had moved very far and very fast. Since the U.S. Army's OB work on the German Army was still at a rudimentary stage, the Americans stood to gain substantial benefits from this partnership. From the beginning, the War Department attached considerable value to these exchanges and understood that they had important political implications. Michela's first report on the OB meetings had gone to both U.S. Army intelligence and the White House. On 11 March, Gen. H. Kroner sent Michela a long list of German divisional locations to be passed to the Soviets and emphasized that this information should simply be given to the Red Army. It "should not be contingent on the reciprocal action on the part of the Soviet G-2," he stressed; "in other words G-2 will not bargain but will make available information . . . regardless of Soviet material which might be forthcoming in return."[46]

President Roosevelt's hope of winning over the Russians by kindness and generosity seized hold of the American intelligence exchange process in Moscow. This approach was naive, as the British had already learned. But the Americans' serious OB intelligence work on the German Army was in its infancy, and the White House was well aware of the fact that the Soviets were carrying the bulk of the weight in the German war and that Stalin's Russia would be a mighty force when the time for peacemaking came. Therefore, at this moment, generosity to the USSR had a real—if narrow—logic behind it.

During the latter part of March, Colonel Exham and his 30 Mission colleagues were forced to reverse themselves again as they got wind of the fact that the American team, which they had scorned for so long, had shaken off its prejudices and lethargy. But bound tight by Whitehall's restrictions, 30 Mission could make only feeble overtures to the Americans. No deal could be cut, and the Soviets were left in the pleasant position of being able to play one Anglo-Saxon army mission off against the other in a great Moscow intelligence exchange festival.

Compared with the troubles, frustrations, and rivalries that characterized Anglo-American army intelligence exchanges with the USSR from the summer of 1942 to the spring of 1943, the Royal and U.S. Navies had a relatively agreeable and successful partnership with the Red fleet. Both Western navy missions had much closer direct contact with their counterparts in the Red Navy than did their army and air force colleagues, who had to struggle through the mazelike "Otdel" Soviet liaison system. As already indicated, the Royal Navy was also the primary long-term beneficiary of "Y" cooperation with the Red fleet, and its "Y" intercept station at Polyarnoe continued to churn out useful intelligence throughout this period and beyond. The Royal Navy organization in the Black Sea and the U.S. Navy's attaché office in Vladivostok, as well as the installations of both navies in Archangel and Murmansk, provided numerous opportunities to collect information and make useful contacts with Red Navy personnel.

This was also a very successful period for the northern convoys—only three vessels were lost in the whole of 1943. Alleged Soviet failure to provide adequate convoy protection and the periodic alarms regarding possible German air and land offensives from northern Norway were not urgent enough to produce serious East-West tension. Problems and irritations certainly existed in the north, ranging from poor security to inadequate billeting. Heavy drinking among Anglo-American crews and shore personnel compounded the troubles, just as it may have for the British and American missions in Moscow. But the Royal Navy's primary assignment, in addition to convoy protection, was to keep the Red Navy happy by providing intelligence about the enemy while quietly gaining all possible information about the Red fleet. By at least November 1942, the Admiralty had received enough data on the Russian fleet to produce a regular, updated report called "The Distribution of the U.S.S.R. Naval Forces," which covered the northern, white, and Black Sea fleets in elaborate and precise detail. Coverage of the Baltic and far eastern fleets, which were outside the Royal Navy liaison net, were covered only thinly and schematically.[47]

The U.S. Navy's ties to the Red Navy were not based on an aura of efficiency and primacy, such as clung to the Royal Navy. Rather, it was clear to all Russians by now that the United States was a far more promising prospect for supplies and technical equipment. Yankee bluntness also may have helped. At a Kremlin dinner, the U.S. naval attaché, Captain Duncan, frankly told Stalin that he "was in Russia for the purpose of getting information," whereupon the Soviet dictator rose and announced, "that is the most honest and straightforward statement I have heard tonight."[48]

In addition, the American ambassador, Admiral Standley, was able to make good use of his special professional link with the Red Navy. The minutes of the 18 August meeting in which Admiral Standley, Captain Duncan, and Comdr. R. H. Allen talked shop with the naval commissar, Admiral Kuznetzov, and Captain Zaitsev read like the record of most naval conferences elsewhere in the world. The men chatted about command systems, joint operations, and how to arrange the relationship between navies and coast guards. Standley put in his plug for information on the Japanese Navy, and Kuznetzov replied with the usual Soviet line that they did what they could but were limited by their neutrality toward Japan. Thereafter the Soviets provided the U.S. Navy with the order of battle of their northern and Pacific fleets but asked that these not be passed along to the British.[49]

The U.S. naval mission seems to have received another helping hand when Captain Duncan, while home on leave in Washington, complained to the Soviet naval attaché in the United States, Captain Yegorichev, that his Red Navy superiors in Moscow were not providing Duncan with sufficient information. Yegorichev then reported to the U.S. naval liaison staff that he would do what he could to open doors for Duncan. But although Soviet Navy personnel had been allowed to visit American PT boats in exchange for U.S. visits to Russian submarines, Yegorichev complained that he had received little information from the U.S. Navy Department.[50]

Perhaps in response to Yegorichev's prodding, in late November, the Red Navy gave Duncan a photo booklet on Soviet aircraft, various charts and pamphlets on German coastal defenses in Norway, and bits of weather information. Two months later, the Americans handed the Soviets general reports on the German Navy, silhouettes of Japanese naval vessels, and data on Axis and Japanese submarines. In February–March 1943, a Soviet-American conference was held on naval supply departments, and the Americans furnished additional information on minelaying by German submarines. Then, for no apparent reason, the U.S. Navy decided that this was the appropriate moment to offer one of its priceless treasures to the Russians and formally presented the Red Navy with a print of Walt Disney's film *Bambi*.

This phase of American naval intelligence cooperation with the Soviets thereby floated away in a cloud of farce. But in the preceding nine months, even though no progress had been made on such delicate matters as Soviet-American sharing of "Y" information, the U.S. Navy had made some limited headway in trading bits and pieces of useful data with the Red Navy about themselves and the German Navy.[51]

However, just as was the case with their British counterparts, American naval liaison personnel often boiled over with resentment and indignation at the Soviets' secrecy, remoteness, and reluctance to cooperate. In March 1943, the Red Navy absurdly overplayed its hand by having the Soviet Ministry of Foreign Affairs ask the U.S. embassy in Moscow for "specifications of the latest American battleship, cruiser, destroyer, and submarine," plus plans and drawings of U.S. torpedoes and details of American naval "secret ciphering devices."[52]

When Captain Duncan learned of this Soviet request, he exploded, sending off a long, angry dispatch to Washington denouncing this "unprecedented request." Duncan argued that the Soviets had used the lend-lease system to secure the "majority of our army's most modern equipment," but they knew that the Navy would "not give another nation the fruits of [our] long technical experience without reciprocal treatment." The Soviets had therefore gone through American "civil organizations"—the U.S. embassy—to get their hands on American naval technology. In Duncan's view, the Soviets repeatedly refused or delayed American requests for Soviet and enemy weapons and were so technically backward that the U.S. secrets they sought could have "no possible value to them in [the present] war." Therefore, only misplaced "sentiment or plain stupidity" could, in the captain's view, possibly prompt the U.S. government to meet the Soviet requests. Duncan concluded that although he had "full sympathy with the Russian people" and "heartily" wanted to assist them in this war, the attempt to be open-handed with the Soviet authorities had failed. The U.S. government should mobilize its lend-lease and public-opinion assets and go over to "a hard boiled horse trading basis" of dealing with the Soviet government.[53]

Duncan's outburst paralleled many of the angry lamentations that Macfarlane and other officers in 30 Mission had sent to Whitehall over the preceding twenty months. The angry British calls for a new approach had invariably been energetically opposed by the Foreign Office and then rejected by the Cabinet. Duncan's March 1943 dispatch, however, received a different reception in Washington. Immediately upon its receipt, the Navy Department passed it on to Undersecretary Sumner Welles of the State Department, who forwarded it to Secretary Hull. It then went to a team of senior foreign service officers—Raymond Atherton, James Dunn, and Loy Henderson (all of whom had years of experience in State Department campaigns against Communist subversives). These men, along with Secretary Hull, concluded that "the advice given by Captain Duncan should be followed."[54]

Admiral Standley had sent his own dispatch from the Moscow embassy echoing Duncan's views, and the State Department arranged for both documents to be sent to the White House. Although the documents and the transmission letter remain in the Map Room files, there is no indication whether President Roosevelt read the documents or whether he gave the red light or the green light or, as frequently occurred, chose the amber light for caution. What is clear is that the State Department and the Navy Department had locked arms to bar any giveaway of battle fleet technology. These two American government departments had also concluded that the time had come to play hardball in the Soviet-American intelligence game.[55]

A hard-line American team was therefore ready to take the field, but only the next six months would show whether those inclined to play a rougher intelligence game with the Soviets would be able to carry the president with them, or whether the prevailing pattern of begging, borrowing, giving, and bartering would remain the order of the day.

7
The First Victorious Summer, April–September 1943

Spring and summer 1943 marked the concluding phase of the fourth year of the European war, as well as the halfway mark in the Pacific war. The advances made by the Allies in this period demonstrated that they were finally well on their way to crushing their enemies. Although the advance in the Pacific continued to be slow, with bitter and brutal slugging matches in New Guinea and the Solomons, the British and American armored forces joined hands at Gafra on 7 April, trapping the Afrika Korps in a huge pocket in northern Tunisia. Five weeks later, all Axis forces in North Africa capitulated, and a vast army of prisoners fell into Anglo-American hands, including 125,000 Germans. For the first time since the war began, Britain and the United States were able to celebrate a truly significant victory over Nazi Germany. The large bag of German prisoners they seized indicated that the West had finally moved into the big leagues of war. As occurred on the Eastern Front, advances were logged in hundreds of miles, and casualties were inflicted in the hundreds of thousands.

To toast their triumph and plan future operations, Roosevelt and Churchill met in Washington (12–25 May). They agreed to invade Italy after the forthcoming invasion of Sicily and set 1 May 1944 as the date for the D-day invasion of northern France. On 10 July, Anglo-American forces landed in Sicily, seizing the island in forty days and so damaging the image of Fascism and its leader that Benito Mussolini fell from power in late July. Once again, Churchill and Roosevelt joined together in the wake of a triumph, this time in Quebec. On this occasion, they agreed on the details of a future operation, deciding to undertake a simultaneous invasion of northern France (Operation OVERLORD) and southern France (Operation ANVIL) to help force the German occupation forces out of Western Europe. The last serious plunge forward by the Western powers occurred in early September 1943 when Montgomery crossed the

Straits of Messina, prompting the Italian monarch to run away from his German partner and capitulate to the Allies on 8 September.

The following day, the main Allied invasion of Italy waded ashore at Salerno, south of Naples. But then things began to go wrong, and the Western powers fell into a bitter slugging match with the German Army in terrain that favored the defense. They managed to take Naples in October, but the advance north was a nightmare. Rome did not fall until June 1944, and the Western powers reached the Po Valley only shortly before Generals Eisenhower and Zhukov crushed the last flickers of resistance in the German homeland during the spring of 1945.

As if to underscore Western disappointment that its great 1943 offensive had slowed to a crawl on the Salerno beaches, the Red Army chose the high summer of 1943 to put on another awesome and decisive display of military power. Between 5 and 15 July, in the greatest tank battle of the war, the Soviets stopped cold the great attack that Hitler hurled at Kursk. Then, ignoring the tradition that had prevailed on the Eastern Front since June 1941—that only the winter belonged to the Soviets, whereas the summer season was for German offensives—the Red Army smashed westward, seized Orel by 5 August, and drove on in the direction of the Dnieper, the Soviet western frontier, and German-occupied Poland.

With Russian triumphs once again exceeding those of the West, mid-1943 was inevitably a time of troubles, as well as successes, in East-West intelligence relations. Military triumph did nothing to lessen Stalinist hostility and suspicion regarding the West. Soviet officials continued to be nearly as difficult and abusive as before, as disparaging about Western military operations, and as eager to secure Western supplies and technology. And they were still calling for the immediate launching of a Second Front. Although Kerr and Molotov enjoyed a cordial patch in their troubled relationship, the Western powers continued to be tormented by the East-West political atmosphere, often playing their hand badly and frequently appearing to be bumbling and incompetent.[1]

After publicly denouncing the Soviets' failure to show gratitude for American supplies in March 1943, Ambassador Standley neither pushed his criticism further nor resigned. Instead, after receiving assurances of support from some American and Allied diplomats and indications from the Soviets that he was now persona non grata, he simply stood (or rather, sat) his ground, while indicating to Washington that he would not serve as ambassador beyond October 1943. The Roosevelt White House, as was its custom, did not react to the situation energetically, so Standley lingered on in the U.S. embassy in Moscow, isolated and ineffectual, as the whole diplomatic corps was returning from Kubyshev and diplomatic business as usual was returning to the Russian capital.[2]

The American Moscow team also continued to be weakened by internecine warfare between Faymonville's lend-lease mission and the office of the military attaché. Faymonville still went his own way—"an enigma inside an enigma" one of his wartime aides recently called him—steadfastly refusing to provide the military attachés with any intelligence information acquired during his own travels through Soviet Russia, although members of his staff filed such reports from all areas of the USSR, including Baku and Vladivostok. The U.S. Army's military attaché office also continued to make its own generous contribution to the ineffectiveness of the American team. Michela and Park declined to grant the Russians any trace of respect, to acknowledge that the process of intelligence exchange had improved, or to recognize that the Red Army and Air Force were clearly winning the eastern war against the much-vaunted Wehrmacht. The backstairs grumbling of the attaché, embassy, and lend-lease staffs also lowered the status of the American mission in British eyes. Hopkins even confided to the British ambassador in Washington during April that Michela and company's anti-Russian attitude had to have bad effects on East-West cooperation.[3]

Although the British had a strong and effective ambassador with reasonable access to Stalin in the person of the wily and frequently inaudible Archibald Clark Kerr,[4] Whitehall also seemed to go out of its way in the summer of 1943 to undercut his position and that of 30 Mission by making a series of damaging military appointments to the mission, as well as embarking on a get-tough policy with the Soviets that it was unable to sustain. As a permanent replacement for Macfarlane, London finally selected Gen. Sir Gifford LeQuesne Martel as head of the mission. Martel had flowered as a tank expert in the 1930s, and his book on armored warfare had even been translated into Russian. But Martel's wartime combat performance had been lackluster, and after a brief and undistinguished assignment in the western desert, he had been put on the shelf. Blinkered and self-satisfied, Martel was excessively "domineering," with a deadly touch of condescension ("The Russian is an Asiatic . . . strangely enough we have never really understood Asiatics"), and he was perfectly tuned to offend the Soviets and turn 30 Mission into a warring camp. The general patronized his British colleagues in Moscow, later even characterizing Kerr as "old and getting past his job" and "somewhat out of touch."[5]

Despite these liabilities, Martel managed to make a good start. His reception by Stalin went well. Martel succeeded in keeping his penchant for condescension under control, only noting later that although Stalin was "quite sound as a whole . . . like all great men he had some special hobbies about warfare," which the general, out of courtesy, "thought it wise to let him get away with." The Soviet leader was "friendly and interested" and warmed up so much as the conversation went on that Kerr thought that Martel "was to be congratulated." Almost immediately, however, serious trouble began. The chiefs of staff had provided Martel with a new "charter" for the mission, calling for him to establish a broad range of order-of-battle and technological sharing arrangements with the Soviets, as well as procedures for the military staffs of the two countries to swap information on their plans and intentions. As Whitehall should certainly have realized by this time, such comprehensive arrangements were completely beyond the realm of the possible. It should also have been obvious that Martel "was not an easy man to work with" and would not make a calm effort to make what headway he could or work quietly with his service and diplomatic colleagues. Whitehall nonetheless pushed on, increasing the troubles by sending Rear Adm. Douglas Fisher from Archangel to Moscow to head the naval section of 30 Mission, thereby confronting Martel with a nominal subordinate who was actually a senior officer from the other service with far more Russian knowledge and experience than Martel would ever acquire. Then, on 16 June, a new head of the air section of the mission arrived in the person of Air Marshal Sir John Babbington, who actually outranked Martel. Though not as eccentric as the new 30 Mission chief (Babbington did not entertain all comers with tales of tiger hunts won and lost), the new head of the air section was highly conscious of his status and was more than willing to defend every inch of his turf.[6]

Martel and Babbington quickly fell into battle. A member of the staff noted as early as 22 June 1943 that "storms are brewing already." Babbington was tough, and he had "lots of medals and an eyeglass."[7] The situation became nearly impossible when, without consultation, General Martel gave the Soviets the Mosquito aircraft that had been provided for Babbington's personal use. The rest of the mission was thereafter compelled to walk softly and snigger in the hallways as the battle of the British mission leaders roared out of control, until Babbington was ordered to return to London in mid-September. Throughout the three months of 30 Mission's civil war, Kerr could only lament that after having long requested that veterans with combat experience be sent to Moscow, he had been saddled with two staff officer peacocks, neither of whom bore "the smell of battle." Martel merely exuded "the vague redolence about him of the petrol and lubricating oil that go with tanks."[8]

In addition to these domestic difficulties within the British and American missions in Moscow, the potential for trouble in East-West cooperation was intensified by the many individuals in those missions who, together with Washington and London, kept badgering the Soviets with requests for information that Moscow was determined not to supply. The Russians had repeatedly indicated an unwillingness to deal with the West on intelligence related to Japan, because of fears that the Tokyo government might attack the USSR. Yet the Americans attempted to use intelligence regarding the Japanese Army as trade bait for barter between April and June 1943. The Soviets rebuffed these overtures, but this did not stop an Anglo-American gathering in Washington, concerned with deception planning, from recommending that Russia's possible entry into the war against Japan be used to frighten the Japanese and pin down Japanese forces in the Home Islands and Manchuria. Such black propaganda activities as these most likely intensified Soviet suspicion of the Western powers if the truth about them ever found its way to Moscow.[9]

Such ill-advised Western adventures were exceeded by the dangerous activities carried on by the Soviet authorities, ranging from the secret-agent work of Philby and company to Communist Party and fellow-traveler pressure on the Western governments to do anything that Moscow desired. The Soviets also combined a rich talent for committing atrocities with an unerring ability to shoot themselves in the foot when their misdeeds became known. April 1943 marked the beginning of the Nazi-Soviet propaganda battles over which of them had murdered hundreds of Polish officers at Katyn. The likelihood that the Soviets had done it—which has been confirmed since the fall of the Soviet system—did considerable damage to East-West relations in 1943, and Moscow's clumsy and frenzied effort to blame the Germans made matters worse. It inflamed anti-Soviet sentiment in the United States and Britain (especially among the Polish population) and added new burdens for the Westerners who had to deal with a Soviet officialdom that thought that stonewalling and counteraccusation were the epitome of political wit and wisdom.[10]

In April 1943, for example, at a time when British officials were increasingly irritated by the Soviet refusal to provide sensitive intelligence, the head of the Soviet mission in London, Admiral Kharlamov, had the gall to complain to the Admiralty that "he was being supplied with insufficient information about the enemy" and that the questions he put to the Naval Intelligence Division were often met with the phrase "we have no information." Kharlamov's complaint drove the Admiralty into a white fury, and the naval staff refuted Kharlamov's accusation by citing the masses of information that had been provided on the equipment and methods of the Royal Navy, as well as those of the Axis and the Japanese.[11] In the process of dealing with what it saw as a Soviet provocation, the Royal Navy took stock of just how much it had been providing to the Soviets and how much they had picked up tangentially through the highly qualified Red Navy engineering officers stationed in Britain. The Admiralty thereupon concluded that much of this intelligence and technical information had been acquired not to defeat the Axis but to reconstruct and build anew the Soviet naval and merchant fleets after the war was over. Admiralty officials consequently resolved (after compelling Kharlamov to retract his accusations) to temper the flow of intelligence and high-grade naval technical information that would be provided to the USSR, although routine matters such as protection for the northern convoys and the intelligence activities of the British naval liaison officer in the Black Sea would continue with little change.[12]

A sterner Admiralty attitude also manifested itself in regard to the delicate matters of "Y" and code breaking. During the late winter and early spring of 1943, Ambassador Kerr had been quietly working to get active Anglo-Soviet "Y" cooperation back on track, even evoking Stalin's help—successfully, it seems—to keep the cooperative process moving. Then in February–March 1943, the British authorities in north Russia faced a threat from the local Soviet commander to close "Wye Cottage"—presumably as part of the crisis involving Soviet police clashes with British sailors—and 30 Mission sprang into action, seeking to mollify the Russians by giving serious consideration to a long-standing Moscow request that two of its naval "Y" staff be allowed to study radio interception measures and methods in Britain. On 29 April, the "Y" board finally approved in principle a two-man Red Navy visit to study British radio intercept procedures (but not the most secret British code-breaking center at Bletchley Park) and also authorized the delivery of material setting out the operation of the Luftwaffe's air-ground signaling system (AUKA), which Crankshaw had brought from Britain the previous year.

British "Y" operations in north Russia proceeded smoothly during the next three months, and interservice rivalries were stilled sufficiently for a member of the British Army section of 30 Mission to tour Wye Cottage. In mid-July, presumably as a sign of comradeship and as a token of gratitude for the "Y" bounty they were receiving in the north, the British government gave the Soviet naval mission in London a sample German ENIGMA machine, although presumably nothing was revealed to Kharlamov's colleagues about the most secret British cipher-breaking activities at Bletchley Park.[13]

Even then Wye Cottage was not completely secure. In early July, the British Navy missions in Archangel and Moscow, as well as the Admiralty, were outraged by the harshness with which the Soviet police continued to treat British seamen in north Russian ports and searched for countermeasures that would force the Russians to abandon their strong-arm tactics. The navy mission in Moscow concluded that everything should be tried, including evacuation from

Archangel, to compel the Soviets to change course—everything, that is, except anything that might put Wye Cottage at risk. During the next four weeks, the highest offices of Whitehall—the Admiralty, Foreign Office, chiefs of staff, and Number 10 Downing Street—echoed the mission's outrage and demand for strong countermeasures, as long as nothing was done that might lead to "the abandonment of the 'Y' service [which] would be a definite loss to our intelligence.[14] By August, the crisis had passed, sailors and police were better behaved, and "Y" cooperation in the north had improved considerably. The chief of Wye Cottage, Lt. C. B. C. Chalkley, proposed that he journey to Moscow to discuss the situation with the Soviet liaison officer for "Y" matters (a Colonel Magnitky), in order to guarantee that British radio interception in the north would not be threatened again. But this scheme was immediately vetoed by Cecil Barclay, the embassy secret intelligence service (SIS) "Y" representative. Barclay was engaged in sensitive discussions with the Soviets, and the ball was in the Russian court. Barclay, presumably speaking for the "Y" board, wished to keep it there and maintain the pressure on Moscow. Chalkley therefore stayed in north Russia, the negotiations in Moscow regarding broader Anglo-Soviet "Y" cooperation ultimately failed, the British "Y" representative was recalled, and the two Red Navy specialists were still not given their "Y" visit to Britain. The great crisis had passed, however, and Wye Cottage continued to function smoothly until the end of the European war.[15]

But even while the northern "Y" crisis was lumbering on from subcrisis to subcrisis in the spring and summer of 1943, other aspects of East-West intelligence cooperation rolled along more smoothly, and frequently with considerable success. During April, the British agreed to give the Soviets information on Luftwaffe RDF; in return, the Soviets allowed General Martel and his staff to examine the Red Army's front-line heavy tank, the T-34.[16] The British also had a useful army OB meeting on 24 April. But overall, it seems that the Americans did better than the British on army and air exchanges during this period, which may have prompted 30 Mission to search out new sources of information on Soviet ground and air forces. In April, the British closely questioned the Canadian military attaché (Brig. H. Lefebvre) to obtain every scrap of information he had on Red Air Force operations and equipment.[17]

Meanwhile, the Americans made the most of their unexpectedly rosy opportunities. Michela even secured some information on German chemical warfare. Boswell and McCabe had lengthy OB meetings with the Soviets on 12 and 19 April, and G-2 Washington was uncharacteristically bullish about the results, noting that the information was "most valuable" and adding that it was "essential" that the meetings be continued, because "Soviet order of battle [on] their front [is] very accurate," though less so for other areas. To keep this flow of information coming, the U.S. Army (in sharp contrast to the British practice) decided on 20 April that it would no longer provide operational OB information to the Soviet military attaché in Washington, concentrating all the exchanges in Moscow to keep as close as possible to the source of the "most valuable" Soviet OB information on the German Army.[18]

The U.S. Navy lagged behind the U.S. Army in acquiring Soviet secrets at this time, but it did obtain a list of Soviet destroyers and small craft in the northern fleet in early April. It also secured a number of worthwhile travel reports on Siberia, including two on the Trans-Siberian Railroad and one on the Vladivostok airport. The U.S. Navy still hoped to get rich intelligence from its newly posted assistant attaché in Vladivostok, and in early April it sent him a report on Japanese vessels in the area to help him "make 'face' by presenting it to such [Red] Naval Official [as] you believe most suitable."[19]

During May and June, intelligence exchange between East and West generally improved, a fact that clashes sharply with the long-held view that summer 1943 marked a low point in Soviet-American relations. The importance given to Eastern Front matters by London and Washington also increased, because the Germans were once again preparing for a knockout blow on the Russian front. After overcoming overly optimistic conclusions that German offensive power in the east was spent, the Western powers correctly concluded that Hitler intended to launch his attack in late May or early June. But the German high command kept delaying the start date, partly because Hitler counted heavily on the new Panther tank and the mammoth Ferdinand self-propelled gun to tip the balance of the battle, and production bottlenecks and repeated modifications delayed their delivery. The British warning of German intentions to strike Kursk in Operation ZITADELLA, which was apparently given to the Russians at the end of April, seems to have come to Moscow much too early. Hitler did not give the final attack order until the beginning of July.[20]

Premature warnings were also provided by the Americans. Beginning on 1 May, a series of highly secret MAGRUS messages (very thinly disguised MAGIC intercepts: MAG[ic] plus RUS[sia] equaling MAGRUS) warned the Soviets to be ready for a German attack. On 1 May, a MAGRUS message declared that in late April the Japanese had tried to persuade Hitler to concentrate his offensive power against Britain and the United States, but "Germany is adhering to [the] decision to launch a great offensive against [the] Soviet Army in 1943." On 5 May, Michela delivered this information to the Russian staff, who "received [it] without comment or display of interest." A week later, Michela was sent a second MAGRUS message: "A German official has informed an Axis diplomat [presumably Oshima, the Japanese ambassador in Berlin] that Hitler on May 7th departed from Berlin enroute to German GHQ in the Ukraine and that a general offensive has reached the stage of active preparations."[21] This message too was presumably passed on to the Soviets, who were also well-prepared by their own sources for an attack on Kursk. In fact, ZITADELLA seems to have been one of the most widely anticipated major offensives of the whole war. British intelligence reported to Churchill on 13 May that the most likely initial German offensive action would be the pinching off of Kursk. But the Nazi command continued to delay, and during this long interregnum, both East and West renewed their efforts to cooperate, as if seeking insurance against the offensive power of Nazi Germany. Even the Western combat commanders realized that the fate of the Allied cause depended on the Russians holding at Kursk. One of Eisenhower's close aides noted in his diary on 27 May 1943, "the real war is still being fought in Russia."[22]

Consequently, both the British and the American missions in Moscow had frequent, and often unusually long, OB meetings with their Soviet counterparts in the run up to Kursk. The American team was strengthened by the arrival from Washington of a trained specialist in German Army OB, Lt. Robert Hall, who was very good at detail but could not easily wheel and deal with the Russians. Four Soviet-American OB meetings occurred in May alone. Those of 10 and 31 May were especially detailed, with the Soviets providing information on Croatian and Fascist Italian units, in addition to German units, and expressing genuine gratitude for the American provision of data on Finnish units. General Strong once again praised the accuracy and detail of the Soviet information on the Russo-German front and told Michela to let "nothing jeopardize [its] continued transmission" to Washington.[23]

The seriousness of the situation on the Eastern Front also brought the British and American OB teams in Moscow together for the first time, with Chapman and Hall conferring on 2 May. In addition to the customary Anglo-Soviet exchanges, General Martel secured extensive information on the declining quality of German divisions in the East, and on 28 May he was supplied with a Soviet diagram of the German order of battle on the Eastern Front that the mission considered to be highly valuable. Along with the usual OB fare in this period, the British gave the Red Army a special ration of information secured from the interrogation of German and Italian officers captured in North Africa who had earlier served on the Eastern Front and therefore had meaningful things to say about the war in the east. London also supplied occasional ULTRA tidbits, and on 28 May, General Dubinen especially thanked the British for all these acts of generosity. In an unprecedented moment of candor, he told Gen-

eral Martel that the Soviets had received a report of "large German troop concentrations at Velikie Luki" from an "untested" source and inquired whether the
British could confirm this information.[24]

Although 30 Mission was unable to do so, this incident is especially interesting because of the oft-told tale of the Soviet agent "Lucy." According to the
story, secret information was given to the Soviets that had been filched from
British secret sources in 1943. One of the noteworthy elements in the story
is the claim that Lucy reported to Moscow in May 1943 that the *Germans*
believed that there were large concentrations of *Russian* troops near Velikie
Luki. The documents now in hand show that the information that the Soviets
held in May 1943 was precisely the opposite (German concentrations rather
than Russian at Velikie Luki). To clarify matters they did not depend on their
secret agents but operated completely above board and asked the British mission for confirmation, all of which adds another quotient of doubt to the already
complicated and highly suspect story of secret-agent Lucy.[25]

Whatever remaining insights conspiracy theories may or may not bring to
the history of Soviet intelligence relations with the West in World War II, it is
clear that the Kursk era created an atmosphere in which General Martel was
able to secure unusually generous treatment from the Soviet authorities. On 21
April, Martel had a lengthy conference with Marshal Vassilevsky, and two days
later, General Dubinen offered the British mission chief a free choice of a visit
to any sector of the Russian front he wished. Martel chose the Upper Donets
Basin, and on 11 May 1943, he began an eight-day visit accompanied by 30
Mission's Col. L. M. Theakstone and Air Commodore D. N. Roberts, as well as
the U.S. military attaché Colonel Michela and the assistant attaché Major Park.
During the visit, Martel and Roberts collected detailed OB on Russian and German units on the southwestern front, which was sent on to London. The British
and American officers had an excellent opportunity to measure the strength and
effectiveness of the Soviet military machine.[26]

Due to his transcendent ego, the acquisition of so much special information
made General Martel even less effective in his post and more difficult to live
with. This situation was compounded when, shortly after his return to
Moscow, Martel was also granted extended interviews with members of the
Soviet general staff, including the head of the Red Army tank directorate. The
British general fairly glowed about the resulting "very much improved relations with the Russians." Since the Soviets' openness with General Martel
occurred precisely when Air Marshal Babbington arrived in Moscow, the
inevitable result was to give the intense civil war within the British mission an
ill-mannered earnestness.[27]

Jurisdictional clashes were also easy to ignite within 30 Mission at this time, because the air mission was having significant successes and was not prepared to hide them under a basket. The RAF team in Moscow had three valuable visits in June. Collier declared that when he went to Stalingrad he saw everything he wanted to see. A close RAF examination of a Soviet YAK 3 aircraft had also been made, and there had been a visit to the Monimo night bomber station. Even more interesting to the Air Ministry was what Cheshire had acquired on the Soviet Air Force signals organization. London stated that this was the first information it had obtained from any source on Russian ground control of combat aircraft. But even this was not sufficient to make the Air Ministry blithely open-handed, and it consistently refused to give the Russians the secret of the RAF's "invisible rays" (i.e., radar) for night operations.[28] But the spring and summer of 1943 produced a bonanza of information on German and Soviet weapons from the Soviet high command. By late May 30 Mission had obtained two types of Soviet antitank rifles, and in June, the British secured samples of Russian rocket artillery. During May, the British were also given a large hoard of captured Wehrmacht equipment, including antiaircraft guns, tanks, and a six-barreled German mortar. All this German equipment was crated up in early June and shipped to Britain by sea.[29]

The Americans were not as fortunate as the British in their Russian journeys in the second half of 1943, although besides the visit Michela and Park made to southern Russia with General Martel (which seems to have been very lightly reported to Washington), Admiral Standley made a tour of Stalingrad. A far more controversial American traveler through Russia was the strongly pro-Soviet former U.S. ambassador to Moscow, Joseph E. Davies, who returned in May 1943 to examine the scene of his earlier diplomatic activities. Davies's arrival drove Admiral Standley to distraction, even though the screening in the Kremlin of Davies's fanciful and fawning film, *Mission to Moscow,* seems to have put nearly everyone to sleep, including that most enthusiastic film fan and august leader, Joseph Stalin.[30]

The American mission was also much less fortunate than the British in securing German or Russian equipment in Moscow. In late June, Michela and company made another fruitless effort to entice the Soviets into exchanging intelligence on Japanese Army OB, just three months before the U.S. Army made its decisive break-in to Japanese Army codes and ciphers. But on 10 June, American officers in Moscow acquired a copy of a highly valuable report on the operation of German tank-buster aircraft, which had been captured by the Soviets.[31] An even greater bonanza for the U.S. Army Air Corps was the "escape" of one of the Doolittle bomb crews that had crash-landed in Soviet territory after the 1942 raid on Tokyo. The Soviets had surreptitiously made the "escape" possible, and the British had slipped the crew into India. This was the first of a series of Soviet-engineered "escapes" of interned American bomb crews, and their release gained the Soviets genuine and undying gratitude from the top brass of the U.S. Army Air Corps. The American Army and Army Air Corps leaders also had reason to hope for better overall intelligence cooperation with the Soviets, because the Red Army indicated that it might be prepared to accept that Michela, not Faymonville, should be the primary recipient of informal Soviet favors.[32]

May and June 1943 brought a trickle of benefits to the British Navy mission in Russia, especially to Captain Garwood in the Black Sea, who visited the Soviet cruiser *Krazny Kaukau* in mid-June and provided the Admiralty with details on the Red Sea base at Poti, which were subsequently forwarded to both the U.S. and Canadian Navies.[33] But generally the U.S. Navy seems to have done better than the Royal Navy, arranging to exchange naval mines and gaining data on Russian submarine strength in the north and details on Soviet anti-submarine and coastal defenses in the same area. Additionally, the U.S. Navy acquired a detailed description of a Soviet destroyer, and U.S. Navy officers managed to explore many points in the Soviet Union during midsummer 1943, including Vladivostok, Baku, Archangel, and Stalingrad. Everywhere they went, these U.S. Navy liaison officers acquired considerable information on Russian military and naval installations, transport systems, and anything else that might conceivably have military significance. In exchange for these new intelligence-acquiring opportunities, the U.S. Navy supplied the Russians with data on some U.S. Navy equipment and methods (although not the highest-level technical and design information the Soviets had recently requested) and turned over significant amounts of intelligence on the enemy, ranging from details on Japanese heavy ships under construction to the arrival of German subchasers in Finland, as well as a copy of the Japanese Merchant Navy's recognition manual.[34]

As high summer approached, East-West intelligence relations came to pivot around three important battles. Kursk dominated the military action, attacks by Russian policemen on British seamen in northern ports was the focal point of East-West political conflict, and the Babbington-Martel clashes were the most significant internal phenomenon of the Western missions in Moscow.

When the Germans struck at Kursk on 5 July, the British mission in Moscow was actually taken by surprise. Colonel Turner noted in his diary that the attack had come "contrary to expectations," a remark that indicates that during the long series of delays in the launching of the German offensive, British intelligence had lost its grip on German intentions. Highly secret reports from a German source, perhaps an agent, prompted MI 14 to observe on 20 June 1943 that the Germans "do not intend to launch a big offensive on the Eastern front this summer."[35] A July 1943 Foreign Office comment stated that the British authorities had known in advance of the German attack set for 1 May but had not known why the German attack plan had been altered and ultimately delayed until mid-July. This information should put yet another nail in the coffin of conspiracy theorists inclined to believe that London refused to give the Soviets full information on the attack due to hostility to Moscow, when the more obvious and likely cause seems to be that Whitehall was at sea once the German attack failed to come on 1 May.[36]

In any event, during the crucial sixteen days of the Kursk battle, 30 Mission sent a steady flow of information to London, tracking Germany's initial "considerable success" and the importance of the fact that the Russians were "holding the haunches of the German break-in with great determination" and were resolved to "avoid mobile warfare in which [the] Germans would have [the] definite advantage."[37] Colonel Turner had a discussion about Kursk with a senior Russian liaison officer on 8 July, and by 9–10 July, the British mission staff had concluded that the German attempt to break through had failed. General Martel, with his customary insensitivity, was already claiming that he was the one who had convinced the Soviets to allow the Germans to make the initial thrust and then counter it with Soviet armor.[38]

No British or American officers were allowed to visit the Kursk battlefront, and much to General Martel's indignation, the Soviets "concealed from the Mission" the launching of their own attack on Orel on 17 July.[39] But Moscow was very generous with information of the technical surprises the Germans sprang during the Kursk battle, and in August, the U.S. ambassador and the British air attaché were allowed to visit Stalingrad. Thirty Mission received some data on Hitler's new secret self-propelled gun, the Ferdinand, by 9 July, although a number of armored experts in London persisted in the erroneous belief that this information was mistaken and that the weapon in question was really a modified Tiger tank. By 26 July, the British mission had been supplied with four pages of technical details on the Ferdinand and the new German Panther tank, information that London called "particularly valuable" because these German weapons had not been used against British forces.[40]

As soon as the critical stage of the Kursk battle had passed, the Red Army also resumed regular OB conferences with the British mission; OB meetings occurred on 19 and 26 July. Relations were so smooth and prospects for Anglo-Soviet military cooperation so rosy that the War Office even had 30 Mission approach the Russians with a request for technical assistance as the British tried to develop their own "heavy rockets." There is, however, no indication in the available files that the Soviets actually provided such highly secret technical assistance to their Western wartime allies.[41]

Even so, Anglo-Soviet military cooperation was definitely much improved, and the same was true of American military relations with the USSR in Moscow. The U.S. mission not only had three post-Kursk OB meetings with the Red Army but also had one on 12 July, while the fighting was still at white heat. Furthermore, the American mission had a protracted meeting with a senior officer of the Red Army tank directorate on 7 July (just as Kursk began). By 28 July, G-2 Washington had concluded that the Eastern Front OB it was receiving from its mission in Moscow was so valuable that it should concentrate all its efforts to exchange Eastern Front information in Moscow rather than Washington. So rich were the pickings for the Americans in the USSR that by 4 August General Michela was complaining that the exchanges were not fair because the Russians had so much more information to give than did the Americans.[42]

Although the Soviets still refused to provide any substantial information on their own forces, no one in the mission or in Washington had grounds to complain about Soviet generosity in sharing technical information with the U.S. Army on the new German Ferdinand self-propelled gun. On 21 July, the mission sent home a long *Red Star* article on the Ferdinand. Three days later, the mission acquired a full report on the Ferdinand from the Red general staff, including details of its armor thickness (ranging from 200 mm on its front plate to 40 mm on the floor of the "combat compartment"), weight, height, speed, armament, and so forth, plus three photographs of Ferdinands that had been captured by the Russians. The next week, Michela sent home another detailed report on the Ferdinand from the *Red Star,* followed by two sketches and a general description of a light Soviet self-propelled gun that Col. Robert McCabe had observed in Moscow.[43]

July brought the successful visit of an Anglo-American surgical mission to Moscow, and the Soviet military mission in Britain was allowed to visit British field exercises. The American World War I air ace Eddie Rickenbacker reported so favorably on his tour of the Soviet Union that he appeared to believe that this land was the home of all things bright and beautiful. Ambassador Standley, who was now definitely on his way out, had been somewhat pacified by a trip to the Urals and a special tour of a collective farm. U.S. Navy personnel also had another useful travel and survey period, with the attaché, Captain Duncan, touring Baku, and another naval officer scouting out the details of a possible air route from Washington to Siberia. The U.S. Navy also received a survey from the Red Navy of Luftwaffe deployment in Norway, plus six documents on Russian naval artillery, more information on Russian naval mines, pilot information on Vladivostok, and some coastal maps of Siberia.[44]

With the survival and future importance of the Soviet Union fully assured by the Battle of Kursk, and the U.S. Navy and Army gaining real intelligence benefits from the USSR, even the OSS showed signs of awakening from its deep hibernation regarding Soviet affairs. In mid-July, William Langer of the Research and Analysis (R&A) Branch made his first effort to station a representative in Moscow to acquire Soviet publications, and by September, the OSS R&A Branch had produced a comprehensive paper titled "The Basis of Soviet Foreign Policy," stressing the tough pragmatism of Stalin's Russia.[45]

In August, the British stationed an RAF photo reconnaissance unit in north Russia to assist a Red Air Force attack on *Tirpitz*. But this was the period when Russian arrests of British personnel in the north reached their zenith, and Churchill ordered preparations to be made to withdraw all British personnel, except, of course, those in "Wye Cottage." The British naval intelligence team in Russia seems to have netted virtually nothing in the way of valuable intelligence (except "Y") during the late summer, even though those in the "other service" were enjoying the rich harvest of the Kursk period.[46]

In mid-July, the positions of all branches of 30 Mission were undermined by the heated exchange between Martel and Babbington, which was now raging in full force. On 1 July, C. F. A. Warner of the Foreign Office voiced his concern. Even a member of the mission who had fought against the Bolsheviks in 1919 (Maj. T. Salt) believed that there were too many people in the mission "who dislike Russia and the Russians and make no particular effort to conceal their feelings."[47] A week later (6 July), a member of the army section of the mission was shocked to discover that a diplomat in the British embassy thought that his job and that of his colleagues would be easier if the whole of 30 Mission was sent packing.[48] Certainly British diplomats were not saints, nor were they always particularly clever, but on 22 July, the 30 Mission chiefs—Martel, Babbington, and Fisher—were compelled to meet with Ambassador Kerr in an effort to iron out their difficulties. All that seems to have resulted from this encounter, however, was another sharp division between Martel, who sang the praises of the mission and its alleged achievements, and Fisher and Babbington, who thought that most of the mission's intelligence activities in Moscow were useless. They wanted to send much of the staff home and thought that the mission itself should be abolished, leaving British service attachés to liaise with the Soviet authorities. There the Babbington-Martel controversy lay suspended, with Kerr unable to resolve the problems and the wheels of Whitehall grinding much too slowly to produce a prompt solution.[49] Then as summer 1943 eased its way toward autumn, high-level military and diplomatic developments began to intervene that would soon shake liaison arrangements, as well as East-West intelligence relations, into a new configuration.

After taking Orel and Byelgorod, the Red Army drove westward, turning the summer into a Soviet offensive campaign season for the first time. At the same time, Patton's tanks shot across Sicily, temporarily creating the impression that perhaps the whole Nazi-Fascist new order in Europe might be on the verge of collapse. The Western powers were gripped by both exaltation at the possibility of imminent victory and serious concern that Soviet power, as well as their own, might crash into the center of Hitler's fortress Europe before East and West had agreed on the form of the next European order or on a balance of Soviet and Western power that could make it viable. Throughout late August, September, and early October, long-distance diplomatic probing continued among London, Washington, and Moscow, culminating in an agreement that the foreign secretaries of the Big Three, Cordell Hull, Anthony Eden, and V. M. Molotov, would meet in Moscow during mid-October to lay the foundation of a general understanding among the Allied powers. A Big Three meeting (Churchill, Roosevelt, and Stalin) would follow in Teheran in November to arrange a new world order.

But many of those in the Western Allied military-political establishment lagged far behind such bold ideas. At the end of July, Churchill cautioned his colleagues that despite the recent military advances in Europe, the British government's date for the probable end of the Pacific war continued to be 1948.[50] During July–August, the bitter struggle in the north Russian ports between Soviet police and British merchant seaman and Royal Navy personnel continued unabated, offering an unintentionally grim forecast of what East-West relations might be like if Soviet and Anglo-American forces ran into each other in Central Europe.[51]

However, as the sailors and police battled in the north and Martel and Babbington remained at each other's throats in Moscow, during August and September, 30 Mission's relations with the Red Army continued to be reasonably harmonious. On 3 August, the Soviets gave General Martel their summary of the general strength of the German armed forces, which concluded that despite recent losses at Kursk and in the Mediterranean, the overall size of the Wehrmacht would continue to increase due to the effect of total war mobilization. To strengthen his hand in the hard bargaining required for intelligence dealings with the Soviets, Martel asked London for (and received) a steady flow of information on Allied operations in Italy to be used as trade bait. But no matter how attractively Martel wrapped up this material, the Soviets showed little interest in anything about this theater of operation, which they persisted in considering a Western sideshow.[52]

In a peculiar parallel to the Soviet attitude toward Western efforts in Italy, Air Marshal Babbington viewed General Martel's activities as a futile magic-lantern show. The air mission continued to send home reports complaining about Soviet noncooperation and citing the fact that five months of pressure had netted the air mission only "two rather disappointing target maps and oblique photographs of the Ploesti oil fields."[53] Then, when army OB meetings slowed to a crawl in September and General Martel joined in the song of failure and pessimism, it was the turn of the authorities in London, especially in the directorate of liaison missions, to take up the optimistic chorus. One official commented in September, "I don't think intelligence can be said to be bad; it is distinctly better than it used to be."[54]

On occasion, the air mission also put aside its most extreme pessimism and doled out a bit of intelligence or technical information to the Soviets, such as the handover of the secret "Upkeep" mine, which took place in mid-September. Martel was also occasionally bucked up by Soviet assurances that liaison matters would soon be straightened out and that OB meetings, at least, would be back to normal. The Soviet presents that arrived from time to time, including detailed information on the German Panther tank and papers on German demolition methods, gave Martel's spirits a brief lift, but he soon sank into disappointment again, lamenting that the Russians were "swollen headed with success" and "tend[ed] to ignore the Mission."[55]

The Babbington-Martel conflict finally stumbled to its end during September, as Babbington reported to London that the Soviets' hostile attitude toward the mission continued unbated, despite the Kursk victory. A deep sense of guilt overcame the air minister (A. J. M. Sinclair) for having put Babbington into a false and rather embarrassing position in the first place. Babbington was therefore recalled, and the rest of 30 Mission slumped back into the task of coping with the other two sources of their misery, General Martel and the Soviet authorities.[56]

As usually occurred during such grim phases in Moscow, one British official or another invariably revealed a special talent for doing silly things that could compound the trials and tribulations. This time it was Colonel Firebrace in London, who thought that he could tempt the Soviets into cooperating on Japanese OB by using as trade bait the same Japanese Army list that the Americans had twice sought to use as an entrée into Soviet cooperation on Japanese intelligence. The Soviets therefore had the pleasure of adding this rejection aimed at the British to the two it had fired at the Americans.[57]

Such incidents indicate how difficult it was to maintain effective East-West intelligence cooperation in good times as well as bad, in the face of Soviet intransigence and a proclivity among Western officials to be hopelessly dense and inconsistent. After Kursk, however, there were also deeper and more significant grounds for East-West tension. Power was definitely slipping away from Germany, and the chief beneficiary of that change so far was the USSR. Western fears and suspicions were inevitably intensified by this situation, and in trying to cope, many Westerners tended merely to reactivate hoary anti-Russian stereotypes and vague slogans instead of developing a new explanatory paradigm.[58] Some Britons still could not get past arrogance and personal caricature. For example, Isaiah Berlin summed up Andrey Gromyko on 4 September 1943 as a very gentle, "dim creature who went through some sort of courses in economics."[59] R. G. Casey, the minister of state in Cairo, had a short chat with Kharlamov when the Soviet admiral stopped in Egypt on his way to visit Moscow, and he tried to bundle up Kharlamov's personal characteristics into a broader vision of the new Russia. In an official dispatch to the Foreign Office on his encounter with Kharlamov, Casey observed that the Russian admiral, "like most officials who come from what Sidney and Beatrice Webb have described as 'the new civilization,'" had "a rather blunt and crude way of expressing himself," which unintentionally gave offense to the more refined people of the West.[60] In this sentence, Casey managed to combine a slap at the British soft Left, condescension toward the Soviets, and a broad hint of the old Gladstonian adage that we must educate our masters. Failing elites have evoked the latter from time to time, and it invariably indicates both that fundamental change is in the wind and that the old order has no idea what to do about it.

Not surprisingly, the greatest power of the Western camp, the United States of America, was not initially as troubled by the behavior of the victorious Soviets as were the British. It saw itself as modern and new, and its power was definitely rising, not falling. The American attitude was different not merely because of naiveté or the illusions of the soft Left but because of what might be called the American ideology of opportunity. As Assistant Secretary of the Navy Ralph Baird wrote to Ambassador Standley (of all people) on 6 September 1943 regarding Russia's future:

> The Russian people from the standpoint of natural resources have as great a future ahead of them as this country of ours had one hundred years ago . . . and, it seems to me that as the natural resources of their country are developing . . . that they individually will want the fruits of their labors . . . and that they will get them, and that no power or totalitarian set-up can hold them back.[61]

Such naive American optimism was possible in 1943, in part because at that point the Soviets were not as eager to rub their successes in the faces of the Americans compared to their attitude toward the British. Although Kharlamov had been rather rough with Casey and earlier had made harsh accusations against the Admiralty, Captain Belikov, the Soviet Navy mission chief in Washington, continued to be all sweetness and light with American officials, only privately confiding to the British assistant naval attaché (Comdr. Richard Miles) his complaints about the "well known . . . lack of cooperation" that the Red Navy faced in Washington, compared with the much more generous attitude that prevailed at the Admiralty in London.[62]

Despite this assortment of pro and anti tendencies in Moscow, London, and Washington, the U.S. Army continued to have rather good OB relations with the Red Army—six extended meetings occurred between 24 August and 16 September[63]—and American diplomats logged two more long survey trips during the early autumn, one to the Urals and the other to Vladivostok.[64] The U.S. naval attaché visited a Soviet shipyard, and the U.S. Navy mission carried on exchanges with the Red Navy on medicine and identification procedures for U.S. and Soviet naval units in the Far East. Additionally, during September, the U.S. Navy passed over a memo on Finnish minesweeping, and the Soviets provided a two-page memorandum on German forces around Murmansk and a fifteen-page paper on the Red Navy's procedures for officer recruitment. But a civilian did far better in acquiring sensitive Soviet Air Force information than did any Anglo-American service representative. Layton Rogers of the Bell Aircraft Company spent two weeks visiting Soviet Air Force fighter bases and training facilities, talked with 60 Russian pilots and 150 mechanics, and learned so much from the Russians that 80 percent of the Soviet suggestions were embodied in a new aircraft being developed by Bell.[65]

These were respectable achievements in intelligence acquisition, but Washington was interested in finding additional ways to gain confidential information from the USSR. The OSS even recruited an American engineering firm doing lend-lease in Russia to provide secret information to Donovan's organization on the construction projects of the Soviet defense industry. Although some in the State Department had come to believe that Michela's loud complaints had improved the situation of the U.S. mission in Moscow, other American officials with longer vision and more prudence believed that the way to increase the flow of sensitive information from the USSR was to recall Michela and the other naysayers in the U.S. Army's attaché office, close that office, and send a higher-level American military mission to Russia. The Moscow foreign ministers' meeting provided a convenient occasion for such a change; the State

Department had already decided to replace Admiral Standley, and the ambassador-designate, Averell Harriman, was to accompany Secretary of State Cordell Hull when he went to Moscow in October. Therefore, the War Department simply appointed Maj. Gen. John Deane—one of General Marshall's favorite young staff officers—as military adviser to Hull's diplomatic mission, with the added duty of remaining on as head of a new American military mission in Moscow that would act as the general liaison and intelligence-trading office for the Pentagon. This move also provided a face-saving means of removing Michela and company, establishing closer control over lend-lease by getting rid of Faymonville, and, in the process, putting the American team on a footing similar to that occupied by Britain's 30 Mission.[66]

Of course, as occurred with a number of organizational arrangements over the course of the war, the Americans were about to adopt the British mission system in Moscow just when the British themselves were most disenchanted with both their organizational setup in Russia and the falling prospects for scoring any successes there. But with American and Soviet power rising, a U.S. military mission in Moscow made sense to Washington, and as George Marshall knew only too well, the timing of this move was vitally important. October 1943 fell just seven months before the scheduled D-day landings in northern France, and Soviet cooperation in the form of a diversionary offensive and the provision of intelligence during the prelude to the landings might go a long way toward making Operation OVERLORD a success.

After years of calling for a Second Front, the Soviets were now going to be asked to assist in making it successful, in large measure by being more generous in sharing intelligence on the German Army. At the same time, the establishment of an American military mission would provide organizational parity for the military representatives of the Western powers in Moscow, so that John Deane and the new head of 30 Mission—whoever that turned out to be—would find it easier for the two countries to work in harness. The downside of the arrangement was that the partnership of the two Western missions might well intensify Soviet fears that the leaders of the capitalist vanguard were joining hands in the shadow of the Kremlin. Another possibility was that 30 Mission personnel might become destructively jealous of a large and well-stocked American presence in Moscow.

Dangers and opportunities were thus rather finely balanced for the Western powers in the USSR during the autumn of 1943, but there seemed no choice but to go forward. All the intelligence-sharing overtures had already been performed during the previous two and a half years. Now the main performance was about to begin.

8

A Winter of More Contentment, October 1943–February 1944

Winter 1943–1944 was an era of real war for all the Allies—tedious, costly, and often slow. On every front, the Soviets and the Anglo-Americans made significant advances but also paid high costs as they gradually learned to use their firepower and mobility more effectively. In the Pacific, American and Australian forces continued to lever the Japanese ground units out of the New Guinea region while inflicting heavy losses on the Japanese air forces and fleet. Moving on into the central Pacific, the U.S. Marines smashed head-on into the strongly held Japanese base at Tarawa in the Gilbert Islands in late November and early December 1943. The result was 3,300 Marine dead and wounded and 4,000 Japanese killed for the seizure of but one of hundreds of tiny clumps of rock in the central Pacific. By early 1944, American strategists and the Marine Corps had learned an important lesson from this hard experience. They by-passed many of the most heavily fortified Japanese-held islands and struck secondary Japanese positions first with overwhelming air and naval force; only then were the Marines sent in to clear out the Japanese garrisons. In consequence, Kwajalein and Eniwetok in the Marshalls were conquered in February 1944 with far fewer casualties than in Tarawa, and U.S. forces made a rapid bound across a third of the Pacific. The moment would soon be at hand when this massive new American amphibious war machine would make a turn toward the "inner line" to Tokyo, smashing west and north through the great Japanese defensive bastions of the Philippine Islands, Iwo Jima, and Okinawa.

The enormous American military-naval machine was at last beginning to roll, and the buildup of American forces in Western Europe in preparation for D day had also begun. Perhaps an even more significant indication of the scale of this midwar American military revolution was the fact that by 1944, over 40 percent of the total armament being produced by all the belligerents was being manufactured in the United States.

Operation OVERLORD promised to provide an effective offensive outlet for this massive buildup of American as well as British power through northern France, the best route into the western portion of Hitler's fortress Europe. During the winter of 1943–1944 however, the Anglo-American forces in Italy continued to slog on alone, battling desperately to cross a procession of rivers and secure an endless series of meaningless molehills. Anzio had failed to open the door to the north, and no other amphibious leaps were possible because OVERLORD, ANVIL, and the Pacific war had first claim on the available landing craft. Montgomery and Mark Clark were therefore left to slug it out through the mud and mountains. Italy was once again a zone of disappointment and mounting losses, as the 5th and 8th Armies found themselves locked into the bloody battles around Casino, vainly trying to batter open a door to the north.

The costly futility of the Italian campaign was thrown into bold relief by the offensives of the Red Army, which thundered westward on a broad front. After taking Kiev in early November, the weight of the Russian advance shifted north, reopening the Leningrad-Moscow railroad in late December and clearing the whole coast of the Gulf of Finland in early February. In the center, Soviet forces also made important gains, driving the Germans across the old Polish border in January, and then punching into Estonia in February. Just as had occurred when the Anglo-Americans had driven across Sicily and toppled Mussolini in the summer of 1943, the winter 1943–1944 advances of the Red Army into Central Europe threatened to pose serious political questions and increase the worries of Britain and the United States.

Bullish thoughts of imminent victory took hold in London and Washington in late 1943 and spawned longings for a German collapse that might somehow provide a victory without opening the door to future trouble with the USSR. In September, in a brief moment of euphoria at the start of the Italian campaign, the British JIC had concluded that Germany's situation was worse than it had been in the autumn of 1918 and that another "11 November" might be at hand. But this expansive fantasy passed before anyone in Whitehall began to toy openly with the thought that if victory was so near the West might be able to dispense with its dependence on Moscow.

By October, the JIC had reversed itself, concluding that the German situation was not so bad after all. Only the Germans' weakened position on the Eastern Front was still deadly serious,[1] and the Western governments were compelled to accept the fact that with Germany still upright and the Soviets continuing to advance, political and military cooperation with the USSR was more important than ever. The three Allied foreign secretaries met in Moscow (19 October–4 November 1943) with the intention of drawing up a blueprint for the European order that would follow an Allied victory. The first Big Three meeting occurred at Teheran soon after (28 November–1 December), emphasizing the appearance of East-West cooperation and Allied unity. Although neither of these meetings produced any fundamental changes in Soviet relations with the West, a strong cooperative tone emerged.

At the Moscow meeting, the representatives of the Big Three agreed again that some form of postwar international organization would have to be established, and this conclusion was confirmed at Teheran. During the Teheran meeting, Stalin toasted American production, without which, he said, the war could not have been won. He removed the silk glove for a moment, proposing with a smile that the best way to deal with Germany after the war would be to shoot 50,000 German Army officers.[2] He also gave the Western powers an informal pledge to enter the war against Japan: "You asked when will the Soviet Government march against Japan, that will be the day the German armies are destroyed." Churchill thought that this declaration was the most important single statement made at the conference.[3]

The Soviet pledge to enter the Japanese war was also welcomed by Washington, which was still deeply troubled by the length of the road to Tokyo and the high casualties of its Pacific Island battles. Of equal importance in improving East-West relations was the appearance of cordiality that accompanied the first face-to-face meeting of the Big Three, as well as the businesslike conferences held by their military chiefs. The Americans in particular tried to use these occasions to erect stronger bridges to Moscow, with President Roosevelt even proposing that the Red Army staff be brought within the Combined Chiefs of Staff machinery, although even Admirals King and Leahy of the U.S. Joint Chiefs of Staff (JCS) opposed the idea. The new U.S. ambassador to Moscow, Averell Harriman, stressed to his staff that he wanted as much openness with the Soviets as possible on D-day matters, and point five of the "military conclusions" at Teheran declared that the staffs of "the three powers should henceforth keep in close touch with each other in regard to impending operations in Europe."[4]

Harriman's desire to be more helpful to the Soviets may have helped East-West relations in Moscow, but it did little to enhance his relations with his British colleague. In 1944 the British ambassador prepared a secret pen sketch of Harriman (just released in the Public Record Office) that was anything but flattering. Declaring that the U.S. ambassador's "intentions are the best," Clark Kerr went on to assert that "he was always on the make" and "so eager to impress, so concerned to beget and nurse a personal prestige that does not by nature dwell in him," that if he stood "well with the Soviet authorities" it was merely because "his hands seem always full of gifts."[5]

In addition to these developments at Moscow and Teheran, there were other signs that a new era of East-West cooperation might be dawning. During October 1943, the head of the American War Production Board, Donald Nelson, had a spectacularly successful tour of Soviet military and industrial facilities, during which he was shown everything he wished to see, was provided with confidential information on Soviet industry, and of course came away singing the praises of the Soviet Union. Even in areas far removed from the USSR, the era of "East-West comradeship" seemed to bring closer bonds between Soviet and Western officialdom. Robert Murphy in Algiers struck up a genuine friendship with the Soviet representative at Eisenhower's headquarters, Alexander Bogomolov, an old-school diplomat who loved Nietzsche, and their cordial partnership lasted until the end of the war.[6]

Certainly not everything ran smoothly even amid the high-level golden glow of the Moscow and Teheran meetings. During the Moscow conference, Stalin and his cronies even made "a concerted effort, headed by M. Molotov," to get Kerr embarrassingly drunk during the ceremonial social gatherings. But this was one seriously misguided Soviet plot, because as one member of the British Navy mission proudly observed, when it came to drink, the British ambassador could hold his own with anyone, and "M. Molotov himself did not come off best."[7] A more serious backward step occurred when Field Marshal Lord Ismay was offered an unrestricted visit to whatever area of the Eastern Front he wished, accompanied by Gen. A. M. Vassilevsky. Even though Eden, Kerr, and General Martel urged Ismay to accept, stressing that the Soviets would probably be offended if he declined, the field marshal refused to delay his departure from Russia to make the visit, and Churchill backed him in this decision.[8]

This was especially unfortunate, because despite the outward show of cordiality, Stalin was certainly not satisfied with the basic attitudes of the British high command, contending that the British generals were insufficiently aggressive and, at Teheran, accusing Brooke of being anti-Soviet.[9] But even such instances of Western poor judgment and Soviet aggressiveness and bad manners were not the nub of East-West troubles. In 1943, British and American efforts to improve relations only thinly veiled their doubts and distrust of the USSR. At the same time, far from Moscow, one British official was given a rare opportunity to come close to the heart of Soviet fears and suspicions. In a chance conversation in Baghdad, the veteran Soviet diplomat Ambassador Maisky observed to a British official that whatever pleasantries occurred in Moscow and Teheran, the Soviets feared American power and economic expansionism, and he added that "President Roosevelt was not immortal, and who could foresee the policies of his successors."[10]

Down on a humbler level, among those who were supposed to make tripartite intelligence cooperation work every day, good and bad omens jostled about during late 1943 and early 1944. Michela, Faymonville, and their aides were ordered by the War Department to leave Moscow on 2 October, well before the foreign secretaries' conference began, and the members of the new U.S. military mission started to arrive soon after. This change did not mean that those with long-term doubts about the Soviet Union had been barred from U.S. Army councils, however. On the contrary, by the end of 1943, General Michela—still moaning about the bad treatment he had received in Moscow—had been assigned to the Russian section of G-2 Washington. That supreme hater of the USSR, Colonel Yeaton, took over direction of the U.S. Army section concerned with exchanging technical information with the Soviets, a move that surely did not contribute to better East-West relations.[11]

This old guard of American Army experts on the USSR helped spearhead a new, highly secret effort to solve the problem of Western ignorance about the Soviet armed forces. Between 4 and 15 February 1944, American and British Army experts on the Red Army and Red Air Force met in London to sort out a picture of the Soviet ground and air forces. The American team, which included Park, Michela, and Lt. Randolph Zander, was headed by Col. J. R. Lovell. Britain was represented by Col. F. Thornton and Maj. N. Ignatieff, the latter a top British expert on Red Army OB. The members of these two groups not only prepared a joint Anglo-American version of Soviet OB in early February but also made arrangements to continue sharing information on the Soviet armed forces (the Ignatieff-Zander agreement). This increased the information that both countries possessed about the ground and air forces of the USSR and consequently left them less at the mercy of Moscow for Soviet OB information. The heart of the Ignatieff-Zander agreement was the sharing of information acquired from ULTRA decrypts of German traffic from the Eastern Front.[12]

This development should not be taken to mean that all those Americans who had returned from Moscow were violently hostile to the USSR, or that the Pentagon and the War Office had embarked on a course of sharp opposition to the Soviet Union. Some representatives of the old outgoing order in Moscow, such as Ambassador Standley's secretary in the embassy, Edward Page, had become upbeat about the Russian situation. When Page returned to the United States, he promoted the view that a fresh and better era might be dawning for Russia itself and for Soviet relations with the West.[13]

Furthermore, the new American military liaison team that arrived in Russia on 1 November, a week prior to the opening of the Moscow conference, had been instructed by General Marshall to do all in its power to cooperate with the

Soviets. It was led by Maj. Gen. John Deane, with Gen. Hoyt Vandenberg (postwar commander of the Strategic Air Command's nuclear deterrent air fleet) and Gen. S. P. Spalding to deal with air and supply matters. Capt. C. E. Olsen replaced Captain Duncan as naval attaché.

The American newcomers made an immediate hit with the British mission, Colonel Turner noting with satisfaction that they were all friendly and intelligent and far better than the previous American military and naval group in Moscow. On 2 November, the Soviets also indicated that they were prepared to make at least a nominal new beginning. General Dubinen was removed as liaison officer with the British and American missions. Henceforth, the Anglo-American teams in Moscow would deal with Gen. A. I. Antonov and his superior, Gen. N. V. Slavin (the chief of the Soviet general staff), who were much higher up the Soviet command system. Although certainly not jolly or especially forthcoming individuals, they were calm, competent, and authoritative.[14]

Deane's brief directed him to be cooperative and to try "to promote the closest possible coordination" of the military efforts of the United States and the USSR.[15] To this end, he was provided with a daily summary of American military and naval operations in the Pacific and Italy, which was passed on to General Antonov. After 6 June 1944, this material was supplemented by a regular summary of Eisenhower's plans and operations, but even so, it was difficult to keep the mission focused clearly and circumspectly. For example, at the Cairo meeting of Churchill, Roosevelt, and their staffs (a meeting that occurred between the Moscow and Teheran conferences), the members of the JCS noted that they wanted to find out "whether the latest Soviet military appreciation of the Japanese position agreed with our own."[16] This query at least raised the possibility that Deane, like Michela and Yeaton before him, might soon be asked to go probing after the USSR's intentions regarding the Japanese, despite obvious Soviet unwillingness to discuss such matters.

Deane's tasks were therefore not defined with precision. Indeed, in some respects, his position was even more complex and tendentious than Michela's had been. The new American organization in Moscow was much larger, Washington's expectations were rising, and as D day approached, the liaison stakes were substantially higher. Furthermore, Deane had been given special and controversial projects to implement, the most important of which was General Arnold's pet scheme, Operation FRANTIC, to establish American air bases on Russian soil to facilitate shuttle bombing of Germany by the U.S. Army Air Corps, which Stalin approved in principle on 2 February. Considering Soviet suspicions, this proposal was so chancy that Anthony Eden stressed to Churchill on 26 October that FRANTIC was strictly a U.S. scheme and that "neither Premier Stalin nor I contemplated suggesting such an arrangement for the Royal Air Force."[17] In the following year, after the Americans actually succeeded in securing shuttle bombing bases in Russia, some British officers had second thoughts about having excluded themselves from the plan, but in late 1943, the campaign for FRANTIC appeared to be a classic instance of British prudence in the face of American tempestuousness.

Yet even in 1943, Whitehall pursued some of its own pet dreams of special cooperative arrangements with the Soviets, dusting off proposals for a comprehensive Anglo-Soviet technical exchange. But the problems of coordinating American and British interests in technology turned out to be so formidable that endless Anglo-American debate finally washed away any enthusiasm that Washington or London had for comprehensive tripartite information-sharing arrangements, although London did continue some technological exchanges with the Soviets.

The organization of secret intelligence coordination between the West and the USSR therefore gradually settled back into the customary goove of exchanges in Washington, London, and especially Moscow, with General Deane's new U.S. team standing in for Michela's old one. A brief threat to the prevailing organization of the British liaison system was made in late 1943, when Colonel Firebrace tried to take over all aspects of British-Soviet exchanges in London, but this intervention was successfully checked by the Admiralty. The liaison structures therefore carried on much as before in all three Allied capitals, and the principal topics of information exchanged continued to be German Army OB, assorted items of naval and air intelligence, plus enemy weaponry, with occasional sorties into such delicate matters as "Y."[18]

Only in regard to Japanese Army OB was the available raw intelligence material radically altered in late 1943. In September 1943, the U.S. Army made its first deep break-in to the Japanese Army's water-transport code and was soon able to track most Japanese troop movements made by sea. This development provided the Pentagon with a flood of detail on the location of Japanese Army units, as well as Japan's general order of battle, and it also revolutionized the Japanese Army OB game. A new and more reasonable approach could now be made to the Soviets with respect to the secret information the two countries possessed on Japanese OB. The one portion of the Japanese Army that was most unaffected by the breaking of the water-transport code was the Kwantung Army in Manchuria, the section of the Japanese Army that moved least frequently by sea and about which the Soviets knew far more than anyone else.[19]

The new American mission was definitely in a more favorable intelligence bargaining position than Britain's 30 Mission in the winter of 1943–1944. The

Americans held more high-quality OB information on the Japanese Army than previously, the flow of lend-lease supplies to Russia had dramatically increased through the Iranian route, and the Red Army's offensive power owed a considerable debt to American supplies. General Marshall and the White House realized the danger of making the Soviets appear to be in hock to the United States and instructed Deane to avoid hard bargaining with the Russians and not to press for information on Soviet weapons, equipment, or tactical methods by open or covert means. When Gen. Clayton Bissell replaced Gen. George Strong as G-2 Washington in early 1944, he stressed the importance of securing intelligence on the Red Army. But Deane refused Bissell's request that one of his G-2 officers be attached to the mission in Moscow, and Marshall confirmed this decision.[20]

Over the two years that his mission was in Russia, Deane requested that the Soviets supply information on matters that the Red Army was especially good at, such as the crossing of rivers and the development of arctic equipment. But during the winter of 1943–1944, the U.S. mission chief kept such informational requests to a minimum and succeeded in sidetracking most of the dangerously expansive intelligence-gathering schemes put forward by agencies in Washington.

One fairly significant exception was a late-1943 OSS proposal to allow an OSS team to liaise in Moscow with the NKVD in a manner analogous to what Britain's SOE and SIS had been doing (with little success) since 1941. Donovan initially sought to send an independent OSS mission to Moscow under Stanley Weinberg, but Donovan himself flew to Russia in January 1944. Following conversations with the same NKVD officer (Colonel Ossipov) with whom the SOE worked in Moscow, he made a tentative arrangement for an exchange of OSS-NKVD missions between Moscow and Washington. It took little time for J. Edgar Hoover, the Justice Department, and General Michela (now of G-2 Washington) to get wind of this proposal to plant the NKVD openly on the banks of the Potomac, and massive pressure was put on the White House to quash the deal. In addition, the secretary of the Joint Chiefs of Staff, Admiral Leahy, was "personally" opposed to the OSS-NKVD arrangement and did his best to block it. In any event, during the third week of February 1943, President Roosevelt and the JCS killed the OSS-NKVD mission exchange plan. But after a short interval to digest the president's 19 February question, "what do we do next?" an arrangement was made in March for the OSS and NKVD to exchange intelligence and information on covert operations through General Deane's office in Moscow. Over the next eighteen months, some items of value to the shadow warriors of the two countries passed back and forth over this link, but the pickings acquired by both sides were limited.

The Soviets certainly had any advantage that did occur, and they could not have debited the account of the U.S. military mission for having raised the issued in the first place.[21]

In fact, during its earliest days, the Deane mission was so sympathetic to the Soviets that some aspects of its activities now seem naively pro-Soviet. In 1943–1944, there was even a tendency to make light of such sensitive and threatening matters as the Polish question. At the time, Moscow was making clear that the USSR would reshape the Polish government and Polish boundaries into something much more "friendly" to the USSR. In a staff meeting with Harriman on 15 February 1944, General Deane—echoing President Roosevelt's patronizing 1941 view that the Polish government in exile should be put under British and American tutelage to learn the ways of democracy—suggested that the Polish question could be easily solved if the Poles would quit "hanging onto archaic ideas" and realize that they had "an opportunity now to come out of this in good shape." Deane even voiced the view that it would be better for everyone if the British would turn up the pressure and make the Poles "see the light" before it was too late.[22]

The American military authorities also carried out a very open-handed policy with their Soviet counterparts in the only operational area where the West was in control and the Soviets had a liaison mission. In late 1943, General Eisenhower established a general policy that the Soviet mission in Algiers would be given AFHQ's version of the enemy order of battle in that theater as well as secret information on Allied operations. Eisenhower stuck to this open-handed policy with the Soviet liaison mission when AFHQ moved to Italy in 1944.[23]

Not surprisingly, as a result of these many favorable factors and Soviet self-interest, the American military mission in Moscow began its cooperative intelligence activities with a string of successes. In early 1944, the Soviets provided the U.S. Army with a number of samples of German artillery, including the "88" and the 55-mm antitank gun, the first of these important German weapons to reach the United States. At the same time, the supply of German Army OB information provided by the Soviets was little short of spectacular, with thirteen OB meetings occurring between 11 November 1943 and 24 February 1944. Sometimes the Soviets were restrained and businesslike, and on other occasions they were warm and friendly, but in all these meetings, the Soviet liaison officer (usually Colonel Pavlov) provided Col. Robert McCabe and Capt. Paul Hall with masses of information, including detail on German divisions in the east. The following short passages from the minutes of the meeting of 10 February 1944 between Pavlov and Hall, with three translators present, illustrate the efficiency and effectiveness of these meetings and the specific detail they encompassed.

Pavlov: Three German Artillery Divisions have been identified on the Soviet-German front, the 18th, 310th and 312th Arty. Divisions. This is the first time the Germans have employed artillery divisions.

Hall: How are these divisions organized?

Pavlov: The exact organization is not yet known, but generally speaking there are three artillery regiments, each with three battalions. The first battalion has two batteries and the second and third, three. There are from 10 to 100 guns in the division.

Hall: What calibers?

Pavlov: Following calibers: 100mm, 105mm, 150mm, and 210mm. These artillery divisions are directly under G.H.Q. These three divisions are in the Southern Army Group.

Hall: Do you know which of these batteries are light, medium and heavy?

Pavlov: As yet that is unknown. This information is from prisoners' testimony and no documents have been captured yet. . . .

Hall: I would like to get the disposition of the 2nd and 6th Finnish Divisions if you have it now. [It is noteworthy that after giving the Soviets information on Finnish units early in the war, the situation was reversed by 1944.]

Pavlov: In the Finnish Army?

Hall: Yes.

Pavlov: We consider both the 2nd and 6th on the front with Kralian Army. Colonel McCabe asked last time about the 2nd and 6th *German* Divisions. The 2nd and 6th German Divs. (rifle) are on the northern sector with the 20th Army at Murmansk.

Hall: You know we are interested in paybooks. I would like to lend you a document which shows how we analyze the books, what information we get out of them, and why we are interested in them.

Pavlov: Can I have it until the next meeting?

Hall: You can have it for several weeks. I regret that it is the only copy I have but you can have it for several weeks for the research section. . . .

Hall	When would it be convenient to meet and what would you like to discuss at the next meeting?
Pavlov:	We can meet next week.
Hall:	We will have the usual changes but would also like to discuss Finnish Order of Battle.
Pavlov:	All right.
Hall:	Do you have any questions you would like me to answer at the next meeting?
Pavlov:	The German Order of Battle in Italy interests us. Could you prepare it for me?
Hall:	I will do that.[24]

Following this meeting, Hall reported to Washington that during the session "Lieutenant Colonel Pavlov was reserved but cordial and the meeting was on a very friendly basis." Hall stressed that "there was none of the sarcasm and disinterest which was often characteristic of our summer conferences" and concluded that "Lieutenant Colonel Pavlov readily answered the questions and proffered information," thereby indicating "a closer and friendlier Russo-American relationship" in Moscow. How well the American Moscow mission was actually doing in acquiring German OB was revealed in early February, when the British Joint Staff mission in Washington began to receive copies from G-2 of the OB reports sent in by General Deane. These were then sent on to London, thereby reversing the situation that had prevailed in 1941–1943, when the Americans had sought such information from 30 Mission.[25]

Hall and McCabe's German OB triumphs were probably the stellar achievement of the American Moscow mission in the winter of 1943–1944,[26] but Deane's staff was also partly successful in its modest requests for information on the delicate matter of German preparations for chemical warfare. They received from the Soviets two samples of the new German gas mask canister being carried by the Wehrmacht in the east, which G-2 requested on 28 January 1944 to help it assess the likelihood of Germany's resorting to some novel and deadly form of chemical warfare. Deane's late-1943 request for information from the Soviets on how they attacked German defensive positions also netted useful information, which, when added to what 30 Mission had acquired on the same subject, produced a nine-page paper that was sent to the White House, the Pentagon, and the military authorities in London.[27]

The U.S. Army Air Corps' efforts to acquire Luftwaffe information from the Soviets were initially not as successful as the intelligence-gathering activities of the main U.S. Army team. Hoyt Vandenberg's stay in Moscow was brief, and without a regular Army Air Corps liaison officer attached to the mission until the FRANTIC shuttle project began, Army Air Corps activities in Russia were at best haphazard. The U.S. Army Air Corps was even reluctant to exchange Luftwaffe OB with the Soviets. As General Arnold informed Deane's staff on 13 November 1943, "all [the] basic intelligence for the German Air Order of Battle" that the U.S. Army Air Corps possessed "comes to us through [the] British Air Ministry. Since Arnold wanted to hold on to "our relationship" with the RAF at all costs, the U.S. Army Air Corps was not prepared to take any chances in intelligence dealings with the USSR.[28] The combined chiefs of staff (CCS) cleared Deane and 30 Mission to provide a four-page secret summary of the POINT BLANK pre-D-day bombing offensive against Germany, and the U.S. Navy mission in Moscow acquired a table prepared by the Soviets on the bomb types used by the Red Air Force in February 1944. But beyond that, exchange on air matters seems to have been a complete blank.[29]

The occasional negative features of the exchanges on Germany that occurred between the U.S. Army and its Air Corps and the Soviets in the winter of 1943–1944 appeared insignificant when compared with the successes of General Deane and his colleagues. Nearly as important, Deane and his naval staff succeeded in nudging open the door on a subject that the Soviets had previously refused to consider: naval intelligence regarding Japan. In late 1943, the Americans continually attempted to prime the pump by giving the Soviets useful bits of Japanese intelligence, including U.S. Navy papers on Japanese ships and the landing methods being used by the Japanese in the Pacific campaign.[30]

On Christmas night 1943, Stalin indicated to Harriman that the USSR would provide the United States with information from "existing sources"[31] on Japan. With U.S. prompting, at Teheran, Molotov agreed that the USSR would enter into an exchange of intelligence on Japan. Two weeks later, the American Army G-2, Gen. George Strong, tried to accelerate matters by sending the mission in Moscow a large shipment of Japanese general staff maps with a promise of more if Deane could persuade the Soviets to turn over the Japanese maps of the Kurile Islands that Washington believed they held. Shortly thereafter, the British authorities accepted War Department proposals to try to arrange an OB exchange on the Japanese Army with the USSR, despite all the previous failures. On 20 January, General Marshall gave General Deane "carte blanche in dealing with the Russians on interchange of Japanese intelligence" and recommended to the War Office that London do likewise. At the same time, Deane was told that he would have a vast quantity of trade bait on Japan at his disposal if he could get exchanges moving, including photostats of the original

Japanese Army register up to May 1943, as well as the current American OB book based on this register and Japanese transfer orders for the period January–October 1942.[32]

By late January 1944, General Strong even offered to send the U.S. Army's top Japanese OB expert, Col. Moses W. Pettigrew, chief of the far eastern unit of the military intelligence service (MIS), to Moscow to carry on exchanges once the Soviets had agreed to play ball. Apparently sensing that this time the U.S. Army might succeed, the U.S. Navy jumped aboard on 28 January and began to push the Russians to exchange information on Japanese air cover over the Sea of Japan. Then on 2 February 1944, Harriman again raised the matter of intelligence exchange on Japan with Stalin. After making the obligatory face-saving statement (in case he later changed his mind on exchanges) that "Soviet information on Japan was not very rich," the Soviet leader declared that Soviet intelligence on Japan "would be made available" to the Americans.[33] Three weeks later, the Red Navy began to turn this pledge into reality. A Captain Eghipke declared in a meeting with Admiral Olsen on 28 February that although the Red Navy would not allow Western naval liaison officers into the Soviet far east, it was prepared to begin exchanges on Japanese naval matters only—no army and no air—in which each side would present to the other a bloc of material it held, along with a list of questions it would like to have answered. Thereupon Captain Eghipke handed Olsen Soviet intelligence on "organization of the Japanese Navy" and three thick intelligence volumes on the waters surrounding Japan, totaling 947 "pamphlets," together with a set of questions relating to these volumes that the Soviets wanted answered.[34]

In other aspects of intelligence exchange during the winter of 1943–1944, the U.S. Navy was not as successful as the U.S. Army. This was no reflection on the new head of the navy section of the U.S. mission, Admiral Olsen, whom General Deane praised after the war for the successes he achieved in cooperating with the Red Navy. Nothing Olsen could have done would have been enough to offset two basic facts that made the Soviet authorities much more tuned to army than to navy matters, especially in this period.[35]

First, with the Persian Gulf supply route now functioning effectively, the north Russian ports and the task of protecting the Murmansk and Archangel convoys were relatively less important to the Soviets, although a huge flow of supplies continued to pour into Archangel and Murmansk. Second, the principal reality of Russian geopolitics was that the USSR was basically a ground, rather than a sea, power. This fact took on added significance in the winter of 1943–1944 as the Red Army smashed westward toward (and in some cases, across) the borders of its western neighbors, just when the Western governments at last seemed serious in their determination to launch a Second Front. Army and air matters, including anxieties about the possible appearance of Western Allied armies in the line of the Soviet advance, therefore had to take precedence in Moscow during 1943–1944, and that, in turn, meant that East-West naval intelligence exchange would inevitably be cast into a secondary role.

Given these unfavorable circumstances, Admiral Olsen and the U.S. Navy mission scored respectable intelligence-gathering achievements during this period, even though they were forced to seek out useful information from hither and yon. This search included questioning the British censorship authorities, as well as carrying out a close examination of Captain Garwood, who had just completed his tour of duty as British Navy liaison officer in the Black Sea. Garwood told the American naval authorities in Moscow that aside from what he had secured from the Russians, the British had "excellent and full information on enemy activities [in the] Black Sea such as sailings[,] mine fields[,] operating units and fixed defenses," presumably acquired through German radio intercepts, and that this information had been "furnished [to the] Red [naval] staff at Gelenjik" on the Black Sea.[36] Supplementing this report, which was sent to the White House and the Navy Department, Olsen and company also secured more information on Soviet icebreakers and the Dvina River ports of the Red Navy. More significantly, the Soviets provided a report on the German methods of defending against seaborne landings—potentially useful in the run-up to D day—and gave the Americans two captured "storm boats," which the Germans had used in their crossing of the Don. Commander Tolley also secured a visit to the Soviet destroyer *Razumny* in February, and in March, Lt. Comdr. E. W. Yorke was permitted to examine the Molotovsk shipyard, a privilege that had been denied to the Royal Navy.[37]

The stellar naval intelligence achievement of the period, however, was scored by Lt. G. B. Bassinger, who was sent to Russia to exchange naval mine information with the Red Navy. Bassinger stayed at his post in Russia until May 1944, filing forty-four reports covering Soviet, German, and Japanese naval mines. In January–February, in addition to providing the Soviets with details of the German induction mine, Bassinger gained data on the Soviet KB, ABD, and AG mines, as well as a full report on the basic VKM-90 detonator used in Soviet naval mines. Bassinger noted on 28 January that his journey had been "quite successful for a beginning," and he seemed to feel that he was in the process of acquiring mine information of considerable value to the U.S. Navy.[38]

The success of Lieutenant Bassinger showed not only that the U.S. Navy could gain intelligence under unfavorable circumstances but also that American official missions in the USSR in late 1943 and early 1944 were enjoying especially good opportunities to travel about the country and get information desired by Washington. In addition to the naval inspection visits mentioned above, U.S. Navy mission personnel made journeys from Archangel to Murmansk and Vladivostok, from Vladivostok to Moscow, from Teheran to a number of points in south-central Russia, day trips out of Moscow, and one journey from Moscow to Baku.[39] Other high-level American visitors, especially those related to lend-lease matters, managed to explore many more areas of the USSR. Eddie Rickenbacker found the USSR highly attractive. Gen. D. H. Connolly visited Leningrad in late 1943 and then passed back and forth through central-western Russia between 17 December 1943 and 2 February 1944, touching at Orel, Kursk, Kiev, Stalingrad, and Moscow, as well as numerous smaller communities. He filed a 75-page report on his travels, including photographs of roads, bridges, and industrial plants in various parts of the country.[40]

These prominent American official travelers were interviewed by the U.S. military authorities upon their return to Washington, and from their experiences, G-2 was able to build up an extensive and reliable portrait of the USSR. Humbler folk, such as officers of merchant ships sailing to Russia and the U.S. Army tank specialists who were in the USSR for ten months in 1943 and early 1944, were also questioned by G-2 and provided detailed accounts of Russian conditions. In addition to drawing on the experiences of these and other Americans doing military and lend-lease work in the USSR, the U.S. government continued to enjoy close relations with the USSR on weather matters and was working to establish partnerships on such relatively delicate commercial questions as the production of synthetic rubber. There was simply no way that the Soviets could continue to keep their country as secret from the Americans in 1943–1944 as had been possible in the earliest phases of the war.[41]

As spring 1944 approached, despite the usual complaints of Soviet boorishness and secrecy, the U.S. government had many reasons to be satisfied with the overall condition of U.S.-Soviet relations in winter 1943–1944, as well as with the many intelligence achievements of General Deane's mission in Moscow. The British government, however, had much less to smile about, either in regard to its general relations with the USSR or with respect to the internal situation of 30 Mission. The British had participated in both the Moscow and Teheran conferences and had managed to sustain their position among the Big Three, even as it became increasingly clear that the United Kingdom was being outdistanced in sheer power by the rising Soviet and American colossi. Churchill had failed to convince his American partners to opt for a mighty attack on the "soft underbelly" of Hitler's Europe, and the main Western blow was now definitely to be the OVERLORD invasion commanded by an American. The U.S. authorities were also showing less enthusi-asm for Churchill's problematic diversionary operations in the Mediterranean. Southeast Asia was also an embarrassment for the United Kingdom in 1944; while the Americans were striking hard in the central Pacific and obviously accelerating the drive toward Tokyo, British forces were moving forward at a snail's pace in a Burma campaign. The Japanese retained the initiative there and continued to endanger British hopes that someday soon the raj would be restored and Britain would somehow retain its empire, despite all the embar-rassments endured and defeats suffered since 1939.

Britain's relations with the USSR were also disturbed by continuing difficul-ties between General Martel and the Soviet authorities, as well as troubles between Colonel Firebrace and the Russian liaison mission in London. In early October 1943, Gen. Sir Leslie Hollis minuted the prime minister that although Anglo-Soviet relations were at that moment "fairly good," there was resent-ment on the part of General Martel and his colleagues in Moscow about what they perceived as shabby treatment from the Russians.[42] Three days later, the CIGS stressed to Martel that "general relations" with the Soviets were more important than getting intelligence, "especially now that [the] Russians are fighting so hard and successfully." This spiked Martel's hope for a "showdown" with the Russians, a showdown that some in 30 Mission looked forward to in the hope that it might hasten the general's departure.[43]

By mid-October, Field Marshal Brooke had become critical of Martel's atti-tude "and had told him so," but the 30 Mission chief continued to grumble that his team had "seen nothing and discussed very little with the Russians for three months." In late October, Martel had a row with Eden during the early stages of the foreign secretaries' conference in Moscow, but after a British staff meeting among Kerr, Ismay, Eden, Martel, and Admiral Fisher, the foreign secretary agreed to try to persuade Molotov that the Soviets should be more helpful to the mission.[44]

Near the end of 1943, some additional developments should have strength-ened Martel's position. The new head of the air mission, Air Commodore D. N. Roberts, was soon echoing Martel's complaints about the Soviets and urging Whitehall to take action to force Moscow to be kinder to the mission. On occa-sion, Martel also showed signs of mellowing a bit toward the Soviet authorities, admitting that the new Soviet liaison officer, General Slavin, was better than his predecessor. But then he immediately minimized the positive effect of this judgment by adding that Slavin was "not making much headway."[45]

But then fate and Russian carelessness delivered into the hands of British officials in Moscow clear proof that Soviet officialdom had little or no intention of cooperating fully and fairly with its Western ally. Instead of sending the routine monthly record of accounts to the Royal Navy mission, a Soviet official inadvertently sent a seven-page set of secret instructions that the Red Navy issued to its own liaison personnel. This document set forth the intelligence targets Soviet liaison personnel were to aim for (new British equipment, especially that for "radio location"), as well as strict orders not to reveal anything of value to the British regarding the methods and equipment of the Soviet armed forces.[46]

When faced with this document, old veterans of the diplomatic and secrecy wars, such as Kerr, took it in stride. They believed that the best way to put the pressure back on the Soviets would be to return the document with a straight face and a smile, to see if anything could be gained from the Soviets' embarrassment. Instead, the mission did nothing about the whole affair except growl, grumble, and complain even more violently about Soviet perfidy and lack of comradeship.[47]

During autumn 1943, British liaison personnel working with the Russians in London also seem to have reached the end of their patience with what they regarded as Soviet obstructiveness and unwillingness to cooperate. In early November, Colonel Firebrace filed a long, detailed, self-righteous report enumerating all that Britain had done for the Russian representatives in London ("we have nothing with which to reproach ourselves") and claiming that the Soviets had done nothing positive in return.[48] Firebrace believed that the Soviets were such barbarians that sensible bargaining with them was impossible; in his view, all that could be done was to suffer their rudeness and, by assuming the "attitude to the grand seigneur," grant them bits of assistance and information in the cause of the Grand Alliance.[49]

Although Firebrace's negative comments were echoed in corners of Whitehall, other officials held that his criticisms of the Soviets were too extreme and that some effective intelligence cooperation with them was possible. Col. F. Thornton of MI 3 noted on 7 November that Firebrace's report "condemns the Russians too strongly," for although it was true that the British had given more intelligence than they had received, "in recent months General Martel has obtained a fair amount of enemy intelligence, particularly technical intelligence [i.e., information on German weapons]" from Moscow.[50] Cavendish Bentinck of the Foreign Office and the Joint Intelligence Committee thought that many of the difficulties with the Russians actually arose from the prejudices of the British Army leaders, whose negative attitudes quickly bounced down the chain of command. "If the upper hierarchy of the War Office are anti-Guatemalan [for example], then gradually the humblest subaltern on Salisbury

Plain will be convinced that the Guatemalans are the lowest of twirps," Bentinck wrote.[51] He contended that the same effects were being engendered by the anti-Soviet passions of the top British generals.

In any case, even the most intense suspicions of Moscow did not prevent British officialdom from bringing forth a seemingly endless procession of new suggestions for exchanges with the Russians. In November, the War Office proposed trading its weekly intelligence review with one from Moscow. In December, the Political Warfare Executive advocated the establishment of a cooperative arrangement with the Soviets on subversive propaganda being used against the Axis. In January, Air Marshal Portal tried to use the occasion of a visit to London by a Soviet general to stimulate "Russian interest in strategic bombing."[52]

However, a lack of clear and systematic liaison procedures, as well as the failure to integrate the views of the Foreign Office with those of the military and naval authorities, left London unable to establish clear liaison policies and execute them. In 1943, the Air Ministry regularly provided copies of its general air intelligence summary to the Russian mission, but the War Office and Admiralty refused to follow suit. When the Foreign Office indicated the absurdity and potential political hazards of the situation, the DMI (Maj. Gen. F. H. N. Davidson) defended the existing arrangement by claiming that the "touchiness" of the Russians would require the "watering down or even excluding altogether . . . of much material" if the army summaries were sent to the Soviet mission. The Foreign Office countered that the army's exclusionary policy was already hopelessly compromised; the War Office distributed copies of its summaries to the Allied governments in exile in London, and someone from at least one of these delegations, or from the War Office itself, was already passing on much of the material to the Soviet mission. In addition, the *Daily Worker* had been able to publish embarrassingly anti-Soviet passages from these British Army intelligence summaries. But the War Office still refused to clean up the situation and put the Soviet embassy on the distribution list.[53]

There was further evidence of the divergent views of the Foreign Office and the military authorities. In February 1944, the Foreign Office had concluded (mistakenly, as it turned out) that unless the West threatened its vital interests, the USSR would be so deeply involved in reconstruction that good East-West relations would prevail for at least five years after the war. In contrast, the service departments were awash with fears and suspicions of the Soviet colossus and its plans for territorial expansion.

No one, of course, better embodied official confusion and heavy-handedness than General Martel. He antagonized high-level Foreign Office visitors to

Moscow, such as Alexander Cadogan (just as he had earlier managed to do in the case of Anthony Eden), and he patronized and quarreled with senior members of his own mission. During December 1943, while making Air Commodore Roberts, the new head of the air mission, as miserable as possible, he had the temerity to report to the vice chief of the air staff (Gen. D. C. S. Evil) that Roberts was "a bit handicapped by the fact that some of the Babbington smell still attached to him."[54]

By January 1944, General Martel had finally shot his bolt. Whitehall dismissed virtually everything he said, ranging from his view that the American cooperation efforts with the Soviets had failed, to his quite sensible plea that British military visitors be sent to Moscow to take advantage of Russian hospitality and secure military intelligence. A steady procession of negative Foreign Office comments regarding General Martel appeared in January—"Far too complacent and patronizing," "General Martel's difficulty is one of personality more than method," "It is General Martel's patronizing attitude . . . that has made it impossible to get along with them [the Soviet authorities]." This certainly helped seal the general's fate, and in early February he was ordered out of Moscow. Whitehall once again turned to the task of choosing a head for 30 Mission.[55]

The selection process rapidly turned into another episode of vaudevillian farce. The candidate ultimately chosen, Lt. Gen. M. B. (Branco) Burrows, was an old friend of Anthony Eden. He spoke Russian and had fought against the Soviets in the World War I era, and he wanted to wear his military medals from that period when he was presented to Joseph Stalin. After much wrangling and travail, Burrows had his way and appeared before the Soviet leader in early March 1944 resplendent in anti-Soviet awards. He then embarked on the duty of securing from the Soviets intelligence data and information on their overall strategy in the run-up to D day (a duty that General Brooke considered "particularly important"), as well as joining with General Deane to share information on Western plans and operations with the Russian authorities.[56]

In addition to his emblematic troubles, Burrows got off to an especially rocky start regarding intelligence-sharing matters because, beginning in the last days of General Martel, the Soviets lodged a series of protests about the British supply of OB information, complaining that the volume was small and the range not comprehensive. During January, the Soviets also objected to any form of complete monthly exchange of German OB with the British. In February, Colonel Firebrace, then in Moscow on a survey visit, added to the trouble by alleging that the Soviets were not supplying 30 Mission with German OB material, especially that regarding the transfer of German units from Eastern

Europe to the west. This accusation produced a denial by the Soviets that they had such information and another round of bitter Soviet complaints and accusations about who was actually bearing the heavy cost of defeating the German Army.

Despite such useless but damaging clashes, the British actually enjoyed a fruitful period of OB meetings on the German Army in February. The four meetings held then were of such length and quality that even General Slavin remarked on "their great value." The British meetings may or may not have been as rich as those of the Americans regarding German OB, but if there were any deficiencies, they were made up by the American dispatch to London, via the Joint Staff mission, of details of the information that Deane's team had received. This was probably a bit galling to the British, who saw themselves as the senior and more mature party in Western intelligence relations with the Russians, but American generosity on this matter meant that London was receiving an unusually rich flow of information on German Army OB from one source or another.[57]

The British Army mission in Moscow was also allowed to visit an exhibition of Soviet military literature during February, and Colonel Hill, the head of the SOE mission, was granted a week's survey visit of Leningrad in late January and early February. Despite its numerous complaints, the Army mission was certainly far better informed on Red Army OB in this period than it had ever been before. After receiving a copy of the War Office version of the Red Army OB in mid-February, it sent London a three-page closely typed list of the errors and omissions therein.[58]

In February 1944, the War Office sent Colonel Bevan to Russia to work with the Soviets on deception activities for D day. Some popular historians contend that this indicated that Moscow had been taken into one of the most secret activities of the Western powers. But although BODYGUARD deception operations were important, they definitely did not have the supreme significance that some attribute to them. On receiving a document stamped "BODYGUARD" on 18 April, Churchill queried Lord Ismay, "What is this?" At the very least, this suggests that if the prime minister did not recognize this deception operation code name eight weeks prior to D day, the Soviets had certainly not been taken into the innermost of Western secret sanctuaries just because they were included in BODYGUARD and agreed on 28 April to carry out deception raids on the coasts of Norway and Finland.[59]

What had taken place was an improvement in the Soviet attitude toward cooperation on German Army intelligence, prompted by the approach of OVERLORD. This change had a positive effect not only on army intelligence matters but also on air and naval matters. Between December 1943 and January 1944, 30 Mission had an unusually fruitful period of exchanges on Luftwaffe intelligence, including information on the number of Luftwaffe sorties and the movement of Luftwaffe units. Another information bonus on the intelligence system of the Red Air Force was supplied to 30 Mission in December 1943 in the form of detailed answers to British questions from an Allied, presumably French, fighter pilot serving in Russia.[60]

During February, exchanges concerning air intelligence matters, in the purest sense, tailed off. But one special aspect of this subject—namely, air support for ground operations—was the topic of an extended meeting between Air Ministry officials and Soviet mission personnel in London on 5 February. The resulting three pages of intelligence on Soviet air support techniques did not provide the Air Ministry with any magical Soviet tricks for dealing with German ground units, but it did supply considerable information about Red Air Force organization and methods. There were also some revealing admissions, such as the great difficulty Soviet pilots experienced in accurately aiming the rocket bomb, which had been the object of so much British intelligence effort and anguish in 1941–1942.[61]

Anglo-Soviet cooperation on "Y" matters in the winter of 1943–1944 went quite smoothly, if thinly. During October, Cecil Barclay had some "Y" meetings with the Soviets and also enjoyed a busy social life with ample Russian female company. In November, the British chiefs of staff noted with satisfaction that the "Y" station in north Russia was functioning smoothly and that "cooperation with Russian 'Y' authorities was reasonably good."[62] But the Royal Navy was worried that its units in north Russia had insufficient radio encoding capacity to transmit the heavy flow of intercepted "Y" traffic to England. By early 1944, the senior British naval officer in north Russia, Admiral Fisher, confirmed this view and called for Typex machines to be sent to Polyarnoe.

During December 1943, the British repaid the Soviets for the benefits they were gaining from this German "Y" traffic by helping them improve the security of their army field codes. On 13 December 1943, General Martel once more informed General Slavin that "according to intelligence on which we place complete reliance [i.e., "Y" and ULTRA], the Germans are reading Russian cyphers."[63] Martel's memo went on coyly to say that "our source is unable to identify the grade of cypher affected but we know that the Germans are thereby gaining a clear picture of the Red Army order of battle." Martel concluded his revelations by explaining the main features of the new British call-sign system and suggested that it serve as a model for reforming Soviet call-sign arrangements. But the mission staff was doubtful that the Soviets would change their call-sign system without "fuller proof of its vulnerability than the Mission is authorized to give." And in any event, it believed that the new British system was "so complicated that the Red Army would probably not adopt it even if wishing to do so."[64]

The Soviets subsequently improved their call-sign system but did not adopt the methods used by the British. On 11 January 1944, they gave a backhanded compliment to the British expertise regarding "Y" and cryptanalytic matters by again requesting authorization to send two Soviet "Y" experts to Britain "to study and exchange information on 'Y' methods." This time, the Soviet petition actually seems to have been fulfilled. British embassy "Y" staff arranged the visit, and the home authorities emphasized that it applied only to "Y" installations; the Soviet visitors would not be allowed to get close to Bletchley Park or the ULTRA secret.[65]

The British authorities certainly went out of their way to assist the Soviets in their late-1943 attacks on Petsamo and on the German battleship *Tirpitz,* providing a comprehensive brief for the Petsamo assault (which achieved little) and stationing a Spitfire photo reconnaissance unit in north Russia to help supply the Soviets with detailed intelligence information for their raid on the *Tirpitz*. But in general, the Royal Navy, even more than the U.S. Navy, had a difficult time with intelligence exchanges during the winter of 1943–1944. In October 1943, Admiral Fisher—although granting that the Soviet mood was friendlier and that the police harassment of Allied seamen had abated—complained bitterly that he was restricted to the environs of Archangel and was able to secure only local intelligence material.[66]

The British Navy liaison officer in the Black Sea (Comdr. W. Lea replacing Captain Garwood in early 1944) continued to make extended survey trips in the Black Sea area and as far as Moscow. Lea secured from the Soviets a large amount of intelligence, including detailed information from German POWs held by the Russians. Although Admiral Miles deprecated the significance of much of the intelligence acquired by Lea, the Royal Navy remained highly wary of British Army efforts to acquire information from the Black Sea area, for fear that the Russians would take fright and shut the door on Commander Lea's operations.

The winter of 1943–1944 thus ended with nearly all aspects of British relations with the Soviets on hold or decline, and the Royal Navy no longer acting as the favored recipient of Soviet generosity. Britain's role as the special, if often abused, intelligence partner of the Soviet Union had been usurped by the United States. In consequence, during the final run-up to D day and in the summer battles that followed, the Americans would take the lead in trying to cooperate on intelligence matters with the USSR. It was a period when battlefield necessity compelled cooperation, and thoughts of what might follow Allied victory in Europe made Washington, London, and Moscow ponder anew the limits that should be set on their sharing of secrets.

9
The D-Day Era, March–June 1944

No period of World War II was more dominated by a single event than the spring of 1944. The preparations for the Anglo-American landings on the coast of Normandy consumed most of the attention of the U.S. and British military leadership from March to June. No major military operation occurred in the Pacific during spring 1944, and on the Eastern Front the Red Army's winter offensive made only a few last-gasp advances between March and May. Only in Italy did any important developments occur in this period, with the Allies finally winning the Battle of Monte Casino on 18 May and then driving toward Rome. Yet in retrospect, even this advance seems to have been almost an overture to OVERLORD, because the outstanding achievement of the Italian campaign was the seizure of Rome, and since this occurred on 4 June, it was immediately overshadowed by the landings on the beaches from Omaha to Sword two days later.

Of course, soon after the successful Normandy landings, other offensives exploded once more. The Soviet summer offensive began on 23 June, and the advance to the Baltic was successfully achieved by 29 July. In mid-June, Hitler struck back at Britain and the D-day buildup, the first V-1 "doodlebugs" smashing into southern England on 14 June. Across the world, in the same period, the American conquest of Saipan produced the great "Mariana Turkey Shoot," in which Japan lost 200 aircraft and three aircraft carriers.

Despite these other Allied triumphs, the spring of 1944 belonged to OVERLORD. This inevitably meant that Anglo-American intelligence relations with the Soviets were keyed to securing as much information and general assistance as possible from Moscow to make the invasion a success.

The new British mission chief, General Burrows, was specifically instructed by the chiefs of staff to pass to Moscow all possible Western information on "German plans and intentions"[1] and to secure as much comparable information from the Soviets as he could. On 21 March, the British and American missions in Moscow were sent a progress report on Operation ANVIL—the projected Anglo-U.S. landing in southern France in support of D day—and on 20 April, Burrows and Deane fulfilled orders from the CCS, telling Moscow that OVER-LORD would occur in early June and asking the Soviets for information on Soviet diversionary operations in support of the landings. Marshal Vassilevsky received this message without comment and did not provide any information about Soviet plans for operations on the Eastern Front to help smooth the way for the Normandy invasion. But the Anglo-Americans stuck with their policy of relative openness toward the Soviets regarding D day. Eisenhower sent Moscow a progress report on OVERLORD, ANVIL, and POINT BLANK (the bombing of Germany in support of OVERLORD) on 9 May, again receiving no comparable report from Moscow.[2]

Although London and Washington were committed to the same goal—joint offensive operations against Nazi Germany—and were now linked together in the new SHAEF machinery commanded by General Eisenhower, as well as in the Combined Chiefs of Staff organization, their national differences and divergent experiences in dealing with Moscow led the great Western democracies down different paths in the run-up to the invasion in the west. Washington was firmly, and perhaps rather blindly, committed to making the partnership with the USSR work, and this stance unquestionably smoothed the way for the American team in Moscow, as did lend-lease and the simple and direct methods employed by Ambassador Harriman, General Deane, and their colleagues in dealing with Soviet officialdom. In consequence, as the British government recognized in March, "the USSR in the past few months have given unheard of concessions to the U.S.A." Although long negotiations were required for some complex projects, including the establishment of direct radio communication links between Moscow and the United States (which took two months just to clear the technical and political obstacles), other exchange arrangements, such as the sharing of weather information, rolled on with a minimum of trouble. When shuttle-bombing arrangements were made in March, American personnel were allowed the unheard-of privilege of entering the USSR without visas.[3]

Harriman was careful to maintain his close links with Stalin, seeing him at regular intervals during the first half of 1944 and twice immediately prior to D day. In return for this special nursing of the Soviet dictator, Harriman received red-carpet treatment. After a survey visit to north Russian ports during April, the ambassador reported to Washington that he had been shown everything he wished "to see at the [Soviet] naval bases and airfields." Although he felt that "the Soviets are not easy to deal with where our interests rather than theirs are involved," Harriman concluded that "the difficulties in the northern ports experienced in the early winter have been overcome." He left the north "with real respect for what had been accomplished," as well as a belief that "there would be ever greater cooperation from the Soviets." Other American officials in Russia, especially the journeyman traveler General Spalding, also testified to Moscow's greater openness by making the long journey from Moscow to Vladivostok in the weeks before D day, carefully studying the Soviet communications system as well as conditions in the Soviet eastern region.[4]

Even though the American policy of securing closer relations with the USSR was enhanced by the appearance in Moscow of "friends" of the USSR, such as Henry Wallace, Washington was also harassed by its own anti-Soviet critics and had to walk rather softly in dealing with some Russian matters. General MacArthur "launched into a tirade lasting 1½ hours against Russia" when he was visited by General Gubbins of Britain's SOE in June.[5] At a time when intelligence cooperation with Moscow was at its peak, General Michela in Washington continued to maintain that the situation was actually worsening because he and his old naysaying colleagues were no longer at their posts in Moscow. The OSS was not outrightly hostile to the USSR, and through its Moscow connection it managed to please the Soviets by sharing some information with the NKVD on an Abwehr organization in Turkey that was targeting the USSR, as well as weighing down the Russians with hundreds of low-level R&A and SI reports. But the NKVD remained at least as coy with the Americans as it did with the British, even though the SOE did its best to make the partnership work, arranging its sixteenth NKVD agent drop—Mission APACHE—into France. Nonetheless, the NKVD complained to both London and Washington when it was not included in a joint SOE-OSS operation in Rumania in early 1944. It was probably amazed, amused, and confused by the way a Western "secret" organization such as the OSS distributed the documentary fruits of its supposedly confidential labors far and wide.[6]

But both Washington and Deane's team in Moscow held firmly to the cooperative tiller in the run-up to OVERLORD. They were convinced that Eisenhower's operation would be best served by working with the Soviets and acquiring all possible data from the Red Army, Navy, and Air Force regarding the armed forces of Nazi Germany. The U.S. Army leaders also realized that most of the important information the West wanted was not held by the Soviet attaché offices in Washington and London but was in Russia. Therefore, unlike the British, they curtailed the information given to the Soviet mission in the U.S. capital and concentrated their information-gathering effort in Moscow. By mid-May, the members of the Soviet attaché's office in Washington were receiving only general intelligence in addition to the special inspection visits they made. On 26 May, General Bissell told Deane that the "Soviet M[ilitary] A[ttaché] makes fewer requests and receives less information than most other United Nations attachés" in Washington.[7]

In consequence, on 1 April 1944, the American Joint Planning Staff noted with satisfaction that the U.S. military mission in Moscow (along with the British military mission) was making steady progress in increasing the scope of information exchanged with the Soviets, and this was a good omen for OVER-LORD. Indeed, in April and May, SHAEF was already securing useful material from Russia including reports that the Germans were using "an entirely new type of machine carbine," the MP 45/1, and had in operation a self-propelled antitank gun on a Panther chassis.[8]

The Americans and Soviets had between three and four OB meetings a month during the run-up to OVERLORD, and these meetings continued to be detailed, serious examinations of the structure and deployment of German Army units on all fronts. Once more, Captain Hall and Lieutenant Colonel Pavlov were the principals, and most of the meeting time was taken up with the details of pure OB—the current location of German Army units. On occasion, however, the meetings lapped over into broader organizational matters regarding the German Army, such as a consideration of the reorganization of panzer divisions on 18 March. On other occasions, they had long discussions of German equipment. For example, on 2 March, Pavlov provided a breakdown of all the main items of German heavy weaponry: "210mm. Chemical Mortar, Model 1942: Barrels—5, Range—7,850 meters; Weight—605 kilograms; Weight of shell—100 kilograms, etc."[9]

The most serious complaint Hall raised about these conferences—aside from the fact that the Russian colonel avoided certain delicate topics, such as the OB of Bulgaria and Rumania—was that by early March, "though pleasant enough," Pavlov was growing a bit indifferent about the meetings. He had not always briefed himself properly and therefore occasionally had to rely on nothing but "his excellent memory."[10] But Hall had no doubt that the U.S. Army was gaining a great deal from these sessions, and he also thoroughly enjoyed them. After the 30 March 1944 meeting, he noted: "I have never seen Pavlov in a better mood. At the end of our conference we spent ten minutes laughing and joking about the difficulty of the Russian language." At this same meeting, Pavlov asserted that some German divisions were being moved from the Western to the Eastern Front, and Hall challenged him, "Where do you get your information?" When Pavlov retorted, "We simply have information," Hall then responded, "We might even say rumor?" Pavlov replied, "OK, we have rumors." Summing up this session, the American observed, "reciprocity is the key note of these meetings, but by and large I believe we are getting the better of the bargain."[11]

G-2 Washington also thought that it was benefiting from these OB exchanges in Moscow. On 8 March 1944, in reply to Hall's report on the 2 March meeting, General Bissell declared that it was "very helpful" and that the Russian OB therein "differed surprisingly little from [the] picture here [,] indicating good service [on] your end."[12] On 12 April, a message from Bissell to Deane regarding recent OB meetings in Moscow was studded with the phrase "now accepted" to indicate that G-2 Washington had come to agree with the Soviet OB expert's claims, ranging from the placing of the 278th German Infantry Division at Trieste to the fact that the German 100th Light and 349th Infantry Divisions were still in Russia.[13]

In early April, General Deane went to work trying to open up more OB doors for Hall, urging General Slavin to authorize provision of Finnish OB to the Americans. It is not clear whether Slavin's promise to "clarify"[14] the situation actually netted the Americans more detail on the auxiliary armies fighting with the Germans on the Eastern Front, but on 6 May, Bissell's praise for the OB exchanges in Moscow knew no bounds. He characterized the material acquired by the Americans in Moscow as "of the greatest importance," and Hall's work as "commendable."[15] In May, Bissell continued to describe the Moscow OB meetings as "very helpful," and on 5 June he passed on the greatest of all compliments, requesting that OB meetings with the Soviets be held daily if possible.[16]

The U.S. Army mission was unable to produce this kind of near miracle and was also unsuccessful in securing front visits during this period—the closest thing to such a visit being General Crist's presence at the swearing-in ceremony when the first Polish Division was inducted into the Red Army on 30 March.[17] But Deane's staff did substantially better with regard to ordnance matters; the first of a series of Soviet-American enemy-ordnance conferences took place on 21 April. By 30 April, the Soviets informed SHAEF, as part of a general account of German armored divisions, that they had never encountered a full Panther tank battalion, and on 2 May, the Americans provided the Soviets with data on a German self-propelled gun.[18] Then on 29–30 May, the very eve of D day, the Soviets topped up their earlier gifts by giving the Americans details on the various demolition techniques customarily employed by the German Army in retreat. Col. Y. M. Rabinovich, the Red Army's top specialist on German demolition methods, gave an extended presentation on the subject to General Crist and Captain Hall, describing in detail how the Germans customarily demolished everything from hydroelectric plants to railroad lines. Rabinovich also presented the Americans with nine diagrams of German demolition methods for destroying industrial targets such as water-pumping stations and open-hearth furnaces. As a special sign of favor, he presented General Crist with his own "personal copy" of the German Army's pioneer manual for demolishing steel bridges and reinforced concrete, as well as a copy of the Soviet manual on the German "road destroyer" used to tear up railroad ties.[19]

These successes regarding intelligence on Germany were paralleled by hesitant steps forward in the direction of Soviet-American Army intelligence cooperation regarding Japan. Colonel Pettigrew, the U.S. Army's leading Japanese OB specialist, received his Soviet visa on 2 March, and a week later, Washington began sending intelligence regarding Japan to the U.S. mission in Moscow, including a summary of Japanese monthly aircraft production figures, for use in exchange with the Russians. Pettigrew arrived in the Soviet capital on 6 April (not two months later because of Soviet stalling on his visa application, as General Deane claimed after the War),[20] and on 11 April, Deane attempted to open the door for Pettigrew, stressing to the Soviets that Washington had sent some "valuable" intelligence that Pettigrew "would like to show and talk over with the Russian intelligence [section] of the General Staff." But when Deane added that this material concerned the Far East, General Slavin immediately declared, "I can say nothing," and the meeting was abruptly terminated.[21]

Deane and company pressed on, especially because the British had now agreed that Pettigrew should handle Japanese matters for both London and Washington in any discussion with the Soviets, thereby eliminating the old Soviet game of playing one Western informational penitent off against the other. Three days after D day (9 June), Pettigrew, accompanied by Deane, made a second attempt to meet with the Russians and gave Slavin "copies of our complete information on North China and Korea." He also loaned the Soviets "volume two of the Japanese Official Army Register, 1942," with apologies that it could merely be loaned, not given, because it was Pettigrew's only copy. Again, however, General Slavin "expressed absolutely no interest in the whole matter" and "made out that he was disappointed and somewhat embarrassed by the present meeting." Not until two more days had passed was Pettigrew finally able to sit down with a Soviet OB specialist on Japan (11 June 1944); then Japanese information began to move east to west, as well as west to east.[22]

Deane immediately sent Slavin proposed agendas for seven more Japanese OB meetings. Initially concerned with north China and Korea, these meetings were to go on to consider general aspects of the Japanese Army organization, together with its specific features, such as post office numbers, that would assist the intelligence-gathering activities of both Russia and the West. On 27 June, Bissell informed Pettigrew that he was "gratified by the progress being made" and "was very hopeful that future meetings will be even more fruitful." "We will cooperate fully," Bissell stressed, "and assume Sinclair [Maj. Gen. J. A. Sinclair, the current British DMI] will do the same." On the following day, G-2 Washington settled into a routine mode of OB exchange work on Japan, accepting most of the information in the Soviet overall summaries in regard to Manchuria, north China, and the Pacific Islands, but challenging some specifics in the Soviet picture (e.g., "see no reason why Kwantung Army should be [credited with retaining] control of 28 [th] Division in preference to others").[23]

This American breakthrough in East-West army OB exchanges on Japan immediately following D day was paralleled by increased Soviet willingness to collaborate on a broad range of intelligence matters regarding the war against Germany. On 13 June, General Crist had an extended meeting with Soviet chemical warfare specialists, who discussed German flamethrowers and gas masks and provided the Americans with specifications on three gas masks and six different German flamethrowers, along with eleven photographs and diagrams. On 17 June, General Bissell and Deane were able to satisfy their hearts' desire when the Soviets acceded to the American request for daily OB conferences.[24] On 22 June, General Spalding also had an important and extended discussion on tanks with Lt. Gen. I. V. Lebedev, deputy chief of the Soviet Armored Corps, which produced eleven closely typed pages of notes for the U.S. mission on the subject of Soviet, American, and German tanks. After the customary opening confusion about what the meeting was supposed to discuss, General Lebedev remarked that "since this is a military meeting, we can discuss these things frankly without political considerations." He then set off on a fairly complimentary survey of American armor, declaring that the American light tank was "a good tank, but it can't fight." In contrast, Lebedev thought that the few Sherman tanks that had been sent to Russia, although they had been "in [only] a few operations so far," were "much better," but they were still no good in mud.[25]

Turning to German tanks, the Soviet general provided much detail on the Panther and its strengths and weaknesses, as well as some observations on the structure, features, strengths, and weaknesses of the Tiger and the Ferdinand. Lebedev was friendly and helpful, although he made it clear at a number of points that he believed that the Americans were neither psychologically ready nor adequately equipped for a showdown battle with German heavy armor (in part, perhaps, because he underestimated the devastating effects of the West's massive tactical airpower). Overall, General Spalding could not have failed to realize that Lebedev was an authentic, tough tank man with vast knowledge of armored equipment and warfare:

> Tigers are no good in mud, neither is the Ferdinand [Lebedev declared]. The Panther can go through mud, but they are not equipped for mud. A big mistake has been made here [by the Germans] and it is too late to correct it now. They would have to change half the tank to correct the defect. The track is all right, but the rim to axle arrangement of the bogie wheels is poor; mud gets into the wheels and stops the tank.[26]

Further on, while considering reports of American tests on a T-34 tank provided by the Soviets, the Russian general remarked:

> I was very much amused in reading that you had difficulty in getting the radio to work in the laboratory, but it worked all right on the tank. Well that is where it is supposed to work![27]

To their credit, the members of the American tank team took all of Lebedev's comments and explanations in good spirit. In grim tank warfare against the Germans, the Soviets were indeed the masters and the Western armies, despite their technological gifts and experience in North Africa and Italy, the novices. Therefore, even well after the D-day landings, SHAEF was happy to receive information on newly appearing German armor from the Soviets, such as the reported encounter in Russia with a "Jagd Panther" in late June.[28]

Some aspects of British Army intelligence relations with the Soviets were also warmer during the spring and summer of 1944 than they had been in the chilly winter atmosphere of 1943–1944. Conforming to instructions, the 30 Mission chief, General Burrows, stressed to the Soviets that exchanges of information on the enemy should not be "one sided,"[29] and after a row with General Slavin on 3 March because of poor OB service for 30 Mission, Anglo-Soviet exchanges on German OB in Moscow rapidly improved. Three full exchanges of OB information took place in March, at least two more in April, another four in May, and three in June. Even the official British history of intelligence in World War II later conceded that "some" OB information was received from the Soviets in spring 1944, but since no minutes or summaries of Anglo-Soviet OB meetings for this period seem to be open to researchers (or, perhaps, even exist), it is impossible to judge just how beneficial they were to the British authorities.[30]

Occasionally, when the British requested information on specific units—as they did in late April on the SS Adolf Hitler Panzer Division—it can be proved that the Soviets provided the desired information; in this instance, the division was on the Eastern Front near Lvov. Also during May, the Soviets gave the British permission to ship home a Panther tank that had been captured by the Soviets, and they provided the mission with pamphlets on German defenses against parachute landings. Near the end of the month, Russia also "finally" provided identifications of German units "down to" the level of regiments.[31]

The British also secured some intelligence from the travels of 30 Mission members, including reports from one British officer who visited Baku in May 1944.[32] They also benefited from the journeys of Dominion officers, including a trip made by the Canadian assistant military attaché from Ottawa to Moscow via Siberia in the second week of May. More importantly, Whitehall received a copy of a long report filed by the Canadian military attaché, Brig. H. Lefebvre, who seems to have been the only Western officer to be granted a front visit by the Russians at this time. A British Foreign Office official was so impressed with Lefebvre's report that he characterized it as "the best account we have yet of what things are like on the Eastern front"; an MI 3 cover note declared, "the contents of this report or the fact of its existence must on no account be disclosed to the Russians."[33]

In May, 30 Mission had obtained from the Soviets a detailed critique of the Dieppe landings of 1942 that had been issued by Berlin to the German 320th Infantry Division, one of two German divisions on the Dieppe coast when the Canadians landed. This critique set out the German view of the main mistakes made by the Allies in the Dieppe assault, including their inability to land their armor at an early stage of the attack; it went on to set forth the principal defensive changes that the German high command had concluded were essential after the Dieppe assault, such as specific improvements in coastal defenses and the maintenance of large German armored reserves. After the 320th Infantry Division had been transferred to the Eastern Front in January 1943, it had been chewed up by the Red Army, its headquarters captured, and its records seized. Soviet intelligence officers recognized the potential value of this Dieppe raid critique to the Western powers and passed it on to the British, who shared it with the Americans. This instance of Soviets-Western cooperation was so important that even after the war, during the early Cold War era, one of the American G-2 mandarins, Col. J. R. Lovell, repeatedly cited the seizure of this document by the Russians as a near-perfect example of good intelligence work. He characterized the Dieppe raid document itself as "probably the most important document exploited in preparation for D Day," although it must be acknowledged that the current poor state of G-2 SHAEF and G-2 Washington records makes this judgment impossible to verify.[34]

This clouded picture has been reflected in contemporary and subsequent official British statements. Although even the British official history of intelligence has acknowledged that the Soviets were "unusually forthcoming" in this period,[35] by 23 June 1944, General Burrows characterized OB meetings with the Soviets as "farcical," and four days later, a high official at the War Office described recent Soviet OB output as "very meagre." On 28 June, the DMI, in a message to 30 Mission, virtually rang down the curtain on the prospects for further useful Anglo-Soviet OB cooperation, declaring that Soviet refusal to impart information on "German divisions below Army Group level renders their already meagre reports of little value."[36]

Also in May and June, General Burrows and his colleagues encountered serious difficulties trying to arrange Russian BODYGUARD diversionary activities for D day. On 28 April, General Slavin told Burrows that the Soviet general staff wished to implement its share of BODYGUARD raids on the northern coast of Norway "between Petsamo and Narvik," but the Soviets' information on this region was "very scanty," and they asked the British to supply the relevant maps. The now traditional inefficiency and failure of cooperation took over on both sides. The British were apparently unable to provide relevant information quickly enough for the Soviets to make up their bureaucratized mind where to carry out their diversionary attack, and the Soviets were too indifferently casual to pick an attack area and then demand that the British provide the appropriate maps and charts.[37] In the end, although General Deane believed that the Soviets were fully cooperative on BODYGUARD matters, no operations in the north were actually carried out, and 30 Mission as well as London made another deposit in the bitterness account brought about by Soviet lack of cooperation.[38]

No matter how much one may discount British grumbles and resentment about any particular Soviet shortcomings on BODYGUARD or specific aspects of the intelligence cooperation effort, it seems clear that the British Army did not do as well as the U.S. Army regarding intelligence-sharing activities with Moscow in the spring and early summer of 1944. It also appears that the Royal Navy came out on the short end of cooperative efforts with the Soviets in this period compared with the U.S. Navy, although perhaps not to the same degree as the British Army. The relative importance of both navy missions was once more undercut by the northern ports' decline in significance for the flow of supplies to the USSR, although as the Red Army advanced toward the Baltic and central Poland, the northern ports' close proximity to the main battlefields again enhanced their significance. In 1944, 18 convoys composed of 530 ships (compared with 431 ships in 1942) sailed for north Russia, with a loss of only 7 ships (compared with 57 losses in 1942), so the value of the northern convoys was still substantial. But as the senior British naval officer in Murmansk reported home, this vast augmentation of Western merchant shipping was due largely to the increased number of American vessels on the northern shipping routes. Only fourteen British vessels arrived in Murmansk during the first five months of 1944, in contrast to seventy-nine American merchant vessels, which was clearly a threatening situation for British prestige and the status of the British Navy mission in the USSR.[39]

The Royal Navy's position in the north was also weakened by recurring troubles with the Soviets over the "Y" station at Polyarnoe. The station was still operating, but the Soviets' refusal to allow British Typex encoding machines to be landed at Archangel during January had decreased the flow of "Y" to the Admiralty. A second attempt in April also failed when the Soviets impounded these machines as well. By May, London realized that the core of the problem was the old failure to master the intricacies of the Soviet bureaucratic maze, and the proper clearances were ultimately secured from Moscow and the Soviet embassy in London. In the meantime, however, the British mission in the north was reduced to a band of moaning complainers by the Typex machine crisis and had lost status and influence in north Russia.[40]

The Royal Navy mission in Moscow did somewhat better than its far northern offspring, energetically pursuing information from the Soviets that might assist the OVERLORD landing operations. In April, the Soviets handed over a rather elementary report on landing methods that the mission sat on for ten days before dispatching it to London. Four days *after* D day, the Red Navy gave the British a German pamphlet on coastal defenses as well as a German POW statement on Axis photo reconnaissance. The British also secured a few bits and pieces of intelligence from the Red Navy, such as information on U-boat and E-boat radio frequencies, a general report on Bremen, and, more significantly, information on the firing mechanism of the German electric torpedo. In exchange, 30 Mission presented the Russians with data on naval mines, copies of German daily secret naval orders, and some of the instructions the German Navy issued to its U-boats and E-boats.[41]

None of this material seems to have been of vital importance to either side. But one important piece of intelligence—the German report on the Dieppe raid that American G-2 prized so highly—may originally have been obtained from the Russians by the British Navy mission. Certainly the Royal Navy mission secured one report on the Dieppe raid from the Soviets on 16 May and as late as 1 June was pressing the Soviets for any additional German intelligence they had regarding the attack on Dieppe.[42] If the Royal Navy mission did the secure the Dieppe raid report, that was the crowning British intelligence achievement of the spring and summer of 1944 in Russia, but if not, that distinction belonged to the British Army.

The British naval liaison office in the Black Sea region, where Commander Lea remained at his post, continued to collect bits of intelligence, but Lea was unable to cut through the red tape to help two special Anglo-American navy missions investigating German methods of destroying ports they were evacuating and the characteristics of a wood-encased mine that the Germans were using. A somber comment on how low the British naval mission and its liaison officer in the Black Sea had fallen was the fact that in May 1944, Commander Lea seems to have spent a considerable portion of his waking hours battling with Red Navy officials about the cook who had been assigned to him.[43]

Only at the very end of May did 30 Mission's main navy section in Moscow enjoy a clear and dramatic intelligence triumph. Between 28 and 31 May, the outgoing head of the mission, Admiral Fisher, and members of his staff went on a four-day tour of Leningrad (perhaps as a reward for the promise of a visit for Admiral Kharlamov to the D-day beaches). The Leningrad visit included a close study of the great Red Navy base at Kronstadt, as well as the Red Navy's capital ships stationed there, permitting the Admiralty to conclude that regarding Soviet heavy ships, "our information on the Soviet Navy is now complete, with the exception of the Far East." Even on this prestigious occasion the British naval leaders could not shake off the cousins; Admiral Olsen and his staff were touring Leningrad and Kronstadt at the same time as the British. In any event, this was Admiral Fisher's swan song, for he returned to Britain shortly thereafter, and Admiral Archer took over command of the naval section of 30 Mission and later became General Burrows's successor as chief of the whole British military mission in Moscow.[44]

Under Archer's direction, 30 Mission enjoyed better relations with the Russians, as well as a closer partnership with the Americans. But when these improvements occurred, the Soviets had been recognized as a victorious great power, and the United States had established itself as the dominant member of the Western partnership. Even in the spring and summer of 1944, the treatment extended to the U.S. Navy by the Soviets was markedly better than that accorded to the British, as if Moscow was reacting to the handwriting on the wall about who the other postwar superpower would be. Consequently, the Navy Department in Washington was the primary beneficiary of the intelligence bestowed on the West by the Red Navy. In addition to detailed reports resulting from the visit of Olsen and his staff to Leningrad and Kronstadt, the

U.S. Navy mission considered Lieutenant Bassinger's exchange work with the Russians on naval mines to be "very satisfactory." Bassinger continued his naval mine survey, preparing reports not only on Soviet mines but also on naval minesweeping devices, including a "German magnetic mine sweeping device which floated," and on the facilities of the Soviet mine technical organizations. In addition, U.S. Navy officers made extended trips across the USSR, with Captain Roullard exploring the Trans-Siberian railroad as well as Vladivostok and its environs. A number of junior U.S. travelers made extensive visits to Russian ports and airfields, including construction sites.[45]

The U.S. Navy moved dramatically ahead of the Royal Navy through its exchanges with the Soviets regarding the Japanese fleet. In early March, the American JIC formally approved naval intelligence exchanges with the Soviets regarding Japan, and in early April, the Red Navy reported that Japanese troops were continuing to move southward and listed their main concentration points in Japan. During May and June, the Red Navy gave the Americans various monographs on Japanese convoys, installations on Sakhalin Island, ground tactics, Pacific naval battles, Japanese naval training and personnel losses, and the total number of Japanese naval personnel "broken down into categories, and complements [of] various ships by speciality."[46] As had been done previously, the more important materials were sent not only to ONI and the chief of naval operations in the United States but also to the White House. Therefore, even though some members of the U.S. Navy mission, Moscow, continued to look down on the Russians—one U.S. Navy official characterized the average Russian as a "primitive," "a child," "quick to anger," and "quick to forget"[47]—the U.S. Navy continued to benefit from its partnership with Moscow.

Nonetheless, the U.S. Navy's intelligence-swapping achievements, as well as those of the U.S. Army, paled considerably in the spring and summer of 1944 in the face of the great triumphs of the U.S. Army Air Corps. As General Arnold and his staff had hoped, the establishment of Operation FRANTIC shuttle-bombing bases in the Ukraine opened new possibilities for closer cooperation with the Red Air Force and, in the process, permitted the Americans to chalk up unparalleled intelligence-sharing achievements, even though on 10 March 1944, General Crist had inspected two of the bases the Soviets had prepared for the Americans and found them to be mediocre.[48]

On 17 March, three U.S. Army Air Corps colonels, accompanied by Captain Hall, met with Lieutenant General Grendle, chief of Red Air Force intelligence and reconnaissance matters. Grendle deferred answering any questions on communications, which were to be taken up in later meetings of "communications experts," and also postponed discussion of Russian antiaircraft defenses until a meeting could be arranged with the Soviet antiaircraft department, which was not an integral part of the Red Air Force. But Grendle stressed that "he would arrange" such a conference and that there would be "no difficulty in securing the information desired [by the Americans] regarding the Soviet Air Defense System" or supplying a map "showing the location" of Russian "airdomes located in the vicinity" of American Air Corps installations.[49]

What Grendle did provide on 17 March was general information on German fighter deployment and the German radar net, as well as the location and strength of German flak batteries. The Soviet air staff also agreed to provide the Americans with six copies of "three-view silhouettes" of Russian operational aircraft, targeting information on German installations in Eastern Europe, and Soviet maps of Poland, Rumania, and western Russia. But the primary intelligence gift to the Americans on 17 March was a list showing the German Air Force dispositions on the Eastern Front. It covered nine locations from Orsha to Odessa and specified the model of Luftwaffe aircraft stationed at each location (ME 109s, ME 110s, FW 190s, and so forth) and whether they were day or night fighters; in all but one location (Ploesti), it also provided the German squadron numbers and fighter group numbers of the German air units stationed there.[50]

This conference alone provided the Americans with more intelligence on the German air force in the east than they had previously received from the Soviets. It also opened the way for them to secure more information on the Red Air Force than they, or the British, had ever dreamed of acquiring. General Grendle was true to his word in arranging additional meetings to cover specific aspects of Soviet and German air defense systems in the east. On 1 April, Col. C. R. Bond Jr. reported home (and to the American military attaché in London) on the information acquired form the Soviets on German flak and fighter distribution. The Soviets supplied data on German flak in twelve main locations in Eastern Europe, for two of which, Baronowizce and Minsk, the number and caliber of guns were specified: "18 to 24 88mm guns and many lighter guns" at Baronowizce, and "3 to 4 batteries [of] 88mm guns at Minsk." The Soviets also gave the Americans another copy of the German fighter distribution summary they had provided two weeks earlier, merely noting that the Luftwaffe units that had been listed as stationed at Balta and Pervomaisk were now unaccounted for, since these two points had been recaptured by the Red Army.[51]

In April and May, the Americans did what they could to reciprocate in providing information on the U.S. Army Air Corps to supplement what the Soviets could see for themselves by close-up examination of American equipment, crews, and air procedures used at Poltava and the neighboring fighter defense base. On 18 April, the U.S. mission gave the Red Air Force a Norwegian bomb sight, and a month later it followed this up with the Norden bomb sight and an extended program for teaching Soviet bombadiers how to use it effectively. Even in the realm of sharing technical equipment, however, the Americans were recipients as well as suppliers. The Soviets provided many samples of Red Air Force crew clothing, plus the specifications for the armored glass used by the Red Air Force. They also allowed the American mission to study the details of German gas masks and at least one report acquired from the interrogation of a German prisoner indicating the effect of Western air raids on German aircraft production.[52]

By 16 May, General Kessler at Poltava had received information on "the performance of certain Soviet aircraft" (although this information may have come from the British test pilot reports of 1941). Whatever the source—Soviet or Western—the American air crews had this information in their possession and considered it "most useful in our planning."[53] On 11 May, a U.S. Army Air Corps officer also had a full intelligence meeting with the Red air staff, and five days later a comparable meeting on communications. In both sessions, the American secured useful data on the enemy as well as deeper insights into the equipment and procedures of the Red Air Force. The Soviets also indirectly indicated that they had excellent sources on Luftwaffe technology, because they requested American information on German jet aircraft well before any such Luftwaffe aircraft had appeared in action in either east or west.[54]

The Americans and Soviets certainly cooperated well enough to permit the first shuttle-bombing raid to go off successfully; 129 B-17s and 64 P-51s landed at the Russian bases on 2 June after bombing marshaling yards and locomotive works in Hungary. Gen. I. Eaker, commander of the 15th Air Force, arrived in Russia on 5 June, meeting with Molotov "to express his sincere appreciation to the Soviet government for the air bases which it had furnished the American Air Force in the Soviet Union." When Molotov queried Eaker about how the shuttle-bombing arrangements were going, the American general replied, "excellently," adding that "the closest cooperation had been shown" by the Soviets and "that the friendliness between Russians and Americans at the airbases was striking."[55] Eaker also observed, completely reversing the negative views of General Crist, that the bases largely built by the Soviets "were better than those on the average that had been constructed in Italy" and "had been prepared in short time, even shorter than the Americans could have prepared them."[56]

This Soviet-American love feast continued through the first half of June, with Soviet and American officers solving every problem that arose about the

Poltava operations. On 10 June, Stalin assured Harriman, in principle, that the Americans would be able to construct air bases in Siberia prior to the USSR's entry into the war against Japan. The Americans even started down the same nearly suicidal road of optimism that the British had trod in 1941. Deane asked Slavin on 10 May for information on the same Soviet airborne rocket equipment that Macfarlane had pursued three years earlier. But before anything could be done one way or the other on the infamous rocket bomb, the Luftwaffe rudely interrupted this happy Soviet-American partnership. Heinkel 111s trailed the second American shuttle-bombing raid to the Poltava bases, destroying forty-seven American B-17s on the ground (the "worst disaster" the Army Air Corps experienced on the ground during the whole war) and achieving the last great Nazi success in the air war on the Eastern Front.[57]

This German air attack took the glow off both shuttle bombing and the special relationship the Air Corps had established with the Soviets. But its negative effects were not grave for intelligence exchange. On 23 June, the Soviets gave the American mission a long summary of German aircraft shot down in the Crimea between 8 and 28 April, including the specific identifying numbers. This was just the kind of information that American intelligence specialists had long sought in vain, for it consisted of factory numbers, operational markings, and aircraft tail markings.[58] A week later, Colonel Bond concluded that the cooperative climate was still so favorable that it should be possible to continue effective cooperation with the Soviets not only on German air intelligence matters but also, "if not pressed too much," on Japanese air intelligence. The U.S. Army Air Corps remained optimistic about air intelligence cooperation with the USSR, even though Bond recognized that "the traditions of the Soviet Government stand in the way to [*sic*] a free exchange of information." If the Americans "acted in good faith" and avoided "snooping," Bond believed that an exchange of "some categories of information" by the air forces of the United States and the USSR would still be possible and would "prove advantageous to both nations."[59]

This was overly optimistic, but such a statement in June 1944 was not surprising, considering the great successes the American Army Air Corps had scored in joint intelligence with the Soviets during the first six months of the year. The length of this leap may best be measured by exploring the fate of British efforts to carry out air intelligence exchanges with the Red Air Force in the same period, for the RAF had remained aloof from the shuttle-bombing program and the Soviet-American intelligence exchanges that accompanied it. In March, the air section of 30 Mission was allowed to visit a Stormavik base, but the Air Ministry in London nonetheless decided to tighten the screws on exchanges with the Soviet air delegation in London, eliminating visits to Bomber Command and reducing to a minimum information about RAF "operations, tactics, and equipment." The RAF remained committed to supplying weapons and intelligence to the Russians "which may be used . . . during the war," as well as "intelligence about the enemy which is of value to Russian operations,"[60] but it was not willing to tell the Russians what it knew about the good "crytographic results" the Germans were "achieving on the Eastern Front" against the Red Air force.[61] Even when the Soviets indicated a willingness to try again on broader intelligence cooperation with the RAF, and members of 30 Mission complained in April that they had "lost a lot of ground in our relations with the Russians in comparison with the Americans" because the RAF was not involved in shuttle bombing, the Air Ministry refused to make any vigorous attempt to improve air intelligence exchanges.[62]

This negative stance by the Air Ministry underscored an important fact regarding Anglo-American intelligence cooperation efforts with the USSR in the spring and summer of 1944. Britain, which had pioneered Western intelligence-sharing efforts with Moscow since June 1941, had surrendered its lead to the United States by at least May or June 1944. In seeking to explain why Washington appeared to make such great headway with the Soviets on intelligence and other matters in this period, since the onset of the Cold War it has been customary to argue that in their naive innocence, the Americans gave so much to the Soviets via lend-lease that Stalin found it expedient in the short run to thinly disguise his hostile intentions, don the mask of good old Uncle Joe, and seize what he could from the Americans while the getting was good. A supplemental, if more partisan, contention has been that "leftists" in the Roosevelt administration were so anxious to pamper the USSR for ideological reasons that Stalin easily enticed them into making enormous comradely bribes to Moscow, only to turn his back on the United States and Britain in 1945 and strike off in pursuit of what he saw as the basic security and ideological interests of Communist Russia by grabbing control of large chunks of Eastern Europe and northern Asia.

In this tale of Stalinist Realpolitik and Rooseveltian naiveté, the British government has usually been cast as the United States' reluctant fellow traveler, whose sense of hard politics, as well as its poverty, kept it from falling prey to the folly of trusting the Soviets or trying to buy their favor, but whose decline and ultimate weakness prevented it from forcing a more realistic policy on Washington.[63] But when one examines the record of British and American intelligence relations with the USSR, especially in early 1944, other contrasting features in the way Britain and the United States dealt with Moscow become clear and take much of the shine off these popular accounts of wartime Western policies and the consequent arrival of the Cold War.

After 1942, the U.S. government did not experience serious internal policy battles regarding what should be done about Russia, in terms of either general policy or specific aspects of military and political cooperation. Roosevelt set out the basic policy—namely, that since the Soviet Union was carrying the heaviest burden of the war against Germany, suffering most of the losses and casualties, and inflicting the bulk of the damage on the Wehrmacht, the USSR should receive all the aid the United States could supply, without carping or undue regard for cost. By midwar, this basically open-handed but self-interested resolve seems gradually to have been supplemented in President Roosevelt's mind by a mixture of admiration for Soviet military achievements and a hope that Western open-handedness would lessen Soviet fear and suspicion. Then Stalin might be inclined to relax Bolshevik fanaticism and join hands with the Western democratic Big Two to create a more prosperous, stable, and peaceful world.

The president did not constantly intervene in the nuts and bolts of Russian policy implementation, any more than he did on most other matters of high policy.[64] After setting a basic line, Roosevelt depended on custom and enlightened self-interest, as well as the power of appointment, to get the right people in the right spots to implement his policies. He did not make scenes or employ dramatic exhortation to get his way, but in the end, he bent nearly everyone to his will with a minimum of crises and controversy. Regarding his policy toward the USSR, as well as that toward many other part-military, part-civil international matters, Roosevelt leaned heavily on the calm but forceful leadership and administrative skill of the U.S. Army chief of staff, Gen. George C. Marshall.[65] Marshall ran the War Department, under the titular direction of Henry Stimson, through a corps of young, able career officers who had learned their trade and established their bona fides under Marshall's direct supervision. As the war progressed, Marshall controlled the various extensions of American military operations (with the notable exception of Gen. Douglas MacArthur's Pacific kingdom) by assigning to crucial overseas posts "his" young men, who knew what Marshall wanted and could be counted on to fulfill his wishes without tantrums or thunderbolts from the Pentagon.

This was especially true of men like Gens. Walter Beddell Smith and Dwight Eisenhower, but also of many now lesser known figures such as Gens. Mark Clark, Albert Wedemeyer, and Jacob Devers. In regard to Russian matters, it was also true of John Deane. He was a Marshall man, had risen rapidly in Marshall's War Department, knew the chief of staff's mind, and also knew how Marshall wanted the game played—namely, through good staff work, loyalty, and no histrionics. So from 1943 to the end of the war, the U.S. military mission in Moscow went through no significant personnel changes, experienced no serious shifts or swings of policy, and enjoyed an absence of suicidal conflicts or any form of the cult of personality.

Needless to say, American civil and military personnel in Washington who were concerned with Soviet matters also exhibited most of these same characteristics. "Leftists" or "rightists" like Henry Wallace and James Forrestal were usually marginalized; feeble figures like Cordell Hull and Edward Stettinius at State were eased aside; and the president, George Marshall, and their trusted handmaidens Harriman and Deane were left to implement American policy toward Russia calmly and consistently. This meant, among other things, that although the CCS had insisted that no Anglo-American "office workers" should receive foreign decorations during the war, the rule had to be relaxed in March 1944 because Stalin insisted on giving a special award not to Franklin Roosevelt but to George Marshall.[66]

Matters were very different in London regarding the formulation of British policy toward the USSR as well as its execution, as has been noted by a number of scholars in the past and at many points above. In June 1941, that seasoned anti-Bolshevik Winston Churchill extended his hand to Stalin, with minimal consultation with his cabinet colleagues. Then, despite the existence of a formal and coherent pyramidal chain of command in Whitehall—moving up from ministers to cabinet and then to the prime minister—as well as a number of lower-level coordinating agencies, including the Joint Intelligence Committee and the Chiefs of Staff Committee, no basic wartime policy toward Russia was ever hammered into a coherent and consistent form. Additionally, many high British officials involved with Anglo-Soviet relations, such as Colonel Firebrace, were bitter anti-Communists or had fought against the Bolsheviks in 1919, as was the case with General Burrows and a number of others.

On the other side of the Russian policy fence in Whitehall, the Foreign Office gradually drifted into a conciliatory stance toward Moscow, again without any clear statement of policy. This attitude was not especially related to the presence of leftist inclinations among Foreign Office mandarins (except for the likes of Donald Maclean and his espionage associates, who had good reasons of personal security not to appear too openly sympathetic to the USSR), but rather because of a quiet recognition that British power was declining and that if the USSR triumphed over Nazi Germany it would emerge as a superpower. As a result of the lack of a clear policy regarding Russia, Whitehall officials continued to squabble through 1944 over what line should be taken with

Moscow on a host of matters, ranging from intelligence to technical cooperation. The difficulties became so serious in May that at least one member of the Northern Department was alarmed by the level of "ill-feeling against the Russians," which he rightly believed "to exist in the Service Departments."[67]

But elsewhere during the winter and spring of 1943–1944, other Whitehall consultative organizations with a strong Foreign Office presence, such as the Post Hostilities Planning Committee, were beginning to state frankly that there might be clashes with the USSR in the postwar era. They cited Iran, Turkey, and over naval matters, but interestingly—and wrongly—neither Central Europe nor the mainland of Asia was mentioned as a likely East-West hot spot. Even so, future prospects for Britain looked so bleak in April–May 1944 that some in London toyed with the possibility of organizing a Western "Free Germany Committee" and approached captured German generals to play parts in such a movement, in the hope of bringing the Third Reich down before Russian power increased and British power declined even more.[68]

Above the departmental differences regarding Russia, the prime minister impetuously hopped from one extreme to another, taking Stalin to his bosom in June 1941 and then falling into fits of rage against the Russians—moaning, stamping, and pouting—during his 1942 visit to Moscow. By April 1944, as the Polish question heated up, he minuted Eden that it was time to "curl up a bit" with the Soviets and "relapse into a moody silence so far as Stalin is concerned." Although Churchill believed that he had tried "in every way "to put himself "in sympathy with these Communist leaders," he did not have "the slightest trust or confidence in them."[69]

But such dog-day moods did not last. By June 1944, with D day successfully accomplished and the West on the Continent in force, the prime minister was more upbeat regarding Moscow. In late June 1944, he even overruled 30 Mission's decision to stop sending home the Soviet daily communiqué, which was merely a rehash of Moscow radio summaries. Churchill insisted that it continue to be dispatched because, he declared, "I am a constant reader of anything you send."[70] In this same period, Churchill lectured the first sea lord on why the *Daily Worker* should not be allowed in operational theaters. "Communists do not hesitate to relay any British or American secret they may find to the Communist Party, no doubt for transmission to Russia," he explained.[71] Yet by autumn he was off for another chat with Stalin, trying to wave a magic wand over East-West clashes of interest in the Balkans.

The failure to grasp the nettle and settle on a definite policy regarding the USSR, combined with the intensity of Churchill's changes of mood, placed British intelligence-exchange relations with the Soviets on an especially unstable and vulnerable foundation. The trouble was increased by London's insistence that all its intelligence interchanges with the Soviets be carried out in London or Moscow. When, in March 1944, the War Office learned that Gen. Sir Henry "Jumbo" Wilson's G-2 office at AFHQ Mediterranean was providing the local Soviet liaison mission with top-secret intelligence summaries, London immediately ordered that this practice be stopped, even if the cutoff offended the Russians, because AFHQ was giving the Soviets "more information than we normally pass to the Russians here." The DMI's main concern was to make the Russians pay for everything they were receiving, thereby, perhaps, improving "the treatment accorded to our Mission at Moscow."[72] This procedure was intended to concentrate the pressure on the Soviets to play ball; Moscow would get no valuable information without being prompted to provide comparable material in return. In actuality, it was merely an exercise in using clever arrangements and pressure as substitutes for policy, because Moscow simply refused to reciprocate, and London was unable to do anything about it.

These troubles were then compounded by a pernicious tendency left over from balmier days in the empire, whereby splendidly clad emissaries were sent abroad to distribute trinkets and woo native rulers while acting as dispensers of political and military wisdom. Nearly everyone in Whitehall knew enough about the United States not to indulge overtly in this form of paternalistic folly in Washington. Halifax and Dill were so careful to avoid patronizing the Americans that many Britons even today believe that Churchill's government bent over backward to accommodate the United States, gratuitously providing the Americans with secrets on the A-bomb, Bletchley's early computers, penicillin, and bacteriological warfare devices (which Marshall and Dill were discussing as early as April 1944).[73] As a result, by the end of the war, Britain's technological cupboard was nearly bare, and American technological supremacy was assured.

But in Moscow, British military appointees echoed the old traditions of the raj, with the mission chiefs from Macfarlane through Martel to Burrows arriving not just to cooperate with an ally but also to instruct the Russians, provide them with occasional nuggets of intelligence, and most of all impress them with British grandeur—and thereby hide British weakness. Macfarlane represented the most boyishly foppish aspect of this tradition, Martel the most pretentious; in 1944, Burrows moved on to manifest the British penchant for expressions of reserved and cold superiority. In all its forms, what may be called the imperial demeanor of the British military mission leaders and many of their staff had the potential to create boundless difficulties. When coupled with the lack of a basic British plan for dealing with the reality of the USSR, the absence of clear

British foreign policy goals, and the prime minister's vagaries, this demeanor ensured that British military intelligence relations with the Soviet Union were always a near disaster waiting to happen.

Almost from the moment he took up his post clad in his medals from the White side of the Russian Civil War, General Burrows embodied the negative aspects of this situation and started out on the wrong foot. Observing in an early dispatch to Eden that "manners are not the strong point of these people [i.e., the Soviets] by any means,"[74] Burrows went on to attack Soviet "zenophobia," which he summarized in a remarkably inappropriate phrase (considering that this was the period of the Nazi *Endlösung*) by asserting that there was a Soviet plot to "decry foreigners" and to "persuade the Russian people that they were the new chosen race."[75] The Foreign Office was troubled by such remarks and by the utterances regarding Soviet Russia recently made by General Martel (now back in London), which "were not likely to do any good to Anglo-Soviet relations." In consequence, C. F. Warner of the Northern Department observed that "we ought in any case to have General Martel told that he must not speak about his experience in Russia at all."[76]

Burrows was nonetheless allowed to march down a portion of the road that Martel had recently trod, peppering London in April and May with complaints of Russian failings, such as the refusal to indicate the location of their planned offensive in support of D day. This particular outburst prompted even Churchill to observe, "I don't know why we should press to know the details of this operation . . . they are fully justified in saying what they do." Stalin explained to Harriman that he was telling the president when the offensive would begin but not precisely where because of poor Western security, a subject about which the Soviet leader was surely very knowledgeable.[77]

Apparently oblivious to the thin ice on which he was skating, Burrows launched his tenure as mission chief in April by revamping 30 Mission's liaison machinery, in preparation for expanded relations with the Soviets as OVERLORD drew near. To this end, he not only established a "Special Intelligence Room," intended to provide OVERLORD information to the Russians, but also overcame opposition from the army section of the mission (which was disinclined to take on extra work) and established an internal mission intelligence "I" room, which, as explained by Group Captain Roberts:

> Under a system called ULTRA [would file and hold] three types of
> messages . . . received from the Air Ministry: Hussar, which can be
> passed to the Russians, Lancer, which is information for [the] head
> of Mission and heads of Sections *only,* and Yeoman, which are

short messages containing hot information from [the] Air Ministry for passing to the Russians.[78]

This was a sensible reform, and it proves that a flow of ULTRA material was still going to the Soviets via 30 Mission at this date. Burrows was also right in arguing that although the Soviets desired a Second Front, they also "fear[ed] that sweeping successes in the West may put in [the] shade [the] previous Red Army victories," not to mention the threat that a large Western offensive might pose to future hegemony in Eastern Europe.[79] But at the same time, Burrows insisted that the Soviets be held to an exacting line of reciprocity, with an end to free Anglo-American gifts for Moscow. This contention was not inherently silly, but since London had not settled with the Americans on this or any other important aspect of policy regarding the USSR, Burrows was in no position to push such a hard-line stand.

Isolated, assertive, and vulnerable, Burrows had sealed his fate. The weakness of his position was soon glaringly obvious. On 10 June 1944, Stalin told Harriman—not the British—that "the present head of the British Military Mission, General Burrows, was not trusted by the Soviet Military authorities."[80] Two weeks later, when Clark Kerr, during a discussion with Molotov and Vyshinsky, mentioned that General Burrows wanted a front visit and also believed that he had received shabby treatment from the Russians, Molotov stated that although "with General Martel there had been minor misunderstandings . . . on the whole relations had been good, and the same with General Macfarlane."[81] But the Soviet foreign secretary went on to emphasize that in the Kremlin view, Burrows was trouble. Vyshinsky chimed in to characterize him as "rather haughty," to which Molotov added in a premature and unconscious takeoff on Arthur Miller's Willie Loman, that Burrows was "haughty and not liked."[82]

From that point on, any possibility that Burrows and the British mission might stand up to the Soviets and effectively champion the cause of East-West intelligence cooperation in the summer of 1944 was probably doomed. Burrows remained at his post through the summer of 1944 and even received a front visit, but the political position of the British mission had been seriously weakened. The post-D-day era would soon show the Americans to be rising in Soviet favor, while Burrows and his colleagues were pushed further away from the centers of Soviet power and influence.

10
The Penultimate Phase Begins, July–November 1944

After years in which the Allied powers had been mainly on the defensive, engaging in only limited or isolated offensives, the high summer and autumn of 1944 found the Allies advancing on every front. In Burma, the British finally ground down Japanese offensive power by midsummer and went over to the offensive in August. The Americans seized Guam and Tinian during summer 1944, and in October, General MacArthur returned to the Philippines while the U.S. Navy nearly obliterated the Imperial Japanese Fleet in the Battle of Leyte Gulf, sinking four cruisers, two battleships, and a large number of other vessels.

Due to this series of military reverses, General Tojo was the first obvious enemy casualty of the final phase of the war, falling from power in Tokyo on 18 July. As the Allies advanced across Europe, Axis leaders there were forced to recognize that dark days were in store for them as well. During August, General Alexander's forces took Florence, freeing all of central and southern Italy and pushing the Germans and their Fascist Italian colleagues into a slice of northern Italy with the Po and the Alps at their backs. Few bright prospects beckoned for Kesselring's army or *Il Duce,* who had placed his fate in Hitler's hands and now found that every day he was closer to a dire and sordid end.

Hitler himself was far from immune from the high price tag attached to failure in World War II. During the week the Americans broke out of the Normandy pocket by smashing east from Saint-Lô, Hitler had his revenge on Stauffenberg and the other unsuccessful plotters against him, but there was no way to check the Allied advance that spelled his doom. By mid-August, the Americans had nearly cleared the Wehrmacht from Brittany, 50,000 German troops had been caught in the Falaise pocket, and Operation ANVIL had landed another large Western force on the coast of southern France and sent it dashing up the Loire Valley. Paris was liberated on 25 August, Lyons a week later. Although the Germans managed to cling temporarily to the extreme northeastern corner of France where the Vosges mountains suited the defense, elsewhere the Western Allied advance could not be stopped.

In September, at a time when 2 million Anglo-American troops were already on the Continent, Montgomery's armies drove northeast, seizing Antwerp on the fourth, Brussels on the eighth, and Luxembourg on the tenth. The following day saw Eisenhower's armies nudge across the German frontier, and although fighting on native soil seemed to stiffen the German defenders, and Montgomery suffered a serious reversal at Arnhem when British paratroops were decimated by panzers, the great summer 1944 Western advance marked the sure doom of Hitler's Germany.

As if to recognize that fact, the Fuehrer struck back with the first V-2 "terror" attack on Britain on 2 September and called out the *Volkssturm* for last-ditch stands on 25 September. But Germany's hour had come in both east and west. Throughout July and August, the Soviets slugged across Poland, Rumania, and Bulgaria. The Rumanian government was the first Eastern European Nazi satellite to jump ship, surrendering to the Soviets on 23 August. The Ploesti oil fields—Germany's last source of nonsynthetic oil—were in Red Army hands one week later. Bulgaria capitulated on 8 September, and the Finns laid down their arms shortly thereafter. By 20 October, the Soviets had also swept through Yugoslavia; Belgrade was quickly in their hands, and the remnants of German units in the southern Balkans were soon fleeing northwest, trying to escape before the advancing Red Army closed the door by seizing Hungary and Austria.

Throughout this triumphant Soviet advance, however, the fate of one city in central Eastern Europe proclaimed that Soviet intentions might not be as kindly as the West would like. The Polish resistance had risen in Warsaw on 1 August 1944 as Russian forces closed in on the city, but while German units systematically destroyed the resisters and the city itself over the next two months, the Red Army remained nearly inert just a few miles to the east. Finally, on 2 October, the Polish resistance capitulated to the Germans, and soon afterward, the Red Army resumed its westward advance, taking Warsaw on 20 October and then crashing into east Prussia.[1]

No one witnessing these great Allied advances, certainly not the Poles, could doubt that the Allies would be unable to keep the political aspects of their war against the Axis and Japan under wraps much longer. As great Allied attacks drove into Europe and Asia, the leaders of Britain and the United States met at Quebec to consider what should be done with postwar Germany, even toying with the idea of turning it into a postwar pasture via the Morgenthau plan. On a more realistic level, the Dumbarton Oaks conference tried to find an effective formula for a world organization that would link the Soviets and the West and establish mechanisms to create and maintain world peace.

Since intelligence sharing with the Soviets was one of the few areas in which the British and Americans had had close relations with Moscow over an extended time, exchanges of secret information might well have been a sensitive gauge of the changes in the cooperative attitude produced by the great Allied military leap forward in 1944. But instead of producing anything new and innovative (except for some exchanges on possible German use of poison gas), East-West relations regarding the sharing of intelligence in the summer and autumn of 1944 seemed to repeat existing patterns, with perhaps a modest overall downturn. This might well have suggested caution to those Western leaders who were eager to start down the road to a brave new world.[2]

Few records of Soviet and American army OB meetings about the German Army remain in open files for the period, but the records that are available show that some valuable material came from the Soviets in July and August. On 7 July, the Red Army gave the Americans a detailed list of German divisions "removed from [the] combat estimate by [the] Soviets," including five divisions "destroyed at Votebsk," three more "mauled and then disbanded," fourteen more "mauled," plus another nine infantry divisions "which have sustained great losses but which are still carried in [the Soviet OB] estimates."[3] In the early part of August, the Americans also received two and a half pages of detailed German Army OB resulting from a long session with the Red Army. In a nearly unprecedented gesture of cordiality, they were also permitted to interview three captured German lieutenant colonels, one from an unidentified unit, and the other two from the 31st and 206th German Infantry Divisions. The German officers told the American interrogators the strength of their divisions, summarized the combat operations in which they had been captured, and added the telling detail that the replacement flow to their divisions had consisted of only "250 men per month," drawn exclusively from those men "reassigned after recuperation from wounds."[4]

The army section of the British 30 Mission may well have had more OB meetings with the Soviets in the summer and autumn of 1944 than did the Americans. The 30 Mission war diary lists six such meetings between July and November, but only one of these, that of 22 August, was characterized as "successful."[5] Burrows acknowledged that the OB meetings were "of value," and this view was echoed by the DMI,[6] although Burrows also told the chiefs of staff during a short visit to London in early August that the Soviet officer handling the exchange could in "no sense be described as an expert and is not sufficiently knowledgeable to be able to answer questions or discuss details."

Burrows went on to hypothesize in an odd bit of fantasy that the Soviet "intelligence system is extremely underdeveloped and over-worked."[7]

As early as July 1944, Burrows lamented that the Russians were not interested in OB information regarding Anglo-American forces. To increase the pressure on the Soviets to cooperate on the pressing matter of German OB, 30 Mission urged London to stop supplying the Soviet mission in London with such information in order to force Moscow to be more forthcoming. By late August, the War office and the Air Ministry had finally cut back on the German OB information they provided to Kharlamov's team, but this change seems to have produced little or no long-term benefit to Burrows. The Soviets still refused to show the British mission in Moscow copies of their "periodic lists" of the German Army that were printed every ten days, even though on "several occasions" the British OB men in Moscow "deliberately made [the] Russian OB representatives aware of [the] existence of our monthly list," to try to tempt them into agreeing to more extensive exchanges. All such efforts drew blanks, however, and by the second week of November, the Soviets flatly refused to give the British any OB data on German units in Army Group Center. All Burrows could think to do in response was to urge London to tighten the screws once again on the Russians in Britain, but since this had been tried repeatedly in the past with no success, 30 Mission was left nearly high and dry on the subject of German Army OB by the early winter of 1944–1945.[8]

The British had a similarly dispiriting season in regard to sharing information with the Soviets on German arms and equipment. They succeeded in carrying out some exchanges on German land mines, and the Red Army provided them with two sample tank heaters and some signals equipment during October. The Americans, however, did much better. In August, the Red Army gave General Deane a highly detailed description of, along with the technical specifications for, the German "240 mm Gun K3"; in September, a similarly detailed report was received on two other pieces of German artillery (the "7.5 cm. Pak 37" and the "15cm.s. F/H 18/40").[9] During late September and early October, the American ordnance staff in Moscow also obtained the specifications for the new German Tiger II Imperial tank and were relieved to discover that it was "just a modernized Tiger."[10] On a somewhat humbler level, the Americans also obtained some German mountain troop equipment. Then, as a result of a 10 September meeting with the Soviets on the likelihood of the Germans resorting to gas warfare, examples of German gas masks, flamethrowers, and some gas warfare equipment, plus more information on the Ferdinand and the Panther tank, were supplied to General Deane.[11]

The British and American missions in Moscow managed to join together in pursuit of information on the German V-2 rocket program, which British officials had begun to seek in late 1943. On 13 July 1944, General Ismay sent Burrows details on the V-1, reported that London no longer required information on the Russian "katusha rocket—[which] is [now] out of date," and told him that Churchill had informed Stalin that the British wanted Soviet assistance in studying "the big rocket" (i.e., the V-2) being developed by the Germans. Stalin immediately authorized the dispatch to Russia of a British-American V-2 technical team, which was supplemented by a Soviet contingent during a short stopover in Moscow. The tripartite team then visited the German V-2 test site at Blizna in Soviet-occupied Poland and returned to Moscow before the first V-2 was launched against Britain.[12]

On 8 September 1944, the British segment of the team relayed an initial report to London via 30 Mission indicating that despite German efforts to remove everything of intelligence value from Blizna, they had been able to establish the type of fuel the Germans were using in the V-2 and also that no "special launching mechanism" was employed in firing the rocket.[13] The Westerners had a few grumbles about stringent Soviet security and red tape, and some skeptics have subsequently dismissed the value of the mission. But overall, the Western mission members themselves, led by Col. T. R. B. Sanders (U.K.) and Lt. Col. J. A. O'Mara (U.S.), had no doubt that they had secured much useful information and been well served by their Russian hosts. The mission had studied the V-2 launching sites, as well as those for V-1 tests; traced the system by which the rockets had been brought in from Germany; determined the general fueling methods and the fuels used; and plotted out the rocket test areas. The team also gathered up the better part of a ton of fragments from Blizna, including bits from the V-2 sites. But the Germans had been so assiduous in clearing the site before evacuation that the fragmentary evidence was much less significant than the few eyewitness accounts that had been secured from Polish laborers and the information that had been obtained about the layout and operation of the test site. By late January 1945, Gen. Carl T. Spaatz reported to General Deane that the information secured from Blizna had "proved to be of inestimable value," and the British were so pleased that they initially gave the Soviets more data on the V-2 than they gave to the Dominions. As late as April 1945, the British JIC still had a highly favorable view of the Blizna mission, stating that "a considerable amount of interesting intelligence was gained by the Mission."[14]

Generals Burrows and Deane then attempted to strike while the iron was hot and proposed technological exchange arrangements, telling the Soviets on 27 August 1944 that in the last stages of the war, East and West should freely share the technical secrets they secured from the Germans. This was much too extreme and politically threatening to the Soviets, who did all in their power to delay serious consideration of the proposal. But in regard to technical and operational cooperation with the U.S. Army Air Corps, the Red Air Force went ahead as if the destructive German raid of 21 June 1944 on Poltava was of little consequence. During July, Maj. Gen. J. K. Cannon came from Washington to discuss ground-support operations with the Red Air Force and joined up with a U.S. Army Air Corps colonel from Poltava for an extended front visit. Also in July, a captain in the U.S. Navy's air arm was given an opportunity to tour the Soviet Naval Aviation School and was supplied with details on the IL-2 attack plane; in August, a U.S. team visited "Stormovik plant Number 30."[15]

At the end of July, General Deane was informed by Poltava that "substantial progress has already been made in the exchange of [air] intelligence and related information." In early August, the Army Air Corps received the first of a series of *daily* reports on German air OB from the Red Air Force. Although usually only one page in length, the reports broke down Luftwaffe deployment into four sectors of the Eastern Front (northwest, central, southwest, and southern) and listed the fighter *Geschwader* at specific locations, such as "Plotsk—4th and 12th Staffeln, 100th Night Fighter *Geschwader*," and "Ismail—3rd Gruppe, 52nd Fighter *Geschwader*."[16]

During September, the Soviets passed over reports on the disposition of the Luftwaffe as of 1 and 20 September 1944, details on downed German aircraft, and even a passage from a report on the interrogation of a Luftwaffe prisoner that mentioned a German jet being shipped, or being prepared for shipment, to combat units. In addition, the Soviets notified the Americans every day at 11:00 A.M. of the specific location of the Russian front line; during the day they reported on the German Air Force dispositions closest to the U.S. bases, plus occasional data on specific bombing targets, such as that supplied on 9 September regarding the environs of Bratislava.[17]

Such unprecedented high levels of Soviet cooperation on air force intelligence were still not enough to satisfy the mandarins in the U.S. diplomatic and military missions in Moscow. On 8 September 1944, General Walsh of the FRANTIC project joined with General Deane and Ambassador Harriman to send General Arnold a stinging telegram denouncing alleged Soviet failures to cooperate with the U.S. Air Force units at Poltava. Declaring that "a studied effort on the part of political elements in the Soviet Government to avoid collaboration with us on all air matters has been apparent during the past two months," the message cited failure to approve *daily* American reconnaissance missions from Soviet bases and delays in authorizing a U.S. air buildup in Siberia as the greatest sins the Russians had committed against the U.S. Army Air Corps. Overlooking the remarkably unprecedented efforts the Soviets had made to assist the U.S. forces at Poltava, the message to General Arnold concluded:

> We believe that in order to keep the Russians in the war, our past policy of fulfilling all Soviet requests without question has been justified. The Soviet attitude that we "will dance to their tune" has however been fostered by our pursuit of this policy. Forcing the Russians to meet us half-way and to give our requests the same consideration as we have always given theirs is considered by all of us as important to the present war effort and to post-war relations.[18]

This notably overstated message had the desired effect on General Arnold, who demanded on 30 September that a tougher stance be adopted toward the Soviets, because generosity had not "paid off."[19] Maneuvering the head of the U.S. Army Air Corps into the position of taking the lead on a get-tough policy with the Soviets was a classic example of how not to deal with the Soviet system or Joseph Stalin. "Hap" Arnold's political acumen was minimal at best, and Stalin's suspicious sensitivity regarding foreign pressures and his nearly medieval pursuit of hints of opposition from "hostile elements" were acute. Such a low-level and impulsive effort to push the Soviets into greater cooperation might well have had serious consequences at a time when the European war had only eight more months to run.

The situation was actually saved by the fact that General Arnold was such a cheerful and happy-go-lucky individual that he did not know how to apply cold pressure effectively, even when he wished to. In addition, the Soviets were so determined to cooperate with the U.S. Army Air Corps that they did not want to believe the U.S. mission in Moscow and the Poltava team had entered into a tough policy of quid pro quo. On 16 September, a Soviet colonel named Kovrishkin and his staff met with a U.S. Colonel Lord. Kovrishkin apparently did not understand that he was being put to the test by the new hard-headed policy of the Moscow mission and General Arnold, so he unconsciously nipped in the bud the American hard-line policy simply by being very generous in providing Soviet air intelligence information. The Russians presented the Americans with a "detailed breakdown of [the] location of German air units," including "18 typewritten pages of information on German air locations and a testimony of prisoners of war" covering the Soviet-German front and Western Europe. Kovrishkin then asked for comparable Western OB information on the Luftwaffe, because American information "on the Western front would be much more complete than the Russian, while the Russians doubtless had much more complete information on the Soviet-German front."[20]

The Russians continued to reach unprecedented heights in cooperation by supplying air intelligence to the Poltava team during October, including information on enemy air sorties and losses, the disposition of the Luftwaffe as of 1 October, and six more statements on German air operations from Luftwaffe POWs. In consequence, Deane reported to Washington that the "Soviets are adopting [a] more cooperative attitude on intelligence matters . . . we were, however, embarrassed owing to [the] lack of information from USSTAF [U.S. Army Air Corps Staff, Washington]" and "suggest you give us as much information as you deem advisable . . . [because] without this information from USSTAF our intelligence section will have great difficulty in obtaining anything from [the Soviets]." Together with this admonition, Deane dispatched to Washington a chart of the organization of the Red Army Air Force and a report on the movements of a Soviet squadron in late June and early July 1944, which Colonel Kovrishkin had given to Colonel Lord.[21]

A week later, Colonels Lord and Kovrishkin met again, and Lord declared that much of the information that Kovrishkin had recently sought—such as that on the Hungarian Air Force—was actually being supplied to the Soviet mission in London by the RAF and there was no point in repeating that portion of the process in Poltava. Lord did give the Red Air Force a summary of German heavy bomber strength and some general data on the V-1, and Kovrishkin played his part by passing along material on the Bulgarian and Rumanian air forces, a list of markings of downed German aircraft, and a map showing a German POW's indication of the German night-fighter northern defense network. Six days later, Lord supplied the Soviets with material on the new German ME 163 and 262 aircraft, for which Kovrishkin expressed appreciation, but he emphasized that what he and his superiors really wanted was information on German "jet propelled aircraft."[22]

Lord subsequently danced around this request from Kovrishkin with a generous ration of double-talk and evasion. But the incident may hold the key to why the Red Air Force was much more patient with the U.S. Air Force than the Soviets usually were with intelligence men from Western organizations. Red Air Force officers surely knew, just from what they saw at Poltava, that the West was ahead of them in most aspects of air warfare. The Soviets probably feared that if they did not catch up, and catch on to the new technological innovations such as jet aircraft, they would be at a serious disadvantage in the postwar era.

Over the next month, little useful intelligence was exchanged, and the American Poltava mission performed two operations perfectly designed to anger the Soviets—an airlift flight to assist the Warsaw rising, and smuggling a dissident out of Russia in a U.S. aircraft. Lord and Kovrishkin met again on 20 November for a final exchange of Luftwaffe intelligence. The material provided by the Russians was one of the richest hauls acquired by the Poltava mission during its stay in the USSR; it included ten pages of statements by German POWs plus "data on captured enemy planes for October, enemy air losses for September and October, [a] break-down of [the] German Air Force by fronts as of 1 November 1944, and enemy plane sorties for September and October on the Soviet Front."[23]

By early December, however, the special U.S. air intelligence link with the Red Air Force had gone silent, and the American mission in Moscow had reverted to its earlier suicidal habits, with the U.S. Navy staff taking its turn in pursuing the secret of the Soviet rocket bomb.[24] This post-Poltava slump brought U.S. Army Air Corps personnel more in line with the situation of the RAF, whose personnel had not been involved in the Poltava operation or its accompanying intelligence-exchange festival. Although the RAF mission in Moscow was responsible for supplying the wrapped-up ULTRA that was still being shared with the Russians, as General Burrows noted in December, "the Air Section of the Mission is worse treated than any of the other sections" of 30 Mission, perhaps "owing to the fact that there is no independent Air Force in Soviet Russia" and therefore no high-level Russian air authorities with whom the air branch of 30 Mission could liaise.[25]

Air Commodore Roberts and his staff consequently received little data on the eastern war or the Red Air Force. They did secure some information as a result of the temporary stationing of RAF heavy bombers at the Red Air Force's Uagedonck airfield in August-September to carry out the successful attack on the *Tirpitz*. Also in August, Commodore Roberts visited a Stormovik base, and his report produced "great interest" at the Air Ministry. Roberts himself declared that the Russians "did very well by him," though even on this occasion the RAF was outnumbered, if not necessarily outgunned, by the U.S. Army Air Corps, for General Walsh, another Air Corps general, and two colonels were included in the same Stormovik base tour.[26]

Other RAF visits were made to the Soviet Central Aero Institute and to a Tsagi aircraft exhibition in Moscow. Vice Air Marshal H. K. Therold had an Intourist-type visit to Leningrad in July, and also during July, an RAF interpreter reported on general conditions in the Crimea. Additionally, the diligent RAF mission closely questioned a high-ranking officer of the French "Normandy" Fighter Squadron attached to the Red Air Force in November and December and filed three pages of reports on operational procedures of the Red Air Force.[27]

But the RAF's efforts could not avoid the appearance of being a minor sideshow compared with the successes achieved by the Americans at Poltava. This was also true of the exchange of army and air force intelligence about Japan, although in this case, the Americans provided London with most of the Japanese information they secured from the USSR. G-2 Washington sent the American Moscow mission new marching orders for Pettigrew on 7 July, indicating that although much material "of a very high order" was being shipped to him: The

> Soviets are not fighting the Japanese and they do not have our immediate requirement for Or[der of] Bat[tle] intelligence on the Japanese for current military operations. A *reasonably liberal attitude* on exchange of Or Bat intelligence material is justified on your part. In general Or Bat intelligence furnished to the Russians should be of approximately the same proportion[al] value as the Or Bat intelligence received from them. Any release of Or Bat intelligence we furnish to Pettigrew should be predicated on above principles. Pettigrew is not to discuss or exchange Or Bat later than 1943 [presumably to keep the Soviets away from decrypted material] . . . [and] he is not to discuss or exchange Navy Or Bat intelligence either surface or air.[28]

Four days later, Bissell sent Pettigrew additional instructions, directing him to discuss with the Soviets:

> detailed intelligence on Japanese strength and dispositions in Manchuria [,] North China [,] Korea and Japan. For other areas discuss only general situation as derived from captured documents and POWs [i.e., not decrypts] unless the Soviets agree to make available to US originals or copies of their intelligence documents . . . discussion should be limited to Or[der] of Bat[tle] intelligence only.[29]

Presumably some exchanges on Japanese army and air OB occurred on this tightly defined basis during August and early September, but no documentary evidence is available. What is clear is that Pettigrew wished to return to the

United States in late October and wanted the Soviets to allow his deputy, Captain Falconer, to take over the OB exchanges with the Soviets. But Moscow would not agree to this arrangement, and on 20 October, Pettigrew began a new series of five exchange meetings with the Red Army expert on Japanese OB, Col. N. P. Tsigichko, which continued until at least 10 November 1944.[30]

At the opening session, Pettigrew loaned Tsigichko a copy of the captured Japanese Army register of 1942, and they discussed "various other matters."[31] Along with a series of questions he wanted the Soviets to answer, Pettigrew requested two copies of "the latest Army Register" on Japan "which the Russians have available prior to 1942."[32] This meeting then adjourned, and five days later (25 October), Tsigichko and Pettigrew met again, but the available notes of the meeting do not indicate that the Soviets provided the Americans with the Japanese Army register or any other Japanese documents. Pettigrew mentioned that the Japanese were beginning to remove one battalion from regiments in a number of divisions, and the two men discussed the Japanese procedure for "refilling or reconstituting" the depleted units. Tsigichko asked for all available information on Japanese Army equipment, especially tanks, and also wanted "all we knew" about the Japanese Air Force.[33]

In the 30 October meeting, the main emphasis of the discussion was "puppet troops," that is, Chinese and Korean auxiliary forces used by the Japanese. Pettigrew also provided "extracts" from the latest American OB bulletins and the final installment of the "loose leaf pages" of the OB information held by the U.S. Army on "the entire area of North China and Manchuria." Tsigichko supplied the Americans with the Soviet picture of the "structure and breakdown" of the "prevalent" Japanese units in the area—"normal divisions" as well as "light mobile divisions."[34] During the 4 November meeting, the Soviets scaled down their earlier high estimates of Japanese forces in north China because of the hard intelligence provided by Pettigrew, and Tsigichko asserted that the Russians held no Japanese Army register later than 1937. Moscow was obviously on the defensive, because the weight and range of American intelligence information so greatly exceeded its own. Tsigichko therefore requested all possible additional information, including that on Japanese air weapons, especially bomb specifications.[35]

The final meeting, which occurred on 10 November 1944, was an all-out exchange festival that included Russian evidence on the removal "from the 'M' [i.e., Manchurian] area" of fifty to seventy Japanese tanks during September, the "presence of the 102 Division . . . on the Island of 'F' [i.e., Formosa]," along with "a request for any American indications that the Japanese 102nd Division had ever been in the 'P' [i.e., Philippine] Islands."[36] All this suggested that it had finally dawned on Moscow that the talks might be useful to check the reliability of secret-agent reports. Tsigichko also indicated that the Soviets had evidence pointing to the presence of the 2nd, 4th, and 8th Japanese Air Divisions in the Philippines and produced some information on Japanese gas masks and shelters, together with an estimate of their effectiveness. Additionally, the Soviet side produced details on Japanese air deployment in Manchuria (600 planes), Korea (100), and the Hokaido-Kraffo-Kuriles area of Japan (450), prompting Pettigrew's peripheral comment that the Russian figure of a thirty-plane complement for a Japanese squadron–air regiment "is very close to the latest American figure," which was twenty-seven.[37]

This was apparently the last of the 1944 OB meetings on Japan held in Moscow, but even after Pettigrew returned to Washington, the Soviets attempted to continue the exchange of air force information on Japan through U.S. Navy channels, providing the U.S. naval mission in Moscow with eyewitness accounts of B-29 raids on the Japanese Home Islands on 11 November and 5 and 9 December 1944.[38] Stalin himself got into the intelligence-exchange game regarding Japan on 10 November, reporting to Harriman that Soviet "radio monitoring" had just learned that the Imperial Japanese Navy had lost a 33,000-ton battleship at the Battle of Leyte Gulf.[39]

Harriman actually sent this report to Washington two weeks after Leyte, and the lateness of its dispatch may have helped cool any enthusiasm Admiral King may still have harbored for intelligence exchanges with the Soviets. On 22 November, the American chief of naval operations instructed the U.S. Navy mission that since the USSR was "still maintaining friendly relations with Japan, we cannot furnish information on Japanese Naval order of Battle" to Moscow. But King assured Admiral Olsen and his staff that the Navy Department would "endeavor [to] furnish other naval information" to the Soviets and agreed "that machinery for rapid collaborative exchange should be perfected" in preparation for when the Soviet Union entered the war against Japan.[40] Since the U.S. Navy mission was thereby directed not to share high-level intelligence with the Red Navy during the autumn of 1944, Admiral Olsen and his team continued to be the poor sisters of intelligence sharing during this period.

The representatives of the two Western navies actually seem to have settled rather contentedly into their sideline roles. In October, although complaining about poor Soviet port security in Archangel, which he labeled "Operation Rigmarole," a British convoy commander found the Russian base commander affable and forthcoming.[41] And although Olsen made a point of discouraging marriages between Russian women and American sailors (ignored by Commander Tolley, who married a Russian woman), the U.S. Navy and the local population had sufficiently warm relations to produce one case of syphilis, three of gonorrhea, and five other cases of unidentified forms of venereal disease among American sailors in late 1944.[42]

Because the Royal Navy was finally allowed to land its Typex machines on 3 July, the flow of "Y" information to Britain increased, and there were no special reasons for official anger. Neither the Western navies nor the Soviet Navy had any serious grounds for complaint concerning the sharing of weather information either, since a senior Soviet hydrometeorologist was stationed in the United States from 4 November 1944 until the end of the war. When any minor meteorological hiccups occurred, the Red Navy was always eager to make matters right. As the U.S. Navy mission reported to Admiral King on 22 July, regarding weather matters, "the Soviets do not refuse criticism."[43] Therefore, even though Soviet reserve on some matters was frustrating, Admiral Olsen concluded on 29 September that this behavior was related primarily to inferiority complexes, bureaucratic rivalries within the Soviet government, and a traditional deep suspicion of foreigners. But since none of this was directed at the Western navies with any special frequency or ferocity, the U.S. Navy mission thought that it was best to just go along and do the best it could.[44]

In intelligence exchanges regarding weaponry, the most ambitious joint Anglo-American effort to cooperate with the Red Navy concerned naval mines. Various German and Soviet mines, along with minesweeping and detection devices, were exchanged with the Red Navy until late July 1944, when Admiral King decided that due to the relatively small amount of information being provided by the Soviets, as well as the obsolescence of some of the mines they turned over, it was time to terminate the effort and withdraw the Western naval mine teams.[45]

But other forms of Anglo-American naval technical exchanges with the Soviets actually increased at this time. The Americans collected twenty pages on Soviet diving escape equipment and another fifteen pages on a German torpedo pistol. The Royal Navy was given ten hours to examine the U-250, which had been captured by the Soviets, and although all the radio equipment and German documents had been removed from the submarine by the Russians, the naval mission still considered the examination worthwhile.

It is important to note why the Red Navy, like other branches of the Soviet government, was always in a strong position in relation to the British and American naval missions. For all the talk of Western comradeship, the smallest whiff of possible special advantage was usually enough for one of the Westerners to try to cut a special deal with the Russians. For example, in August 1944, the British Navy liaison office in the Black Sea region began to receive detailed reports on Axis naval matters acquired from Soviet interrogation of captured Rumanian personnel. The DNI immediately ordered that the contents of these reports should not be sent to any U.S. representative in the Soviet Union, Middle East, or Turkey.[46] Although the British may have had legitimate fears about American cipher security, this was not an issue for other items the British received from the USSR; therefore, an element of territorial protectionism seems to have been at work. The Royal Navy was also quite tightfisted with information it received from British telegraphists aboard refitted Soviet submarines going from Scotland to the USSR in September 1944, as well as with reports on aspects of Red Navy procedures acquired during the transfer of the *Royal Sovereign* to Red Navy service in September 1944.[47]

Beyond the special opportunities to observe Soviet nautical operations, the British and American naval missions, as well as those of the armies and air forces, had a number of useful but certainly not sensational opportunities to travel and observe conditions across the USSR in mid-1944. Staff members from both Western navy missions explored the regions of the northern ports, examining everything from ship repair facilities to airports. U.S. Navy Capt. D. Roullard, stationed in Vladivostok, as well as a number of American visitors to Siberia filed reports on the USSR's eastern region, because planning for a Soviet-American air buildup in Siberia was scheduled to begin soon, in preparation for the USSR's turn against Japan.[48]

Yet even in regard to opportunities for visits, the Western navies fell behind the Western armies and air forces during the summer and autumn. General Connolly made an extended tour of Kiev, and Generals Spalding and Bond were able to survey Leningrad. The American Army's highest-profile visit to the front was made by General Deane in July, when he rejoiced in the fact that Red Army combat officers were much friendlier and more forthcoming than the Soviet liaison personnel in Moscow.[49] The British Army also had a good visiting season. Two officers toured Simferopol in November, two more spent eight days in White Russia in early August, General Thornton received a front visit in October, and General Burrows finally had his dreams fulfilled in July by a three-day tour of the Minsk sector of the front in the company of Marshal Vassilevsky.[50]

In later years, some veterans of the Western effort to collaborate with the USSR would consider the achievements of summer 1944 the glory phase of East-West wartime intelligence cooperation. Even the OSS managed to arrange liaison with the NKVD in London during August, although this agreement was of little practical value, because the OSS was merely twinned with Col. I. Chichayev, the same man the SOE was using for most of its linkups with the

NKVD. The OSS exchanged some information with the NKVD on economic targets in Germany suitable for special operations and air attacks, and it even agreed to supply the USSR with small microfilm units that would further the activities of Soviet secret agents. But by late summer and early autumn, things had gone seriously wrong with the OSS-NKVD partnership. Donovan's men insisted on trying to dash into Rumania, Bulgaria, Hungary, and Czechoslovakia (just as the USSR overran these countries), ostensibly to gather intelligence and rescue downed American fliers, but actually operating under the aegis of a JCS order authorizing the OSS to carry out activities aimed at overthrowing governments in the Nazi bloc.

Inevitably, the Soviet authorities struck back in anger, and OSS operatives were rounded up by the highly efficient Soviet security forces. A full-blown East-West crisis was averted when—after the Soviets insisted that the OSS could function within the Soviet-controlled zone only if Moscow authorized it to stay—Washington, London, and the OSS yielded to the inevitable and provided the Russians with the names of all of their supposedly secret operatives assigned to the new Soviet-controlled zone of Eastern Europe.

OSS relations with the NKVD thereupon outwardly improved, but this was rather like putting the corpse in a more handsome coffin. OSS teams managed to get a bit of information about Soviet looting of Western-owned oil equipment in Rumania, and Western diplomats in Moscow, including George Kennan, praised general OSS reports on the USSR that were produced in this period (which may have helped bring about the OSS's later transformation into the CIA, thus giving it eternal life). But at the time, none of these marginal OSS successes either netted much useful intelligence or set the stage for the kind of broad secret intelligence cooperation with Moscow that Donovan desired. This failure was only one of a broad range of indicators in the autumn of 1944 that the current round of Soviet military successes and increases in political power might not bring good long-term relations with the Western powers.[51]

With regard to technical exchanges, in July, General Burrows had been willing to implement CCS orders that the two Western missions in Moscow provide information on a long list of Western technological developments to the Soviets, only indicating to General Deane that it had occurred to him that they should keep "a little something up our sleeves here which may be of use at certain moments."[52] By autumn, however, Western officials in Washington, London, and Moscow were having second thoughts. On 12 September, Ambassador Harriman made the abrupt and surprising claim to Washington that the Soviet attitude had taken a "startling turn during the last two months," that the USSR was definitely less cooperative, and that unless something was done in the direction of taking a firmer line with the Russians, "the Soviet Union will become a world bully."[53]

Deane and Olsen quickly fell in with Harriman's sudden shift toward a harder line with Moscow. On 20 September, they reported home that "since the [recent] successes on both fronts"—that is, the Soviets' in Eastern Europe and the Anglo-Americans' in the west—"there had been a general stiffening of the Soviet attitude toward us and the British."[54] The leaders of the American military mission in Moscow therefore urged the War Department not to proceed with its plan to provide Moscow with more high-level American technology. Apparently before receiving a JCS authorization to cease high-level technology exchanges with the Soviets, Deane told Burrows on 30 September that he and Admiral Olsen "had changed their minds" on the exchanges with the Russians because, "with the war with Germany coming to a close and doubts existing about Russian participation in the war with Japan," it was no longer clear that disclosure "to the Soviet General Staff" of such information would "aid the prosecution of the present war."[55]

Burrows, and presumably the British chiefs of staff, chose to proceed with the technology exchanges despite Deane's message, "dribbling out" British items until early October, when, on "Russian initiative," the meetings "assumed [the character] of two boys swapping stamps—ASDIC set against some fifth rate intelligence about captured Rumanian Ports."[56] Why the British chose to continue technological exchanges with the Russians when the Americans did not is only one indication of a confused and confusing Western irritation and belligerence toward the Soviets that is difficult to explain. Perhaps it is explicable only in terms of letting off steam generated by earlier frustration and disappointment, or because the approaching victory provided the opportunity to vent long-held dislikes, fears, and resentments regarding the Soviet leaders and the Communist system.

The rising contentiousness of the Western mission leaders is especially curious, because in such matters as German weaponry and air intelligence, the Soviets had recently been cooperating to an unprecedented degree. They had dealt with Pettigrew on Japanese OB—one of the most sensitive intelligence issues of all—as well as doing good service to the West (and themselves) regarding front visits and the inspection of V-1 and V-2 sites. The Soviets had even agreed to assist the Americans in their odd scheme of driving 500 trucks loaded with supplies for China across the wilds of southern Russia (Operation LUX). The Soviets had not miraculously become open-handed or open-minded in late summer 1944, but they were definitely more cooperative than they had been in the past.[57]

Yet the U.S. mission in Moscow raised a chorus of calls for more restrictive measures against the Soviets, and some high London officials were stumbling toward the same position. During July, Admiral Cunningham had warily noted how rapidly the Red Army was advancing, and near the end of the month, in an extended and intense session of the Chiefs of Staff Committee, Britain's military leaders concluded that hereafter British planning should rest on the assumption that there was only one possible future military threat to Britain—the USSR. By August, some in the Foreign Office appeared to have reversed themselves and were now inclining toward restrictions on handouts to the Russians relating to all forms of military information. The Air Ministry was quick to note that it had been advocating, and practicing, such a policy for the previous six months—which may have been the reason its mission had received the worst treatment of any of the British or American teams in Moscow.[58]

In mid-August, some Foreign Office officials repeated the call for more pressure to be exerted on the Soviets to gain reciprocity. The British chiefs of staff were reluctant to go along, however, observing that it might lead to trouble with the Americans. This double fear of Soviet hostility and American withdrawal of support threatened to paralyze Britain's military decision-making process.

But then, just as the Foreign Office and the chiefs of staff were about to swap their traditional positions—with the Foreign Office being tough with the Soviets and the chiefs of staff being soft—the two groups managed to catch hold of themselves and sank back into their customary roles. On 18 August 1944, the Foreign Office's Sir Orme Sargent began mumbling that there were "increasing signs that the Chiefs of Staff and their subordinate organizations are thinking and speaking of the Soviet Union as being enemy number one and even [of] securing German assistance against her."[59] Twelve days later, Sargent returned energetically to the charge, claiming that "certain high placed officers in the W[ar] O[ffice]" had been speaking of "the impending Russian danger," which prompted Eden to note that "this is very bad. I am inclined to speak to Ismay about it."[60]

Nothing, however, actually seems to have been done to get a grip on either current military attitudes or future British policy. Apprehension and anger toward the USSR existed, but uncertainty and reluctance to take plunges were even stronger forces in London in 1944, where approaching poverty and colonial unrest had been added to British hesitation and weakness. On 5 July, Churchill expressed his deepest feelings about such matters when, in a minute to Ismay, he noted, "considering the difficulties we have in getting on between the British and American staffs [in the CCS] it is surely better not to complicate matters by dragging in the Russians at this juncture."[61] The British position in the summer and autumn of 1944 was, therefore, to have no policy beyond trying to soldier on, smoothing out as many troubles as possible with the rising superpowers, and trying to steer a creaking Britian into safe water by war's end.

Since their more experienced British cousin was thus paralyzed, and they themselves were suffering from a severe case of anger-and-frustration blues (which afflicted all Western missions in Moscow at one time or another), Deane and Harriman turned their backs on the fact that their intelligence relations with the Soviets were uncommonly good. Amid moans and pouts, they raised a cry for the United States to get tough with the Russians. Washington, which was still held in the single-minded but weakening grip of Franklin Roosevelt and George Marshall, paid little heed, and no reply seems to have been sent to Harriman's 12 September plea for authority to get tough with the Russians. The American mission chiefs in Moscow therefore had no choice but to back down, and just eight days later, they cabled home the preposterous assertion that their "somewhat firmer and uncompromising policy"[62] had miraculously done the trick; all was now fine in Moscow, and they could go back to the old stand— giving things away, struggling to get what they could from Soviet liaison officers, and running to Stalin whenever they sought any really important special favors.

The latter portion of this American modus operandi—calling on Stalin— was also employed by the prime minister during October, after Stalin rejected Western requests for another Big Three meeting. The Soviet leader had begged off a general meeting, claiming illness, and after visiting Stalin on 23 September, Harriman reported that he actually "looked more worn out than I have ever seen him and not yet fully recovered" from the grippe. Since Harriman could not move Stalin toward a Big Three meeting or budge Molotov from his claim that he and "his associates felt Stalin must protect his health and that traveling was not good for him," there could be no immediate top-level tripartite gathering.[63] Churchill thereupon tried to seize the initiative and protect what he saw as Britain's basic interests from disturbing American interference. He flew to Moscow to cut a deal with Stalin covering Greece and the Balkans. The Roosevelt White House—no matter the subsequent claims that Roosevelt was a foreign policy simpleton—was not naive enough to accept the idea of a secret Churchill-Stalin deal on anything and insisted that Ambassador Harriman be present as an observer during all sessions of the conference.[64]

Forced to accept this rather humiliating demand from its American partner, Britain faced another disconcerting snub from the Russians. Since July, General Burrows had been on his good behavior, avoiding confrontation and, in the British view, being more successful in dealing with the Soviets. But on 23 September, Stalin put an end to this impression by telling Kerr and Harriman that Burrows tended to act as if he thought Russians were "savages" and the 30 Mission chief would have to go. Kerr did his best to defend Burrows, but in the end, he had to yield to Stalin's demand that Burrows be withdrawn, noting that the Soviets had memories as long as elephants, and elephantine vindictiveness when they were patronized. Harriman, however, was inclined to agree with Stalin's view, noting that Burrows was "typical of the 'high hat' approach of some British officers in the Soviet Union." By November, sections of the British press were also accusing Burrows of having made anti-Soviet statements during his passage through Cairo, and although the government officially denied the truth of these reports in the Commons, confidential Foreign Office comments indicated that they may have been true.[65]

By the end of September, Burrows's role in the USSR was effectively finished, although he remained as head of the mission for another month because London wanted no major changes during the prime minister's stay in Moscow. In the interim, the general was treated politely by the Russians, and some within the British team in Moscow, including the ambassador, believed that he was just an unlucky individual whose position had been undermined by the "jellyfish attitude of the Americans," who had failed to support him when the Soviets had turned up the pressure.[66] Kerr therefore enjoyed a bit of *Schadenfreude* as the American shuttle-bombing project came to an end, since he believed that it would now be John Deane's turn to take the heat "and fret."[67]

The Churchill-Stalin meeting of October 1944 had fewer histrionics than that of 1942, but the prime minister made absurd efforts to entice Stalin into agreeing to a division of the Balkans into Soviet and British zones of interest behind the United States' back. The prime minister managed to get Stalin's blue-penciled tick on his Balkan zone-of-influence paper, but there was no explanation of what this gesture actually meant, and future events were to show that it meant virtually nothing. The USSR had the power to do as it wished in the east and would, in fact, do so. Britain lacked the muscle to go it alone in Eastern Europe and, in any event, would soon slip to a point where it could do very little in most areas of the world without American encouragement and support.[68]

But with regard to the sharing of military information, the Churchill-Stalin talks broke new ground in East-West cooperation. Extended strategy and operational discussions occurred on 14 and 15 October, featuring not only Burrows, Deane, and Antonov but also the Soviet commander in the Far East (General Schevchenko) as well as Ismay, Molotov, Harriman, Churchill, and Stalin. During these sessions, Stalin and Antonov put forth the Soviet view of the military situation more frankly and comprehensively than had been done at any time in the past, and they outlined the Soviet intention of chewing up the large German formations on the northern and southern sectors of the Eastern Front before crashing directly into Germany in the central sector. During the discussion, Stalin indicated that he was troubled by the possibility that the Germans might open the door to the West at this point, thereby depriving the Soviets of the great victory they deserved. During a Churchillian ramble about the possibility that the German front in the west might collapse, Stalin broke in to remark, probably ruefully, "that a break in the west would decide the war."[69]

The discussion of this Kremlin nightmare did not prevent Stalin from going into Soviet plans for entering the war against Japan. Together with Generals Antonov and Schevchenko, Stalin provided detailed estimates of Russia's own organization and that of the Japanese in the regions of Siberia, Manchuria, and north China. Although Deane thought that Soviet estimates of Japanese forces were too large, being "considerably in excess of ours"[70]—a judgment that was subsequently proved correct ten months later when the fighting began—the American Moscow staff was appreciative of Soviet promises to enter the war against Japan three months after the end of the European war, as well as the greater openness with which Stalin and his staff discussed Soviet strengths and weaknesses.

In the aftermath of these "Big Two, plus" meetings in Moscow, the participants and observers counted up the wins and losses, including those from the various drinking bouts in the Kremlin, during which, as one of the Royal Navy staff admitted, there had been "many casualties among the home and visiting teams."[71] In London, the chiefs of staff voiced serious reservations about sharing any military technology with Moscow: "We do not wish to add unnecessarily to the Russians' postwar technical information on military equipment." But at the same time, Brigadier Firebrace was criticized in London for being too hard on the Russians. Such muddled developments as these prompted the Royal Navy war diarist in Moscow to note that trying to produce an effective East-West cooperative policy "would try a saint."[72]

Only the American wallflowers at the Moscow conference, who had seen, heard, and said much but had not committed themselves or officially participated, seem to have emerged from the proceedings both optimistic and relatively satisfied. Despite grumbles about Soviet caution and reserve during late autumn, the American mission had done very well in intelligence exchanges with the Soviets, the war had gone favorably in both Europe and the Pacific, and American military and economic power was increasing by leaps and bounds. Optimism was ascendant in Washington and, by and large, in the U.S. mission in Moscow during November 1944.

But shortly thereafter, a military reversal in the Ardennes, increasing friction with the Soviets over developments in Eastern Europe, and the death of a president would show even the high-flying U.S. government and the American people that the last mile to V-E Day would not be a crystal stair.

11
Victory on One Front, December 1944–May 1945

When painted in the broadest strokes, the war in the Pacific during the winter of 1944–1945 was yet another great American advance toward the Japanese Home Islands. On 19 February 1945, after many months spent mopping up in the Philippines, the United States unleashed massive air and naval softening-up attacks against Iwo Jima, a vital island on the inner line toward Tokyo, and then once again sent in the Marines. A vicious month-long battle followed, reminiscent of the earlier clashes at Guadalcanal and Saipan. At Iwo, 22,000 Japanese troops and 7,000 American Marines died—a high price for victor as well as vanquished—but the American high command thought that the sacrifice was worthwhile, because the rest of the inner line, stretching through Okinawa to the Japanese Home Islands, now lay open before them. With Iwo and the neighboring islands in American hands, the great fleets of B-29s would soon be swathed in fighter escorts from takeoff to landing, which, judging from the first mass attack on Tokyo, might literally burn Japan into submission. The light construction of the Japanese capital had produced such ferocious firestorms on 9 March 1945 that 83,000 people died, nearly three times as many as all those who fell on both sides at Iwo Jima.

A visionary, or even a far-sighted military analyst, might have seen from these developments that whatever military assets the Japanese still possessed—and despite the Japanese determination to resist to the point of suicide, which was inherent in their culture—nothing Japan could do would prevent the Americans from smashing Japanese military power and seizing the Home Islands. To someone willing to ponder the matter, such a conclusion might have indicated that the United States had little need to seek additional armed forces to subdue Japan. This was especially true if a high price tag was likely to be placed on the use of the Red Army in Asia.

But those holding power in Washington overestimated the military obstacles awaiting them on the road to Tokyo. They were also keeping a nervous eye on American casualty figures, which, after the post-D-day battles in Europe, had already risen to about half a million dead and wounded by late 1944. U.S. leaders thus found it extremely difficult to relinquish the dream that Stalin might be willing to unlock the door to an easy victory in Asia and, after donning the cloak of power and responsibility in Eastern Europe, might also be ready to assist the United States in securing worldwide peace, prosperity, and security.[1]

As autumn 1944 drew to a close, East-West relations were, if not cordial, certainly much improved from what they had been in earlier eras. Stalin had been rough and tough on Warsaw, and the Red Army's march through the Balkans had been no children's crusade, as hoards of refugees from the Red Army amply testified. But the Soviet leader had gone out of his way to stress the limited nature of Soviet military and political objectives, speaking just like the capitalist leaders of the importance of having "friendly" countries on his borders. In mid-December 1944, he even suggested to the U.S. ambassador that the West should land forces on the Dalmatian coast (Churchill's favorite invasion prospect in his dream of attacking the "soft underbelly" of Europe) so that they could drive north to clasp hands with their Russian ally in Vienna, or perhaps even Budapest. In addition, he repeatedly indicated to Westerners within the secret sanctuary of the Kremlin that he identified completely with the Anglo-American cause in the Pacific war, telling Ambassador Harriman on one occasion that he was always interested in hearing about Western operations "where Japs are being killed."[2]

Of course, there were still those in the American Midwest, in the cozy remoteness of London's West-end clubs, and in the Western military missions in Moscow who believed that a hard line with the Soviets was required, even in these balmy days for East-West relations. General Deane's demand for hard bargaining extended as far as lend-lease supplies. The crassness with which Stalin danced around Western governmental requests to get involved in Eastern Europe—from Churchill's desire to arrange joint Anglo-Soviet relations with Tito to General Donovan's and the SOE's attempts to run independent intelligence operations in the Balkans—provided solid grounds for dreary thoughts about the future.[3] By January 1945, Admiral Archer of the British military mission, Moscow, had become so devoid of good cheer about East-West relations that he observed to London, "I feel it would be advantageous if all officers coming to this country would read and re-read the Old Testament Book of Job before taking up their appointments."[4]

Still, the great Allied pincers closing on Germany from east and west compelled even the greatest Stalin haters and those most disillusioned by Soviet intransigence to concede that some measure of Allied cooperation had to continue if the war was to be won and the cost to the Allies kept within reason. Western military commanders were made acutely aware of this truth in mid-December, when Hitler's "Bulge" offensive threw them badly off balance and led British and American officials to beseech Stalin to move the date of his spring offensive forward to take the German pressure off the Americans. The brave "Rats of Bastogne" and their American and British liberators actually thwarted Hitler's hopes of a breakthrough and Germany's last dream of a turn in the tide, but Stalin did advance the date of his spring offensive to mid-January, convincing at least Admiral Cunningham that the Red Army had helped the Western armies by drawing significant numbers of German units to the Eastern Front.[5] In addition, reasonably routine matters, such as the exchange of weather information, the treatment of U.S. fliers interned after crash-landing in Russia from raids on Japan, and repatriation of Soviet and Western troops rescued from German POW camps, were actually handled much more reasonably and smoothly in this period than many Western skeptics (or postwar conspiracy theorists) believed possible.[6]

East-West intelligence cooperation during the "Bulge era" of December 1944 therefore resembled a muddled picture of pluses and minuses. On 30 November, General Slavin told the British with a straight face that no German OB meetings had been held during the previous month because the Soviets had no information to exchange, an explanation that 30 Mission, with commendable understatement, found "hardly credible." Soon thereafter, Captain Chapman had two useful OB meetings in Moscow,[7] and the U.S. mission also had meetings with the Red Army regarding German OB in December, with some of the resulting information being forwarded to the White House. G-2 Washington specifically indicated how "grateful" it was for Moscow's assistance in definitely identifying and locating German panzer divisions on the Eastern Front.[8]

Although Colonel Pettigrew had returned to Washington in Early December, some American links with the Soviets regarding military intelligence on Japan were continued, and Pettigrew himself returned to Moscow in mid-January 1945. In early December, G-2 Washington sought Russian assistance in evaluating a dubious Chinese intelligence report on Japanese Army OB in north China, and on 23 December, the Soviets were given a copy of the summary of Japanese fighter aircraft tactics they had requested earlier. Air intelligence exchanges regarding the Luftwaffe also continued. General Deane's mission periodically received Russian charts on captured enemy aircraft and Luftwaffe sorties during October–November 1944, as well as some information the Russians had gained from German POWs. On 27 December 1944, the Soviets even presented General Deane with a copy of their complete order-of-battle report on the Luftwaffe on the Eastern Front—a nearly unique act of Soviet openness. In return, the Red Air Force was given various items of general Luftwaffe intelligence, as well as the photo reconnaissance reports it sought on airfields in Austria and Hungary.[9]

Regarding naval intelligence matters, Soviet-American relations in the Far East had improved. In late December 1944, the Soviet naval authorities in Vladivostok not only supplied the American consul with information on Japanese merchant navy activities in the region but even invited him to dinner. In western Russia, both British and U.S. Navy officers secured survey visits. A number of trips were made to Red Navy installations from Leningrad to Molotovsk,[10] and once again a senior Royal Navy officer (in this case, Capt. W. B. Walker) felt justified in observing that "the Russians had always a professional respect for our Navy, something like contempt for the Army, and knew little of the Royal Air Force."[11]

In late December 1944 and early January 1945, Stalin reacted favorably to Churchill's request that a special British-American team be permitted to examine a German U-boat captured by the Red Navy that had been carrying the new German "Gnat" torpedo, and that the team be provided with some of the documents the Russians had found on that submarine. As had previously occurred when the Soviets had hosted a special Western mission, Anglo-American security worries greatly complicated matters. London was unwilling to tell Moscow that the Royal Navy had already acquired a similar torpedo from an earlier U-boat capture, for fear that the Soviets might request access to other aspects of the technical intelligence the Admiralty possessed on the German Navy.[12]

The OSS also went the cautious extra mile in cooperating with the USSR in late December. In addition to flooding Moscow with survey (research and analysis) reports, Donovan reduced the OSS missions in the Soviet "sphere" of the Balkans, including the mission in Rumania that featured Frank Wisner, the future CIA guru. He also gave Moscow a large number of field reports on conditions in Germany, including some from Bern written by future Cold War CIA chief Allen Dulles. Donovan seems to have been willing to send nearly everything he had to Moscow, except for secret information on the zones of Germany to be occupied by the Western powers. But at the same time, he was inclined to look ahead and gather up whatever vital information he could regarding secret aspects of Soviet operations. In December, the OSS acquired (apparently from the Finns) copies of a series of Russian military and NKVD codes. Donovan thought that this material was of such importance that he went through with the purchase of the Soviet codes, despite strong opposition from the State Department. In mid-December, the OSS director reported to the president that he had bought the codes, but later in the month, Secretary of State Edward Stettinius (who had recently replaced Cordell Hull) and his colleagues succeeded in striking back, convincing President Roosevelt that the code purchase was fraught with political dangers and that the material should be sent back to Russia.

During January 1945, Donovan yielded and agreed to return the codes, declaring that the OSS had not and would not study them. This declaration was most likely metaphorical, because Donovan's men had already held the Russian codes for at least three weeks and surely must have examined them. But since the OSS had no cryptanalytic section at the time, anything Donovan's people could have accomplished would have been limited. In any event, by 9 January 1945, the NKVD had been informed that Donovan had the codes, and after a bit of confusion about how they should be returned to Russia, on 15 February the OSS director himself gave them to a grateful Soviet Ambassador Gromyko in Washington.[13]

If and when all Soviet and American intelligence records for the wartime period are finally released to the public, it may still be difficult to assess the importance and impact of this peculiar incident. The degree to which it whetted the appetite and increased the knowledge of OSS Russian specialists and their CIA and NSA successors is extremely difficult to gauge, and the impact of the affair on that most impenetrable of enigmas, the mind of Joseph Stalin, is not likely to be recorded on any bit of paper. But it seems safe to conclude that the saga of the Soviet codes demonstrated to the Washington bureaucracy and the Soviet government that in early 1945 the Roosevelt administration continued to be committed to a policy of cultivating good long-term relations with the USSR. But it also demonstrated that Western intelligence services, while following general orders and playing the game, were able, willing, and perhaps eager to prepare for the day when Nazi Germany and Japan were beaten and other priorities, and other potential enemies, would hold their attention and interest.

In dealing with the situation immediately facing them in early 1945, however, the intelligence chiefs of East and West were compelled to keep their eyes focused primarily on the present. The Soviets were certainly not willing to expand their range of intelligence cooperation with Western secret agencies in January 1945, rejecting both an OSS effort to coordinate black propaganda operations and an SOE attempt to expand its agent-dropping partnership with the NKVD to cover Eastern Europe. But General Fitin did step in to assist Donovan in his attempts to locate and rescue survivors of one of the OSS teams that had been lost in Czechoslovakia, and he also allowed a small OSS unit attached to the U.S. embassy in Moscow to collect Soviet publications on Eastern Europe, Asia, and the USSR itself.[14]

During the early-1945 run-up to the Yalta conference (which was held between 4 and 11 February), little of real importance occured in regard to East-West intelligence cooperation. Western naval officers still gathered useful bits of information about Russian ports from Vladivostok to Odessa, and the Red Army mission in London provided the Anglo-Americans with a detailed breakdown of German Black Sea naval losses. Until 31 January 1945, Russian merchant ship masters in San Francisco also routinely provided ONI with useful details on Japanese minefields and shore defenses in the north Pacific. In the same period, American Army G-2 staff members prepared a special report on Japanese tactics and weapons for the Soviets, which was given to them at the end of January.[15]

But as had happened frequently in the past, the most marked upswing in information and intelligence cooperation occurred during high-level East-West military visits. Between 13 and 22 January, the head of the air section of the Soviet mission in London, General Sharapov, visited the British Second Tactical Air Force in the Low Countries. The Russian visitor was given the red-carpet treatment and was allowed to see all aspects of RAF tactical operations. Sharapov reciprocated by supplying detailed explanations of Russian tactical air operations and methods, answering numerous RAF questions "without hesitation," and generally being "prepared to be far more communicative than he had been on any of the visits [he had] paid to R.A.F. establishments in England."[16]

Air Chief Marshal Sir Arthur Tedder had a comparably free exchange of views with Stalin when he was sent to Moscow by Eisenhower in January 1945 to thank the Soviet leader for the Russian supportive offensive during the Battle of the Bulge, to brief the Soviets on Western operational plans, and to inquire about Soviet plans and intentions. General Marshall had told Eisenhower that whoever was sent on this mission should use a "simple Main Street Abilene style" when talking to the Soviet leader, because "he likes it."[17] Although Tedder probably did not rise to these lofty midwestern oratorical heights, he seems to have convinced the Soviet dictator of his forthrightness. Stalin spoke to Tedder candidly about Soviet procedures, deployment, and general offensive intentions, punctuated by blunt remarks on the need for "Cheka"-type troops to control German espionage in conquered areas. He also offered his view that although the German people had "more stubbornness than brains," they were nonetheless "frugal and enduring." Near the end of the conversation, Stalin stressed that East and West had compelling reasons to cooperate because:

We have no treaty, but we are comrades. It is proper and also sound selfish policy that we should help each other in times of difficulty. It would be foolish for me to stand aside and let the Germans annihilate you; they would only turn back on me when you were disposed of. Similarly it is to your interest to do everything possible to keep the Germans from annihilating me.[18]

This vision of the need to cooperate based on the principle of mutual survival, which seemed so reasonable at the highest levels of East-West contact, continued to be difficult to implement further down the chain of command. On the eve of the Yalta conference, General Deane was able to send home some information on the latest version of the German Tiger II tank, but the Soviets refused to allow any visits to the Red Army battlefront. Only to the area of the front held by the Lublin (i.e., Soviet-controlled) Polish units were they willing to grant a Western visit, but London and Washington concluded that this was too high a political price to pay for marginal intelligence benefits, because it might be construed to be informal recognition of the legitimacy of the Lublin Polish government.[19]

The Western effort to carry out broad exchanges with the Soviets with regard to technical "targets" likely to be found in their respective zones of Germany also made no headway during January, despite much pushing by London and Washington. Some documents related to this subject are even now withheld by the U.S. and British governments, but such obsessive and now probably ludicrous secrecy is not surprising if one puts aside romantic notions of the role that trust and love should play in relations between wartime allies. Intelligence is a game to be played against all comers, and no partnership or "friendly relationship" gives anyone total immunity. So it is important to note that while the British were complaining about Soviet deviousness, reluctance to share, and secrecy, they themselves were acquiring "Most Secret information" (i.e., information from agent or cryptanalytic sources) regarding the dispatches of their ally, the French ambassador in Moscow.[20]

The cold and rough features of the world of international intelligence did not offer much hope of improvement in East-West relations during the Yalta conference, which took place in February 1945. Since Yalta itself has become notorious as the scene of the general dishing out of territorial concessions to Stalin—including a slice of Poland, Port Arthur, part of Sakhalin, the Baltic states, and the Kuriles—it seems an implausible venue in which the Big Three or their military advisers would show any loftiness of vision or imagination regarding intelligence sharing or anything else. This was especially true because, by a miracle of improvisation, the Soviets had made the scene of the meeting so comfortable that it engendered slothful sentiments among the guests. Churchill reported to Atlee on the fifth day of the conference (8 February) that "this place has turned out very well so far," with amenities laid on by the Soviet hosts, "regardless of cost."[21]

Nonetheless, General Marshall and Field Marshal Brook swept aside all the temptations of the palate and the flesh, as well as a dismal Foreign office briefing on the Soviets' failure to play ball on technical and intelligence matters during the preceding three and a half years. During an interval between plenary sessions on 9 February, the two men considered increasing the flow of high-grade intelligence to the Russians. Although it is not clear whether the British or the American team initiated this discussion, Brook reported to the British JIC following his talk with Marshall that the two of them had agreed "that at the present critical stage of operations on the Russian front we are no longer justified in withholding from the Russians intelligence[,] however gained[,] of major strategical importance affecting their front." While emphasizing that it was "still essential not to disclose to the Russians the source of our most secret information,"[22] Brooke and Marshall had decided that henceforth a large flow of critical ULTRA and MAGIC information would be sent to the U.S. and British missions in Moscow for relay to the Soviets. The Washington authorities, the British JIC, and Churchill having agreed to the Brooke-Marshall decision on ULTRA-MAGIC transmissions, 30 Mission immediately implemented the policy. On 15 February, Archer met with General Slavin and informed him that while "in the Crimea" he had received instructions "to approach Army General Antonov on certain intelligence matters," and he requested that Slavin arrange a meeting for him with Antonov. In the meantime, Archer gave Slavin "certain information to pass on to the Soviet General Staff," which presumably included the first of the new series of ULTRA reports that were to be given to the Soviets.[23]

No copies of this series of ULTRA transmissions are available in the British Public Record Office, nor have such documents from earlier stages of the war been opened to the public there. But through Freedom of Information Act appeals in the United States, copies of three such ULTRA transmissions (5 and 8 March and 9 April 1945) located in American records have been obtained, as well as a copy of an Ultra document sent to Moscow but not given to the Soviets because "it was known that it [the information contained therein] was already in their possession."[24] These documents consist only of nuts-and-bolts details about German military movements that might or might not have indicated German overall intentions, such as the movement of the 10th Panzer Division toward Stettin, the composition of Army Group "Vistula," the construction of a defense line from Maribor to Brno by 11 April, and the positions of the 1st, 2nd, 9th, and 12th SS Panzer Divisions as of 8 March. No additional information or comment was included in the transmissions, except that in the case of the 9 April message, which marked out the Maribor to Brno defense line, a sentence was appended stating that "the British General Staff add that they have no indication as to the extent to which this position has already been developed by the German."[25]

The British and American military authorities were nonetheless sure that this kind of detailed and accurate information would be of great value to the Red Army field commanders. They also knew from hard experience that the military bureaucracy in Moscow was often more of a brake than an accelerator regarding the flow of intelligence information to the field. Therefore, on 26 February, Admiral Archer and Colonel Brinkman met with General Antonov in order to "speed up the delivery of high grade intelligence regarding German troop movements inside Germany to the Soviet General Staff[,] who had hitherto been very dilatory in arranging meetings to discuss such matters."[26] This time Antonov was all speed and efficiency—the word on the availability of top-secret material from the Western powers having reached the Kremlin inner sanctum—and he told the British officers that as long as they "always used the codeword LIGHTNING he would arrange for one of his staff officers, General Slavin or Colonel Diakonov, to receive this intelligence" and speed it on its way to the Red Army field commander. But London insisted that 30 Mission should give the ULTRA information only "to General Antonov, or some immediate deputy . . . NOT to General Slavin," and also requested that the Red Army not divulge the ULTRA information below the level of "Commanders of Russian Army Groups."[27]

Running parallel to these British ULTRA transmissions to the Soviets in the spring of 1945 was a series of MAGIC reports sent to Moscow by the Americans, whose cryptanalysts acquired considerable information on German intentions and the general course of developments on the Eastern Front from the dispatches sent home by Japanese Ambassador Oshima and his staff in Berlin. During February, MAGIC intercepts were sent to Moscow indicating that "Allied air attacks against production and communications," along with German withdrawals, would delay Nazi counteroffensives. But one MAGIC intercept sent on 20 February to the Red Army in Marshall's name produced serious trouble. This dispatch indicated that the SS Panzer Korps was about to be transferred to the east and would be committed against the center of the advancing Soviet line. The report also carried a notation that this information came from a report "we have intercepted from Japanese sources in Berlin," a comment that not only emphasized the report's accuracy and value to the Russians but also indicated most strongly that this was in fact a product of cryptanalysis.[28]

Unfortunately, in this case, the information also turned out to be incorrect; Hitler changed his mind at the last minute and committed the SS Panzer Korps in Hungary. The Soviets, however, made no mention of the error to the Americans for nearly a month and a half. In the middle of the East-West shouting match over American efforts to arrange a German surrender in northern Italy with SS Obergruppenführer Karl Wolff (Operation SUNRISE), Stalin accused Washington of not being straight with him and added that some of the intelligence material sent to Moscow was inaccurate, especially General Marshall's 20 February MAGIC message indicating that the SS Panzer Korps was about to strike the center of the Red Army line.

To clear the air and defend what he had done, Marshall took the extraordinary step of informing the Soviets not merely that the information he had sent on 20 February came from reliable sources but also that it had come from cryptanalysis. Marshall told the Soviets that the message had been "*intercepted* from Japanese sources in Berlin," thereby surely leaving the Soviets in no doubt that American MAGIC had cracked Japanese diplomatic ciphers.[29] Furthermore, Marshall did not permit the troubles with Stalin over SUNRISE to deter him from sending even more high-grade intercept intelligence to the Soviets, informing General Antonov on 9 April that the 16th SS Panzer Army had been moved to the Western Front and that the West also had "indications" that the Germans would make a stand against the Red Army in Thuringia.[30]

The Red Army leadership was thus well aware from official Western sources as well as from their secret agents not only that the Anglo-Americans were reading German and Japanese codes and ciphers but also that the Western leaders, especially General Marshall, had gone out of their way to pass some of this material to the Red Army. On 12 April 1945, General Antonov took the occasion of a meeting with General Deane to indicate to the Americans that he understood and appreciated what Washington had done by asking Deane to "extend his greeting to him [i.e., Marshall] and thank General Marshall for the regular information which he keeps supplying" to the Red Army.[31]

The provision of ULTRA-MAGIC material to the USSR between February and May 1945 was undoubtedly the most significant aspect of East-West intelligence cooperation during the final phase of the European war. But other, more conventional exchanges were also carried on in this period. As had frequently been the case in the past, Royal and U.S. Navy personnel appear to have been the most successful in arranging journeys to gather helpful information. One U.S. Navy officer visited a Red Air Force base in March, another examined a number of Russian shipyards between March and May (thereby gaining an opportunity to study a Soviet submarine chaser), and a third was able to examine an automobile assembly plant in Odessa. The members of a special Anglo-American SHAEF mission who had been sent to Russia to examine Soviet methods of crossing large rivers (in preparation for the Western armies' attack on the Rhine) found the Soviets "most frank and helpful," although they never actually witnessed any Red Army river-crossing operations.[32] The Western personnel dispatched to Russia to assist in the repatriation of Western troops who had been liberated from German captivity by the Red Army also had good opportunities to examine conditions in the Odessa area. Although some British troops freed in Poland had a number of complaints about their treatment at the hands of the Red Army, those in Odessa did not. These men had not been subjected to any Russian questioning "on subjects other than personal details required to establish [their] identity as British."[33]

As German power waned, however, a number of now traditional entrées into cooperation with the Russians that the Western navies and armies had enjoyed in 1941–1944 gradually withered. The northern convoys were no longer as important to Soviet supply needs, and the German Navy and Luftwaffe were less able to threaten the Western ships headed for Archangel and Murmansk. Royal and U.S. Navy officers thereby lost much of their special relationship with the Red fleet, and East-West naval technological exchanges apparently ceased completely. With the exception of the ULTRA and MAGIC transmissions, the British and American army missions in Moscow also found that their intelligence exchange links with the Red Army had gone cold. No German Army OB meetings appear to have occurred with either Western military mission in this period, and exchanges on German Army equipment also ceased. The sole Red Army request for special assistance from the West, which Eisenhower answered favorably, came in February; the Soviets wanted information on the artillery measures the Anglo-Americans employed prior to the launching of offensives.[34]

Beyond that, the only subject the Red Army was prepared to discuss even moderately seriously was the possibility that, faced with total defeat, the Germans might resort to gas warfare. In mid-February, General Slavin gave the British mission a detailed memorandum on what Moscow believed were stepped-up German measures to counter possible Allied poison gas attacks.[35] The Soviets and some Western officials thought that these might be precautions the Germans were taking before they themselves resorted to gas. The British therefore responded positively to this Soviet initiative by supplying the Russians with two JIC memoranda that weighed the likelihood of Germany's resorting to gas warfare. But within a few weeks, when no clear indications emerged that Hitler was actually ready to use poison gas and the Allies had caught the German armies in a final death grip, these tentative East-West probes on chemical warfare quite fittingly evaporated.

In sharp contrast to the gradual pullback in army and navy intelligence cooperation during the final stage of the European war, there was a last burst of Russian interest in exchanges with the U.S. Army Air Corps in late February and early March. In addition to the fact that Moscow needed American assistance to mount a Red Air Force offensive in Siberia against Japan, this may well have been a final effort to acquire as much high-level American air warfare advanced technology as possible. Near the end of February, the Soviets gave the U.S. Moscow mission a series of reports, ranging from summaries of Luftwaffe deployment on the Eastern Front to details of German planes captured by the Russians since January 1945. Totals of sorties by plane type in December 1944 and January 1945 were also provided to the Americans, as were figures on German air losses for this period. More interestingly, the Soviets supplied the U.S. Army Air Corps with copies of interrogation reports of "German aviators shot down in the period 20 January to 10 February" 1945.[36] In early March, Moscow went on to supply the American mission with targeting information for an unbombed German munitions plant and additional information secured by interrogations of Luftwaffe personnel shot down over Russian-held territory. Near the end of March, the Americans were given another detailed three-and-a-half-page report on Luftwaffe OB, including that for central Germany.[37]

Throughout the winter 1944–1945 phase in which the Soviets showed some generosity to the U.S. Army Air Corps, the Royal Air Force was again left out in the cold. The only clearly documented exception to the blackout of 30 Mission occurred when the Americans shared the information received from Moscow on 12 March regarding the specifications and exact location of the German Army staff headquarters at Zossen, along with a Russian request to "Dear General Deane" that the Anglo-American air forces destroy it. U.S. Army Air Corps chose not to carry out such a raid, and this particular intelligence gift to 30 Mission also failed to bring joy to British hearts. Bomber Harris's night bombing armadas were not designed to hit pinpoint targets, and at this stage of the war, Whitehall was leery about undertaking anything that might resemble an assassination operation. Zossen was therefore not obliterated, and in early March, the RAF also fended off Russian requests that they be allowed to send observers to examine Bomber Command's Pathfinder Force, a highly secret navigational unit that led the waves of Halifaxes and Lancasters that were pulverizing German cities.[38]

These negative British responses to Russian requests were instances of a new Air Ministry decision to be increasingly tightfisted and uncooperative with the Soviet mission in London and the Red Air Force high command in Moscow. The atmosphere had not gone frigid between East and West in late February and March, but it showed signs of turning distinctly chilly. In February–March, Admiral Cunningham believed that the Soviets could be both darkly useful, proposing that captured SS troops be gathered in one place so "they will be handy to be shipped to Siberia," and a threat, because the most worrisome political fact from London's point of view was that the Soviets were entrenched in Poland, and the West had no sure means of getting them out. The first week of March also witnessed the beginning of Operation SUNRISE, which soon left East-West relations dominated by Stalin's rage at the doings of Allen Dulles and SS Obergruppenführer Karl Wolff. Although the Western powers would consistently maintain that they had not negotiated with the SS—and in fact seem not to have clearly promised Wolff immunity from war-crimes prosecution—the SUNRISE dealings in Italy dragged on, leaving Stalin suspicious, angry, and willing to make wild accusations against both Churchill and Roosevelt.[39]

Yet none of these dark signs dampened the enthusiasm for East-West cooperation exhibited by Lord Ismay and General Eisenhower and his staff at SHAEF. As late as 24 May, Ismay said, "more use has been made of the [30] Mission during the last two months than ever before." On 15 March, SHAEF even tried to secure Moscow's agreement to the immediate dispatch of Western military representatives to the USSR "to discuss security problems in Germany." But of course, Eisenhower had no luck with this idea, and 30 Mission was no more successful in its plan of procuring Red Army information regarding which German divisions had actually been destroyed in the east.[40]

By early April, although Pettigrew returned to Moscow and the American mission held limited Japanese OB discussions with the Soviets, overall East-West intelligence exchanges were at a low ebb and falling fast. The NKVD rejected OSS requests for new exchanges as well as American proposals for meetings between NKVD officials and William Donovan.[41] After months of fruitless wrangling, Churchill also said no to any further technical exchanges with the USSR, and on 12–13 April, Eden finally acknowledged that open-handedness with the Soviets did not work and swung around to the Air Ministry view that liaison staffs in London and Moscow should engage in a subtle game of barter with the Soviets on intelligence matters. Although the appointment of a new head of the air section of 30 Mission, Air Vice Marshal H. K. Thorold, in mid-April was not intended to indicate to either the Russians or other officials of 30 Mission that the British government's policy on intelligence exchanges had changed, the RAF was certainly acting in that spirit. In April, for example, the Air Ministry routinely reclassified as "secret" a captured Luftwaffe chart on "Russian aircraft" that the Germans had classified as "restricted" and then added this document to the Air Ministry's confidential intelligence files.[42]

In mid-April, the death of Franklin Roosevelt jolted not only the American people and Anglo-American officials but also Joseph Stalin, who apparently realized that any changes in American policy that occurred as a result of the passing of FDR would certainly not be in the direction of increased generosity to the USSR. Even the NKVD sent condolences to Washington on the president's death, and in the presence of Harriman and Kerr, Stalin brusquely ordered Molotov to drop his objections and attend the United Nations organizational conference in San Francisco as a sign of respect for the late president and to give support to the general agreements that had been made by the wartime Big Three.[43]

Such personal gestures could not smooth out worsening East-West diplomatic difficulties, however, any more than a magician's wand could wave away the dilatory and troubled intelligence and military relations between the West and Moscow. In April, some members of the CCS, including Admiral Cunningham, had serious doubts about Eisenhower's decision to direct his attack at south Germany while leaving Berlin to the Red Army. Stalin simply lied to Harriman about Soviet intentions, telling him on 16 April that the principal goal of the Red Army's offensive thrust was not Berlin, because the "main blow would be [made] in the direction of Dresden."[44]

Finding common ground between East and West was becoming extremely difficult, except when it came to heaping more and now largely pointless destruction on shattered Germany. On 16 April 1945, the British mission in Moscow asked the Soviets whether they objected to the Western powers bombing the targets on a long list of cities in eastern Germany, Austria, and Czechoslovkia. The Soviets approved the bombing of every one of them, including shattered Dresden, only asking that the Anglo-Americans make no more attacks on Prague.[45]

But this reflex-like meeting of the minds of Moscow, Washington, and London regarding the demolition of Germany did nothing to slacken the march toward East-West confrontation once the Third Reich had been destroyed. By 15 April 1945, the planning staff at AFHQ Mediterranean in Italy was already preparing the countermeasures it would employ in the event of a "Russian inspired invasion of Turkey."[46] A day later, OSS headquarters in Washington ordered the staff of its main radio intercept station on the East Coast of the United States to begin monitoring Soviet radio broadcasts. Although the broadcasts in question were open, *en clair* transmissions from Moscow, the OSS had avoided monitoring them for three years so as not to give offense to the Soviets. But by 2 May 1945, with FDR dead, V-E Day at hand, and East-West relations less than smooth and harmonious, such civilities were a thing of the past. Even the secretary of the British JIC, F. W. Cavendish Bentinck of the Foreign Office, was forced to admit that although "in the days of Mason Macfarlane and Martel" he "was of the opinion that the Military Mission at Moscow were to blame for their lack of success," he had now changed his mind and "reached the conclusion that the Russians were to blame."[47]

Even at this point, though, not all voices of calmness and caution had been stilled. On 2 April 1945, the U.S. secretary of war, Henry Stimson, lectured the new secretary of state, Edward Stettinius, that, in retrospect, "Russia had been very good to us on the large issues," and although Russia had "poor manners," "she had kept her word." On 23 April, a week prior to Bentinck's conversion to the view that 30 Mission's difficulties should be blamed on the Russians, Stimson dismissed the aggressive and angry moans of Ambassador Harriman and General Deane by observing in his diary that the only reason they "wanted the U.S. Government to get tough with the Russians" was because of "their past bad treatment."[48]

Similarly, in the run-up to V-E Day, Churchill struggled to keep focused on securing as much influence and prestige for Britain as he could, since the British role in victory was likely to be overshadowed by the activities and triumphant posturing of the Russians and Americans. Three days prior to V-E Day, London hurriedly appointed a new head of 30 Mission, Lt. Gen. J. A. G. Gammell, an army man of higher rank than Admiral Archer, but this change was not made to indicate any special respect for the Russians. Too late, Churchill had concluded that in the event of large-scale German surrenders, a British Army officer of high rank in Moscow might help raise British status and prestige with the Russians. But as fate would have it, when Hitler committed suicide and the German Army came to surrender, Admiral Doenitz and General Jodl chose to approach SHAEF, and neither Deane nor Gammell, nor the Red Army high command, were to stand in the front rank of triumphant glory at Rheims on May 7, 1945.[49]

Of course, the Soviets arranged another formal surrender ceremony in Berlin, which Admiral Archer would attend (since General Gammell had not yet taken up his post in Moscow). This ceremony ritualized Stalin's triumph over Hitler, and the Russian people received a slip of international glory for the enormous sacrifices they had made in the defeat of Nazism. The two divisive surrender ceremonies, like the post-Yalta political troubles between East and West and the increasingly futile attempts to make intelligence cooperation work, demonstrated all too clearly that London, Washington, and Moscow were at this point not real allies, nor even "comrades."

The war, of course, was still not over. Japan remained unsubdued, and as the Iron Curtain began its initial descent over Eastern Europe, the Western and Eastern military "allies" were faced with a final opportunity in the Far East to make wartime intelligence cooperation work effectively. This time, the Americans held most of the political high cards, the most powerful weaponry the world had ever seen, and a multitude of intelligence materials on Japan and the Japanese armed forces. The summer of 1945 would test Washington's ability to smash Japanese military power quickly and at low cost. May to August 1945 would also test whether the U.S. government would use its enormous stock of Far Eastern intelligence to establish a better basis for trust and cooperation between East and West and thereby lessen the force of the approaching Cold War tide.

12
An End to War?
May–August 1945

V-E Day finished the European war, and in the weeks immediately following 8 May, East and West made reasonably harmonious efforts to carry out the
Three Power agreements made at Yalta regarding zones of occupation and the
general policies to be followed in occupied Germany. To avoid giving offense to
the Soviets, Western advance units that had fought their way into portions of
Czechoslovakia and what was to become the Soviet zone of Germany quickly
withdrew to the west, and in the initial European postwar phase, the Soviet
Union and the Western powers managed to maintain traditional civilities, albeit
with a minimum of warmth.[1] During May, Harry Hopkins visited Stalin in
Moscow again, and Roosevelt's old confidant briefly recaptured enough of the
high-level cordiality that had prevailed at Teheran and Yalta to give the public
and some Washington officials reason to hope that all would yet be well and that
the Big Three might continue to be linked together as closely in peace as in war.[2]

But many officials in Washington, and even more in London, were already
deeply troubled by the armed might that Stalin and his armies had spread across
central Eastern Europe. Equally worrying were the harsh cleansing policies that
the Soviets began to employ in Germany and the Soviet-occupied territories of
Germany's former satellites, including Bulgaria, Rumania, and Hungary. On 15
May, in a meeting with Ambassador Kerr, Churchill lamented that the "Soviets
were dropping an iron screen across Europe from Lübeck to Trieste, behind
which we have no knowledge of what was happening."[3] A month later, the
prime minister gloomily lectured the War Cabinet for nearly an hour on the
dangers posed by Russian power and belligerence. Other British officials also
concluded that the Soviets were closing themselves and their zone off from
the West. The 30 Mission chief, General Gammell, noted in a July report on the
USSR that the West was now faced with the question of how to deal with
the Russian "iron curtain now drawn across Eastern Europe."[4]

Initially, the top echelon of American leadership seems to have viewed the post–V-E Day situation in the East with less alarm than did senior British officials, partly because of the calming effect of a 3,000-mile-wide expanse of water, which often lessened American apprehension about developments in central Eastern Europe. In addition, the U.S. government was much more deeply engaged than the British or the Soviets in pressing home the Pacific war, and this focus apparently allowed Washington fewer opportunities to worry about Russia than were available to Whitehall. But although the Truman White House, as well as the State and Defense Departments, succeeded in reining in their worst concerns about the USSR in the short run, fears about the Soviet Union were dancing energetically in a number of Washington executive branch offices, as well as in Congress and among broad sections of the American public. Irregular organizations such as the OSS, which were eager to make a mark and perhaps acquire a postwar life, were understandably quick to react to the possibility of a Russian menace. Donovan's men, even as they carried out anti-Nazi counterintelligence operations with the USSR in Europe, quickly set to work preparing studies that delineated possible threats from the East and pondered why the USSR needed a military budget as huge as the one that had just been announced for 1946.[5] By 22 July, even the U.S. Army had produced a 200-page highly secret report on "the German G-2 service in the Russian campaign."[6]

These worries and uncertainties about Eastern Europe that surfaced during the summer made the West less eager to carry out intelligence exchanges with Moscow, and the Soviet "iron hand" in Eastern Europe made it difficult for Anglo-American intelligence agencies to gather useful information about what was actually happening in the new Soviet zone. The British chiefs of staff were initially inclined to play intelligence hardball in Eastern Europe; they wanted Western advance military units that penetrated "the Soviet sphere" of eastern Germany and Western Czechoslovakia to seize all the secret German equipment they could find and destroy everything else. But by the time the Western withdrawals actually occurred in midsummer, the cautionary views of the U.S. Army and of the British Foreign Office prevailed, and the Western units took only the German equipment whose seizure could be justified as useful in the war against Japan; everything else was left to the USSR. Even though the Pentagon championed moderation in such matters, the Joint Chiefs of Staff issued new orders to General Deane and the U.S. military mission in Moscow directing them to deal with the Soviets on a basis of strict reciprocity and requiring that "nothing should be asked from [the] Russians which the United States Government cannot force the Russians to accept" by retaliatory action.[7]

On the ground in Moscow during the summer of 1945, the British and American missions saw their intelligence-gathering opportunities seriously reduced but not entirely eliminated. The Royal Navy mission in the north continued to gather data on Soviet ships and bases, and the British naval liaison officer in the Black Sea region remained at his post. The Royal Navy teams in the USSR still characterized their Soviet counterparts as courteous and helpful,[8] and although there were few such feelings of camaraderie with the Russians among the members of the RAF branch of the mission, the airmen surveyed Leningrad and acquired data on Torvay and Moscow airports. By 12 June, these reports from Moscow allowed the RAF to declare that it held detailed information on twenty-one Soviet airports, which the Air Ministry had already cross-filed under ninety-five different subject headings in London's secret files.[9]

American officials also picked up details on Russian installations and institutions through travels around the USSR. In the summer of 1945, George Kennan prepared a long account of his trips to Novosibirsk and Stalinsk in June, and another State Department officer chronicled his trans-Siberian journey in August. None of the information acquired by Westerners in Russia or the Russian "satellite zone" during the summer of 1945, except for that picked up by U.S. Army Air Corps air and weather teams moving into Siberia, surpassed in value what could have been gained by outsiders in other comparably "closed" societies. Admiral Archer and his staff were permitted to visit Danzig in early September, but they gained little information of significance, aside from the fact that the Russians had already seized and removed eleven unfinished German submarines from this Soviet-occupied Polish port, which had ostensibly been the cause of the outbreak of war in 1939.[10]

Exchanges of intelligence documents confronted even more serious opposition and obstacles in both East and West. Within three weeks of V-E Day, Whitehall turned over a new leaf and instituted a get-tough policy with the Soviets on all forms of informational exchange. Characterizing the main features of Soviet officialdom and the Soviet negotiating stance as "suspicion," "centralization of control," "security," and "hard bargaining," the British JIC observed that since V-E Day, East-West relations had definitely deteriorated. The British intelligence departments then went on to conclude, incorrectly, that although the USSR's political and propaganda power was great, since the West no longer needed Russian military might, the balance of power had actually shifted against Stalin and his colleagues. The JIC held that Russia would soon be compelled to play a less aggressive tune, because it would be desperately dependent on Western economic aid. Building on this dangerously false premise, the Whitehall mandarins argued hard for a rough-edged policy in which "reciprocity" would be basic to every aspect of Anglo-Soviet relations, including the sharing of intelligence, technical cooperation, and access to military facilities. "Nothing," the JIC concluded, "should be given to the Russians gratuitously," and all British officials should speak with one voice, being "firm and correct rather than overtly friendly."[11]

By mid-June, the Royal Navy was already applying the new harder line to Soviet requests for access to German naval bases in Western Europe, declaring that this should occur only when the British and Americans were permitted to see bases in Eastern Europe. On 1 July, British pressure intensified. All military, air, and naval staffs were instructed to answer Soviet requests for information with the stock response that "higher authority might be more favorably inclined to agree to the information being supplied if the Soviet Military Mission could show that some information of a comparable kind had been given by the Russian Government to our Mission in Moscow."[12] A week later, Churchill demanded that British authorities carry out a comparably stern policy of reciprocity with the Soviets in regard to technical information, because "our attitude to the Russians must be determined by their attitude to us."[13] The Foreign Office once more tried to put a brake on the headlong Whitehall dash toward confrontation with Moscow. A Foreign Office memo of 22 July declared that the "hardline anti-Soviet attitude" in the British armed forces might be difficult to control. It noted that "Firebrace himself has pretty strong Czarist associations," and his deputy had greeted the German attack on Russia in 1941 by proclaiming "with relish that the Bolsheviks would be defeated within six weeks."[14]

But such admonitions did little to check the British dash toward confrontation or the concomitant shift in British intelligence priorities from securing intelligence from the Russians about Germany to acquiring intelligence about Russia from the Germans. As early as 29 June 1945, MI 3 declared that the bulk of its information on the Red Army had been derived from the Germans and their satellites, especially from German "Y" and German documents, as well as from Japanese intercepts and material secured from the Poles. In the judgment of MI 3, the time had come to interrogate German POWs in British hands in the hope of gathering more such intelligence on the Soviet Union.[15]

By 22 August, when the air section files of 30 Mission were screened to see what was worth saving, everything on the Japanese Air Force was destroyed, and only three files on the Luftwaffe were preserved. But twenty-eight files on Russia and the Russian Air Force were retained for their intelligence value.[16] By 27 August, the former German naval attaché in Moscow, Capt. Otto von Baumbach, had been intensively interrogated about the Red Navy, although he had not been in the USSR since 1941 and many Royal Navy officers had much more recent acquaintance with the Red Navy.[17]

London's reversal of intelligence priorities, coupled with a definite British movement in the direction of hard-line policies toward the USSR, a rise in mutual suspicion between Moscow and Washington, and Soviet repression in Eastern Europe, was hardly a good omen for the Potsdam Big Three conference that opened on 17 July and continued intermittently until 2 August. Yet despite definite tensions, the new Big Three—with Truman replacing Roosevelt and Clement Attlee taking Churchill's place halfway through the proceedings— managed to maintain appearances and a measure of consensus on the broad questions of German occupation policy and the holding of the Nuremberg war- crimes trials. During an interval in the Potsdam proceedings, President Truman also casually informed Stalin that an American wonder weapon (the atomic bomb) had become operational. The Soviet leader took this news with no out- ward sign of emotion; in all probability, Russian agents had done their work effectively enough to prepare the Kremlin for the existence of the bomb. Stalin then went on to repeat his earlier pledge to enter the war against Japan in the near future. The reiteration of this Soviet promise discomfited Churchill, who had already lost his enthusiasm for Soviet participation in the Pacific war and hoped that the Americans had also turned cool toward the prospect of the Red Army overrunning Manchuria.[18]

But this time the prime minister was certainly off base. On at least two occa- sions by 23 July, American officials had informed the British that they would provide the Russians with intelligence on Japan whether or not the Soviets re- ciprocated. Stalin had also indicated a number of times since Yalta that he fully intended to fight Japan, and on 2 June 1945, he had raised a secret toast in the Kremlin with the British ambassador present "to the meeting of the Allied Commanders in Tokyo."[19] Even more important, the U.S. government had accepted Moscow's promises to intervene as genuine and continued to wel- come them, because American politicians were under great political and mili- tary pressure to end the war in the Pacific as quickly and as cheaply as possible. Traces of war weariness were apparent in the United States, and public and Pentagon concerns about the level of American casualties were rising. Okinawa had finally been taken by the 10th U.S. Army on 21 June, and the remaining large ships of the Japanese high-seas fleet had been destroyed by the U.S. Navy. But the Okinawa victory had required two and a half months of bitter conflict and had resulted in 10,000 American dead and 30,000 wounded, as the reality of kamikaze exacted its costly toll. Great nervousness about what might happen if the Americans were required to hit the beaches in the Japanese Home Islands was still very much alive in Washington and among U.S. Army leaders in the Pacific. Two and a half months before the 10th Army had gone ashore at Okinawa (13 February 1945), even that old hater of Communists, Gen. Douglas MacArthur, had made clear to a visiting Pentagon officer that the ideological and geopolitical complications that might accompany Russian intervention counted for nothing compared with the need for Russian assistance in defeating Japan:

> He [MacArthur] emphatically stated that we must not invade Japan proper unless the Russian Army is previously committed to action in Manchuria. He said this was essential and that it [Russian intervention] should be done without the three month delay upon the conclusion of the defeat of Germany as indicated by Marshal Stalin to the President. . . . *He* [MacArthur] *understands Russia's aims; that they would want all of Manchuria, Korea and possibly part of North China. This seizure of territory was inevitable;* but the United States must insist that Russia pay her way by invading Manchuria at the earliest possible date after the defeat of Germany.[20]

Three months later, and just two months prior to the Potsdam conference, General Marshall himself made absolutely clear to Field Marshal Wilson that the United States was still counting heavily on Soviet intervention against Japan. On 12 May, Marshall told Wilson that he was determined not to use American forces on the Asian mainland and was relying on the Russians to deal with the Japanese Kwantung Army. Wilson sent this information to Brooke, who relayed it to the British chiefs of staff, thereby guaranteeing that British Army authorities had no doubt that the Americans wanted to let the Russians do any dirty work that might be necessary against the Japanese on the Asian mainland. Since the British Army had just completed three years of ruthless and bloody struggle to lever the Japanese out of the comparatively narrow zone of Southeast Asia, having someone else dispose of the Kwantung Army, whatever the political side effects, could hardly have been a matter of deep regret for British military leaders, any more than it was for those of the United States.[21]

Any possibility that Churchill might have been successful in opposing Russian entry into the Pacific war was eliminated on 26 July, when Labour won the general election and Clement Attlee became prime minister. Eleven days later (6 August), Stalin declared war on Japan, and Soviet forces stormed into

Manchuria and Korea, quickly overrunning the Japanese defensive positions, which turned out to be more weakly held than had been posited by Western and Soviet intelligence. The second atomic bomb was dropped on Nagasaki on 9 April, and following five days of secret dickering, the Japanese government surrendered on 14 August (V-J Day). Two weeks later, American occupation troops began to take possession of the Japanese homeland.

However, it must be emphasized that in the two months prior to V-J Day, as the British sank deeper into a policy of tightfistedness and hard bargaining with the Russians, even in regard to intelligence on the Japanese, the U.S. authorities had consistently pursued a policy of sharing Japanese intelligence with Moscow. On 26 June, the Air Ministry issued a general order that "*all* intelligence reports, technical and otherwise which have hitherto been sent, or made available, to the Russians, either by automatic inclusion on a distribution list or otherwise are no longer to be so disclosed except when a comparable quid pro quo is arranged."[22] On the same day, General Deane had a discussion on Japanese antitank and antipersonnel mines with General Slavin. On that occasion, the American general told the Red Army staff representative:

> If there was anything else of interest to the Russian General Staff regarding Japanese intelligence . . . or if there are other pieces of Japanese equipment, or any experience gained from fighting with the Japanese which might interest the Russians, we would be very glad to make everything available.

In the same session, General Deane remarked that "if the Russians wished," the U.S. Army "would be very glad to have them [the Soviets] send observers to our units where they are fighting the Japanese." To top off the American Army intelligence open-handedness regarding Japan, General Slavin was told that Colonel Pettigrew was returning to Moscow and "would be pleased to meet any Russian specialists" who wished to discuss Japanese intelligence questions.[23]

Pettigrew was soon back at his post in Moscow, where he remained until the third week of August. He was made acting head of the American military mission in General Deane's temporary absence. On 21 July, the War Department provided Pettigrew with detailed information on Japanese-controlled railways in Manchuria and northern China, the American estimate of manpower and equipment losses for both the Japanese Army and the Japanese Air Force, overall Japanese casualties, aircraft losses, and "monthly production figures" for heavy equipment.[24] On 2 August, a special U.S. Army intelligence team had been assembled in the Pentagon, led by the chief of the War Department's Special (i.e., cryptanalytic intelligence) Branch, Col. Alfred McCormack, and a lieutenant colonel from G-2 named William R. Perdue. The primary duty of this team was to pass to the U.S. military mission in Moscow an extended series of high-grade intelligence messages regarding the Japanese Army and Air Force for relay to the Soviet Army high command. Most of the data contained in the messages had been acquired from top-secret ULTRA decrypt sources and constituted the highest grade of intelligence information on the Japanese armed forces held by the U.S. Army.

Maj. Robert Hall, who had worked for a number of years as a specialist on Red Army intelligence matters in the Pentagon, had been seconded to Pettigrew to aid him in Japanese "exchanges with the Soviet Government."[25] Maximum secrecy regarding these exchanges had to be maintained due to "the extreme importance of [the] source," and on 3 August, Pettigrew began to pass the ULTRA material to General Antonov, beginning with a "summary of OB in Japan" itself. Lively Soviet-American discussions on Japanese OB soon followed. Pettigrew reported to Washington on 3 August that the Red Army believed that only one regiment of the Japanese 121st Division had actually been moved from Manchuria to Japan.[26]

During early August, Washington officials transmitted to London some of the Japanese intelligence materials and comments they had received from the Russians, and by 11 August, portions of this material had been relayed from London to Air Marshal Gammell in Moscow. Since 30 Mission was still not receiving any high-grade intelligence on Japan directly from the Russian authorities, London and Gammell's mission remained on the periphery of the main Soviet-American intelligence exchange loop. Not until the USSR declared war on Japan on 8 August, two days after the first atomic blast on Hiroshima, did 30 Mission discuss Japanese intelligence with the Soviet authorities. Air Marshal Gammell then told General Antonov that 30 Mission was prepared "to furnish to the Soviet General Staff operational intelligence regarding the enemy in areas under the control of the British Chiefs of Staff." But by this time, the Americans had shown that they were bolder and more successful than the British in dealing with Moscow on Japanese intelligence.[27] By 8 August, they had already given the Russians secret material that was much more valuable than anything Moscow was likely to receive from the British Southeast Asian Command, which was now an operational backwater.

The four and a half years of Western intelligence cooperation with the USSR therefore ended with the Americans riding high. The East-West intelligence-sharing process pioneered by the British in 1941 in the face of American doubt and hesitation ended with the British on the sidelines and the

Americans dishing out masses of top-secret intelligence to the USSR. Since none of the information provided by the Americans in the last week of the war could have reached the Soviet attacking units in Siberia soon enough to have significantly helped their assault on the Kwantung Army, this final festival of American open-handedness regarding secret intelligence appears to have done little to speed up Japan's defeat or lessen the cost in casualties during the last week of World War II offensive action in Asia.

But even if the final phase of East-West intelligence cooperation in World War II yielded few, if any, important military or political benefits to the Allied cause, that certainly does not mean that the broad sweep of East-West intelligence exchange between 1941 and 1945 was devoid of significance. Certainly the fact that the U.S. Army high command supplied top-secret operational ULTRA to the Soviets in August 1945 should incline historians to question the arguments of Gar Alperovitz and others that the final phase of the war against Japan was primarily an early Cold War political performance in which the U.S. government dropped atomic bombs on Japan to warn the Russians to stay out of the Asian war and to make their invasion of Manchuria unnecessary.[28] If that had been the guiding principle of American military policy and strategy in the final weeks of the war, the War Department's provision of operational ULTRA to the Red Army authorities in mid-August 1945 would have been an act of madness so bizarre that it would have few parallels in all of modern history. The ULTRA transmissions prove that Alperovitz is wrong. The historical record set forth above indicates that the American government, and to a large extent the British government as well, frequently put its desire to produce effective intelligence exchange with the Soviets ahead of other considerations throughout 1941–1945. Of course, they grumbled about Soviet secrecy and Russian boorishness, as well as harboring fears about Moscow's future intentions. But during the European war, both Western governments consistently sought to cooperate on intelligence matters with the USSR. The British became more hesitant after V-E Day, but since they held little valuable intelligence related to the last stage of the war against Japan, the Americans were the dominant intelligence exchange force, and they supplied the USSR with high-grade Japanese intelligence right up until V-J Day, even though the intelligence the Soviets supplied in return was of marginal value.

The history of the final phase of East-West intelligence cooperation in World War II therefore shows that the U.S. government did not put Cold War and balance-of-power considerations foremost in its relations with the USSR and in the war against Japan during August 1945. By sharing its highest-grade intelligence on Japan with the Red Army right up to the end of the conflict, the U.S.

government revealed that the principle of "military necessity" and Allied cooperation remained the dominant themes of its military-political calculations and
operations until the last days of the war.[29]

That this policy was naive has been suggested by many political observers
inside and outside the U.S. government at the time and by an army of Cold War
activists of varying persuasions in the years that have followed. The Western
military missions in Moscow were provided with hard evidence that this was so
within two months of V-J Day. On 24 October 1945, during the dismantling of
30 Mission's office building in Moscow, British authorities discovered Soviet
secret listening devices throughout the building, including especially sensitive
bugs in the mission's main conference room. In retrospect, it was also apparent
to most observers that the Western attempt to neutralize the political nature of
warfare by pushing many political considerations to the sidelines in World War
II was probably a serious error.[30]

It must now be recognized that although the West avoided making serious
intelligence attacks on the USSR during World War II, within days of its conclusion, British intelligence was working on Soviet military codes and ciphers.
A 10 October 1945 MI 6 document (just released), citing as its source decryption of secret Soviet coded traffic "from mid-August 1945," set out such a
broad sweep of general characteristics of the Soviet military structure that one
of its War Office recipients in MI 3 queried in the margin, "who intercepts and
descrambles Russian W/T [wireless] traffic?" Due to the slow pace of declassi-
fication (despite the end of the Cold War), that question still cannot be
answered, but that the British military intelligence establishment was breaking
some portions of Soviet enciphered traffic in August 1945 is, in light of this
document, undeniable.[31]

The speed with which this change occurred, and the ferocity with which
East-West hostility exploded on the world, quickly produced a massive case of
international amnesia, wiping away public and governmental memory of East-
West wartime cooperation. The record of four years of East-West intelligence
cooperation presented here, however, shows that this was the most extensive
and successful such effort carried out by reluctant allies in the history of modern warfare. As such, it suggests that, half a century later, existing histories of
World War II may need to be reconsidered. Russia and the West can join
together in pride over a wartime cooperative effort that, against long odds,
brought genuine benefits to both the Eastern and Western wings of the Allied
cause.

Notes

Preface

1. DEFE 1/34, PRO, Hess 23 May 1941.

2. For John Chapman's most recent contribution, "The Imperial Japanese Navy and the North-South Dilemma," see John Erickson and David Dilks, eds., *Barbarossa: The Axis and the Allies* (Edinburgh: Edinburgh University Press, 1994), pp. 150–206.

3. Diane T. Putney, *Ultra and the Army Air Forces in World War II* (Washington, D.C.: Office of the Air Force, 1987), p. 46, and David Syrett, "The Secret War and the Historians," *Armed Forces and Society* 9:3 (Winter 1983): 296.

Chapter 1. Overture

1. Some British documents on intelligence in the Russian civil war were not released until 1995. See WO/160, 17–21, PRO.

2. April 1919 memo in WO 32/21382, PRO (new release).

3. 29 April 1927, CO 273/539, PRO (new release).

4. 25 January 1939, FO 115/799, PRO, and CO 323/1611, PRO (both new releases).

5. Drs. Keith Jeffrey (Belfast) and Eunan O'Halpin (Dublin), together with the author, are preparing a volume on antisubversion in the interwar period. In general, all U.S. filing numbers ending in B, such as 824B, can be translated in 824 Bolshevik. See also Christopher Andrew, *Her Majesty's Secret Service* (New York: Penguin, 1987), pp. 174 ff.

6. See Joan M. Jensen, *Army Surveillance in America, 1775–1980* (New Haven, Conn.: Yale University Press, 1991), and Roy Talbert Jr., *Negative Intelligence: The Army and the American Left, 1917–1941* (Jackson: University of Mississippi, 1991).

7. Charles Bohlen, *Witness to History* (New York: Norton, 1973), and Daniel Yergin, *Shattered Peace: The Origins of the Cold War and the National Security State* (Boston: Houghton Mifflin, 1980).

8. 11 November/12 December Hughes-Coolidge exchange in 1924, 811.00B/394A, DB, NA.

9. Yergin gives a balanced summary of these trends in *Shattered Peace*.

10. War Office intelligence summaries, WO 287/228, 236–37, and 240, PRO.

11. 6 August 1940 report, DEFE 1/57, PRO.

12. 29 September 1939, HO 45/25521, Special Branch to Undersecretary of State (new release), PRO.

13. 11 June 1940, Far East Central Bureau, WO 208/2053, PRO.

14. Late 1939, WO 208/11, PRO.

15. Air attack plans, CAB 104/259, PRO; SOE, Alexander Cadogan diary (unpublished portions), 1/10, 14 January 1941, Churchill College, Cambridge.

16. 18 October 1940, COS (40) 842, WO 193/659, 25 April and 20 May 1941, FO 371/29465/N1955 and N2410, PRO; 20 and 21 December 1940, Diary "O" series, F. H. N. Davidson papers, Kings College, London.

17. 10 August 1049, INF 1/611, PRO.

18. See Gabriel Gorodetsky, *Stafford Cripps' Mission to Moscow, 1940–1942* (Cambridge: Cambridge University Press, 1984), passim.

19. 20 June 1941, FO 371/29479/N1366, PRO. On the intelligence setting of the Nazi-Soviet war, see John Erickson and David Dilks, eds., *Barbarossa: The Axis and the Allies* (Edinburgh: Edinburgh University Press, 1994), especially "British Intelligence and Barbarossa," by F. H. Hinsley, pp. 43–75.

20. 3 April 1941, FO 371/29479/N1366, PRO.

21. 23 May 1941, JIC (41) 218 Final, CAB 81/102, PRO.

22. 23 May 1941, CAB 120/691, PRO.

23. 21 April 1941, Box 579, Entry 57, RG 319, Suitland, NA.

24. 9 June 1941, JIC (41) 234, FO 371/29483/2906, PRO.

25. "German Agents in Connection with Possible Moves Against Russia," 11 June 1941, ADM 223/298.

26. 12 June 1941, COS 59 (51) 2, CAB 65/18, PRO.

27. 13 June 1941, FO 418/87, PRO.

28. 14 June 1941, JIC (41) 234 (revised), CAB 81/102, PRO.

29. 14 June 1941, JP (41) 451 (s), CAB 84/32, PRO.

30. Raymond H. Dawson, *The Decision to Aid Russia, 1941* (Chapel Hill: University of North Carolina Press, 1959), pp. 64–66.

31. Ibid., and Henry Stimson diary, 17 July 1941, Yale University.

32. 17 June 1941, FO 371/39483/2904, PRO.

33. 17 June 1941, INF 1/913, PRO.

34. 30 June 1941, COS (41) 218, CAB 79/12, PRO; Gorodetsky, *Stafford Cripps' Mission to Moscow,* pp. 230–231.

35. JP (41) 49th and JP (41) 465, CAB 84/3 and 32, and WO 193/645A, PRO.

36. 23 June 1941, CAB 62(41) 4 and CAB 65/18, PRO; Henry Stimson diary, 22 and 23 June 1941, Yale University.

37. 24 June 1941, Army projects 336-2, Russia, Box 1052, RG 407, MR, NA.

38. JPS, Washington, 23 June 1941, CAB 122/100, PRO.

39. 20 November 1941, CAB 122/100, PRO.

40. 23 June 1941, FO 371/29560/3065, PRO.

41. 23 June 1941, R. G. Turner diary, Imperial War Museum.

42. 23 June 1941, WO 193/645A, PRO.

43. 22 June 1941, FO 371/29358/N3048, PRO.

44. The best indicator of the range of Britain's decryption is the new HW 1 series of intercepts for the prime minister in the PRO.

45. 21 June 1941, CAB 122/101, PRO.

46. 23 June 1941, JP (41) 478, CAB 84/32, PRO.

47. 26 June 1941, FO 371/29560/N3090; ADM 1/11158, and WO 208/1763, PRO.

48. 1 July 1941, WO 208/1578, PRO; emphasis added.

49. 6 July, Macfarlane to Nelson, WO 193/623, and 10 July, Macfarlane to CIGS, WO 193/644, PRO.

50. Stalin to Cripps, 22 July 1941, FO 371/29594/BN136610, PRO.

51. "G(R) 16," WP (41) 145, 4 July 1941 and subsequent papers, WO 193/623 and 655, PRO. Cadogan diary, Churchill College (22 August 1941). On Axis agents, 5 August 1941, WO 178/25, PRO.

52. 19 September planning, FO 371/29597/N5500 and N5539, PRO.

53. 23 and 24 June 1941, Dalton diary, LSE. George Hill memoir, Hoover Institution, Stanford, Calif., and the great assistance of Mark Seaman of the Imperial War Museum.

54. Ibid.

55. George Hill, *Go Spy the Land* (London: Cassell, 1932), passim, and George Hill, "Four Years with the NKVD," Hoover Institution, Stanford University. See especially the newly released SOE-NKVD files, HS 4 series, especially HS4/332, 351, and 355, PRO.

56. Cadogan diary, 25 and 27 June 1941, 1/10, Churchill College, Cambridge; James MacGregor Burns, *Roosevelt: Soldier of Freedom* (New York: Harcourt Brace, 1970), p. 103; Edward M. Bennett, *Franklin Roosevelt and the Search for Victory* (Wilmington, Del.: Scholarly Resources, 1990), p. 28.

57. 11 December summary of events, INF 1/913, PRO.

58. 25–26 June 1941, Turner diary, Imperial War Museum; 24 June, WO 193/645A and ADM 1/12671, PRO.

59. 24 June 1941, WO 193/645A and ADM 1/12671; Flight over Iran, 24 June 1941, FO 3781/29560/N3086. The trip, Turner diary, later summer to autumn, Imperial War Museum. See also Ewan Butler, *Mason-Mac: A Life of Lieutenant General Sir Noel Mason Macfarlane* (London: Macmillan, 1972), p. 131; 24–28 June 1941, WO 178/25, and FO 3371/29466/N3250, PRO.

60. 26 June 1941, FO 371/29560/N3289, PRO.

61. 24 June 1941, FO 371/29560 and WO 216/124, PRO.

62. Mason Macfarlane, see esp. Folder 31, Box 2, Mason Macfarlane Papers, Imperial War Museum; Butler, *Mason Macfarlane,* passim; Wesley J. Wark, "Three Military Attachés at Berlin in the 1930s: Soldier-Statesmen and the Limits of Ambiguity," *International History Review* 9:4 (November 1987): 586–611; Cheshire report, 2 January 1942, FO 371/36969/N706, PRO; A. H. Birse, *Memoirs of an Interpreter* (New York: Coward, 1967), p. 65.

63. 24 June 1941, WO 216/124, PRO.

64. 22–29 June 1941, ADM 1/11158, ADM 199/604, ADM 223/252, WO 193/645A, and AIR 20/8049, PRO; Mason Macfarlane Papers, Folder 31, Box 2, Imperial War Museum.

65. "Draft," Folder 31, Box 2, Mason Macfarlane Papers, Imperial War Museum.

66. 24 June 1941, WO 193/645A, PRO.

Chapter 2. Searching for an Intelligence Partnership

1. Dimitri Volkogonov, *Stalin: Triumph and Tragedy,* trans. Harry Shulman (Rocklin, Calif.: Prima, 1992); David M. Glantz, *Soviet Operations in the Initial Period of War, 22 June–August 1941* (London: Frank Cass, 1987); John Erickson and David Dilks, eds., *Barbarossa: The Axis and the Allies* (Edinburgh: Edinburgh University Press, 1994); John Erickson, *The Road to Stalingrad* (London: Grafton, 1985); Hans Adolf Jacobsen and Charles Burdick, *The Halder Diary, 1939–1942* (London: Green Hill, 1982).

2. 3 July 1941, WO 193/644; 15 July War Office estimate, WO 208/1777, PRO.

3. 3 July 1941 file, Box 43, NHC 76, RG 38, MR, NA; 10 July 1941, WO 193/645A, PRO.

4. 10 July 1941, FO 371/29561/N3519 and Cadogan diary, 1/10, 3 July 1941, Churchill College, Cambridge.

5. 28 June and 12 August 1941, INF 1/676 and 913, PRO.

6. 3 July and 25 October 1941 and 27 January 1942, WO 193/645A and WO 193/652, PRO.

7. 26 July and 27 August 1941, WO 208/1775, 1778, and 2060. See also F. H. Hinsley, E. E. Thomas, et al., *British Intelligence in the Second World War: Its Influence upon Operations,* 4 vols. (London: Her Majesty's Stationery Office, 1979–1985), 2:69–70.

8. Hinsley, Thomas, et al., *British Intelligence,* 2:69–70, and Bradley F. Smith, *The Ultra-Magic Deals* (Shrewsbury: Airlife, 1993), pp. 54 ff. Since these two works appeared, ULTRA transmissions to the prime minister have been released in the HW 1 series, PRO.

9. 18 August 1941, FO 371/29586, Pika report examples FO 371/29586 and adjacent files. The Polish mission chief appointed on 28 August was Gen. S. Bohusz-Szyszko, and the ambassador was Stanislaw Kot. See CAM 2/27/64 and HW 1/235, PRO, as well as Frantisek Moravec, *Master of Spies: The Memoirs of General Frantisek Moravec* (London: Sphere, 1981), pp. 202 ff.

10. For the U.S. embassy and military attachés in general, see RG 319, Entry 57, Moscow, Boxes 579 and 585, Suitland, NA; Entry 59, Transcripts, Russia file, Box 252, Suitland, NA; Stimson diary, 23 June–31 July 1941, Yale; Sect. of State to U.S. embassy Moscow, June–July, 740 00118 EW/939/360, DB, NA; Ambassador Clinton Olson and General James Boswell interviews, October–November 1993.

11. Such doubts about Soviet military competence also remained in the British War Office, one officer noting on 28 August 1941, after receiving a report on the high technical level of the Red Air Force, "if all this is true, how is it that they bleat for us to send them assistance and planes?" WO 208/2060, PRO.

12. Yeaton's exit, 3 November 1941, CAB 122/100, PRO; 6 August 1941 ff., August Files 2 and 3, Box 579, Entry 57, RG 319, Suitland, NA.

13. Cadogan diary, 1/10, 4 August 1941, Churchill College, Cambridge; 6 August 1941, FO 371-294983/N6516, PRO, and George C. Herring, Jr., *Aid to Russia 1941–1946* (New York: Columbia University Press, 1973), pp. 1–24.

14. 6 July list of mission members, and general on the USSR, FO 371/29561/N3463, N3450, N3848, and N3855. For Soviet misconceptions, Firebrace to DMI, 12 August 1941, WO 178/90, PRO.

15. 6 July 1941, CAB 84/32, CAB 120-678, and FO 371/29561/N3559, PRO.

16. 8 July 1941, WO 178/90; 7 July 1941, WO 32/15548, and 9–12 July, ADM 223/290, PRO.

17. 9 July, Eden talk, FO 954/24/338; 9–12 July AIR 8-937 and WO 178/90; 13 July, WO 193/659; 9 July CAB 80/58, COS (41) 133 (O). The British knew from a decrypt that the Germans had given up plans to take Spitsbergen (ADM 223/3). For later developments regarding Spitsbergen, see WO 106/1996, PRO. Short biographies of Russian mission members are in FO 371/32945/N1160, PRO.

18. Soviet Military Mission and British Liaison Groups, WO 178/90; FO 371/29561/N3559 and CAB 122/101, PRO. Bombing targets, WO 178/90 (28 July 1941); AIR 20/8049 (18 July 1941); ADM 223/290 (30 July). On the Soviet test pilot, WO 178/90 (5 August 1941), PRO. In September 1941, the British and the Soviets refined their special operational partnership and thereby excluded the NKVD from joint operations in much of the Arab world, 30 September 1941, HS4/334, PRO.

19. 21 July, CAB 122/101; 26 July, Firebrace, WO 178/90. The original members of the British team were Firebrace; Maj. R. S. Landale, Royal Marines; Maj. A. D. Blank, Army; and Flight Lt. F. W. Wilton, RAF.

20. 16 July 1941, Macfarlane to DMI, WO 193/653, PRO.

21. History of the Liaison Organization, WO 208/4115, PRO; regarding the British Army as the "dominant partner" and the independent navy section, see COS (41) 235 and 242, 7 and 11 July 1941, CAB 79/12, and ADM 223/107. Regarding the British Army "on leave," see August 1941, WO 178/90 and FO 371/29562/N4433, PRO.

22. Navy Exchange, COS (41) 235 and 242 (7 and 11 July 1941), CAB 79/12, PRO. For Soviet naval visits, ADM 223/32; Baltic and Black Sea naval intelligence, WO 178/90 and ADM 223/251. See also ADM 1/15824, PRO, for British unhappiness with the Firebrace team.

23. 29 June 1941, WO 178/25 and FO 371/29562/N4433, PRO.

24. 29 June meetings, WO 178/25; FO 371/29562/N4433; FO 371/29485/N3300, N3277, N3300; FO 371/29594/N3347, ADM 199/1106, and WO 31/15548, PRO.

25. 10 June 1941 JIC (41) 16, and 26 June JIC (41) 19, CAB 81/88 (thanks to Richard Aldrich for the latter reference), and 26 June 1941, WO 193/645A and FO 371/29560/N3203, PRO.

26. 15 July, AIR 8/564, PRO.

27. 19 September 1941, WO 32/15548; 1 July 1941, FO 371/29485/N3300; 15 July, AIR 8/564 (Eden and Consular Offices, FO 418/87). India, FO 371/29562/N4120, N29563, N4558, and N4892 (26 July, 14 and 26 August). Malaya, 16 August, FO 371/29563/N4614. Also 18 August, WO 193/645A, and 12 September, WO 32/15548. Beaverbrook mission and Siberia, 16 September, FO 371/29563/N4978 and N5219, 19 September, WO 32/15548, PRO.

28. 4 July 1941, WO 193/645A and WO 32/15548, PRO.

29. 3 July, WO 193/645A; 28 June and 4 July, WO 32/15548; War Diary entry, 29 June, WO 178/25, and 29 June 1941 report, AIR 8/564, PRO.

30. Bradley F. Smith, *The Ultra-Magic Deals* (Shrewsbury: Airlife, 1993), pp. 43–65; Ralph Erskine, "Churchill and the Start of the Ultra-Magic Deals," *International Journal of Intelligence and Counter Intelligence,* in press.

31. 30 June and 1 July 1941, COS (41) 236, CAB 79/12, and FO 371/29466/N3349;

DMI order, 27 June 1941, WO 193/645A and HW 1/2, 6, and 8 for Churchill's June 1941 notations, PRO.

32. 28 June 1941, HW 1/8; COS (41) 223, 30 June 1941, in FO 371/29466/N3349; COS (41) 228, CAB 79/12; DMI order, 27 June 1941, WO 193/645A, PRO.

33. 29 June 1941, FO 371/29475/N3240; FO 371/29485/N3277; FO 371/29494/N3347, plus WO 32/15548 and WO 178/25, PRO.

34. 29 June 1941, AIR 8/564; 30 June, ADM 199/1106; 1 July, FO 371/29485/N3300, PRO.

35. 30 June 1941, WO 78/25, PRO.

36. 1 July 1941, WO 32/15548 and FO 371/29485/N3300; 5 July 1941, ADM 199/1106, and 6 July 1941, WO 193/649, PRO.

37. 5–6 July 1941, Naval Mission War Diary, ADM 199/1106, PRO.

38. 6 July 1941, WO 193/649 and WO 178/25, PRO.

39. A. H. Birse, *Memoirs of an Interpreter* (New York: Coward, 1967), pp. 71 ff.

40. 4 July 1941, WO 32/15548, PRO.

41. Ibid.

42. 4 and 7 July 1941, WO 193/649 and 652, plus AIR 8/564; WO 32/15548 and HW 1/14, PRO, for these dates. See also Robert Cecil, "C's War," *Intelligence and National Security* 1, no. 2 (May 1986): 179, Peter Calvocoressi, "When Enigma Yielded Ultra," *The Listener* 97, no. 3 (27 January 1977): 114; F. W. Winterbotham transcript, pp. 215 and 217, 7462/36/27, Imperial War Museum.

43. WO to 30 Mission, 4 and 7 July, and 30 Mission to WO, 7 and 8 July 1941, WO 193/649 and 652, plus AIR 8/654, PRO. The British official history is at odds with the open documentary evidence; it suggests that Churchill simply forced through the dispatch of wrapped-up Ultra but does not mention that he also withheld it. Hinsley et al., *British Intelligence,* 2:59.

Chapter 3. Moaning and Dealing

1. Private CIGS to Marfarlane, 11 July 1941, WO 193/644; DMI to VICS, 11 July 1941, WO 178/25. On "C," see CIGS to Macfarlane, 4 September 1951, WO 32/15548, PRO.

2. 12 July 1941, FO 371/29487/N3836; 11 July 1941, WO 178/25, PRO.

3. Test flights, August–September 1941, AIR 40-27; AIR 8/654 and AIR 40/29; and FO 371/29490/N5180, PRO.

4. 11 August 1941, AIR 8/564, PRO.

5. Meeting with Stalin, 12 July 1941, AIR 8/564, WO 178/25; 22 July 1941 reflection, FO 371/29594; 14 July 1941 estimate to CIGS, WO 216/124, PRO. Mason Macfarlane memoir, Folder 31, Box 2, Mason Macfarlane Papers, Imperial War Museum.

6. 13 July 1941, Macfarlane to DMI, WO 193/654A, PRO.

7. F. H. Hinsley, E. E. Thomas, et al., *British Intelligence in the Second World War: Its Influence upon Operations,* 4 vols. (London: Her Majesty's Stationery Office, 1979–1985), 2:72. 15 July 1941, WO 178/25; 13 July, WO 193/645A; 17 July, AIR 8/564; 14 July, HW 1/10; 18 July, WO 32/15549, PRO.

8. 17, 18, 19, and 27 July 1941, AIR 8/564, PRO.

9. 19 July 1941, WO 178/25, and 20 July 1941, FO 371/29488/N4017, PRO.

10. 19 July and 15 September 1941, WO 32/15548. Macfarlane was fully aware that the "hot results [come] from our 'Y' service or from very secret sources." 19–21 July 1941, WO 178/25; 20, 21, 23 July 1941, AIR 8/564; 21 July 1941, FO 371/295621/N4000; AIR 20/2075. Churchill and "C," 17 July 1941 HW 1/14, PRO.

11. 22 July 1941 handovers, WO 178/25 and WO 32/15548; Luftwaffe, WO 193/644; to DMI, WO 193/649 and 652; to Air Ministry, AIR 8/564 and 575, PRO.

12. 22 and 31 July 1941, WO 193/649 and WO 32/15548; 25 and 31 July, WO 178/25 and FO 371/29488/N4281; 28 and 30 July, AIR 8/564, PRO.

13. Ibid.

14. Ibid.

15. 5, 6, and 31 July and 1 August 1941, ADM 199/1106, PRO.

16. 12 July 1941, ADM 1/11158; 14 July, Kharlamov report, ADM 223/251; 20 July 1941 visit, AIR 8/937; Air defenses, 30 July 1941, ADM 11503 and 20023, PRO.

17. 19 July 1941, ADM 199/1106, PRO.

18. 29 July 1941, FO 954/24/361, and 17 July 1941, ADM 199/1106, PRO.

19. 23 July 1941, WO 32/15548 and "Y" AIR 20/8049, PRO.

20. 26 July 1941, Chemical Warfare WO 193/649. Hinsley et al., *British Intelligence,* 2:675–676.

21. 27 July 1941, AIR 20/8049 and WO 193/649, PRO.

22. 25 July 1941, FO 371/29562/N4070, and 29 July, FO 954/24/361, PRO.

23. 31 July 1941, FO 181/962, PRO.

24. Change in Cripps's view by mid-August, FO 371/29489/N4587; Admiral Miles, 31 December 1942, ADM 223/252; Vyshinsky, 31 July 1941, FO 181/962. By mid-August, Cripps was accepting Stalin's views of the battle situation. 15 August 1941, FO 371/29489/N4587. Panfilov on German censorship, 10 August 1941, WO 193/652. As early as 26 June 1941, Whitehall had been anxious to get hold of the "American Mail in transit on the Trans-Siberian Railway." JIC (41)193, CAB 31/88, PRO.

25. 31 July 1941, WO 32/15548, PRO.

26. 7 August 1941, WO 32/15548, PRO.

27. 3 and 5 August 1941, AIR 8/564; 7 August, WO 31/15548 and ADM 199/1106, PRO.

28. HW1/40 and 51, PRO.

29. 10 August 1941, AIR 8/564, PRO.

30. Naval Issues, 7, 9, and 20 August 1941, ADM 199/1106; 1 and 10 August, 3, 20, and 21 September, ADM 199/1102. See also 20 September, WO 32/15548, and 26 August, WO 193/644, plus 20 and 21 September, AIR 8/564 and 937, PRO.

31. 7–9 and 20 August and 5 September 1941, FO 371/29491/N5863, and Turkey and BNLO Black Sea Reports, 6–8 and 23 August 1941, WO 193/649 and AIR 8/564 (other such reports in ADM 199/1106 and 1107 and WO 193/652 and 653); Churchill and Soviet scuttling, ADM 205/10; Fawkes, 7 October, ADM 223/248, PRO.

32. 13 September–2 October 1941, War Diary, ADM 199/1106, PRO.

33. 2–14 September 1941, FO 371/29563/N5219 (Cavendish Bentinck); 9 and 12 September, Siberia, WO 31/15548; 2 September 1941, JIC (41) 25th Meeting, CAB 81/88; 14 September, FO 371/29563/N5031 and 6084, PRO.

34. 8 August 1941, CAB 120683, PRO.

35. 29 August 1941, WO 32/15549 (this file was officially closed but came up in error), PRO.

36. 10 September 1941, WO 32/15548, PRO.

37. 10 and 11 September 1941, AIR 8/564; 14 September, WO 178/25, PRO. See also A. N. Birse, *Memoirs of an Interpreter* (New York: Coward, 1967), p. 75, and 10 September 1941, WO 32/15548, PRO.

38. Ibid.

39. 14 August 1941, FO 371/29489/N4612, PRO.

40. 4 September 1941, WO 31/15548, 14 September 1941 Air Mission, AIR 8/564, PRO.

41. 4 September 1941, WO 32/15548; 7 September 1941 (Cripps), FO 371/29490/N5113; 14 September 1941, AIR 8/564 and CAB 120/36, PRO.

42. August–September, esp. 4 September 1941, WO 32/15548, PRO.

43. 1–4 August 1941, WO 178/25; 1 August, WO 193/649; 2, 3, and 19 August, AIR 8/564; 22 September, WO 32.15548, PRO.

44. Ibid.

45. 19 August 1941, WO 178/25, PRO.

46. 27 August–2 September 1941, WO 178/25; 17 September, WO 32/15548; 1 and 2 September, WO 193/645A, and 10 September, WO 193/649; 27 August, AIR 8/564; 2 September, FO 371/29594/N3970; 10 September 1941, WO 193/649, and Murmansk OB, 13–17 September 1941, WO 32/15548, PRO.

47. 26 August and 8 September 1941, WO 193/49; 29 August 1941, WO 178/25; 14 September, WO 32/15548, PRO.

48. 31 August 1941, WO 193/644; 9, 16, and 23 September 1941, FO 371/29563/N5219 and N5302, PRO.

49. 1, 15 August and 9 September 1941, AIR 8/564; 10 August, WO 193/652; 20 September 1941, WO 32/15548, and 8–9 August, FO 371/29562/N443 and N4489, PRO.

50. 1, 15 August and 9 September 1941, AIR 8/564, PRO.

51. 6–9 August 1941, FO 371/29562/N4434 and N4502; for other technology exchange, see 7 and 16 August and 20 September 1941, AIR 8/54; 22 September 1941, AIR 40/1559; 15 August 1941, WO 193/652; 19 August 1941, FO 371/29571 and 29466, PRO.

52. 30 June 1941, COS (42)223, and 11 August, FO 371/29466/N3349, PRO.

53. 11, 14, and 15 August 1951, AIR 8/564; 11 August, WO 193/649; 19 August, FO 371/39571/N4807, PRO; 20 September 1949, G2 Memo, Box 585, Entry 57, RG 319, Suitland, NA.

54. 19 August 1941, Mason Macfarlane to DMI, FO 371/29571/N4807; see also 20 September 1941, G2 Memo, Box 585, Entry 57, RG 319, Suitland, NA.

55. 15 August 1941, WO 193/652, and 16 August 1941, AIR 8/564, PRO.

56. SOE—12 and 16 September 1941, Hugh Dalton diary, BL of PS, London; George Hill reminiscences, "Four Years with the NKVD," Hoover Institute.

57. 10 August 1941 quote, WO 193/649; examples of Polish and Czech material in 30 Mission reports, FO 371/29493 and 29494, plus WO 193/652. See also 19 August 1941, FO 371/29571/N4781 and WO 32/15548, PRO, and Ewan Butler, *Mason-Mac: A Life of Lieutenant General Sir Noel Mason Macfarlane* (London: Macmillan, 1972), pp. 137–138.

58. 22 July 1941, FO 371/29487/N3988, and 5 August, FO 371/29562/N4289; Macfarlane and the War Office, 3 August, AIR 8/56, PRO.

59. 4 August 1941, FO 371/29562/N4289, PRO.

60. 17 August 1941, WO 193/649 and 652; 22 September, FO 371/29491/N5615; 25 October, AIR 8/564; 23 October, WO 32/15549; 21 August 1941, CAB 66/18, PRO, and Butler, *Mason Macfarlane,* pp. 139–140.

61. 22 September 1941, WO 32/15549, and Tiflis trip, 21 October 1941, AIR 8/564, PRO.

62. 23 October 1941, WO 32/15548, PRO.

63. 15 September 1941, G-2, Entry 182, Box 802, RG 164, MR, NA.

64. Ibid.

Chapter 4. The Turning Points of Late 1941

1. Dimitri Volkogonov, *Stalin: Triumph and Tragedy,* trans. Harry Shulman (Rocklin, Calif.: Prima, 1988), passim; David M. Glantz, *From Don to Dnieper: Soviet Offensive Operations December 1942–August 1943* (London: Frank Cass, 1991), passim; John Erickson, *The Road to Stalingrad* (London: Grafton, 1985), passim.

2. In late 1941, see AIR 8/564, AIR 20/2325; WO 208/1798, PRO.

3. 3 December 1951, WO 178/90, plus AIR 8/564; AIR 46/22, WO 193/649 and 645, ADM 223/250 and 252, and FO 954/24/53, PRO.

4. 2 November 1951, Box 802, Entry 182, RG 165, MR. NA; November 1951, Box 252, Entry 59, RG 319, Suitland, NA; on Harriman, 23 October 1951, General File, Entry 86, RG 165, Suitland, NA; Boswell interview, November 1993; Olson interview, October 1993 (Author's Collection, Hoover Institution); Naval Attaché Reports, December 1951, Box 4, RG 38 (Moscow) MR, NA.

5. 30 December 1951, G-2, Paraphrases Files, RG 319, Suitland, NA.

6. 1 December 1951, Box 252, Entry 59, RG 319, Suitland, NA.

7. 7 November 1951, WO 193/645A and 655, plus WO 178/25 and WO 165/38, PRO.

8. 2 July 1943, FO 181/973/2, also AIR 2/7861; AIR 45/22 and AIR 8, 564, plus WO 32/15548, PRO.

9. Macfarlane complaints and London's response, PREM 3/397/17; WO 32/15548; FO 371/29558/N6065; WO 32/15548. For intelligence, WO 193/649, PRO.

10. FO 371/29471/N6749 and N6774, PRO. For lack of intelligence, see gaps in WO 32/15548 and in the WO 193 series. On Kubyshev, FO 371/29471/6749 and 6774, PRO; also Folder 3, Box 2, Macfarlane Papers, Imperial War Museum.

11. WO 178/90; ADM 199/72, 757, 1102, 1106, and 1107, and FO 371/29493/N6326, N3298, and N1162, PRO, plus Documents F, Moscow File, PSF Box 66, Roosevelt Library, Hyde Park.

12. ADM 223/290, ADM 199/1107, and FO 371/29494/N6616, PRO.

13. 12 October 1941, FO 371/29563/N6084; 11 November 1941, JIC (41) 32, CAB 81/88, and WO 32/15548, PRO.

14. 4 December and 1 December 1941, WO 178/90, PRO.

15. FO 371/32898/N1162 and ADM 199/1102, E. Kordt in Shanghai, 11 December 1941, WO 178/25; Russians at War Office, 22 December 1941, WO 178/90, PRO.

16. 103.9182/22C, Box 63 (11 December 1941), DB, NA. U.S.-Soviet exchanges, 16 and 22 December 1941, Naval Aide Intelligence File, Box 63, Map Room, Roosevelt Library; 22 December, Correspondence File, Box 2, ONI, Eastern Europe, RG 38, MR, NA.

17. October 1941, INF 1/147; 14 October 1941, INF 1/676; 12 and 25 November 1941, INF 1/913, PRO.

18. HW 1/206 and WO 178/25 and 90, PRO.

19. WO 178/25 and 90, PRO.

20. Thanks to the Imperial War Museum's Mark Seaman for information on SOE-MI 6 cooperation with the Soviets. For the political warfare executive's role, see FO 298/27, PRO.

21. WO 32/15548 and 178/90, PRO.

22. FO 371/29491/N5679 and PREM 3/395/8, PRO.

23. WO 32/15548; WO 193/645; FO 371/29469/N5585 (1–2 October 1941); FO 181/962/8, PRO.

24. 29 September 1941, WO 32/1558 and FO 371/2949/N5542; 22 September 1941, WO 178/90, PRO.

25. Ibid., and FO 371/29469/N5585, PRO.

26. WO 178/25, FO 371/29491/N5616 (25 September 1941); AIR 8/564; WO 193/649, FO 371/29469/N5585, PRO. See also F. H. Hinsley, E. E. Thomas, et al., *British Intelligence in the Second World War: Its Influence upon Operations,* 4 vols. (London: Her Majesty's Stationery Office, 1979–1985), 2:73, although it seems (surprisingly) to understate the scale of the British contribution.

27. JIC, 4 October 1941, WO 193/649, 6 October 1941, WO 178/25, plus 8 October 1941, WO 32/15548, PRO.

28. 10 and 14 October 1941, FO 371/29469/N5585, N29563, and N6084, and 14 October 1941, WO 178/25, PRO.

29. Ibid., and Georgi K. Zhukov, *Marshal Zhukov's, Greatest Battles* (New York: Harper, 1969), p. 52.

30. 10 and 14 October 1941, AIR 8/564; 27 October, AIR 7861; 20 November, AIR 46/22; 3 November, FO 371/29471/N6705; 5 November, WO 193/645A; 14 November, WO 193/647; 19 November, WO 178/90; 11 November, WO 178/25; see also 28 January 1942, AIR 46/23, PRO.

31. 8 November 1941, HW1/203; 16 October 1941, Knox to Alexander, ADM 1/14994; 4 October 1941, Churchill/Davidson, CAB 120/681 and WO 193/644, PRO.

32. 16 October 1941, ADM 1/14994, and 24 October 1941, JIC (41) 452 final, CAB 120/681, PRO.

33. 24 October 1941, JIC (41) 452; Panfilov, 7 December 1941, WO 32/15548, PRO.

34. WO 32/15548, PRO. For scholarly historians, there is a special pleasure in watching a Soviet general reading and criticizing a JIC report in 1941, because the British government then kept the general collection of JIC reports closed for fifty years (except for accidents such as this one), allegedly because Whitehall wanted to keep such sensitive material out of the hands of the Soviets.

35. FO 371/29599/N7233, PRO.

36. 9 and 13 December 1941, WO 178/25 and 90; 16 December 1941, AIR 2/7861; 20 December 1941, WO 193/649; 3 December 1941 ff., FO 371/29495/N7304, PRO.

37. 7 October 1941, CAB 120/36, and 14 October 1941, AIR 20/2386, PRO.

38. Harriman-Beaverbrook materials (including many duplicates), Harriman File, Stimson Papers, Top Secret, Box 8, Entry 74A, RG 107, MR, NA; 28 September, though listed as November, 1941, FO 371/29578/N6312; 3 October 1941 File, FO 371/29578/N5883; Beaverbrook to Cripps, 2 November 1941, PREM 3/340/117, PRO. 17 September 1941, British military estimate for Harriman, 22 September–10 October Chronological File, Box 10, and Balfour diary, Box 164, Harriman Papers, Library of Congress; Beaverbrook to Cripps, 3 November 1941, FO 181/962, PRO; George C. Herring, Jr., *Aid to Russia 1941–1946* (New York: Columbia University Press, 1973), pp. 41 ff; Olson and Boswell interviews.

39. 22–27 September 1941, File 22–27, Box 160, Harriman Papers, Library of Congress; John Deane, *Strange Alliance* (New York: Viking, 1947), p. 72.

40. September 1941, Box 8, Entry 74A, Top Secret, Stimson, RG 107, MR, NA; Transcaucasia, 19/1041, MI 3(c), WO 193/654B; Mason Macfarlane's opposition, 25 October 1941, FO 371/29492/N6224, PRO.

41. Stalin-Beaverbrook, 28 September 1941, Box 8, Entry 74A, Top Secret, Stimson, RG 107, MR, NA.

42. Ibid.

43. Ibid., and Cripps Message, 28 September 1941, WO 193/656, PRO.

44. 22 and 16 November 1941, FO 371/29598/N6734 and N6797, PRO.

45. 18 December 1941, FO 371/32874/N109 and WO 32/15548, PRO.

46. 19 December 1941, FO 371/32898/N1162, PRO.

47. Alan Brooke "Retrospect," 13 August 1972, 3/A/VI, Liddell Hart Centre, King's College, London.

48. For complex intelligence considerations on the other side, see John W. M. Chapman, "Signal Intelligence Collaboration Among the Tripartite States on the Eve of Pearl Harbor," *Japan Forum* 3, no. 2 (1961): 231–255.

Chapter 5. Difficult Times

1. Macfarlane estimates, 27 March and 20 April 1942, FO 371/32907/N1695 and N2202. British warning, 21 April 1942, WO 178/26, PRO. See also, John Erickson. *The Road to Stalingrad,* (London: Grafton, 1985) and Dimitri Volkogonov, *Stalin: Triumph and Tragedy,* trans. Harry Shulman (Rocklin, Calif.: Prima, 1988).

2. 18 May warning, WO 193/645A, PRO.

3. 1 June 1942, JIC (42) 200 (final), and Churchill comment, CAB 79/21 and 120/68, PRO.

4. 8 February, WO 216; PM to FDR, 7 March 1942, FO 954/31/316; Macfarlane estimate, 27 March, FO 371/32907/N1695. See also 20 April 1942 report, same file, N2202, PRO.

5. February OB meeting in London and Soviet requests, WO 178/90 and 193/649, PRO.

6. 5–6 February, FO 371/32897/N801, PRO.

7. OB meetings: 7 March, WO 178/26 and 193/645A; 27 January, WO 178/26; May and June, FO 371/32955/N3219 and 371/32908/2894, as well as WO 178/26. See also FO 371/32907/N2368 and WO 178/26 (for 22 and 23 April). For Panfilov's view in June, WO 193/645A. On flak, 24 April, WO 178/26, PRO.

8. Panfilov talks, and 22 January 1942, FO 371/32904/N141 and 371/32905/N609. Artillery, 6 February, WO 106/3270; ammunition, 27 March, FO 371/32955/N343; tanks, 24 January and 11 February, WO 106/3270 and 193/649, plus May 1942, WO 208/1826; chemical warfare, 30 May, FO 594/25/74, and 15 June, WO 178/26, PRO.

9. 27 February 1942, WO 208/1796; 3 March 1942, WO 106/3270 and 193/654a; 5 March 1942, WO 178/26, PRO.

10. 1 March 1942, FO 371/32955/N1560, PRO.

11. 12 February 1942, FO 371/32876/N939. Regarding U.S. alleged insecurity in winter–spring 1942, FO 371/32897/N936, 371/32955/N343, and 371/32905/N933. Regarding bargaining material, 17 February 1942, FO 371/32898/N988, PRO.

12. Atrocities, March 1942, FO 181/965/5; Britain as the main enemy of Germany, February 1942, FO 371/32905/N1021; on the need to bargain, 17 February 1942, FO 371/32898/N988, PRO.

13. January–February 1942 front visit: AIR 20/3050, WO 106/3270, WO 193/649, and WO 208/1819, Vodka remark, 1 February, WO 193/645A, PRO.

14. Exham and Michela front visit, 26–28 June 1942: FO 181/964/4, WO 32/15548, WO 193/659, and AIR 20/795, PRO.

15. 7 February quotation, WO 193/658; War Office pressure, WO 178/26 (1 January 1942). Meetings: 27 January and 17 February, WO 178/90; Japanese grenade, FO 371/32897/N707; exchanges, Moscow and London, 9 February, WO 193/645A; 11 March, WO 106/3270 and 178/26; 13 March, WO 208/1787; and 7 and 29 May, WO 178/26, PRO.

16. 16 January 1942, JP (42) 56, FO 371/32955/N343, PRO.

17. For the BNLO Black Sea: ADM 199/1107; ADM 223/248; AIR 40/2344; FO 371/32907/N2015; FO 371/32899/N2016; WO 208/1783; and WO 193/649, PRO.

18. 10 February 1942, ADM 199/1102. See also FO 371/32899/N2016 and Maclachlan Collection, MC-1 File, Churchill College, Cambridge.

19. 29 April and 15 June 1942, ADM 199/1102, PRO.

20. For general provision of naval intelligence in January–February 1942, see ADM 223/289 and 290; FO 371/32898/N1162 and 371/32899/N2016, plus ADM 199/1102 and WO 208/1787. On Estonians and Latvians, ADM 1/6179. Captured documents, 13 January 1942, FO 371/32898/N1162, PRO.

21. 15 and 27 February 1942, ADM 199/1102, PRO.

22. 18 May and 9 June 1942, ADM 199/1102, PRO.

23. Churchill warning to Stalin, 13 April, ADM 223/3; threats to convoys, ADM 223/3; air cover, FO 371/32955/N2791, ADM 116/4544, and especially 7 June 1942, ADM 237/167, PRO.

24. Conditions in Archangel, ADM 199/6944 and FO 371/32910/N3557, PRO.

25. Macfarlane comment, March (no day indicated) 1942, ADM 199/72, PRO.

26. 19 April 1942, AIR 46/23, PRO.

27. For potential protests: FO 371/32898/N1523 and N1622. Visits: AIR 8/930; AIR 19/290; AIR 20/2075 and 2325; AIR 46/22 and 23; AIR 2/7871; AIR 19/291; AIR 20/2309 and ADM 223/252, PRO.

28. Generally on exchanges, FO 371/32902/N1480; organization and output, AIR 20/2324 and FO 371/32890/N895; and FO 372/32897/N495, plus AIR 46/23 and 20/2311, PRO.

29. *Verlobungsring*, 23 April 1942, AIR 20/2311. Rocket bomb, 6 January 1942, ADM 199/1104; 16 April 1942, AIR 46/23; 27–29 May, AIR 46/22; 30 May, AIR 19/291; 23 June, AIR 2/7861; 24 June, AIR 19/291 and ADM 199/1102, PRO.

30. 4 January and 15 April 1942, AIR 20/2311; 18 April 1942, AIR 2/7861; 23 April 1942, AIR 46/23; 8 May and 11 June, AIR 2/7861, PRO.

31. 2 January and 1 February 1943, FO 371/36969/N702, PRO.

32. 3 March 1942, AIR 2/7861 and general files, January–March, FO 371/32904/N244; FO 371/32906/N133; and FO 371/36969/N702, PRO.

33. 19 March 1942, FO 371/32906/N1480; 3 March 1942, AIR 2/7861, PRO.

34. 24 January and 14 February 1942, AIR 20/2311. For general material on air exchange, see AIR 2/7861; FO 371/32897/N495 and N555; plus FO 371/32907/N609, PRO.

35. 1–4 February 1942, AIR 46/23, and 2 February, AIR 2/7861 (also general information in AIR 20/2310, PRO.

36. 25 February 1942, AIR 46/23. See also 1 February, AIR 2/7861; 5 February, FO 181/964/7; 8 February, AIR 20/2311 and 46/23; 11 February, AIR 46/26; 12 and 13 February, AIR 46/23; 19 February, AIR 20/2311; 21 February, AIR 46/23; 18, 24, and 25 February, AIR 2/7861 and 46/22, plus 26 February, AIR 46/23, PRO.

37. 30 March and 4 April 1942, AIR 2/7861; 5 April, AIR 20/2311; 14 April, AIR 46/23, PRO. On Japanese OB, 18 April 1942, AIR 46/26, 22 April 1942, FO 371/32955/N2197, PRO.

38. 2 May 1942, AIR 2/7861 and 46/22. On Goering, 16 June 1942, WO 178/26. Stalin-Clark Kerr, 29 March, FO 371/32878/N1688, and 30 March 1942, CAB 81/107, PRO.

39. 15 May 1942, AIR 20/3014, PRO. Freeman's view that the Russians were fighting and the British were not, though largely accurate, would have shocked the prime minister and the chiefs of staff.

40. 20 January 1942, FO 371/32898/N1162, and Appendix BBB, WO 178/26 and 193/653 (January 1942), PRO; MI 6 and the services, 29 January 1942, Cadogan diary (unpublished), Churchill College, Cambridge; Mitchell to Stewart, 10 August 1975, MLBE, Churchill College, Cambridge.

41. For the general "Y" situation in January–February 1942, see Appendices B, BBB, and NNN, WO 178/26, PRO.

42. Call sign, squadron number, and related matters, Appendices B, BBB, and NNN, WO 178/26. See also 20 February, AIR 46/23, and 24 February, AIR 2/7861. Crankshaw to Tulbovitch, 16 April 1942, Appendix NN 1, WO 178/26, PRO.

43. NKVD contacts with 30 Mission, 2 February 1942, FO 371/32905/N933, PRO, and George Hill reminiscences, Hoover Institution; Way Mission, 15 January 1942, FO 371/32904/N324, PRO. On oil, 1 March 1942, WO 193/632, PRO; MEW, January–April 1942, FO 371/36421/W2058. Too many Polish reports and those from Pika reached the British in this period to make itemized citation possible; see guide to FO holdings in the PRO, Kew. Pika reports also reached the War Office and prime minister; see, for example, WP (42) 98, CAB 66/22, and April 1942 file, PREM 3/395/18, PRO.

44. A 160-page document on the bugging of Italian officers in Khartoum as early as January–March 1941 had just been released in the PRO (WO 208/2759). See also WO 208/1819 for other new releases and note that under the 1995 release policy, a great deal of CSDIC material is becoming available in various portions of the DEFE series. It was the high quality of such British intelligence, not just ULTRA, that apparently led the authors of the official history to be so dismissive of cooperative efforts with the USSR. F. H. Hinsley, E. E. Thomas, et al., *British Intelligence in the Second World War: Its Influence upon Operations,* 4 vols. (London: Her Majesty's Stationery Office, 1979–1985), passim (consult "Soviet Russia" entries in all volumes).

45. R. H. Parker, 20 January 1942, INF/1/677; Soviet propaganda drops, FO 371/32888/N1563, PRO.

46. Eden, WM (42) 1/4, January 1942, CAB 65/29, PRO.

47. 11 February 1942, FO 181/964/7. On Polish evacuation, see, for example, FO 181/966/8, PRO.

48. Macfarlane, 1 January, CAB 122/101; 21–27 March 1942, FO 371/32955/N343 and WO 178/26, PRO.

49. 11 March and 1 April 1942, Churchill Brook, and Eden, PREM 3/395/18; DNI and Eden, 23 March, FO 371/32898/N1294; 1–13 April, CIGS/Eden/Maisky, FO 371/32899/N1951 and N1743; May 1942, Gubbins, FO 371/32899/N2470 and N2563 plus CAB 120/683 and 690, PRO.

50. 14 and 21 April 1942, Clark Kerr, Eden, A. V. Alexander, and Cadogan, FO 371/32864/N2087 and 371/32955/N1986; 13 November 1942, ADM 1/12060; 4 May 1942, Clark Kerr, CAB 120/678; April 1942, Cadogan and CIGS, Cadogan diary, unpublished, 1/11, Churchill College, Cambridge, plus Cadogan and Eden comments, FO 371/32955/N1823, PRO.

51. 15 May, Panfilov, FO 371/32908/N2695; Macfarlane in London, especially 13 June 1942, CAB 105/67; COS (42) 178 (8), CAB 79/21, and FO 371/32908/N3098, PRO.

52. 10 April 1942, CAB 105/38, PRO.

53. Colonel Ratay to Edward Mason (COI-OSS), 22 April 1942, 820.02, Box 9, Confidential File, London, RG 84, Suitland, NA. For COI and the Communist Party, 22 April 1942, 13–28 April File, Box 165, PSF, Roosevelt Library; Obolewski message to Admiral Standley, spring 1942, Mission Memoranda File, Box 17, Standley Papers, USC.

54. 1 January 1942, Correspondent 3 File, Box 2, ONI, Eastern Europe, RG 38, MR, NA; Steinhardt to Ankara, S-T File, 1942, Box 38, Steinhardt Papers, Library of Congress; George C. Herring Jr., *Aid to Russia 1941–1946* (New York: Columbia University Press, 1973), pp. 83 and 103. Macfarlane's views, 1 January 1942, CAB 122/101, PRO. Michela, 21 May 1942, File 4, Box 585, Entry 57, RG 319, Suitland, NA; Michela's resignation attempt, 3–5 March, 11-26-41 to 3-30-42 File, Box 585, Entry 57, RG 319, Suitland, NA. Standley briefing, Memos 4-25-42 to 3-13-43 File, Box 17, Standley Papers, USC; Olson and Boswell interviews, B. F. Smith collection, Hoover Institution.

55. 1 January 1942, Togo reference, Correspondence 3 File, Box 2, ONI Eastern Europe, RG 38, MR, NA; Macfarlane's view of U.S. mission in Moscow, 19 July, JIC (42) 276 (o), CAB 81/109, PRO; 17 January 1942 report, Kubyshev File, Box 4, ONI,

Naval Attaché Moscow, RG 38, MR, NA; Ward to Standley, 17 June 1942, Moscow Confidential, RG 84, Suitland, NA. Courier report (13 April–20 May), files 800 and 802, Soviet Union, Box 7, Entry 59A, 546 (P6), Entry 59, RG 319, Suitland, NA.

56. Courier report (13 April–20 May), Files 800 and 800.2, Soviet Union, Box 7, Entry 59A, 543(P6), RG 84, and May 1942, folder 5/1/42 to 3/31/43, Box 1043, Entry 47, RG 319, Suitland, NA; 19 March 1942, German OB File, 8/5/41 to 10/10/41, Box 252, Entry 59, RG 319, Suitland, NA. Soviet apology and weapons, 13 April 1942, File 711, Box 5, Steinhardt Papers, Library of Congress, and Box 7, Entry 59A, 543 (P6), RG 84, Suitland, NA; April–May intelligence, File 4/7/42 to 11/19/42, Box 580, Entry 57, RG 319, and folder 5/1/42–8/31/42, Box 1043, 350.05, Entry 47, RG 319, Suitland, NA. Walter Isaacs and Evan Thomas, *The Wise Men* (New York: Simon and Schuster, 1986), p. 218.

57. Examples of Macfarlane reports, 12 February 1942, in OPD 385.2/29, Box K275, Entry 921, RG 156, Suitland, NA. 12 May 1942, Admiral Start to Admiral King, Double Zero files 1941–1946, Box 38, Naval Historical Center, Washington Navy Yard; 18 May 1942 File, "British Intelligence Summaries," Box 22, Entry NHC 76, RG 38, MR, NA; ONI Files, Naval Attaché Moscow, Subject Files, RG 38, MR, NA.

58. 5 May 1942, File 4, Box 585, Entry 57, and Box 1044, Entry 47, 350.051, RG 319, Suitland, NA; 25 March, 30 April, and 9 May 1942, ONI Correspondence File (3), Box 2, ONI Eastern Europe, Naval Attaché Moscow, Box 8, CNO RG 80, MR, NA; G-2 reports, 5 April, Correspondence File 3, Box 2, Eastern Europe, ONI, RG 38, MR, NA.

Chapter 6. Converging and Dividing Paths

1. Cadogan diary, unpublished, 26 July 1942, Churchill College, Cambridge.

2. See especially Philip H. Bell, "Grossbritannien u. d. Schlacht v. Stalingrad," in Jürgen Foster, ed., *Stalingrad, Ereignis-Wirkung-Symbol* (Munich-Zurich, 1985), pp. 351–365. Thanks to Charles Burdick for this reference.

3. For a Red Navy reception in Rosyth during 1942, see ADM 199/604, PRO.

4. Martin Kitchen, *British Policy Toward the Soviet Union During the Second World War* (London: Macmillan, 1986), pp. 124–140, and Clark Kerr Papers, FO 800/300 ff., PRO. No historian has weighed Stalin's calls for a Second Front on the basis of the intelligence data then available.

5. 11 October 1942, FO 371/33036/N5272, PRO.

6. Churchill minute, 2 January 1943, WO 259/77, PRO.

7. 4 September 1942, FO 181/964/8, PRO.

8. 12 January 1943, WO 208/4564, PRO.

9. 8 July 1942, FO 181/964/7; 29 September 1942, WO 193/644, PRO. 22 September 1942, R. G. Turner diary, Imperial War Museum; OB summary on Russia, March 1943, 336.2, Entry 47, RG 319, Suitland, NA. 4 August 1942, comment on JIC (42) 285, CAB 105/30. The 4 September memo was sent on to the British embassy in Washington, FO 181/964/8, PRO. Dubinen response to DMI, 20 January 1943, WO 32/15548, PRO. (Note that the British often followed the procedure of written responses to questionnaires; see, for example, 22 September 1942 NID response in London, ADM 223/290.) POW interrogation, ADM 223/32 and 23 December 1942, WO 178/26, PRO.

10. 3 March 1943, FO 181/976/8; January 1943, FO 181/976/6/4; 19 December 1942 to 14 October 1943, FO 181/976/6/4; 19 December 1942 to 14 October 1943, FO 181/978/14, PRO. A great many versions of Pika's 23 July report may be found in WO 208/1794. On railroad intelligence, see 4 September 1942, FO 371/32955/N455, and 26 September 1942, FO 371/32956/N4933, PRO; 17 October 1942, Commander Tolley Report, Russia File, Box 99, MR, Roosevelt Library; 28 February 1943, File 2 January to 3 March 1943, Box 579, Entry 57, RG 319, Suitland, NA, and Clark Kerr to CCS, 14 December 1942, CAB 79/87, PRO.

11. August–September 1942, ADM 199/1102 and 1004. 1 September 1942, WO 178/26, PRO. On relations between missions, see Boswell interview, October 1993.

12. 15, 22, and 25 September 1942, WO 178/26, PRO. By 6 October 1942, "C" had provided the NKVD with twelve special radio sets, which may indicate a special British effort to gain Soviet favor. HS 4/334, PRO.

13. October–December (especially 11 October and 1 December) 1942, WO 178/26, PRO.

14. 26 October, 19 and 28 November, 1 and 29 December 1942, WO 178/26; 21 February 1943, WO 178/27; 16 and 26 October, 1 December 1942, and 5 and 21 January 1943, plus 2 February 1943, ADM 199/1102; 26–31 August 1942, ADM 199/1104; 31 December 1942, ADM 223/252; 18 and 28 November plus 2 December 1942, WO 178/26, PRO. Maclachlan Memo (undated), Maclachlan Papers, 1/7, Churchill College, Cambridge; 26 November 1943 letter, R. G. Turner Papers, Imperial War Museum.

15. 23 February 1942, AIR 20/1063; 24 February 1943, ADM 199/604; 5, 20, and 21 March 1943, ADM 199/1102; 24 February and 5 March 1943, FO 371/36989/N1159 and N1414, PRO. F. H. Hinsley, E. E. Thomas, et al., *British Intelligence in the Second World War: Its Influence upon Operations,* 4 vols. (London: Her Majesty's Stationery Office, 1979–1985), 2:64, states that the "Y" station was closed by the Soviets, but these open documents repeatedly and clearly state that the problem concerned the transmission of results, and the "Y" station itself was never under direct threat. 13 October 1942, File 4/7/42 to 11/19/42, Box 580, Entry 57, RG 319, Suitland, NA. Bacteriological warfare, 29 October 1942, FO 954/25/461, PRO.

16. Gas warfare, 7 March 1943, Box 580, Entry 57, RG 319; 8 March 1943, File 7, Box 586, Entry 57, RG 319; 10 March 1943, Box 1044, 350.0511, Entry 47, RG 319, all Suitland, NA. General gas file, December 1942 on, WO 208/2127, PRO. SOE-NKVD, George Hill memoir, p. 217, Hoover Institution; 2 September 1942, File 710, Great Britain, Box 5, Entry 59A, 543 (P6), Moscow embassy, RG 84, Suitland, NA. Doubts existed about agent drops in Whitehall as well; see 24 November 1942 entry, Cadogan diary, unpublished, 1/11, Churchill College, Cambridge. As of 8 December 1942, "C" was striving to get his own man, i.e., an MI 6 man, into Moscow at a time when the NKVD and the SOE had already exchanged 90 percent of their secret "gadgets." HS4/328, PRO.

17. 25 and 26 July 1942 memos, 4-25-42 to 3-13-45 File, Box 17, Standley Papers, USC; 26 July 1942, ONI, Eastern European Section, Box 16, RG 38, MR, NA; 2 October 1942, AIR 20/2311, and 19 September plus 8 October 1942, AIR 2/7861, PRO. 10 October 1942, Naval Attaché Moscow, Box 1, CNO, RG 38, MR, NA; 6 and 14 September 1942, 4/7/42–11/19/42 File, Box 580, Entry 57, RG 319, Suitland, NA, 27 November 1942, WO 178/26, and material on Russian units, December 1942, CAB 122/104, PRO.

18. Tizard mission and related matters, ADM 1/13368; AIR 19/371 (11 March 1943), AIR 20/7961, and CAB 122/104 (December 1942), PRO.

19. October 1942, FO 371/31836/F6885, PRO. Vladivostok, Lt. Comdr. George C. Rolland replaced Taecker in March 1943, Naval Attaché File, Box 1, ONI, RG 38, MR, NA; the British and Vladivostok, 1 October 1942, FO 371/31836/F6885; British visits: AIR 20/2325 and 2075, ADM 199/604, ADM 223/248, AIR 20/2075, WO 208/1792, 1793, and 1826, PRO. U.S. visits: Moscow Serials File, Box 38, ONI, Eastern Europe, and Boxes 4 and 5, USSR, CNO, RG 38, MR, NA.

20. The Black Sea in 1942: ADM 199/604, ADM 223/248, and 24 March 1943, FO 371/36959/N2348, PRO. Constantine Fitzgibbon, *Secret Intelligence in the Twentieth Century* (London: Hart Davis, 1976), p. 276, seems to have been the originator of the claim that the post of BNLO Black Sea was abolished in 1942.

21. For example, the U.S. Navy in Archangel visited not only Soviet ships and dockyards but also Soviet prisons. Archangel reports, 1942–45, CNO, RG 38, MR, NA.

22. Vladivostok: FO 371/32955/N3889; ADM 205/20; ADM 1/11862; and FO 800/301/frames 10–11 (13 February 1943), plus FO 371/329555/N3889 (27 July 1943), PRO.

23. Stalin approval for U.S. flyers, Box 53, Entry 42, RG 165, Suitland, NA; Clark Kerr complaint, 5 March 1943, "Russ Memos" File, Box 17, Standley Papers, USC. Visits: Standley Papers, ibid., Willkie File, Box 3, Entry 422, RG 165, MR, NA; 2 December 1942, ONI, Eastern Europe, RG 38, MR, NA; Exham to DMI, 10 December 1942, FO 371/32916/N6335, PRO. The British were nervous about possible "malpractice," i.e., secret Western intelligence activities related to VELVET. 28 November 1942, WO 178/26, PRO.

24. 27 August and 21 September 1942 reports, 4/7/42–11/19/42 File, Box 580, Entry 57, RG 319, Suitland, NA; 18 July and 11 and 16 September 1942, Eastern Europe, ONI RG 38, MR, NA. March 1943 Official Visits File, Box 7, Moscow Attaché, CNO, RG 38, MR, NA. "Armour Protection of German Ships" File, Box 1213, Entry 98A, RG 83, MR, NA (my thanks to Dr. Timothy Mulligan for this reference). "Refueling and Repair" File, Box 133, Map Room, Roosevelt Library.

25. 17 August 1942, WO 193/650; 10 November 1942, AIR 20/2311, PRO. 29 December 1945 copy of Russian report, "Details of Ship Construction Germany" File, Box 1213, Intelligence Division, Entry 98A, RG 38, MR, NA. 28 June 1942 and 27 July 1943 entries, ADM 199/1102, PRO. In November 1942, "C" sent at least eleven ULTRA items to the mission, including one on 7 November on German plans to bomb Baku, which carried the note, "you may inform the Russians." HW1/1141, PRO.

26. July through 27 August London exchanges, WO 178/90; Luftwaffe, 2 July 1942, AIR 46/23; Japanese OB, 12 July 1942, FO 371/32955/N3889; 31 July 1942, 4/7/42–11/19/42, Box 580, Entry 57, RG 319, Suitland, NA.

27. Churchill, 15 August 1942, PREM 3/395/18. See also FO 800/300; Colonel Exham, 7 August 1942, WO 176/391; Cheshire, 6 August 1942, AIR 19/291; MI 3's estimate, 15 August 1942, FO 371/32912/N4348, PRO.

28. 21 August 1942, FO 371/31836/F6022, and 16 September 1942, AIR 2/7861 for meetings. London meeting, 1 September 1942, WO 178/90; WO circular, 25 August 1942, WO 178/26; 23 September 1942, FO 371/32914/N4995, PRO. 25 and 29 September 1942, Turner diary, Imperial War Museum.

29. July 1943, WO 193/54A, PRO.

30. 1, 16, 18, and 23 September plus March 1943, 4/7/42–11/9/42 File, Box 580, Entry 57, and 7 September G-2 Order, File 5, Box 585, Entry 57, RG 319, Suitland, NA.

31. Ibid.

32. 17 October 1942, Russia File, Box 99, Map Room, Roosevelt Library (thanks to Warren Kimball for this reference).

33. 31 December 1942, Box 3, Entry 422, RG 165, MR, NA; 28 and 30 October 1942, Box 1044, 350.051, USSR, Entry 47, RG 319, Suitland, NA. See also Edward Drea, *MacArthur's ULTRA: Codebreaking and the War Against Japan, 1942–1945* (Lawrence: University Press of Kansas, 1991), passim, and Bradley F. Smith, *The Ultra-Magic Deals, 1940–46* (Shrewsbury: Airlife, 1993), pp. 105 ff.

34. 19 October and 17 November 1942, WO 178/26; 1 October 1942, JP (42)615, CAB 119/39; 19 November 1942, AIR 46/24; 4 November 1942, PREM 3/395/18; 30 November 1942, Japanese Army list, WO 208/1787, PRO, and 13 November 1942, Turner diary, Imperial War Museum.

35. 6 January 1942, WO 178/26, PRO.

36. WO 178/26 and 27; Belgians, December 1942, FO 371/36958/N207; Stalingrad, 2 December 1942, FO 371/32916/6217, PRO.

37. 10 December 1942, WO 178/26, PRO.

38. 6 January 1943, WO 178/26; 7 January 1943, FO 371/36969/N261; 10 January 1943, WO 208/1787, PRO.

39. 3–11 January 1943, FO 371/36927/N624, and 12 January 1943, WO 32/15548, PRO.

40. 2 February 1943, JIC (43) 60, Final, and JIC (943) 72, Final; 23 February 1943, AIR 20/7961, PRO. Hinsley, Thomas, et al., *History of British Intelligence in the Second World War,* vol. 3, pt. 2, p. 20.

41. 23 January and 4 February 1943, WO 178/27, and 23 January 1943 Report, FO 371/36958, PRO. For the Caucasus withdrawal plan, 4 February 1943, WO 178/27, PRO.

42. 23 January 1943, WO 178/27, PRO.

43. 3 and 13 February, WO 178/27, PRO.

44. 15 March 1943, WO 178/27; 9, 14, 15, and 18 March 1943, WO 208/1826, 15 March 1943, WO 32/15548, PRO. 14 March 1943, R. G. Turner diary, Imperial War Museum.

45. 3 March 1943, AIR 2/7861; 15 March 1943 and enclosures, WO 32/15548, PRO. See also 23 December 1942, WO 178/26, 16 February 1943, PREM 3/396/13, as well as 16 February 1943, FO 181/975/3, PRO.

46. 3 March 1943 on, Box 1044, 350.0511, Entry 47, RG 319, and 11 March 1943, File 7, Box 586, Entry 57, RG 319, Suitland, NA. Claims of Anglo-Soviet air cooperation, 17 October, Map Room, Box 99, 300, Roosevelt Library (my thanks to Warren Kimball for this reference). Interview with General Boswell, October 1993.

47. 26 November and 1 December 1942, FO 371/32916/N6117, PRO. Drinking: ADM 1/13272, PRO, R. G. Turner diary, Imperial War Museum, especially October–November 1942. Anti-Soviet reporting from northern ports (especially January–March 1943), ADM/199/73, PRO. Complaints about Russian failings, 13 August 1942, ADM 237/165; Navy liaison system, ADM 223/252; requests, 26 November and 1 December, FO 371/32916/N6117, PRO.

48. 19 August 1942, Box 99, Russian Files, MR, Roosevelt Library.

49. 18 August 1942 meeting, Memos 4-25-42 to 3-13-42 File, Box 17, Standley Papers, USC; March 1943 reports, Boxes 5 and 7, Naval Attaché Moscow, Correspondence and Visits Files, Boxes 5 and 7, CNO, RG 38, MR, NA.

50. 19 November 1942, File EF 61, USSR, Box 6, RG 38, MR, NA.

51. 1 February–5 April, Archangel reports, Box 4, RG 38, MR, NA; 1 February to 29 March, Reports of Official Visits File, Box 7, Moscow Attaché, CNO, RG 38, MR, NA.

52. 17 March 1943, 300 Russ (1), Sec. 2, Box 100, Map Room, Roosevelt Library.

53. Ibid.

54. Ibid.

55. Ibid.

Chapter 7. The First Victorious Summer

1. Molotov-Clark Kerr, 18 July 1943, FO 800/301, frame 68, PRO.

2. Hopkins and Loy Henderson's views, April 1943, FO 954/30, PRO, and Correspondence File, Box 33, and Joe Davis File, Box 17, Standley Papers, USC.

3. Forrest G. Pogue, *George Marshall: Organizer of Victory, 1944–1945* (New York: Viking, 1973), pp. 74–75. Interview with Ambassador Clinton Olson, November 1943, author's papers, Hoover Institution.

4. 24 August 1943, Turner diary, Imperial War Museum.

5. 5 and 12 April and 23 August 1943, Turner diary, and 4 May 1943, Martel Papers, Box 240, Imperial War Museum, and Gifford Martel, *The Russian Outlook* (London: Michael Joseph, 1947), p. 65. See also Clark Kerr, 12 April 1943, FO 371/36969/N2226, and H. M. Waldeck to VCNS, 12 September 1943, ADM 1/13383, PRO.

6. 12 April 1943, FO 371/36969/N2226; 5 April, Turner diary, and April comments, Martel Papers, Box 240, Imperial War Museum. Admiral Fisher, April and June 1943, MC-1, Maclachlan Papers, Churchill College, Cambridge.

7. 22 June and 23 August 1943, Turner diary, Imperial War Museum; June–September 1943, AIR 20/5401; 24 June 1943, AIR 19/293, PRO. Clark Kerr, 20 June 1943, FO 800/301 frame 41, and Babbington's appointment and orders, 15 and 22 May and 16 June, AIR 20/5401 and FO 371/36969/N3557, PRO.

8. 20 June 1943, FO 800/301 frame 41, PRO (staff letter to Clark Kerr); Marshal Babbington, 24 June, AIR 19/293; Mosquito aircraft, 9 June 1943, WO 193/655, and 22 June, Turner diary, Imperial War Museum; Babbington's orders, 16 June, FO 371/36969/655, PRO. How bad 30 Mission's situation was compared with earlier periods is difficult to determine, because the embassy records in Moscow were destroyed on 2 July 1941 when the Germans neared the city. FO 181/973/2, PRO.

9. 15 April and 29 June 1943, File 8, Box 596, Entry 57, RG 319, Suitland, NA. 29 June and 24 July 1943, WO 178/27, PRO; May–June cover and deception, Anglo-American Meeting File, Box 3, Entry 422, RG 319, MR, NA.

10. Allen Pauli, *Katyn: The Untold Story of Stalin's Polish Massacre* (New York: Macmillan, 1991), passim.

11. 1 May 1943, Russian Naval Mission London, FO 371/36969 and ADM 223/289 (March 1942–December 1943 period), PRO.

12. 5–29 April 1943, ADM 223/32, 107, and 290; 1 May 1943, FO 371/36969, PRO; Maclachlan memo, MC 1, Churchill College, Cambridge. 22 May 1943, NID 16 memo, ADM 223/32. On BNLO Black Sea, see 13 April 1943, FO 371/36959/N2346; May–June 1943, ADM 199/1107. Also, 5 May 1943, WO 208/1793, and June–September 1943, ADM 199/1105, PRO.

13. 3 April 1943, FO 371/36959/N2346; 27 April 1943 ff., ADM 199/1102; 11 April 1943, ADM 199/1104, PRO. 30 June 1943, Turner diary, Imperial War Museum. See also Peterborough section, *Daily Telegraph* (London), 28 December 1987, p. 15. Subsequently, Dr. Alan Harris Bath kindly provided me with the original reference, ADM 223/289, PRO.

14. Early July 1943, ADM 199/1102 and CAB 122/100 (COS [43] 461 [0]), PRO.

15. April 1943, ADM 199/1102 and 1107, plus FO 371/36959/N2346, PRO; R. G. Turner diary (30 June 1943), Imperial War Museum; on the recall, 7 May 1943, AIR 2/7861; 5 August and 1 September, ADM 199/1102, PRO, and Turner diary (26 August and 26 September 1943), Imperial War Museum.

16. 20 April 1943, AIR 20/8046, PRO.

17. 24 April meetings, WO 178/26. The T-34, 28 April and 1 May, Box 240, Martel Papers, Imperial War Museum; 2 April, Brigadier Lefebvre, AIR 20/2325, PRO.

18. 3, 11, 17 April 1943, File 8, Box 586, RG 319, and chemical warfare information in April, Binder VIII, Box 804, Entry 182, RG 165, comment of 25 October, Suitland, NA. U.S. Navy comments, 20 April, File 5, Box 2, Eastern Europe, Attaché, ONI, RG 38, MR, NA.

19. 6 April 1943, Box 50, Attaché, Moscow, MR, NA; 20 April, Report on Trans-Siberian, Russia (1) File, Box 100, Map Room, Roosevelt Library; 1 April, Trans-Siberian reports, Box 5, CNO, Moscow, RG 38, MR, NA.

20. Timothy P. Mulligan, "Spies, Ciphers, and "Zitadella," *Journal of Contemporary History* 22, no. 2 (April 1987): 235–260. Anthony Read and David Fisher, *Operation Lucy* (London: Hodder and Stoughton, 1980), p. 162; F. H. Hinsley, E. E. Thomas, et al., *British Intelligence in the Second World War: Its Influence upon Operations,* 4 vols. (London: Her Majesty's Stationery Office, 1979–1985), 2:624. See also 13 May 1943, PREM 3/396/13, and JIC conclusion of 15 February 1943, JIC (43) 64, CAB 81/113, PRO. Note too that the newly released Churchill ULTRA files (HW 1, PRO) show that although the prime minister received Kursk information on 16 and 30 April 1943, and the latter item was sent on to the Soviets, no Kursk ULTRA was received by Churchill thereafter, indicating that British intelligence was at sea regarding the German attack timetable.

21. 1–12 May 1943, MAGRUS, Box 3, Entry 422, RG 165, MR, NA.

22. Butcher diary, Box 143, Eisenhower Files, pre-presidential, Eisenhower Library, Abilene; 13 May 1943, 396/13, PREM 3, PRO. For Whitehall's intelligence picture during the battle of Kursk, see Hinsley, Thomas, et al., *British Intelligence in the Second World War,* 2:624–627.

23. 10 May 1943, File 9, Box 586, Entry 57, and Box 1044, Entry 47, 350.051, RG 319, Suitland, NA.

24. 28 May and 20–21 June 1943, WO 178/27, and 2 May 1943, WO 178/26, plus 3 July 1943, HW 1/1789, PRO.

25. Ibid.

26. Vassilevsky, 21 April 1943, R. G. Turner diary, Imperial War Museum; Martel front visit, 11–19 May, WO 208/1829, WO 216/133, and WO 178/27; 4 and 25 June, FO 371/36969/N3165 and N3349, and FO 371/32909/N3533. May 1943, Box 240, Martel Papers, Imperial War Museum. See also June reports, FO 371/36959/N3752 and WO 216/133, PRO.

27. 21 June 1943, 5p. report, Box 240, Martel Papers, Imperial War Museum, and June 1943 report #2, WO 178/26, PRO.

28. AIR visits, etc., April–July, AIR 46/26, AIR 20/2325, AIR 2/7861, PRO. Babbington's estimate, 12 August 1943, FO 371/36960/N6277, PRO; negative views in air mission, 15 August 1943, AIR 2/7861; radar, 12 June 1943, WO 178/26, PRO.

29. 28 April and 29 May, 1943, R. G. Turner diary, Imperial War Museum; 23 May 1943, AIR 20/7961. The material was shipped to the United Kingdom on the *Empire Portia,* 14 June 1943, WO 176/391, PRO.

30. On Davies, Visit File, Box 17, Standley Papers, USC; on the negative general tone, 15 April 1943, Files 6 and 8, Box 586, Entry 57, RG 319, Suitland, NA.

31. 10 June 1943, Ordnance File, Box K280, 385.21/81, Entry 921, RG 165, MR, NA. See 12 January 1943, WO 32/15548; 8 July and 28 September 1943, WO 178/27, and January 1944, WO 208/1787, PRO.

32. May 1943 ff., FO 371/35098/E2872, PRO.

33. 12 June 1843, ADM 199/1107, and 27 June 1943, ADM 199/1105, PRO.

34. April–July 1943, Russia (1) File, Box 100, Map Room, Roosevelt Library; Murmansk Files, Moscow, CNO, RG 38, MR, NA; and File Op-FA5 and Vladivostok File, Moscow, ONI, Boxes 2 and 5, RG 38, MR, NA; plus May–July 1943, Moscow Misc. Serials File, ONI Eastern Europe, Box 38, RG 38, MR, NA.

35. 3 June 1943, WO 208/4565, PRO (new Release 1995).

36. 5 July 1943, Turner diary, Imperial War Museum.

37. 8–9 July 1943, Martel to War Office, FO 371/32910/N3687, PRO. See also the summary of the conspiracy vision and its rebuttal in Mulligan, "Spies, Ciphers, and Zitadella," p. 235.

38. 8 July 1943, Turner diary, Imperial War Museum. Martel to COS, 5 July–30 August 1943, PREM 3/400, and 10 July 1943, PREM 3/396/13, plus 9 July 1943, FO 371/36959/N4068, PRO.

39. 17 July 1943, FO 371/36959/N4228, PRO; 10 July 1943, Turner diary, Imperial War Museum.

40. 26 July 1943, M.I.3.C., WO 208/1835; 9 and 15 July, FO 371/36959/N4068; 10 July 1943, Martel to COS, PREM 3/396/13, and 20 August 1943, AIR 46/28, PRO.

41. July 1943, FO 371/36959/N4068; 26 July and British rockets 23 July 1943, WO 178/27; see also 21 July 1943, WO 208/1829, PRO.

42. 7 July–4 August 1943 items, Box 1044, 350.0511, Entry 47, and 28 July, File 10, Box 586, Entry 57, RG 319, Suitland, NA.

43. 21, 24, 28, and 31 July 1943, Box K228, 473.955/5, Entry 921, Ordnance, RG 165, Suitland, NA; on Russian silence on their own forces, JIC (43) 102, CAB 81/114 (but General Martel and a Soviet general did have a discussion on Red Army armored forces on 15 June 1943). AIR 46/28, PRO.

44. 2 August 1943 report, Box 7, Reports of Visits File, and 8 July 1943, A82 Information File, Box 2, CNO, Moscow, RG 38, MR, NA. Rickenbacker visit, July

1943, Russia-Bradley File, Box 3, Entry 422; G-2 Interview File, Box 898, Entry 93, RG 165, MR, NA; 16 July and 11 August, Russ Memo File, Box 17, Standley Papers, USC.

45. 13 July 1943, 103.91802/1146A, Box 92, RG 59, Diplomatic Branch, NA.

46. "Y" termination, 28 July 1943, ADM 199/606, and July 1943, FO 371/37040/N4397, PRO (general on Royal Navy in north Russia).

47. 1 July 1943, FO 800/301 frame 55; "Y," 11 August 1943, COS (43) 461 (0), CAB 122/100, and 15 August, ADM 199/1109 (Admiral Fisher), PRO.

48. 8 July 1943, Turner diary, Imperial War Museum.

49. Martel and Babbington, 16 July, Babbington-Evill, AIR 20/5401; July (no day) 1943, FO 371/36970/N4593; service heads and Clark Kerr, 22 July 1943, FO 800/301/71-73, PRO.

50. 31 July 1943, Churchill minute, CAB 120/744, PRO.

51. 21 July 1943 summary and 25 July 1943 Churchill minute, CAB 120/690, PRO.

52. 3 August 1943 summary, WO 178/27; 3 September 1943 (Italy), WO 208/1837, and 3 September 1943 (also Italy), FO 371/36960/N4813 (plus FO 181/979/14) PRO.

53. 15 August 1943, AIR 2/7861, PRO.

54. 10 August 1943, FO 371/36960/N4655; 2 September, Martel, FO 371/36970/N4813 and N5566; 28 September 1943, WO 208/1838, PRO. ULTRA must have been the source of the huge Russian OB lists in British files; see WO 33/1790, 1904, and 2002, PRO.

55. August (no day) 1943, FO 371/36970; 3 August 1943, FO 181/979/13; 14 August 1943, FO 371/36960/N4517 and N4813; 3 and 20 September meetings, WO 178/27, PRO. 1 September gift of German guns, WO 176/391, PRO.

56. 12 August 1943 (Babbington), FO 371/36960; 28 August 1943, AIR 19/293; general mission, 1 July 1943, Warner to Clark Kerr, FO 800/301 frame 55, PRO. 23 August, Turner diary, Imperial War Museum.

57. 15 July 1943, lack of Japanese OB, WO 208/1829, PRO.

58. A naval memo of July 1943 refers routinely to Russian and Asiatic peoples and semicivilized countries. MC-1, Maclachlan Papers, Churchill College, Cambridge.

59. 4 September 1943, FO 371/34586/C10283, PRO.

60. 28 August 1943, FO 371/36925, PRO.

61. 6 September 1943, Baird to Standley, Box 33, Standley Papers, USC.

62. 14 September 1943, FO 371/37005/N552, PRO.

63. 24 August–16 September 1943, Box 1044, Entry 47, RG 319, Suitland, NA.

64. 3–19 August 1943, Box 389, Entry 57, RG 319, Suitland, NA.

65. 24 July to 8 September 1943, Official Visits File, Box 7, CNO Moscow, RG 38, MR, NA; 23 September 1943, MR 300, Russ (1) Sec. 3, Box 100, Roosevelt Library.

66. 23 September 1943, Harriman to Marshall, Box 3, Entry 422, RG 165, MR, NA, and 10 July 1943 reports of Michela's situation, File 15, Box 587, RG 319, Suitland, NA; Harry Hopkins views, as of 22 April 1943 (in talk with Lord Halifax), FO 954/30, PRO. For the general situation, see Forrest C. Pogue, *George Marshall: Ordeal of Hope, 1939–1942* (New York: Viking, 1966), passim, and John R. Deane, *Strange Alliance* (New York: Viking, 1947), passim.

Chapter 8. A Winter of More Contentment

1. JIC reports, (43) 367 and 409 (0), 9 September and 2 October 1943, CAB 120/744, PRO.

2. For Teheran, see Keith Eubank, *Summit at Teheran* (New York: Morrow, 1985), passim; William M. Franklin et al., *The Conferences at Cairo and Teheran* (Washington, D.C.: U.S. Government Printing Office, 1961), passim; and Charles E. Bohlen, *Witness to History* (New York: Norton, 1973), p. 147.

3. George C. Herring Jr., *Aid to Russia, 1941–1946* (New York: Columbia University Press, 1973), passim, and 10 February 1944, FO summary on probable Soviet postwar policy, ADM 116/5118, PRO. Quotation from Churchill, 23 October 1944, referring to 28 November 1943 meeting, PREM 3/397/3, PRO.

4. Teheran file, Top Secret Ambassador's Files, USSR, Box 2, RG 84, Suitland, NA.

5. 1944–45 Foreign Office yearly report, Moscow, p. 197, FO 490/4, PRO.

6. Robert Murphy, *Diplomat Among Warriors* (New York: Doubleday, 1964), pp. 256 ff. Nelson visit, 27 October 1943, ONI, Moscow, Box 1, RG 38, MR, NA.

7. 7 November 1943, Stalin File, ADM 199/1102, PRO.

8. 29 October 1943, Ismay to Churchill, FO 800/409 and PREM 3/396/13, PRO.

9. Edward M. Bennett, *Franklin Roosevelt and the Search for Victory* (Wilmington, Del.: Scholarly Resources, 1990), p. 116.

10. 7 October 1943, ADM 199/605, PRO.

11. Herring, *Aid to Russia,* p. 103; 25 October Michela report, Binder VIII, Box 804, Entry 182, RG 165, MR, NA; 22 December 1943, CAB 122/936, PRO.

12. Bradley F. Smith, *The Ultra-Magic Deals* (Shrewsbury: Airlife, 1993), pp. 198–199.

13. 4 October 1943, G-2 Interview File, Box 898, Entry 193, RG 165, MR, NA.

14. 2 November 1943, Turner diary, Imperial War Museum.

15. Mission History, Harriman Papers, Box 190, Library of Congress.

16. Keith Sainsbury, *The Turning Point: The Conference at Teheran* (New York: Oxford, 1985), p. 208.

17. On preparations for the OVERLORD invasion of France, see Teheran Conferences, point 5, 28 November–1 December 1943 File, Top Secret, Box 2, RG 84, Suitland, NA, and 26 October 1943, FO 800/409, and 5 November 1943, JP (43) 396 (S) CAB 119/39, PRO.

18. October 1943, ADM 1/158/24, PRO; Firebrace's Moscow survey, 22 November 1943, Turner diary, Imperial War Museum; Firebrace report to chiefs of staff, 24 November 1943, COS (43) 729, FO 371/36970/N7241; technology exchange, ADM 199/605 and 1332, PRO.

19. Edward Drea, *MacArthur's ULTRA: Codebreaking and the War Against Japan, 1942–1945* (Lawrence: University Press of Kansas, 1991), passim, and Ronald H. Spector, ed., *Listening to the Enemy: Key Documents on the Role of Communications Intelligence in the War with Japan* (Wilmington, Del.: Scholarly Resources Press, 1988), passim.

20. John Deane, *Strange Alliance* (New York: Viking, 1947), p. 49. For the British mission's pleasure at the new American team, see 25 October 1943, Turner diary, Imperial War Museum.

21. CCS 385, USSR (11-4-43), RG 218, MR, NA. For General Michela's harsh view of OSS-NKVD exchange, see 8 February 1944 memo, 4 November 1943 to February 1944 File, Box 84, Entry 182, RG 165, MR, NA. See also Bradley F. Smith. *The Shadow Warriors* (New York: Basic Books, 1983), pp. 330 ff. For the SOE in this period, see agent drop information in HS 4/328, PRO.

22. 15 February 1944, File 15-21, Box 171, Harriman Papers, Library of Congress.

23. 2 December 1943, Eisenhower to Deane, WO 204/1342, PRO. Deane, *Strange Alliance,* p. 152.

24. Conferences File, Box 783, Entry 203, RG 165 MR, NA (seven OB meetings are covered in this file).

25. Deane to Strong, 5 February 1944, AIR 40/2344, PRO. Some reports also went to the White House—4 February 1944, Box 100, Map Room, 300 Russ., Sec. 4, Roosevelt Library.

26. For reports of other OB meetings in 1944, see Box 1044, 350.0511, Entry 47, RG 319, Suitland, NA. For OB sent to Deane by G-2, see File 1, Box 587, Entry 57, RG 319, Suitland, NA.

27. Gas masks, 28 January 1944, File 1, Box 587, Entry 57, RG 319, Suitland, NA. For defenses, December 1943 file, MR 300, Sec. 3, Warfare Russ, Box 100, Map Room, Roosevelt Library.

28. 13 November 1943, File 1, Box 587, Entry 57, RG 319, Suitland, NA.

29. 20 February 1944, CAB 122/937, PRO; Red Air Force bombs, 24 February 1944, Folder 1, Box 16, Eastern Europe, ONI, MR, NA.

30. 18 November and 10 December 1943, Box 7, CNO, Moscow, RG 38, MR, NA.

31. History of the Military Mission, p. 26, Box 190, Harriman Papers, Library of Congress.

32. 10, 12, and 20 January 1944, File 1, Box 287, Entry 57, RG 319, Suitland, NA.

33. 26 January 1944, File 1, Box 587, Entry 57, RG 319, and 2 February 1944, Top Secret Ambassador, Box 1, RG 84, Suitland, NA; 29 January, July 1941–January 1944 File (SC) A-3, Box 16. Eastern Europe, ONI, MR, NA.

34. Official Visits File, CNO, Moscow, RG 80, MR, NA; attachment, CCS 350.05 (2-9-44), JCS, RG 218, MR, NA. G-2 also wanted to expand U.S.-Soviet exchanges on Japan; see Bissell to Deane, 16 February 1944, File 2, Box 587, Entry 57, RG 319, Suitland, NA.

35. Deane, *Strange Alliance,* pp. 237–238. Of course, one could also argue that the Royal Navy always had an easier time than the British Army in Russia.

36. 5 February 1944, Sec. 4, File 300, Box 100, Map Room, Roosevelt Library.

37. October 1943–February 1944, Eastern Europe, ONI, RG 38, Boxes 16 and 39; 22 February 1944, Vladivostok (I) File ONI, Moscow, Box 5, RG 38, MR, NA.

38. 28 January 1944, Eastern Europe, ONI Box 11, RG 38, MR, NA; 24 July 1943, Moscow, CNO, Box 7, RG 38, MR, NA; January–March 1944, Box 1, Moscow ("Weather History" File), RG 84, Suitland, NA.

39. 22 February 1944, Vladivostok I File, Box 5, ONI, Moscow, RG 38, MR, NA; Harriman final report, Military Mission File #3, Harriman Papers, Container 190, Library of Congress.

40. E. Rickenbacker, January 1944, Box 898, Entry 193, RG 165, MR, NA; Connolly report, Box 5, RG 334 (Moscow), MR, NA. British versions, WO 208/1867, AIR 20/7951, and PREM 3/396/14, PRO.

41. See Box 898, Entry 193, RG 165, MR, NA.

42. 1 October 1943, CAB 120/683, PRO.

43. 4 October 1943, Turner diary, Imperial War Museum.

44. Late October, AIR 20/5401, 23 October FO 181/950/10, PRO, and 21 October 1943, Turner diary, Imperial War Museum.

45. November–December 1943, AIR 20/8059 and FO 371/43288/N258/9, PRO.

46. 8 and 9 October 1943, FO 371/36970 and 371/43361, PRO.

47. 2 January 1944, FO 371/43361/N469, and 1 February 1944, FO 800/302 frame 5, PRO.

48. CAB 122/942, PRO (this file became COS [43] 729).

49. Ibid.

50. Ibid.

51. Ibid.

52. 3 January 1944, ADM 199/77, and 26 November 1943, WO 193/651, PRO.

53. 15 September 1943 on, FO 371/37054/4932, PRO.

54. 13 December 1943, AIR 20/2606, PRO.

55. January ff., FO 371/43288/N346 and N376, plus FO 371/43289, PRO.

56. COS (44) 52 (O), FO 371/43288/N928, N1196, and N2913, PRO.

57. 2 and 4 February 1944, WO 193/651; 3 and 23 February 1944, WO 178/27 and 208/1837, PRO.

58. Military literature exhibit, 5 February 1944, WO 208/1844; Hill's visit to Leningrad, 29 January–4 February 1944, WO 208/1842 and 1844, plus FO 490/3; Red Army OB, 23 February 1944, WO 208/1850, PRO.

59. 5 February 1944, CAB 120/769, PRO. Anthony Cave Brown, *Bodyguard of Lies* (New York: Harper and Row, 1973), passim.

60. French pilot report, 18 December 1943, AIR 20/2324, and 18 February 1944 report, AIR 46/27, PRO.

61. 3 February 1944, AIR 20/956, PRO.

62. November 1943, COS (43) 729 (O), AIR 20/8059; 8 October 1943, WO 178/27, PRO. 29 August, 10 October, and 2 November 1943, Turner diary, Imperial War Museum.

63. 13 December 1943, WO 178/27, PRO.

64. Ibid., and 11 January 1944, ADM 199/1102, PRO.

65. 11 January 1944, ADM 199/1102, and 24 November 1943, AIR 20/8059; "Y" matters, January 1944, FO 371/43288/N1197 and 371/43289/N2812, plus November–December entry, ADM 199/1104, PRO.

66. 11 February 1944, FO 181/989/7/1; 5 October 1943, AIR 20/2606. Fisher's lament, 26 October 1943, FO 371/36970/N6385, all PRO.

Chapter 9. The D-Day Era

1. 18 March 1944, COS (44) 82 (O), FO 371/43288/N1743, PRO.

2. On ANVIL, 21 March 1944, CAB 122/942; D day, 20 April 1944, WO 178/27, 24 April, CAB 120/429, 9 and 26 May, CAB 122/937, PRO.

3. 24 March 1944, ADM 199/605, PRO. Weather, 25–30 1944 File, Box 172, Harri-

man Papers, Library of Congress; 2 June 1944, Summary, Pending File, Box 3, Top Secret, RG 111, Suitland, NA.

4. 19 April, Top Secret. Ambassador, Moscow, RG 84, Suitland, NA. For General Spalding, see Chapter 8.

5. 17 June 1944, FO 371/38708, PRO.

6. Information from the SOE adviser, Mark Seaman of the Imperial War Museum, and David Carpenter, whose generosity I appreciate (information in the author's collection, Hoover Institution). See also Bradley F. Smith, *The Shadow Warriors* (New York: Basic Books, 1983), pp. 347 ff. See also the new HS4 series in the PRO.

7. 26 May 1944, General Information File, Box 10, Moscow, RG 334, MR, NA.

8. April–May 1944, WO 219/5216, PRO; JPS 429, in CCS 381, (9-2-43) CCS, RG 218, MR, NA.

9. 2 March 1944, 350.0511, Box 1044, Entry 47, RG 319, Suitland, NA (also for OB meetings to 28 April 1944).

10. Ibid.

11. Ibid.

12. 8 March 1944, File 2, Box 587, RG 319, Suitland, NA.

13. 12 April 1944, File 3, ibid.

14. 11 April, Box 15, RG 3334, Moscow, MR, NA.

15. 6 May 1944, File 3, Box 587, Entry 57, RG 319, Suitland, NA.

16. 9 May 1944, ibid.

17. 30 March 1944, ABC 452.1, Poland (26 November 1942), Sec. 2-B, RG 165, MR, NA.

18. 18 May 1944, WO 219/5221, 13 April 1944, WO 219/5216; 30 April 1944, WO 219/5214, PRO.

19. Germany File, Box 9, RG 334, Moscow, MR, NA.

20. 2 March 1944 (visa), File 5, Box 390, Entry 57, RG 319, Suitland, NA; 14 March 1944, Meetings with the Soviets File, Box 15, Moscow, RG 334, MR, NA; John R. Deane, *Strange Alliance* (New York: Viking, 1947), p. 238.

21. 11 April 1944, Meetings with the Soviets File, Box 15, Moscow, RG 334, MR, NA. See also Deane, *Strange Alliance,* pp. 238–239. British agreement—no day, March 1944, WO 208/1787, PRO. A large Japanese OB meeting in Washington was scheduled for 10 May 1944, and MID wanted Pettigrew to get all possible such OB from the Soviets by that date. File 3, Box 587, Entry 57, Suitland, NA.

22. 9 June 1944, Meetings with the Soviets File, Box 15, Moscow, RG 334, MR, NA.

23. 27 and 28 June, File 4, Box 587, Entry 57, RG 319, Suitland, NA. Deane's suggestions, 23 June, Information Exchange File, Box 10, Moscow, RG 334, MR, NA; gas, 13 June 1944, Meetings with the Soviets File, Box 15, Moscow, RG 334, MR, NA.

24. 17 June 1944, WO 208/1787, PRO.

25. Information Exchange Air Force File, Box 10, Moscow, RG 334, MR, NA (many thanks to Timothy Mulligan for this reference).

26. Ibid.

27. Ibid.

28. 3 June 1944, WO 219/522, PRO.

29. 4 March, FO 371/43289, JIC (44) 81 (O), final, PRO.

30. F. H. Hinsley, E. E. Thomas, et al., *British Intelligence in the Second World War: Its Influence upon Operations,* 4 vols. (London: Her Majesty's Stationery Office, 1979–1985), vol. 3, pt. 1, pp. 19–20. 3 March 1944, Turner diary, Imperial War Museum; see also OB meetings, 10 February to 10 May, WO 178/27, PRO.

31. 4 June 1944, FO 800/302/46; A. H. Panzer Division, 10 May 1944, WO 178/27 and 208/1837; Panther tank, 7 May 1944, and Regimental OB, 4 June 1944, WO 178/27, PRO. See also 9 May 1944, FO 371/43289/N3040, PRO.

32. May (no day) 1944, WO 208/1844, PRO.

33. 9–17 April 1944 visit, FO 371/43362/3983; other Canadian reports, 6–11 May 1944, WO 208/1847, PRO.

34. G-2 Teletype Net File, Box 792, Entry 303, RG 165, MR, NA; see also 26 February memo, SHAEF/116G/4/INT, WO 219/1867, PRO.

35. Hinsley, Thomas, et al., *British Intelligence,* vol. 3, pt. 2, p. 282.

36. COS (44) 212th Mtg, CAB 122/942, and 28 April 1944, WO 178/27, PRO.

37. 28 April 1944, WO 178/27, PRO.

38. Also on BODYGUARD, 5 February 1944, Ismay to Churchill, CAB 120/769, and 9 May 1944, CIGS to Burrows, AIR 20/5401, PRO. Deane, *Strange Alliance,* pp. 147–149.

39. Ship totals and significance, ADM 199/2112 (1941–1945) and ADM 199/605 (January–May 1944), PRO.

40. Typex machines and "Y," 10 May 1944 report, ADM 199/606; 29 March 1944 report, FO 371/43399/N1749, and 5 May 1944, ADM 199/1102. As late as December 1944, the SOE believed that SIS was getting valuable "Y" and counterintelligence information from Moscow. HS 4/334, PRO.

41. 3 April–10 June 1944, ADM 199/1102, PRO.

42. 16 May 1944 and 1 June 1944, ADM 199/1102, PRO.

43. April–May and June–July 1944, ADM 199/1105, and 4 April 1944 ff., ADM 223/248, PRO.

44. 6 July 1944, FO 371/43290/N4749. On Fisher's visit, 28–31 May 1944, ADM 223/252, and 4 May 1944, FO 800/302 frame 66 ff., PRO.

45. 25 April 1944, Navy-Olsen File, Box 172, Harriman Papers, Library of Congress; March–June 1944, Weather History File, Moscow, Ambassador, Top Secret, RG 84, Suitland, NA; Boxes 1, 3, 16, and 39, ONI, Eastern Europe, RG 38, MR, NA; March–June 1944, Boxes 1, 2, 4, and 7, Moscow, RG 38, MR, NA; March–June, Box 100, MR 300, Roosevelt Library.

46. May–June 1944, Box 110, Russia, MR 340, Roosevelt Library; March–April 1944, Box 2, Moscow, CNO, RG 38, MR, NA, and 3 March 1944, JIC 171/1, CCS 350.05 (2-29-44), Box 251, RG 218, MR, NA.

47. 24 March 1944, ONI, Eastern Europe, Box 16, RG 38, MR, NA.

48. 10 March 1944, 9–15 March File, Box 171, Moscow, Harriman Papers, Library of Congress.

49. Meetings with the Soviets File, Box 15, Moscow, RG 334, MR, NA.

50. Ibid.

51. 1 April 1944, Air Intelligence File, Box 1, Moscow, RG 334, MR, NA.

52. 2 April 1944, Germany File, Box 9, Moscow, RG 334, MR, NA.

53. Air Intelligence File, Box 1, Moscow, RG 334, MR, NA.

54. 5 June 1944, 1944 Miscellaneous File, Box 2, Ambassador, Top Secret, Moscow, RG 84, Suitland, NA.

55. See also 16 May 1944, Colonel Kessler to Washington, Air Intelligence File, Box 1, and 21 May 1944, General Aderson File, Box 1, Moscow, RG 334, MR, NA. W. F. Cramer, *The Army Air Forces in World War II* (Chicago: University of Chicago Press, 1951), vol. 3, pp. 308–319; 30 May 1944, Deane to Slavin, Box 2, Russia, CNO, RG 38, MR, NA.

56. 5 June 1944, 1944 Miscellaneous File, Box 2, Ambassador Top Secret, Moscow, RG 84, Suitland, NA.

57. Thomas A. Julian, "Operation at the Margin: Soviet Bases and Shuttle Bombing," *Journal of Military History* 57 (October 1993): 644, and 8 March 1944, File 2, Box 587, Entry 57, RG 319, Suitland, NA.

58. 23 June 1944, German Air Force File, Box 9, Moscow, RG 334, MR, NA.

59. 28 June 1944, Information Exchange File, Box 10, Moscow, RG 334, MR, NA.

60. 21 March 1944, AIR 20/7961, PRO.

61. 16 April 1944, AVIA 39/37, PRO.

62. April (no day) 1944, AIR 20/3221, PRO.

63. A good corrective to what might be called the wise-Britain view is Martin Kitchen, *British Policy Toward the Soviet Union During the Second World War* (London: Macmillan, 1986).

64. For Roosevelt's general foreign policy, see Robert Dallek, *Franklin D. Roosevelt and American Foreign Policy, 1932–1945* (New York: Oxford University Press, 1979).

65. For George Marshall in the later war period, see Forrest Pogue, *George Marshall: Organizer of Victory, 1944–1945* (New York: Viking, 1973).

66. 18 March 1944, CAB 105/35, PRO.

67. 9 May 1944, AIR 19/294, PRO. See also Kitchen, *British Policy Toward the Soviet Union*, pp. 170 ff.

68. 3 April 1944, PHP (43) 1 (O), CAB 119/28, and the Foreign Office's "Probable Post-war Tendencies in Soviet Foreign Policy," ADM 116/5118, PRO.

69. 1 April 1944, PREM 3/396/14 and CAB 120/678, PRO. On the Moscow visit, see Kitchen, *British Policy Toward the Soviet Union*, pp. 124 ff.

70. June 1944, WO 178/27, PRO.

71. 29 May 1944, ADM 205/39, PRO.

72. 29 March 1944, DMI to AFHQ, WO 204/900, PRO.

73. April–November 1944, Army Intelligence Top Secret Decimal Files, 1942–1952 (countries), Box 1, RG 319, Suitland, NA.

74. 15 April 1944, FO 954/26/382-386, PRO.

75. Ibid.

76. May 1944 (no day), FO 371/43420/3363, PRO.

77. 24 April 1944, CAB 120/429, PRO, and 26 June 1944, Conversations File, 1943–1948, Box 1, Top Secret, Ambassador, RG 84, Suitland, NA.

78. 17 and 22 April 1944, WO 178/27, PRO.

79. 19 May 1944, FO 371/43417/N3220, PRO.

80. 10 June 1944, Ambassador Files, Top Secret, Moscow, Box 1, RG 84, Suitland, NA.

81. 23 June 1944, FO 800/302 frame 95 ff., PRO.

82. Ibid.

Chapter 10. The Penultimate Phase Begins

1. On the U.S. military and the Warsaw rising, see Earl F. Ziemke, *Stalingrad to Berlin* (Washington, D.C.: U.S. Government Printing Office, 1968), pp. 340–341.

2. Poison gas questions, 14 June–8 August 1944, Information Exchange File, Box 10, Moscow, RG 334, MR, NA.

3. 7 July 1944, MR 300, Box 100, Russ War Sec. 5, Roosevelt Library.

4. 5 August 1944, Germany File, Box 9, Moscow, RG 334, MR, NA.

5. 22 August 1944, WO 178/27, PRO.

6. 1 August 1944 ff., CAB 120/690, PRO.

7. Ibid.

8. 3 July and 10 November 1944, WO 178/27, PRO.

9. August (no day) and 11 September 1944, Information Exchange File, Box 10, Moscow, RG 334, MR, NA; 2 October and 3 November 1944, WO 208/1837, and 6 October 1944, WO 178/27, PRO.

10. 28 September 1944, Meetings with the Soviets File, Box 15, and 7 October 1944, Exchange File, Box 10, Moscow, RG 334, MR, NA.

11. 8 August 1944, Information Exchange File, Box 10, Moscow, RG 334; and 11 September 1944, ibid., plus 28 September 1944, Meetings with the Soviets File, Box 15, RG 334, MR, NA, and 17 October 1944, File 7, Box 588, Entry 57, RG 319, Suitland, NA.

12. 13 July, 11 and 27 August, plus 2 September 1944, WO 178/27, and 23 July 1944, FO 181/983/1, PRO.

13. 3 September 1944, Bomb Sites File, Box 3 and Intelligence Teams File, Box 11, Moscow, RG 334, MR, NA. 10–16 September 1944 report, WO 208/1844, PRO.

14. 28 January 1945, Information Exchange File, Box 10, Moscow, September 1944; Intelligence Teams File, Box 11, and Bomb Sites File, Box 3, Moscow, RG 334, MR, NA, plus CAB 122/938 and 10 April 1945, JIC (45) 119 (O), CAB 81/128, PRO.

15. General Cannon visit, Cannon File, Box 3, and Meetings File, Box 15, Moscow, RG 334, MR, NA, and 1 August 1944, Army Intelligence Reports File, Box 2, Attaché Moscow, RG 38, MR, NA. Navy visits, 6 July 1944, File 1, Box 16, ONI, Eastern Europe, RG 38, MR, NA; 19 August 1944, Stormovik plant, Air Intelligence File, Box 1, Moscow, RG 334, MR, NA.

16. 30 July 1944, Air File, Box 10; Moscow, 10 August 1944, German Air Force File, Box 9; 31 August 1944, Air Force Dispositions File, Box 9; and 9 September, Air Intelligence File, Box 1, Moscow, RG 334, MR, NA.

17. 11 August–5 October, "Soviet Recon. Summary," Red Air Force File, Box 29, Moscow, RG 334, and 9 and 16 September reports, Air Intelligence File, Box 1, plus 16 September 1944, Meetings with the Soviets File, Box 15, Moscow, RG 334, MR, NA.

18. 8 September 1944, Cables File, Ambassador, Top Secret, Moscow, RG 84, Suitland, NA.

19. George C. Herring Jr., *Aid to Russia, 1941–1946* (New York: Columbia University Press 1973), p. 137.

20. 16 September 1944, Meeting with the Soviets File, Box 15, Moscow, RG 334, MR, NA.

21. 12 and 13 October 1944, Meetings with the Soviets File, Box 15, and Air Intelligence File, Box 1, Moscow, RG 334, MR, NA.

22. 23 October 1944, Meetings with the Soviets File, Box 15, and Air Intelligence File, Box 1, Moscow, RG 334, MR, NA.

23. 20 November 1944, Meetings with the Soviets File, Box 15, Moscow, RG 334, MR, NA.

24. November–December 1944, Aircraft Ordnance File, Box 8, Moscow, CNO, RG 38, MR, NA.

25. 9 December 1944, ADM 223/252, PRO.

26. 20 August and December 1944, AIR 46/27 and AIR 20/7951 and 8060, PRO; for *Tirpitz* attack, see FO 371/43442/N5858, PRO.

27. Thorold report, 2 August 1944, AIR 2/7862; July–August institute visits, etc. and Normany squadron talks (November–December 1944), AIR 46/27, PRO.

28. 7 July 1944, File 4, Box 587, RG 319, Suitland, NA. Emphasis added.

29. 11 July 1944, Box 587, File 4, Entry 57, RG 319, MR, NA.

30. Ibid., File 3.

31. 20 October 1944, ibid.

32. 25 October 1944, ibid.

33. Ibid.

34. 30 October 1944, ibid.

35. 4 November 1944, ibid.

36. 10 November 1944, ibid., and Meetings with the Soviets File, Box 15, Moscow, RG 334, MR, NA.

37. Ibid (a second document of 10 November is in the Meetings with the Soviets File).

38. 5 and 9 December 1944, Official Visits File, Box 7, Moscow, CNO, MR, NA.

39. 10 November 1944, Presidents File, Ambassador, Top Secret, RG 84, Suitland, NA.

40. 22 November 1944, Map Room 40 (Russia), Box 10, Roosevelt Library.

41. 27 October 1944, ADM 199/352, PRO.

42. 28 August 1944 report, Box 2, Moscow, CNO, RG 38, MR, NA.

43. 22 July 1944, Inter Office File, Box 1, Attaché, Moscow, CNO, RG 38, MR, NA.

44. 29 September 1944, Folder 2, Box 16, Eastern Europe, CNO, MR, NA, Weather and hydrographic information, Box 11, Eastern Europe, ONI, and Box 1, Moscow, ONI, RG 38, (August–November 1944), RG 38, MR, NA. Weather, 22 July 1944, Box 1, Moscow, CNO, RG 38, MR, NA.

45. Mines, 2, 14, and 20 July, Boxes 16, 17, and 39, Eastern Europe, ONI, RG 38, MR, NA.

46. 23 August 1944, ADM 199/1105; from ULTRA, the British knew that the Germans had been desperate to prevent the Russians from salvaging the U-250. 21 August 1944, HW 1/3181, PRO.

47. 9 and 12 September 1944, ADM 199/605, PRO.

48. 1 September 1944 ff., Boxes 5 and 28, Files Vladivostok I and 32-J, ONI, RG 38, MR, NA, and Boxes 4 and 26, Moscow, CNO, MR, NA.

49. USAAC visits: Deane, 25 July 1944, WO 193/45A, PRO; Hurley, File 820, Box 48, Moscow, RG 84, Suitland, NA; Connolly, Box 27, Moscow, RG 334, MR, NA.

50. Burrows, 6–9 July 1944, WO 193/650, and 6 October 1944, WO 178/27; Simferopol visit, 18–24 November 1944, WO 208/1844, PRO.

51. Bradley F. Smith, *The Shadow Warriors* (New York: Basic Books 1983), p. 381.

52. 10 July 1944, Burrows to Deane, Technical Information File, Box 31, Moscow, RG 334, MR, NA.

53. Significantly, this dispatch, "Gunfire 76," is in Winston Churchill's files, PREM 3, 96/4, PRO.

54. 20 September 1944, Technical Information File, Box 31, Moscow, RG 334, MR, NA.

55. 30 September 1944, AIR 20/8048, PRO.

56. 1 September 1944, AIR 20/8048, PRO.

57. Operation LUX, China File 1944, Box 4, Moscow, RG 334, MR, NA.

58. 26 July 1944, DD 52577, Cunningham Papers, British Library.

59. 18 August 1944, FO 371/43290/N5224 and N6202 (see also ADM 116/5118), PRO.

60. 30 and 31 August 1944, FO 371/43290/N6202, PRO.

61. 5 July 1944, CAB 120/690, PRO.

62. 29 September 1944, Roosevelt File, Ambassador, Box 1, Moscow, Top Secret, RG 84, Suitland, NA.

63. 24 September 1944, Harriman to FDR, Presidential File, Box 59, Entry 422, RG 165, MR, NA.

64. Martin Kitchen, *British Policy Toward the Soviet Union During the Second World War* (London: Macmillan, 1986), pp. 242 ff.

65. 23 September 1944, FDR File, Box 1, Moscow, Ambassador, Top Secret, RG 84, Suitland, NA, and 25 September 1944, Clark Kerr to London, PREM 3/396/7. See also FO 371/43290/N6202 and 371/43306/N5126, PRO.

66. Clark Kerr to Eden, 25 September 1944, FO 954/26/463-4, PRO.

67. Ibid.

68. Kitchen, *British Policy Toward the Soviet Union,* pp. 233–234.

69. 14 October 1944, CAB 127/34. For the American military aspect, see Meetings and Milestone Files, October 1944, Boxes 12 and 16 Moscow, RG 334, MR, NA.

70. 16 October 1944 (Leahy Papers), Russia, Moscow, 1944 Files, RG 218, MR, NA.

71. November (no day), ADM 1/16837, PRO.

72. Ibid., and November 1944 (no day), CAB 119/128, PRO.

Chapter 11. Victory on One Front

1. For the dynamics of the Pacific War, see especially John Dower, *War Without Mercy: Race and Power in the Pacific War* (New York: Pantheon, 1987).

2. December 1944, Milestone File, Box 16, and 14 December 1944, Anglo-American-Soviet Planning File, Box 2, Moscow, RG 334, MR, NA. For a recent brisk reappraisal of the Cold War, see Thomas G. Paterson, *On Every Front: The Making and Unmaking of the Cold War* (New York: Norton, 1992).

3. See Bradley F. Smith, *The Shadow Warriors* (New York: Basic Books, 1983), pp. 350 ff.

4. January 1945, ADM 199/1105, PRO.

5. 16 and 24 January 1945, 52578, Cunningham Papers, British Library.

6. Weather—December 1944, Special Branch File, Box 785, Entry 203, G-2, RG 165, MR, NA. Internees, POWs, etc., December 1944, AIR 46/25; 10 April 1945, FO 371/47881/N4594; April–August 1945, FO 181/1003/8; and FO 181/1005/4, PRO. Air Crews File, Box 11, Moscow, RG 334, MR, NA.

7. 6, 8, and 12 December 1944, WO 178/27, PRO.

8. 8 December 1944, MR 300, Sec. 4, Russia, Roosevelt Library; 29 December 1944, File 9, Box 588, Entry 57, RG 319, MR, NA.

9. 8 December 1944, Bissell to Peabody/Deane, File 9, Box 588, Entry 57, RG 319, Suitland, NA; Pettigrew, 4 December 1944, File 8, Box 588, Entry 57, RG 319, Suitland, NA; 14 December, Air Intelligence File, Box 1, and 14 December Meetings with the Soviet File, Box 15, as well as 23 December Air Force Exchange File, Box 10, and 27 December German Air Force Disposition File, Box 9, Moscow, RG 334, MR, NA; 8 January 1945, British and Pettigrew's role, WO 208/4704, PRO.

10. 15 December 1944, Vladivostok, Box 62, Entry 422, RG 165, MR, NA. 21–23 December visits, Leningrad, Moscow File, Box 39, ONI, Eastern Europe, RG 38, MR, NA; Sevastopol, December 1944, ADM 199/1105, and Murmansk, December 1944, ADM 199/1105, PRO.

11. 2 January 1945, ADM 205/48, PRO.

12. 15 December 1944, FO 181/9831; 29 December, FO 371/47847/N2; 30 December, ADM 205/43, Sec. A; December 1944–January 1945, ADM 205/18A; 2 January 1945, ADM 205/48, PRO.

13. 12 December 1944, CCS 091.411 Balkans (8-21-44), Sec. 1, RG 218, MR, NA, and Smith, *Shadow Warriors,* p. 354.

14. SOE deals, January–February 1945, FO 371/47709/N1184, and 12 January 1945, WO 204/1931, PRO. Czechoslovakia, 29 January 1945, USSR Division, 1945 File, Entry 1, Chiefs Papers, Box 5, RG 226, MR, NA; Czechoslovakia, 29 January 1945 ff., WO 205/10184, PRO, and 2 January 1945, OSS File, Moscow, RG 334, MR, NA.

15. 28 January 1945, MR 100 and MR 300, Russ. War Sec. 5, Roosevelt Library; 31 January 1945, Box 44, CNO, Moscow, RG 38, MR, NA; 11 January 1945, Germany File, Box 9, Moscow, RG 334, MR, NA; 31 January 1945 on Japanese tactics, General Information File, Box 10, Moscow, RG 334, MR, NA.

16. 13–22 January 1945, AIR 20/7952, PRO.

17. Forrest Pogue, *General C. Marshall: Organizer of Victory, 1944–1945* (New York: Viking, 1973), p. 531.

18. 15 January 1945, Stalin File, Box 26, W. B. Smith Papers, Eisenhower Library.

19. 14 February 1945, Information Exchange File, Box 10, Moscow, RG 334, MR, NA; 22 January 1945, AIR 20/7952, PRO; French ambassador, 27 December 1944, FO 371/39421/C18086, PRO.

20. 27 December 1944, FO 371/39421/C18086, and 21–24 January 1945, WO 178/27, PRO.

21. 8 February 1945, FO 800/416, frames 113–116, PRO.

22. 9 and 15 February 1945, AIR 20/2606 and WO 178/27; briefings of British mission at Yalta on situation of 30 Mission, 4 February 1945, FO 371/47848/N1285 and 800/415, plus 9 February, FO 371/47911/N1507, PRO. F. H. Hinsley, E. E. Thomas, et al., *British Intelligence in the Second World War: Its Influence upon Operations,* 4 vols. (London: Her Majesty's Stationery Office, 1979–1985), vol. 3, pt. 2, pp. 655–656.

23. 15 February 1945, WO 178/27 and CAB 120/690, PRO.

24. Brinkman to Deane, 22 February and 5 March 1944, Technical Office File, Box 31, 8 March 1944; Information Exchange File, Box 10, 9 April 1945; Germany File, Box 9, Moscow, RG 334, MR, NA. Peter Calvocoressi (a Bletchley veteran) acknowledged in 1980 that some ULTRA went to the Soviets, but not specifically in this period. Peter Calvocoressi, *Top Secret Ultra* (London: Cassell, 1981), p. 94.

25. Ibid.

26. 26 February 1945, WO 178/27; see also 27 February 1945 note, WO 32/15548, and 28 February 1945, HW 1/3555, PRO.

27. Ibid.

28. 20 and 28 February 1944, Antonov File, Box 2, and Deane-Antonov File, Box 1, Moscow, RG 334, MR, NA. John Erickson, *The Road to Berlin* (London: Grafton, 1985), p. 686, and Carl Boyd, *Hitler's Japanese Confidant: General Oshima Hiroshi and MAGIC Intelligence, 1941–1945* (Lawrence: University Press of Kansas, 1993).

29. Emphasis added. 10 April 1945; Planning File, Box 2, Moscow, RG 334, MR, NA; Bradley F. Smith and Elena Agarossi, *Operation Sunrise* (New York: Basic Books, 1979), pp. 108 ff.

30. 9 April 1945, Germany File, Box 9, Moscow, RG 334, MR, NA.

31. 12 April 1945, Meetings with the Soviets File, Box 16, Moscow, RG 334, MR, NA.

32. 17 February 1945, CAB 120/679 and FO 371/47848/N2944. U.S. Navy trips, March–May 1945, Boxes 2 and 5, Moscow, CNO, RG 38, MR, NA.

33. 10 April 1945, FO 371/47881/N4595 and FO 181/1005/4 and 5, PRO.

34. 14 February 1945, Eisenhower to Soviets, Exchange File, Box 10, Moscow, RG 334, MR, NA.

35. 26 January 1945, German gas mask filters, Equipment File, Box 7, Moscow, RG 334, MR, NA, and 15 and 28 February 1945, Chemical war information to Soviets, WO 178/27, PRO.

36. 20 and 25 February 1945, Air Intelligence File, Moscow, RG 334, MR, NA.

37. 4, 7, and 24 March 1945, German Air Force and Air Intelligence Files, Boxes 1 and 9, Moscow, RG 334, MR, NA.

38. 12 March 1945, CAB 105/87, and March 1945 (various days), AIR 20/7952, PRO.

39. 28 February, 6 and 27 March 1945, vol. 52578, Admiral Cunningham diary, British Library. Smith and Agarossi, *Operation Sunrise,* pp. 101 ff. RAF go-slow policy, 23 March 1945, FO 371/47848/N3802, PRO.

40. 15 March 1945, AIR 20/7952; 24 May 1945, FO 371/47849/N6129, 15 March, CAB 122/1048; 19 March, WO 178/27, PRO. 18 March 1945, Antonov File, Box 2, Moscow, RG 334, MR, NA.

41. 3 April 1945, Meetings with the Soviets File, Box 16, Moscow, RG 334, MR, NA. Churchill, 8 April 1945, CAB 120/679; Eden, 13 April 1945, AIR 19/294; Thorold appointment, 13 April 1945, AIR 20/5401; reclassification, 6 April 1945, AIR 40/3, PRO.

42. 6 April 1945, AIR 40/3, PRO.

43. 14 April 1945, FO 181/1001/7, PRO.

44. 16 April 1945, PREM 3/395/14, PRO, and vol. 52578, Cunningham diary, British Library.

45. 16 April 1945, AIR 20/3230, PRO.

46. 15 April 1945, WO 204/1345, PRO.

47. 2 May 1945, FO 371/47895/N5116; Air Ministry declining cooperation, 5 May 1945, AIR 20/8061, PRO. 16 April 1945, Radio Advisory Committee, Box 8, Chiefs Papers, R and A, Entry 1, RG 226, MR, NA.

48. 2 and 23 April 1945, Henry Stimson diary, Yale University.

49. Churchill to Archer, 4 May 1945, FO 954/26/654, PRO.

Chapter 12. An End to War?

1. A 14 May 1945 SHAEF intelligence report was most troubled by alleged German efforts to pit the Western powers against the Soviets. JIC, SHAEF (45) 22 (final) in JIC (45) 165 (O), 17 May 1945, CAB 81/129, PRO.

2. For a British view of the Stalin-Hopkins talks, see C. Kerr to Foreign Office, 6 June 1945, FO 181/997/5/7 and 999/7/9, PRO.

3. FO 800/32/101, PRO. On 6 June 1945, Churchill ordered the record of this remark destroyed, which was done, but a handwritten copy remained.

4. FO 371/47850/N8935, PRO. Both of these "iron" remarks came a year prior to Churchill's use of the phrase at Fulton, and on 11 June 1945, Churchill spoke for nearly an hour in cabinet on how dangerous the USSR was. Cunningham diary, vol. 52578, British Library. For the Foreign Office and JIC view of 23 May 1945, see FO 371/47849/N6045, PRO.

5. 1945 File, State Department–OSS, 103.918/3-2145 (especially 31 May 1945); 31 May 1945, John Balfour, etc., FO 371/47883/N8125, PRO; 16 May 1945, Magruder to Deane, and 31 May, Robineson to Deane, Moscow, Subject File, OSS, RG 334, MR, NA. On OSS counterintelligence with the Soviets, see 11 July–30 August, OSS Files, Moscow, RG 334, MR, NA.

6. 22 July 1945, WO 208/4343, PRO.

7. 28 and 30 May 1945, FO 371/47849/N6137, N6309, and N6491; 13 and 27 June 1945, FO 371/47850/N6883; 13 August 1945, AIR 20/8049; 12 July 1945, AIR 20/8061; and 13 July 1945, CAB 122/943, PRO.

8. 1 September 1945, AIR 20/1945, 24 May 1945, ADM 223/252, and 8 September 1945, north Russia, ADM 1/18908, PRO.

9. 19 May 1945, AIR 20/5507; 12 June 1945, AIR 20/2325; 20–25 July 1945, AIR 46/27, PRO.

10. 30 May 1945, ADM 199/606, and September 1945, AIR 20/7952, PRO.

11. 23 May 1945, FO 371/47849/N6045, PRO. Admiral Archer also thought that the USSR would initially walk softly. 8 June 1945, Cunningham diary, vol. 52578, British Library; 19 June 1945, JP (45) 141, FO 371/47850/N6876, PRO. For later British military mission general assessments, see especially 26 September 1945, FO 181/1000/12, and 3 October 1945, COS 945, 597 (O), ADM 223/32, PRO.

12. 13 June 1945, FO 371/47850/N6883, and 1 July 1945, JIC (45) 163, AIR 20/7952, PRO.

13. 9 July 1945, COS (45) 172, AIR 20/2610, PRO.

14. 22 July 1945, FO 371/47850/N8507, PRO.

15. 29 June 1945, MI 3 Minute, WO 208/1862, PRO.

16. 22 August 1945, AIR 2/8071, PRO.

17. 27 August 1945 ff., ADM 223/255, PRO.

18. 2 June 1945, FO 181/1004/14, PRO. For Stalin and the bomb, see also 23 July 1945, Cunningham Diary, vol. 52578, British Library.

19. 23 July 1945, Foreign Office minutes, FO 371/4780/N8570, and 19 July 1945, CCS 196th Meeting Potsdam, CAB 122/946. Stalin—2 June 1945, FO 181/1004/14, PRO.

20. 13 February 1945, MacArthur to Col. Paul L. Freeman, OPD Executive Files, 1940–1945, Box 12, Entry 422, RG 165, MR, NA. Emphasis added.

21. Wilson to Alanbrooke, 12 May 1945, File 52572, Admiral Cunningham Papers, British Library.

22. 26 June 1945, AIR 20/2610, PRO; emphasis added. An ill Major Birse returned to the United Kingdom on 22 June (WO 178/27), and no OB expert replaced him; see 11 July 1945, FO 181/1005/4, PRO.

23. 26 June 1945, Meetings File, Box 56, Moscow, RG 334, MR, NA.

24. 15 July 1945, Pettigrew made acting head of mission, Antonov File, Moscow, RG 334, MR, NA; G-2 to Pettigrew, 21 July and 21 August 1945, File 15, Box 589, Entry 57, RG 319, Suitland, NA.

25. 3 August 1945, Milepost Files, Box 6, Moscow, RG 334 and SRH 198, Box 38, RG 457, MR, NA.

26. Ibid. This was two weeks *after* the first successful atomic test in New Mexico.

27. 8 August 1945, WO 178/27, PRO, and Meeting with the Soviets File, Box 16, Moscow, RG 334, MR, NA.

28. Gar Alperovitz, *Atomic Diplomacy: Hiroshima and Potsdam* (New York: Elizabeth Sifton, 1985); p. 161: "American policymakers, aware that Russia could conquer the Japanese armies on the China mainland in less than two months, desperately hoped to end hostilities before Soviet military operations paved the way for Soviet military domination of Manchuria and North China."

29. Another instance of East-West cooperation, although not completed until after V-J Day, was the creation of U.S. weather stations in Siberia in August 1945. See Box 1, Chief Signal Officer, Top Secret, 1942–1945, Box 1, RG 111, Suitland, NA, and G. Patrick March, "Yanks in Siberia," *Pacific Historical Review* 58, no. 3: 327–342.

30. 24 October 1945, FO 371/47851, PRO.

31. 10 October 1945, MI 6(a) to MI 3, WO 208/4566, PRO. As all sides have conceded, the West received substantial intelligence on Russia during the war by decryption of German messages. Recently released documents show that this material included German operational transmissions in the USSR (as well as reports back to Germany), so the British did not have serious difficulty receiving operational radio traffic in the territory of the USSR, whether German or Russian. 23 September 1945, NID 12 memo, ADM 223/298, PRO.

Bibliography

Books

Aldrich, Richard, ed. *British Intelligence, Strategy, and the Cold War, 1945–1951.* London: Routledge, 1992.

Allen, Paul. *Katyn: The Untold Story of Stalin's Polish Massacres.* New York: Macmillan, 1991.

Alperovitz, Gar. *Atomic Diplomacy: Hiroshima and Potsdam.* New York: Elizabeth Sifton, 1985.

Andrew, Christopher. *Her Majesty's Secret Service.* New York: Penguin, 1987.

Antonov-Oveyenko, Anton. *The Times of Stalin: Portrait of a Tyranny.* Trans. George Saunders. New York: Harper and Row, 1981.

Beaumont, Joan. *Comrades in Arms: British Aid to Russia, 1941–45.* London: David Poynter, 1980.

Beitzell, Robert, ed. *Teheran, Yalta, Potsdam: The Soviet Protocols.* Hattiesburg: University of Mississippi Press, 1970.

Bell, P. M. H. *John Bull and the Bear, 1941–1945.* London: Routledge, 1990.

Bennett, Edward M. *Franklin Roosevelt and the Search for Victory.* Wilmington, Del.: Scholarly Resources, 1990.

Berezhov, V. *History in the Making.* London: Collets, 1983.

Bialer, Seweryn, ed. *Stalin and His Generals.* New York: Pegasus, 1969.

Birse, A. H. *Memoirs of an Interpreter.* New York: Coward, 1967.

Bohlen, Charles E. *Witness to History.* New York: Norton, 1973.

Bosworth, Richard J. *Explaining Auschwitz and Hiroshima: History Writing and the Second World War.* New York: Routledge, 1993.

Bourke White, Margaret. *Shooting the Russian War.* New York: Simon and Schuster, 1942.

Boyd, Carl. *Hitler's Japanese Confidant: General Oshima Hiroshi and MAGIC Intelligence, 1941–1945.* Lawrence: University Press of Kansas, 1993.

Brown, Anthony Cave. *Bodyguard of Lies.* New York: Harper and Row, 1973.

Bryden, John. *Best Kept Secret: Canadian Secret Intelligence in the Second World War.* Toronto: Lester Publishing, 1993.

Burns, James MacGregor. *Roosevelt: Soldier of Freedom.* New York: Harcourt Brace, 1970.

Butler, Ewan. *Mason-Mac: A Life of Lieutenant General Sir Noel Mason Macfarlane.* London: Macmillan, 1972.

Calvocoressi, Peter. *Top Secret Ultra.* London: Cassell, 1981.

Chalou, George C., ed. *The Secrets World: The Office of Strategic Services in World War II.* Washington, D.C.: National Archives, 1992.

Clayton, Aileen. *The Enemy Is Listening.* London: Hutchinson, 1980.

Cramer, W. F. *The Army Air Forces in World War II.* Vol. 3. Chicago: University of Chicago Press, 1951.

Cunningham, Viscount of Hyndhope. *A Sailor's Odyssey.* New York: Dutton, 1951.

Dallek, Robert. *Franklin D. Roosevelt and American Foreign Policy, 1932–1945.* New York: Oxford University Press, 1979.

Dawson, Raymond H. *The Decision to Aid Russia, 1941.* Chapel Hill: University of North Carolina Press, 1959.

Deane, John R. *Strange Alliance.* New York: Viking, 1947.

De Jong, Alex. *Stalin and the Shaping of the Soviet Union.* New York: Morrow, 1986.

Dilks, David, ed. *The Diaries of Alexander Cadogan.* New York: Putnam, 1971.

Dower, John. *War Without Mercy: Race and Power in the Pacific War.* New York: Pantheon, 1987.

Drea, Edward. *MacArthur's ULTRA: Codebreaking and the War Against Japan, 1942–1945.* Lawrence: University Press of Kansas, 1991.

Dunn, Walter S. *Hitler's Nemesis: The Red Army, 1930–1945.* London: Praeger, 1994.

Erickson, John. *The Road to Berlin.* London: Grafton, 1985.

———. *The Road to Stalingrad.* London: Grafton, 1985.

Erickson, John, and David Dilks, eds. *Barbarossa: The Axis and the Allies.* Edinburgh: Edinburgh University Press, 1994.

Eubank, Keith. *Summit at Teheran.* New York: Morrow, 1985.

Feifer, George. *Tennozan: The Battle of Okinawa and the Atomic Bomb.* New York: Ticknor and Fields, 1994.

Fitzgibbon, Constantine. *Secret Intelligence in the Twentieth Century.* London: Hart Davis, 1976.

Franklin, William M., et al. *The Conferences at Cairo and Teheran.* Washington, D.C.: U.S. Government Printing Office, 1961.

Gaddis, John L. *The United States and the Origins of the Cold War.* New York: Columbia University Press, 1972.

Glantz, David M. *From Don to Dnieper: Soviet Offensive Operations December 1942–August 1943.* London: Frank Cass, 1991.

———. *Soviet Military Intelligence in War.* London: Frank Cass, 1990.

———. *Soviet Operations in the Initial Period of War, 22 June–August 1941.* London: Frank Cass, 1987.

Gorodetsky, Gabriel. *Stafford Cripps' Mission to Moscow 1940–1942.* Cambridge: Cambridge University Press, 1984.

Harriman, W. Averell, and Elie Abel. *Special Envoy to Churchill and Stalin.* New York: Random House, 1975.

Herring, George C. Jr. *Aid to Russia, 1941–1946.* New York: Columbia University Press, 1973.

Hill, George. *Go Spy the Land.* London: Cassell, 1932.

Hinsley, F. H., E. E. Thomas, et al. *British Intelligence in the Second World War: Its Influence upon Operations.* 4 vols. London: Her Majesty's Stationery Office, 1979–1985.

Isaacs, Walter, and Euen Thomas. *The Wise Men.* New York: Simon and Schuster, 1986.

Jacobsen, Hans Adolf, and Charles Burdick. *The Halder Diary, 1932–1942.* London: Green Hill, 1982.

Jensen, Joan M. *Army Surveillance in America, 1775–1980.* New Haven, Conn.: Yale University Press, 1991.

Kahn, David. *Seizing the Enigma: The Race to Break the German U Boat Codes 1939–1945.* London: Souvenir Press, 1993.

Keeble, Curtis. *Britain and the Soviet Union, 1917–1986.* London: Macmillan, 1989.

Kharlamov, N. M. *Difficult Mission.* Moscow: Progress, 1986.

Kimball, Warren. *America Unbound: World War II and the Making of a Super Power.* New York: St. Martin's Press, 1992.

Kitchen, Martin. *British Policy Toward the Soviet Union During the Second World War.* London: Macmillan, 1986.

Knightly, Philip. *The Second Oldest Profession.* New York: Norton, 1987.

Kot, Stanislas. *Conversations with the Kremlin.* Trans. H. C. Stevens. London: Oxford University Press, 1963.

Lewin, Ronald C. *American Magic,* New York: Farrar, Straus, Giroux, 1982.

Lukas, Richard C. *Eagles East: The U.S. Army Air Force in the USSR, 1941–1945.* Tallahassee: Florida State University Press, 1970.

McJimsey, George. *Harry Hopkins,* Cambridge, Mass.: Harvard University Press, 1987.

Maisky, Ivan. *Memoirs of a Soviet Ambassador.* New York: Scribner's, 1967.

Marks, Frederick W. III. *Wind over Sand: The Diplomacy of Franklin D. Roosevelt.* Athens: University of Georgia Press, 1988.

Martel, Gifford. *The Russian Outlook.* London: Michael Joseph, 1947.

Moravec, Frantisek. *Master of Spies: The Memoirs of General Frantisek Moravec,* London: Sphere, 1981.

Murphy, Robert. *Diplomat Among Warriors.* New York: Doubleday, 1964.

Nadeau, Remi. *Stalin, Churchill, and Roosevelt Divide Europe.* New York: Praeger, 1990.

Pauli, Allen. *Katyn: The Untold Story of Stalin's Polish Massacre.* New York: Macmillan, 1991.

Peake, Hayden B., and Samuel Halpern. *In the Name of Intelligence.* Washington, D.C.: NIBC Press, 1994.

Perlmutter, Amos. *FDR and Stalin: A Not So Grand Alliance.* Columbia: University of Missouri Press, 1993.

Piekalkiewicz, Janusz. *Unternehmen Zitadelle.* Bergish Gladbach: Gustav Lübbe, 1983.

Pogue, Forrest. *George Marshall: Ordeal of Hope, 1939–1942.* New York: Viking, 1966.

———. *George Marshall: Organizer of Victory, 1944–1945.* New York: Viking, 1973.

Putney, Diane T. *Ultra and the Army Air Forces in World War II.* Washington, D.C.: Office of the Air Force, 1987.

Read, Arthur, and David Fisher. *Operation Lucy.* London: Hodder and Stoughton, 1980.

Richelson, Jeffrey. *American Espionage and the Soviet Target.* New York: Morrow, 1980.

Sainsbury, Keith. *Churchill and Roosevelt: The War They Fought and the Peace They Hoped to Make.* London: Macmillan, 1994.

———. *The Turning Point: The Conference at Teheran.* New York: Oxford University Press, 1985.

Seaton, Albert. *Stalin as Warlord.* London: Batsford, 1976.

Smith, Bradley F. *The Shadow Warriors.* New York: Basic Books, 1983.

———. *The Ultra-Magic Deals.* Shrewsbury: Airlife, 1993.

Smith, Bradley F., and Elena Agarossi. *Operation Sunrise.* New York: Basic Books, 1979.

Spector, Ronald H., ed. *Listening to the Enemy: Key Documents on the Role of Communications Intelligence in the War with Japan.* Wilmington, Del.: Scholarly Resources Press, 1988.

Standley, William H., and Arhur A. Angleton. *Admiral Ambassador to Russia.* Chicago: Regnery, 1955.

Talbert, Ray Jr. *Negative Intelligence: The Army and the American Left, 1917–1941.* Jackson: University of Mississippi Press, 1991.

Tarrant, V. E. *Stalingrad: Anatomy of an Agony.* London: Leo Cooper, 1992.

Tucker, Robert C. *Stalin as Revolutionary, 1879–1929.* New York: Norton, 1974.

Ulam, Adam B. *Stalin: The Man and His Era.* New York: Viking, 1973.

Urban, G. R., ed. *Stalinism: Its Impact on the World.* London: Maurice T. Smith, 1982.

Volkogonov, Dimitri. *Stalin: Triumph and Tragedy.* Trans. Harry Shulman. Rocklin, Calif.: Prima, 1992.

Weinberg, Gerhard I. *A World at Arms: A Global History of World War II.* New York: Cambridge University Press, 1994.

Werth, Alexander. *Russia at War.* New York: Dutton, 1964.

Yergin, Daniel. *Shattered Peace: The Origins of the Cold War and the National Security State.* Boston: Houghton Mifflin, 1980.

Zhukov, Georgi K. *Marshal Zhukov's Greatest Battles.* New York: Harper, 1969.

Ziemke, Earl F. *Stalingrad to Berlin.* Washington, D.C.: U.S. Government Printing Office, 1968.

Articles

Calvocoressi, Peter. "When Enigma Yielded Ultra." *The Listener* 97, no. 3 (27 January 1977): 110–114.

Cecil, Robert. "C's War." *Intelligence and National Security* 1, no. 2 (May 1986): 170–189.

Chapman, John. "Signals Intelligence Collaboration Among the Tripartite States on the Eve of Pearl Harbor." *Japan Forum* 3, no. 2 (October 1961): 231–255.

Julian, Thomas A. "Operations at the Margin: Soviet Bases and Shuttle Bombing." *Journal of Military History* 57 (October 1993): 627–652.

March, G. Patrick. "Yanks in Siberia." *Pacific Historical Review* 58, no. 3: 327–342.

Mulligan, Timothy P. "Spies, Ciphers, and Zitadella." *Journal of Contemporary History* 22, no. 2 (April 1987): 235–260.

Wark, Wesley J. "Three Military Attachés at Berlin in the 1930s: Soldier-Statesmen and the Limits of Ambiguity." *International History Review* 9, no. 4 (November 1987): 586–611.

Index